A Research Agenda for Energy Politics

Elgar Research Agendas outline the future of research in a given area. Leading scholars are given the space to explore their subject in provocative ways, and map out the potential directions of travel. They are relevant but also visionary.

Forward-looking and innovative, Elgar Research Agendas are an essential resource for PhD students, scholars and anybody who wants to be at the forefront of research.

For a full list of Edward Elgar published titles, including the titles in this series, visit our website at www.e-elgar.com

A Research Agenda for Energy Politics

Edited by

JENNIFER I. CONSIDINE
Senior Research Fellow, CEPMLP, University of Dundee, Scotland

SYLVAIN COTE
Former Program Director and Research Fellow, KAPSARC, Saudi Arabia

DOUGLAS COOKE
Founder and Principal, Majura Energy Consulting, Canberra, Australia

GEOFFREY WOOD
Lecturer in Energy and Environmental Law, School of Law, University of Stirling, Scotland

Elgar Research Agendas

EE Edward Elgar
PUBLISHING

Cheltenham, UK • Northampton, MA, USA

Published by
Edward Elgar Publishing Limited
The Lypiatts
15 Lansdown Road
Cheltenham
Glos GL50 2JA
UK

Edward Elgar Publishing, Inc.
William Pratt House
9 Dewey Court
Northampton
Massachusetts 01060
USA

A catalogue record for this book
is available from the British Library

Library of Congress Control Number: 2023931366

This book is available electronically in the **Elgar**online
Political Science and Public Policy subject collection
http://dx.doi.org/10.4337/9781789901764

Printed on elemental chlorine free (ECF)
recycled paper containing 30% Post-Consumer Waste

ISBN 978 1 78990 175 7 (cased)
ISBN 978 1 78990 176 4 (eBook)

Printed and bound in the USA

This book is dedicated to Miranda Considine, Melvin A Conant, William A Kerr, and Alex Kemp, whose commitment, dedication, and support have been invaluable throughout the years. Also, our greatest gratitude goes to Géraldine Escofet, as well as to Mathieu and Benoit Côté, for their unconditional love and support.

Contents

Contributors

Abdullah Aldayel is a Research Associate in the Markets and Industrial Development program, with a focus on oil markets and energy policies. He holds a BS in petroleum engineering from King Fahd University of Petroleum and Minerals.

Greg Baiden has been Chairman and CEO at Penguin Automated Systems Inc. since 2001. Dr Baiden began his career in mining research at Inco Limited in 1986. He conceptualized and implemented the world's first robotic mine prototype. This was the beginning of a professional career dedicated to creating robots to make the mining industry safer. Dr Baiden completed his undergraduate and master's degrees at Queen's University in mining engineering and earned his PhD at McGill University in mining engineering. From 2001 to 2014, he taught robotics and mine automation at Laurentian University. Dr Baiden was also the Dean of Engineering at Laurentian University from 2002 to 2007. One of his projects is a new vision for the underground mining of water in the form of ice on the Moon using a series of transformational teleoperated machines. These systems are built on the thinking of the current TeleR-S&R (Search and Rescue) system, which can operate 12 hours a day on land and in water. Dr Baiden considers the current TeleR-S&R a system available to the public for help in the search and rescue of missing persons or equipment. The project has received international interest.

Arnault Barichella is completing his PhD in political science at Sciences Po Paris and has spent a year as Visiting Fellow affiliated with the Department of Government at Harvard University. He received his BA in modern history from Oxford University and his master's in European affairs from Sciences Po Paris. His interest in cybersecurity issues is linked to his experience as a Research Assistant for a French Senator on the Foreign Affairs and Defense Commission. He was subsequently hired by the French Institute of International Relations (Ifri) and the Jacques Delors Institute to write policy papers on cybersecurity and data protection in the energy sector.

Arnault is also the Editor-in-Chief of the forthcoming *Palgrave Handbook on Cybersecurity and Energy Transitions.*

Brad R. Blair is a General Partner with NewSpace Analytics LLC in Idaho Springs, Colorado. He is a professional consultant on advanced mining technology, the economic use of space mineral resources, and the analysis and modeling of emerging space market opportunities. Brad holds degrees in engineering geology (BSc), mining engineering (ME), and mineral economics (MSc) from the Colorado School of Mines (CSM). He began researching lunar in-situ resource utilization (ISRU) technology in 1989 under the NASA Space Exploration Initiative funding as a graduate student at CSM. During the summer of 1999, as a visiting professional at Douglas Cooke's NASA/JSC Exploration Office, he learned and practiced the art of cost estimation in support of a design reference mission for human exploration of Mars. From 2001 to 2005, he and a small team at CSM conducted research for NASA on topics related to ISRU technology, cost estimation, and space resource economic analysis. Since that time, Brad has worked under US and Canadian government research contracts and consulted for aerospace and mining industry clients on ISRU systems development and economic analysis. He directly participated in two NASA centennial challenges, and he advises and participates in NewSpace start-up companies. His previous nonprofit service includes those as Member of the Board of Directors of United Societies in Space since 2006, Chairman of the Board of the International Space Development Authority Corporation since 2011, and Advocate of the Space Frontier Foundation since 2011.

Elizabeth Carey is an Associate Researcher at the Centre Thucydide for Analysis and Research in International Relations, at Université Paris II Panthéon-Assas, France, from which she graduated with a doctorate in Political Science. Her work is focused on international climate change policies and governance in a post-Paris world, with a particular emphasis on UNFCCC processes and low-carbon policies. She has worked as a researcher and public affairs professional for international organizations, think-tanks and governments. Elizabeth was New Zealand's Energy Advisor at the IEA and a researcher in the Climate and Environment Team at King Abdullah Petroleum Studies and Research Center (KAPSARC), Saudi Arabia.

Dongmei Chen is a Research Fellow at the King Abdullah Petroleum Studies and Research Center (KAPSARC) with a focus on energy trade, energy investment, and regional energy cooperation. She has more than 20 years of experience in China's energy and climate change policy development.

Alberto Cisneros Lavaller is CEO/President of Global Business Consultants—an outsourcing consulting firm specializing in the Latin American oil/gas business, particularly in the areas of E&P, downstream, and planning—a position he has held since 2003. He is a Professor at the Master of Hydrocarbons at Sergio Arboleda University, Bogota, and at the Institute of Graduate Studies in Business Administration, Caracas.

Jennifer I. Considine is an Honorary Senior Research Fellow at the Centre for Energy, Petroleum and Mineral Law & Policy (CEPMLP) in Dundee, Scotland. Dr Considine has worked with a number of international energy companies, including Husky Energy, Pieridae Energy, Ecopetrol, TransCanada Pipelines, Westcoast Energy, Coastal Corporation, Duke Energy, and ANR Pipeline. She is currently a Research Council Member of the J.P. Morgan Center for Commodities (JPMCC). Dr Considine is a former member of the Board of Directors for Canada Post and founding member of a number of initiatives to promote Scottish–Canadian relations, including the Canadian Friends of Scotland.

Timothy J. Considine is the School of Energy Resources Professor of Energy Economics at the Department of Economics, University of Wyoming. He previously worked at the Pennsylvania State University, Bank of America, and the US Congressional Budget Office. Considine holds a PhD from Cornell University, an MS from Purdue University, and a BA with honors from Loyola University Chicago.

Douglas Cooke is a Senior Public Policy Analyst with over two decades of experience advising the Australian government on energy market reform, energy security, and international energy dialogue. Douglas has served as a senior executive with the IEA and KAPSARC and as Vice Chair of the IEA Global Energy Dialogue. He has led Australian delegations to the Asia–Pacific Economic Cooperation Energy Working Group, the International Energy Forum, and the Energy Charter. Douglas has contributed several publications for the IEA and the Organisation for Economic Co-operation and Development (OECD) and served on several IEA peer reviews of member country energy policy and emergency response arrangements.

Sylvain Cote is an Economic and Policy Advisor with over 30 years of experience leading research and providing policy advice on issues such as energy transition, labor market, and entrepreneurial performance. During this period, he has been Director and Senior Research Fellow at the King Abdullah Petroleum Studies and Research Center (KAPSARC) and has held senior advisory positions in the Canadian federal government, the Organisation for Economic Co-operation and Development (OECD), and the North American Commission for Labor Cooperation. Sylvain has also served on several expert advisory committees: the UNDP Knowledge Index Advisory Board, College of Business Administration Industrial Advisory Board at Prince Sultan University, Labor Market Strategy Advisory Committee (Saudi Arabia), EcoMod School of Modeling and Data Science, Global Entrepreneurship Monitor National Expert Group (Saudi Arabia), Eurostat–OECD Entrepreneurship Indicator Development Programme, and International Consortium for Dynamic Entrepreneurship Benchmarking. He holds master's degrees from the University of Victoria and the University of Alberta, Canada.

Carol A. Dahl is a Senior Fellow at the Payne Earth Resources Institute and Professor Emeritus in the Mineral and Energy Economics Program at CSM. She has served annually as an Adjunct Professor at the Chinese University of Petroleum in Beijing since 2014 and has been a Visiting Professor, Department of Business Administration, Technology and Social Sciences, Luleo University of Technology, Sweden, since 2016. She received her PhD in economics from the University of Minnesota, having studied under Christopher Sims, who shared the Nobel Prize in economics in 2010. She received a BA in economics with distinction from the University of Wisconsin and has published widely in peer reviewed energy journals, regularly presents her work at international conferences, has been a Visiting Scholar at a number of well-known universities worldwide, has sat on a number of national technical review panels, and is on the technical expert list of the US Fulbright Program. She received the Adelman–Frankel Award in 2010 from the United States Association for Energy Economics for unique and innovative contributions to the field of energy economics and the Outstanding Contributions to the Profession Award in 2013 from the International Association for Energy Economics for contributions to the field of energy economics and its literature.

Tilak K. Doshi holds an MA and BA in economics and history from the Victoria University of Wellington, New Zealand and gained his PhD in Economics from the University of Hawaii's East-West Center. Tilak's area of expertise is in energy economics with a focus on the downstream oil and gas sector. He has worked in a number of organizations: the Institute of Southeast Asian Studies in Singapore as a Fellow and the Head of the Energy Project, Arthur D. Little as the Principal Consultant for Energy Practice, Saudi Aramco as a Specialist for Business Analysis and Corporate Planning and for Crude Oil Sales and Marketing. He was previously the Chief Economist and Principal Fellow at the Energy Studies Institute, National University of Singapore, and the Program Director and Senior Research Fellow at KAPSARC, Riyadh, Saudi Arabia. He was a Managing Consultant at Muse, Stancil & Co. (Asia), based in Singapore, from 2016 to 2019. He is also a regular *Forbes* contributor.

Joseph Eagleeye is a Principal of the commodity research firm Premia Research LLC and its trading affiliate Premia Capital Management as well as an Advisor for Omnium, a quantitative consulting firm within the Consumer Packaged Goods industry. He is also the Associate Editor of the *Global Commodities Applied Research Digest* at JPMCC. Eagleeye holds a BS in applied mathematics from Yale University and an MBA from the University of California at Berkeley.

Philipp Galkin is a Visiting Researcher at KAPSARC working on the economic and policy aspects of energy supply and energy trade. Before moving to Saudi Arabia, Philipp worked in the spheres of economics and finance in the private and government sectors. He holds a PhD in economics from the St Petersburg State University of Economics and Finance and an MBA from the University of Southern California.

Louis L. Grenier is a former Mission Manager, Space Exploration, Canadian Space Agency. His past positions include Senior Advisor, Audit and Evaluation, and Acting-Director, Strategic Development, at the Canadian Space Agency.

Andrey A. Konoplyanik is an Energy Economist by background, with his major professional areas being international energy economics, energy and investment legislation, energy financing, and international energy market development trends. He holds a PhD and Dr of Science in international energy economics, Professor in International Oil & Gas Business. His current positions include Adviser to Director General, Gazprom export LLC; Professor at the chair of World Economy, Diplomatic Academy, Russian Ministry of Foreign Affairs; Co-chair from Russian side of Work Stream 2 Internal Markets, Russia–EU Gas Advisory Council; and Member of Scientific Council on System Research in Energy, Russian Academy of Sciences. His detailed professional career, publications and presentations are available at www.konoplyanik.ru.

James S. Logan, MD, MS, board certified in aerospace medicine, served 22 years as a Senior Space Medical Officer at NASA Johnson Space Center in multiple positions, including Chief, Flight Medicine; Chief, Medical Operations; and Chief, Medical Informatics and Health Care Systems. Mission Control certified, he supported numerous space shuttle missions as Crew Surgeon or Mission Control Surgeon. After serving as Project Manager for the design of the first clinical medical facility in space onboard the International Space Station, he became a founding board member of the American Telemedicine Association, first Provost of the International Space University, and co-founder of the Space Enterprise Institute.

Michael C. Lynch is a Distinguished Fellow at the Energy Policy Research Foundation and President of Strategic Energy and Economic Research. Mike spent nearly 30 years at MIT as a student and then researcher at the Energy Laboratory and Center for International Studies. He was a Chief energy economics at IHS Global Insight. His past roles include President of the US Association for Energy Economics and service on the editorial boards of two publications; he is also a senior contributor for *Forbes*. Mike's books have been translated into six languages, and his book *The Peak Oil Scare and the Coming Oil Flood* was published in 2016 by Praeger.

Tara K. Righetti joined the University of Wyoming College of Law faculty in the fall of 2014. Prior to that, she served as CEO and General Counsel of a privately owned upstream oil and gas company with operations in six states and on the outer continental shelf. She is admitted to practice in Texas and California and is a Certified Professional Landman. Professor Righetti teaches classes related to oil and gas and commercial law. She also teaches the natural resources field practicum. Her research interests include split estate issues, royalty payments, subsurface trespass, and energy development on public land. Professor Righetti's research focuses on legal issues related to oil and gas regulation, land use, contracts, and development.

Jitendra Roychoudhury is a Research Fellow at KAPSARC, Riyadh, Saudi Arabia. His ongoing research portfolio at KAPSARC covers various economic, energy, and policy developments and the impact of policies on global commodity markets. Before joining KAPSARC, Jitendra was Director and Chief Consultant at HDR|Salva, India. He has worked extensively as a commodity consultant within India's energy and infrastructure sectors, advising on developing market entry strategies.

Dale Tietz is an Aerospace and Space Entrepreneur running and contributing to several organizations. His experience as a senior Pentagon official in national security, science and technology, and space and military is second to none.

Hilary Till is the Solich Scholar at JPMCC, University of Colorado Denver Business School and the Contributing Editor for JPMCC's *Global Commodities Applied Research Digest*. She is also the Director of Portfolio Risk Analysis at a top-10 US wealth manager. Till has a BA with general honors in statistics and concentrations in economics and computer science from the University of Chicago and an MSc in statistics from LSE, where she studied under a private fellowship administered by the Fulbright Commission.

Richard Wheeler is a Policy Analyst and Practitioner in the areas of energy security and regional security. Richard worked for nearly a decade in the upstream oil and gas industry in both external relations and project management roles on exploration and development projects in three continents. He has also worked as a Senior Energy Security Advisor for the Organization for Security and Co-operation in Europe (OSCE), the world's largest regional intergovernmental security organization, and has recently concluded a series of assignments as an accredited multilateral diplomat focusing on a broad range of security sector issues for the OSCE. He is a member of the Pacific Council on International Policy. His works include Energy Security and Intergovernmental Organizations (OGEL 2, 2014); "Multilateral Engagement with Central Asia on Energy Issues," *Central Asia in the Era of Sovereignty: The Return of Tamerlane?* (Eds Daniel L. Burghart and Theresa Sabonis-Helf, 2018); and "Regional Integration as an Energy Security Strategy: Lessons for Central Asia From Europe's Efforts Towards Security of Supply Through Regulatory Integration" (Policy Brief No. 49, OSCE Academy in Bishkek, September 2018). He obtained his MA in Russian studies at Georgetown University's Center for Eurasian, Russian and East European Studies, speaks fluent Russian and conversant Ukrainian and Turkish, and has lived and worked in Central Asia for over a decade.

Geoffrey Wood is a Lecturer in Energy and Environmental Law at Stirling University Law School, Scotland. He holds a PhD in low carbon energy governance from the Centre for Energy Petroleum and Mineral Law and Policy (CEPMLP) at the University of Dundee, Scotland. An interdisciplinary energy and environmental law, policy and regulatory specialist, his research and teaching focuses on the development of legal and governance frameworks for sustainable energy transitions to optimise policy delivery in terms of environmental, social, economic, political and technological outcomes. Recent research includes exploring the impact of austerity on environmental decision making in Scotland, local content and offshore wind in the UK post-Brexit, a critical analysis of policy risk and politics on low carbon energy deployment in the UK and Scotland, the role of definitions in renewable and low carbon energy governance. He has published extensively on energy and environmental issues, and has published over 40 articles, books, book chapters and other publications, including five books on a diverse range of topics: *From Fossil Fuels to Low Carbon Energy Transitions: New Regulatory Trends in Latin America* (2022); *New Zero Carbon Energy Systems and Energy Transitions* (2022), *Social License to Operate and Energy Transitions* (2022); *The Palgrave Handbook of Managing Fossil Fuels and Energy Transitions* (2019) and *A Critical Review of Scottish Renewable and Low Carbon Energy Policy* (2017). He is also Series Editor of the major new Palgrave Studies in Energy Transitions (PSET) handbook series (Palgrave 2022). Currently also a Researcher in global energy transitions at the University of Dundee and a Guest Lecturer in energy, climate and environment at Glasgow Caledonian University, he has previously held research, lecturing and consultancy positions for various organisations including the Scottish Government, the Offshore Renewables Institute, the Royal Society of Edinburgh and the Extractives Hub (a joint UK Government–University of Dundee project).

Xiaoliang Yang joined the Global CCS Institute as China Country Manager in March 2022. Prior to joining the institute, Xiaoliang served as Technology Director at China Oil & Gas Climate Investments. Xiaoliang has also held various positions at the World Resources Institute (WRI). During his time at WRI, Xiaoliang supported the US–China Climate Change Working Group and the US–China Clean Energy Research Center as well as led the theme on knowledge sharing on large-scale carbon capture and storage demonstrations. In addition, Xiaoliang has worked in the Department of Social Affairs at the UN Headquarters and at KAPSARC in Saudi Arabia. Xiaoliang holds a PhD in environmental science from the State University of New York College of Environmental Science and Forestry and an MPA from Maxwell School, Syracuse University.

Acknowledgments

The editors would like to acknowledge members of the editorial committee of the *Geopolitics of Energy* for their wisdom, encouragement, and advice: John A. Hill, Dr Joseph J. Malone, Max K. Morris, Charles K. Ebinger, G. Henry M. Schuler, Ian Smart, Grenville Garside, Christa G. Conant, Robert E. Ebel, Adam Sieminski, John Devlin, John Roberts, Alex Kemp, Peter Adam, Paul Tempest, Michael C. Lynch, Alberto Cisneros Lavaller, Napier Collyns, Murray Gart, Elena Turner, Campbell Watkins, and Anthony Reinsch. We would also like to thank Nina Booth and the staff at Edward Elgar; the Centre for Energy, Petroleum and Mineral Law & Policy, University of Dundee; and the King Abdullah Petroleum Studies and Research Center for their valuable support. The editors would like to give a special thanks to KAPSARC for their invaluable support and contribution to the OPEN Access for Chapter 2 and 5 of the book.

Abbreviations

BCM	billion cubic meters
BnetzA	Bundesnetzagentur (German Federal Network Agency)
BRICS	Brazil–Russia–India–China–South Africa, an informal grouping (first appeared as just a statistical exercise when this abbreviation was presented by analyst Jim O'Neil from Goldman Sachs in November 2001; in June 2006, a formal union was organized at Russia's initiative)
CEGH	Central European Gas Hub (in Baumgarten)
CEPMLP	Centre for Energy, Petroleum and Mineral Law & Policy, Dundee University
CC CPSU	Central Committee of the Communist Party of the Soviet Union
CCS	carbon capture and sequestration
CMEA	Council of Mutual Economic Assistance and Cooperation (between USSR and other socialist, mostly European, countries), alternatively COMECON (1949–1991)
COMECON	Council for Mutual Economic Assistance and Cooperation (between USSR and other socialist, mostly European, countries), alternatively CMEA (1949–1991)
DG COMP	Directorate General for Competition of the European Commission
DG ENERGY	Directorate General on Energy of the European Commission
DP	delivery point (in LTC)
EAEC	European Atomic Energy Community, alternatively EURATOM (signed 1957, in force from 1958 to date)

EC	European Community (1993–2009)
ECSC	European Coal and Steel Community
ECT	Energy Charter Treaty (legally binding treaty, signed 1994, in force from 1998 to date)
EEC	European Economic Community (signed 1957, in force from 1958 to 1993)
EIB	European Investment Bank
EU	European Union (signed 1992, in force from 1993 to date)
EURATOM	European Atomic Energy Community, alternatively EAEC (signed 1957, in force from 1958 to date)
FID	final investment decision
FDI	foreign direct investment/investor
FSU	Former Soviet Union
GAATSA	Countering America's Adversaries Through Sanctions Act (US Law)
GAC	Russia–EU Gas Advisory Council
GATT	General Agreement on Tariffs and Trade (1947–1995, succeeded by WTO)
GMT	Gazprom Marketing & Trading
GPB	Gazprombank
GTM	EU Gas Target Model
GTS	gas transportation system
H2	hydrogen
IEA	International Energy Agency
IRR	internal rate of return
KPMG	international consultancy firm
LTC	long-term contract
MHM	methane–hydrogen mix
MSR	methane steam reforming
MTPA	mandatory third-party access
NC CAM INC	Network Code on Capacity Allocation Mechanisms for Incremental Capacity
NIS	newly independent states (of the FSU and COMECON)

NGO	nongovernmental organization
NPS	nuclear power station
NRES	nonrenewable energy sources
NS-1	Nord Stream 1 (offshore gas pipeline)
NS-2	Nord Stream 2 (offshore gas pipeline)
OECD	Organisation for Economic Co-operation and Development
OIES	Oxford Institute of Energy Studies
Politburo CPSU	Political Bureau of the Central Committee of the Communist Party of the Soviet Union (the highest political body of the USSR)
PPP	public–private partnership
PSA	production-sharing agreements
RenH2	renewable hydrogen
RES	renewable energy sources
ROR	rate of return
RROR	reasonable rate of return
SMO	special military operation (of Russia in Ukraine since February 24, 2022)
TOP	take-and/or-pay contractual provision in LTC
TPA	third-party access
Transit Protocol	draft Energy Charter Protocol on Transit
UIOLI	use it or lose it
UKNS	UK sector of the North Sea
UPU	Urengoy–Pomary–Uzhgorod (gas pipeline)
USD/US$	United States dollar
USSR	Union of Soviet Socialist Republics (1922–1991)
WS2	Work Stream 2 Internal Markets (of the Russia–EU Gas Advisory Council)
WTO	World Trade Organization (since 1995, successor of GATT)
WWII	Second World War

Foreword: move to an energy transition, but cleverly

Michael C. Lynch

There is strong evidence that the world is entering a great Energy Transition that will ultimately see minimal greenhouse gas (GHG) emissions and a reliance on electrons rather than combustion for energy. Although there are many uncertainties about the precise path and impacts of climate change, the world's governments have accepted that it must be addressed—and quickly. Unfortunately, how that translates into action remains uncertain, with recent high energy prices creating resistance to some higher-cost alternatives to fossil fuels. Still, the combination of policy imperatives and advancing technologies implies a significant evolution in global energy production and consumption.

Expectations

Governments covering most of the world's population and economic output have set a variety of goals for the reduction of GHG emissions, primarily focused on carbon dioxide, which is the biggest source of anthropogenic climate change. These goals include commitments to decarbonize power generation and substitute fossil fuels with electric power in buildings and vehicles. The International Energy Agency (IEA), in Paris, has described a scenario that achieves net-zero emissions in 2050, which would require an estimated 75 percent decline in the consumption of petroleum, an 80 percent drop in coal consumption, and a 70 percent reduction in natural gas usage. Biofuels and other synthetics would take the place of some of that, while the production of photovoltaic power would grow by a factor of 20 and wind by a factor of 10. Figures F.1 and F.2 show projections of fuel use in the IEA World Energy Outlook 2021 for the Stated Policies and Net Zero 2050 scenarios.

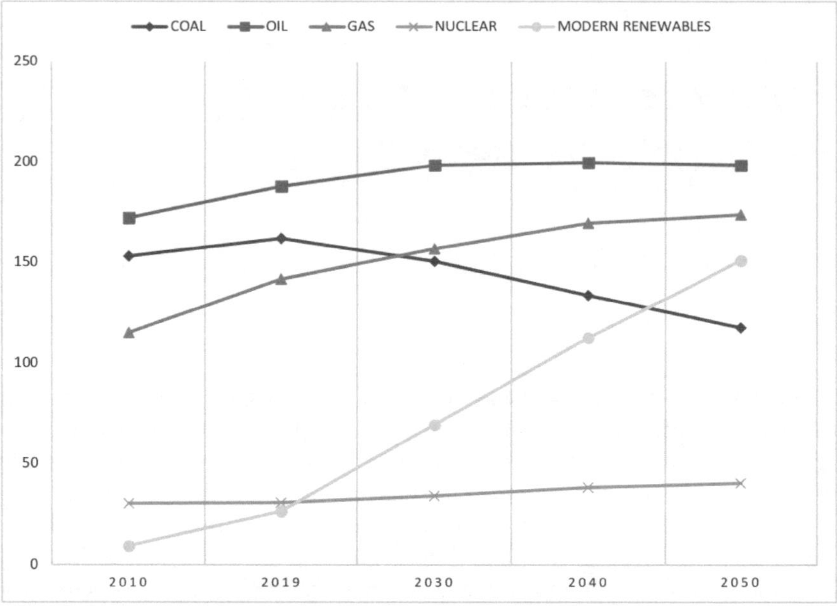

Notes: Modern renewables exclude hydro and traditional biomass.

Figure F.1 Fuel use in the Stated Policies scenario (EJ)

More immediately, analysts have argued that the pandemic will cause a major change in the energy sector, as increasing numbers work from home and rely on internet meetings instead of travel. Of course, this is hardly certain: The rise of the internet two decades ago led many to think that both travel and in-person shopping would decline sharply. The former proved untrue, and while the latter has occurred, the effect has not been as strong as anticipated.

Certainly, oil demand has not shown the effect of most of these changes. The IEA estimates that while jet fuel usage in 2022 will be over 20 percent lower than in 2019, consumption of other oil products will be near pre-pandemic levels. The global economy has, however, grown by over 10 percent since the pandemic arrived, thanks largely to economic stimulus, implying that some savings have occurred. Still, current trends do not support the claims that the demand for oil—or even fossil fuels—has peaked.

Before looking ahead, it is worth looking at the past to provide some context for the expected Energy Transition and, in particular, to understand what has

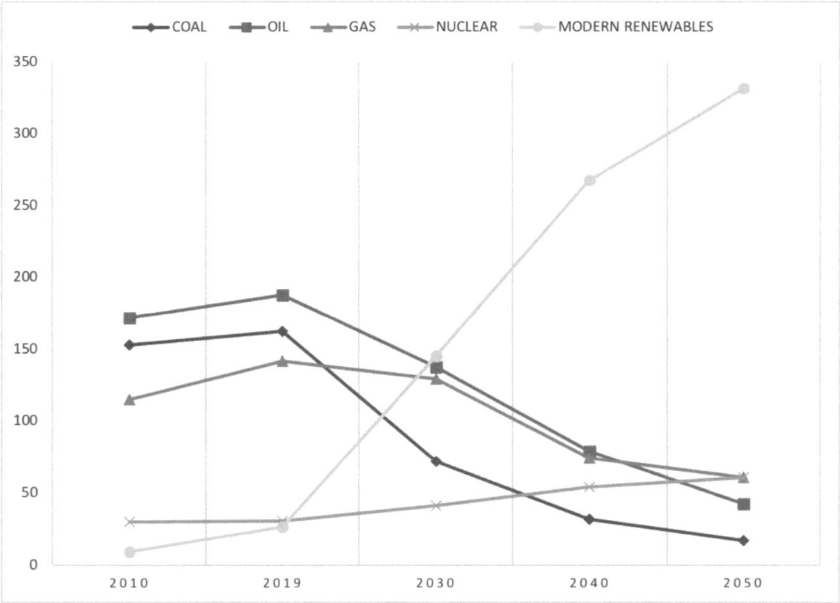

Notes: Modern renewables exclude hydro and traditional biomass.

Figure F.2 Fuel use in the Net-Zero 2050 scenario (EJ)

and has not worked to change energy production and usage in the past, as well as many of the misconceptions that should be avoided now.

Misguided Theory

The failure of many past policies has been aided and abetted by bad advice from advocates, analysts, and academics, including some very prominent ones. Most disconcerting has been the embrace of the so-called Hotelling Valuation Principle, which argues that mineral prices should rise exponentially and has been interpreted to prove mathematically that oil prices should rise at the rate of interest. This was first described by Solow (1973), but adopted by many others, including Dasgupta and Heal (1979) and Slade (2009). Numerous energy economists, such as Adelman (1990), have shown that the theory, as interpreted, is incorrect, primarily because of faulty assumptions; yet, it remains accepted by some as valid.

Similar to this was the use of the Hubbert curve, which purported that the production of oil (or gas) in a region should follow a bell-shaped curve, with the area under the curve representing the total recoverable resource. This would not only allow any region with a sufficient history of production to have its resource estimated, but also enable extrapolation of trends to predict future production. As Lynch (2016) demonstrated, this method was not scientifically based; rather, it was an example of curve fitting and failed repeatedly to produce accurate forecasts, often spectacularly.

Another theory proved useful in financial markets but was misapplied to corporate management, that is, the Capital Asset Pricing Model, for which William Sharpe, Harry Markowitz, and Merton Miller received the Nobel Prize in Economics. They showed that the correlation between asset values could be measured to enable portfolio managers to reduce risk by diversifying their holdings. Others then applied this model to corporate strategy and argued that corporations should diversify their businesses. For example, an oil company, whose profit was positively correlated with oil prices, should invest in an airline, whose profit was negatively correlated with oil prices. However, this assumed that management would not affect profitability, which proved fallacious. As described in one case, "In the fall of 1984, after 10 years and at least a US$500 million investment, 'the world's largest company concluded that oil and office products do not mix.'"[1]

Ultimately, the oil industry was urged to end diversification and focus on its core business.

Irrational Exuberance

Although the past half century has seen major changes in the world's energy landscape, much still remains the same. Nuclear power has increased but is nowhere near the levels expected in the 1970s due to high costs and public resistance, coal use has declined in many places but globally remains near record-high levels because of heavy reliance on the cheap fuel in China and India, and oil still dominates the transportation sector despite decades of enthusiasm for synfuels, biofuels, and electric vehicles.

Past failed efforts at Energy Transition include the 1970s push for synthetic fuels, such as the liquefaction and gasification of coal, production of oil products from kerogen (shale), and liquefaction of methane to produce clean petroleum products. In all of these cases, failure was due to an unrealistic assessment of conventional resources, which proved to be more abundant and cheaper than analysts believed and, thus, made expensive substitutes uncompetitive.

Electric vehicles have been promoted many times in the past because the simpler and cleaner nature of the engines is appealing from an engineering viewpoint. Unfortunately, poor performance and high costs, plus the need for massive infrastructure investments, meant that, as recently as the 1990s, exuberance about their prospect proved to be misplaced (MacKenzie 1994). Similarly, belief at that time that hydrogen fuel cell vehicles were near commercial viability proved premature.

All of the aforementioned does not mean that the belief in an Energy Transition now is irrational exuberance or based on flawed theories, but merely that irrational exuberance is all too common and solid analysis is necessary to differentiate between that and reliable predictions. This volume makes a valuable contribution toward that end.

Successful Transitions

In a very general sense, the historical Energy Transition is thought of as proceeding from wood to coal to oil to gas to nuclear. However, this ignores many smaller steps that were just as important to the energy landscape and to people's lives. Lighting went from sunlight and wood fires (in prehistory) to vegetable oils and animal fats in candles and lamps from ancient to near-modern times. In the 19th century, kerosene began to be used in lamps; then, urban households relied on synthetic natural gas from coal before electric lights became viable. And electric lights have evolved over the years: Incandescent bulbs dominated most uses for decades, but, more recently, were replaced by fluorescent lamps and now light-emitting diodes. Although some advances involved reductions in the quality of light (fluorescent lamps in particular), they typically involved improvements in cost and quality.

The case of the automobile highlights the interaction of cost and performance, where the Model T was initially more expensive than a horse (Table 0.1). However, it provided much greater carrying capacity, speed, and range and removed the need for constant maintenance and disposal of manure. Although cars quickly replaced horses in transportation, in farm use—two decades after the first Model T tractor version had been introduced—the number of horses had declined only by 50 percent.

Table 0.1 Transportation Options in 1920

	Model T	Horse
Horsepower	20	1
Speed	35-40	10-17
Passengers	2-7	1 to 2
Cargo Capacity (lbs)	2000	200-300
Exhaust	n.a.	22 lb manure
Range	200	40
Price	4740	2280
Fuel Cost/year	1752	840

Source: Lynch and Sandrea (2021).

A New World

The past few decades have seen a growing recognition of anthropomorphic climate change as data has accumulated and science has improved. While there are uncertainties, most governments appear ready to decarbonize their economies in whole or in part, depending on the timescale. The Paris Accords, whose goal is to limit global temperature increases to 2°C above preindustrial levels, were adopted in 2015 and ratified a year later. In response to these, many countries have adopted plans to promote renewable energy, electric vehicles, and a variety of other measures in order to bring their emissions to net zero. Nearly all nations have offered National Determined Contributions describing their commitments, and 53 countries and the European Union have agreed to net-zero goals (IEA 2021, pp. 91–92).

The costs and performance of many new energy technologies have also improved dramatically. Lithium-ion batteries have greatly improved in terms of cost and performance, and the current generation of electric vehicles outperform those promoted three decades ago. This has led to much greater adoption and, in some areas, dominance in terms of new investment.

Solar and wind power have been used for millennia in a variety of ways, but the current employment represents a quantum leap. Wind turbines are a perfect example of how numerous factors can improve the viability of a technology, with advanced designs and materials, plus larger structures, bringing costs down from US$3.5/kw to less than US$0.5/kw now (Lantz et al. 2012; Stehly and Bieter 2018).

Solar panels have seen the same advances, but cost reductions appear to reflect improved manufacturing more than different materials. Whereas half a century ago solar energy was primarily promoted for water heating, now rooftop installations of solar panels are widespread and larger ground-level projects abound. Generous subsidies have played a role, but lower costs mean that many locations are economically viable even without them.

Any number of technological developments could aid, alter, or halt the Energy Transition. Most important, better, cheaper batteries would not only improve the attractiveness of electric vehicles but also make intermittent renewable supply much more competitive with conventional power generation. Ongoing efforts to develop new methods of biofuel production would greatly reduce demands for electrification of transport. New models of fission reactors, such as small modular reactors, could become the baseload power of choice, and there have even been suggestions that advances in materials will finally make fusion power viable. Either would diminish the demand for wind and solar power. On the other hand, a breakthrough in open-air carbon capture would mean that the more expensive carbon-reduction schemes would be unnecessary and leave a significant amount of fossil fuels in the mix.

The Geopolitical Impact of the Transition

The geopolitical implications of the Energy Transition will be significant. On the one hand, less reliance on fossil fuels will decrease energy trade, especially for petroleum, which has loomed large in the political landscape. Half a century of attempts to reduce dependence on vulnerable fuel supplies has yielded only modest gains, but that could change in the coming decades.

Certainly, the possession of massive petroleum reserves has translated into some political power for Middle Eastern countries, but it has hardly given them the kinds of dominance so often feared by analysts (Vitalis 2022). Iran and Iraq have variously been under sanctions as the international community chose to punish their political behavior regardless of the impact on oil markets. After an initial burst of activity in the early 1970s, oil power has not helped resolve the Arab–Israeli conflict, for example, and while Europe has, to date, been unable to wean itself off Russian oil and gas supplies despite the current war in Ukraine, it has nonetheless imposed significant sanctions on Russia and not been shy about providing Ukraine with military support.

Still, a significant drop in world oil demand will have strategic implications. For one thing, it is more likely that production in the OPEC countries and Russia will not decline as much as in the rest of the world compared with demand—and presumably price—decline. Increased dominance of the oil market will give them more political power, although largely with the non-OECD countries, as OECD oil demand dwindles (Lynch 2021).

It is also possible that lower oil demand and prices will translate into sharply reduced oil income in a number of nations that rely on it for their budgets, which could lead to more political instability and oil price spikes, although the economic impact will fall heaviest on countries that have not transitioned from fossil fuels. Still, as the Russo–Ukrainian War has shown, globalization means that political instability in one country can have broad impacts.

The dominance of a few suppliers for both renewable energy equipment and minerals has raised some concerns, especially China's role in providing photovoltaic cells and batteries and processing some minerals. Raw materials needed in the Energy Transition include many minerals, most of which are theoretically abundant but whose production is heavily concentrated in certain nations that are not politically stable, such as the Congo (cobalt). Unlike disruptions of fuel supplies, however, a cessation in minerals production will affect new project development, not energy production from existing sources, and so will be less harmful than past oil crises. Longer-term diversification should reduce the vulnerability.

The growing interconnectedness of power grids to offset renewable energy variability could create disputes over power supply in the future, as weather-related production dips in one country might see it reduce contracted-for exports, a growing problem in the broader economy. Exports of goods ranging from palm oil to vaccines have been embargoed as countries hoard them to mollify their citizenry, and this could be a source of conflict in future power trade. Additionally, the interconnectedness might make larger grids more vulnerable to problems like cyberattacks in the future.

The Potential for Pushback

Finally, although opponents of the Energy Transition often cherry-pick problems and exaggerate dangers, there are some real challenges. The high cost of renewable power and electric vehicles tends to be downplayed by their advocates but remains an impediment to their widespread usage. The variability of solar and wind adds to their costs and lowers their convenience, although storage and load management have improved and are likely to advance further as time passes. Despite improvements in lithium-ion batteries, electric vehicles still have a limited range and recharging can be a lengthy process, causing some purchasers to revert to conventional vehicles (Dua and Bansel 2021).

In addition, increasing political resistance to reliance on a handful of politically unstable or distasteful nations for the minerals needed for many parts of the Energy Transition could delay the uptake of some technologies, as could opposition to the land needs for renewables like wind and solar, as well as transmission lines necessary to move power from renewable-rich areas to those in need. Political pressure to focus more on energy poverty and less on GHG emission reductions seems unlikely to succeed, but cannot be completely ruled out.

Already, there have been populists in a number of countries arguing against increased spending on the Energy Transition and/or the higher prices that can result. The IEA has, for years, been arguing for reduced subsidies for fossil fuels, but they remain at US$440 billion globally, little changed from a decade ago.[2] Although most of that is outside the OECD countries, which are leading efforts to address climate change, post-pandemic financial constraints and public resistance could also mean a turn away from the Energy Transition.

Future Research

The Energy Transition, however it occurs, will almost certainly need some major questions to be answered better than they have been to date. These include the following:

> What is the best way to spur innovation? Although innovation is widely regarded as the great contributor to civilization's advances, there is still disagreement about the best way to enable it. Some argue that research money generates breakthroughs; others think government mandates will require industries to develop new technologies, while some advocate for the importance of an open society—but with patent protections. Beyond a doubt, each plays some role, but the balance between costs

and benefits remains unclear. Did the California electric vehicle mandate in the 1990s make any contribution to battery technology, and what were the costs to the subsequently abandoned effort? Do Renewable Fuels Standards simply reward existing players or encourage the development of lower-cost alternatives?

Convenience remains a major intangible element in some new technologies, in particular electric vehicles. To what degree would an expansion of charging stations reduce inconvenience and thus boost sales? How much cheaper should electric vehicles be to offset inconvenience?

What is the best way to cope with public resistance to projects related to the Energy Transition, from land-hungry renewable power to electric transmission lines? Are financial inducements enough, and how much would be necessary?

Energy efficiency has long been touted as not only inexpensive but profitable. However, consumers have not responded as expected, with only gradual improvements over time, primarily as a result of evolving technology not consumer choice. Various explanations have been offered—from imperfect information to high discount rates to inaccurate cost accounting. Establishing what would encourage more efficiency would be useful.

The Way Forward

An apocryphal story describes a sculptor who—asked how to make a statue of an elephant—said, "I get a block of stone and carve away everything that doesn't look like an elephant." Needless to say, this is a great simplification, but it highlights one important element of trying to foresee the future: avoid errors. And, after half a century of intensive energy economics research, some are obvious:

Resources are enormous, and scarcity is typically transient and often reflects political decisions or events.

Resource availability does not translate into automatic adoption or consumption.

Seeming expert opinion and analysis are quite possibly flawed, and sometimes egregiously so.

Large-scale transformation of the energy industry will require action not by governments or companies, but by consumers deciding in large numbers to adopt new fuels and/or technologies.

The economics of a given fuel or technology is not the only factor determining consumer choice. Convenience and quality also matter, but it is a combination of the three that will determine the transition.

No energy source is perfect in terms of either security and reliability or zero emissions. Therefore, diversification should always be a primary goal.

The transition to coal helped make Great Britain a global power, and oil did much the same for the United States; however, the globalization of the economy and the greater diversity of energy supplies reduced, but hardly eliminated, the geopolitical power of petroleum resource holders. The evolution of the energy industry has great consequences for society, and understanding what is likely—and why—requires intense analysis and, especially, that researchers remain open-minded.

Notes

1. Richard B. Schmitt and Laurie P. Cohen, "Exxon's Flop in Field of Office Gear Shows Diversification Perils," *Wall Street Journal*, September 3, 1985.
2. See https://www.iea.org/topics/energy-subsidies.

References

Adelman, M. A., "Mineral Depletion Theory with Special Reference to Petroleum," *Journal of Economics and Statistics*, 1990.

Dasgupta, Partha and Geoffrey Heal, *Economic Theory and Exhaustible Resources*, Cambridge University Press, 1979.

Dua, Rubal and Prateek Bansal, "Once Consumers Adopt an Electric Vehicle, Do They Go Back?" KAPSARC Instant Insight, June 16, 2021.

International Energy Agency, *World Energy Outlook*, 2021.

Lantz, E., M. Hand and R. Wiser, "The Past and Future Cost of Wind Energy," 2012 World Renewable Energy Forum.

Lynch, Michael C., *The Peak Oil Scare and the Coming Oil Flood*, Praeger, 2016.

Lynch, Michael C. and Ivan Sandrea, "The Pandemic and the End of Oil? The Pandemic, Peak Oil Demand, and the Oil Industry," EPRINC 2021.

MacKenzie, James J., *The Keys to the Car: Electric and Hydrogen Vehicles for the 21st Century*, World Resources Institute, 1994.

Slade, Margaret E. and Henry Thille, "Whither Hotelling: Tests of the Theory of Exhaustible Resources," in *Annual Review of Resource Economics*, volume 1, 2009, p. 252.

Solow, Robert "The economics of resources or the resources of economics?" *American Economic Review Proceedings*, 1974.

Stehly, Tyler and Phillip Bieter, "2018 Cost of Wind Energy Review," National Renewable Energy Laboratory.

Vitalis, Robert, *Oilcraft: The Myths of Scarcity and Security that Haunt U.S. Energy Policy*, Stanford University Press, 2022.

Introduction to *A Research Agenda for Energy Politics*

Jennifer I. Considine

The future research agenda for energy politics is concerned primarily with the future evolution of the geopolitics of energy in a rapidly changing landscape. As we are reminded by Mel Conant (1994),[1] "'geo' refers to the location of oil reserves; 'politics' reflects the decisions of importing and producing governments affecting access to supplies. The basic ingredients will always be a mix of politics, economics, and security objectives. All of the factors have to be kept in mind since overlooking one or more may invite serious trouble." The scope and complexity of these issues increase with the rise of technology, cybersecurity, and environmental concerns.

Designed to be visionary and provocative, *A Research Agenda for Energy Politics* takes a hard look at the pressing issues facing researchers in the new world order. Starting with a concise history of Energy Politics that brings us to the present era, the book looks at the evolution of energy politics through three unique lenses or perspectives: affordability, security, and sustainability. The Research Agenda asks pressing questions about the sources of geopolitical risk, problems of capital allocation to finance a growing demand for smart and renewable energy, and benefits and costs of global geo-economic shifts. Leaders in the field present their futuristic visions of energy and energy politics, and the book concludes with a futuristic look at artificial intelligence and its applications in the energy industry.

The book is divided into four sections: (i) Navigating emerging geopolitical risks: politics, economics, and business in a new world (dis) order; (ii) Financing the transformation: mobilizing capital in a competitive landscape; (iii) Global scenarios: harnessing the benefits of global geo-economic shifts;

and (iv) The future of energy policy: meeting the macro challenge—domestic reform or unsustainability.

> Oil is high profile stuff, for it fuels much more than automobiles and airplanes. Oil fuels military power, national treasuries, and international politics. Because of this it is no longer a commodity to be bought and sold within the confines of traditional supply and demand balances. Rather, it has been transformed into a determinant of well-being, of national security and international power for those who possess this vital resource, and the converse for those who do not (Robert E. Ebel[2]).

The first section—Navigating emerging geopolitical risks: politics, economics, and business in a new world (dis) order—contains four chapters addressing the sources of instability in world energy markets.

In the first chapter, the authors review the factors determining the stability of world oil markets and the potential for oil shocks. We are reminded of the key determinants of geopolitics, including "the location of energy sources and strategic reserves; domestic and foreign government policies affecting energy supply and distribution; price; anticipated demand and supply and the geopolitics of choice for importers and exporters alike" (Considine and Paik, 2018). The chapter draws the reader's attention to the unprecedented troika threatening world energy markets: war in Europe, Covid, and climate change. The possibility that one, or all of these, might be exacerbated by haphazard and contradictory policy prescriptions and the unintended consequences of political sanctions is proposed as a subject for future research.

The second chapter looks at critical geopolitical and energy security issues in India with a focus on securing access to reliable and affordable energy sources and the economic drivers that motivate domestic and international energy policy. The role of Indian energy policies will be of increasing importance to domestic and international markets alike as the country charts a delicate course between climate obligations and the just transition from a fossil fuel-based economy. The implications of the transition for energy affordability, accessibility, and sustainability are recommended as a promising area for future research.

Alberto Cisneros Lavaller's chapter, "Renewables and hydrocarbon price climbing," draws our attention to the geopolitical implications of low capital investment in hydrocarbon energy sources and rising energy prices for Latin America and the developing world. Future research is needed to monitor the evolution of hydrocarbon prices and domestic and local subsidy schemes as these are likely to determine the pace, and success, of the transition to renewables.

The second section—Financing the transformation: mobilizing capital in a competitive landscape—contains three chapters examining the challenges facing the world's energy industry. The section investigates the increasingly complex web of energy politics that evolves as capital investments and valuable, scarce resources are torn between the competing ends of energy security and the green transformation.

Andrey Konoplyanik, in Chapter 4, discusses the complex issue of European and Russian energy economics, drawing the reader's attention to the threats inherent in war and an accelerated transition to a zero-carbon energy economy. Harsh lessons learned from the past and the oil shocks of the 1970s exemplify the need for informal dialogue and mutually beneficial cooperation between Russia and the EU in the energy sphere.

In Chapter 5, Dongmei Chen and Philipp Galkin remind us that geopolitical considerations at the cost of intensified relations with major developed economies have the potential to spill over and impact international cooperation on the non-energy element of the BRI (Belt and Road Initiative). The development of valuable liquefied natural gas infrastructure has reduced risks associated with the shipment of energy through chokepoints like the Malacca Strait and South China Sea. While China has a leadership role to play in the transition to clean energy, the battle for scarce rare earth metals threatens to politicize valuable supply chains. Political instability in crude oil–producing nations threatens to render some of China's overseas investments as unprofitable, stranded assets. On the financing side, high levels of political and economic risk in the BRI nations provide an excellent opportunity for China-backed development financing of large-scale energy infrastructure and coal projects.

In Chapter 6, Elizabeth Carey examines the outcomes of the COP26 Conference in Glasgow in 2021. The most prescient of these, the negotiation of Article 6 proposes a number of market and nonmarket approaches for signatories to fulfill existing climate pledges. The chapter focuses on the role of viable business solutions such as Carbon Capture and Storage (CCUS) and the need for more flexible and innovative energy policy to overcome historical barriers to their implementation. The implications of the situation in Ukraine on global energy and climate policy have yet to be fully determined and are recommended as a subject for research.

The third section—Global scenarios: harnessing the benefits of global geo-economic shifts—contains three chapters addressing potential future scenarios for the world oil industry, as well as the ability of big data and futures prices to forecast and hedge the political and economic risk present in these same scenarios.

Hilary Till and Joseph Eagleeye, in Chapter 7, outline the role of trading, speculation, and futures markets as means of harnessing the benefits of global geo-economic shifts. The chapter outlines the potential benefits to be drawn from the inference of crude oil market fundamentals through price-relationship data. The promise of 'big data' and the reality of data 'black holes' are discussed in detail through several fascinating examples, including proxying the physical market with future spreads, using futures price relationships to understand the complexities of Chinese demand, and determining the marginal cost of crude oil production. Given these considerations, the most pressing subjects for future research include the 'best practices' required to provide transparent and accurate data on world oil markets and new methods to produce insightful and pragmatic forecasts of these critical markets.

Chapter 8, "Scenario analysis: imagining the unimaginable!", suggests future energy scenarios, including (i) a technological advance in one specific fuel type and (ii) a change in approach toward energy governance and regulation. Richard Wheeler focuses on how a specific technical advance or a shift in regulatory approach—in isolation—might alter the energy landscape, thus influencing the use of specific fuels in national and regional energy systems. A look into alternate technical advances, how global markets might be affected, and how this might alter the geopolitical landscape is suggested as an area for future research.

In Chapter 9, Tilak Doshi demonstrates that, despite considerable progress in the Gulf, including Saudi Arabian reforms and the Abraham Accords, historical divisions and internal conflicts linger in the GCC (Gulf Cooperation Council). The flashpoints include Iran's continued intrusions in Saudi Arabia and the UAE by proxy Houthi allies in Yemen; Qatar's ties with Turkey based on support for Hamas and the Muslim Brotherhood; and Turkish intervention in Libya, which represents a 'red line' with the potential to inspire Egyptian military intervention in support of Cairo's ally Khalifa Haftar. Inflation and higher food prices promised by the Russia–Ukraine war have the potential to trigger severe trade imbalances, and domestic social unrest in Egypt and other "fragile and conflict-ridden states such as Iraq, Syria, Yemen, Libya, Jordan, and Lebanon." The US–EU sanctions blocking Russian access to the SWIFT international payments system present a new risk factor to the GCC's Sovereign Wealth Fund managers. China, India, and Russia are all exploring commodity-based alternatives to SWIFT, perhaps signalling the end of the petrodollar.

The final section—The future of energy policy: meeting the macro challenge—domestic reform of unsustainability—contains 2 chapters concerning the complexities involved in the design, implementation, and ultimately the success of contemporary energy policy.

In Chapter 10, Arnault Barichella discusses the critical issue of cybersecurity and the increasing potential for cyberattacks on power networks and generators, including nuclear plants. A number of policy choices are examined in detail, including: (i) the 'security in depth' approach favored by the United States, (ii) the 'comprehensive and flexible' approach chosen by the EU, and (iii) the 'detailed regulatory framework' utilized by France. The rapid development and globalization of digital technology requires international collaboration and further research into the future of privacy and data protection frameworks.

Timothy Considine and Tara Righetti, in Chapter 11, discuss the highly politicized subject of production of oil and gas from federally owned and managed lands in the United States. The chapter outlines the challenges presented by land fragmentation and overlapping regulatory authorities, to applied economic research and efforts to estimate the costs and benefits of the restriction on leasing and drilling. The implications of federal oil and gas policy for GHG emissions and future implications for world oil prices, production on private land, and consumption have yet to be fully determined and are recommended as an important area for further study.

The last two chapters, "Establishing a lunar underground outpost" and "Questions to ask before we commence mining in space," remind us that our energy future is far from certain. The promise of an abundance of cheap and reliable energy remains a distant but achievable goal.

The Role of Russia

In light of recent developments in Europe, we begin with an extract from "The Geopolitics of Oil," which, although written more than 25 years ago, provides a historical overview of the role of Russia, the former Soviet Union, and its continued relevance to contemporary issues in the geopolitics of energy (Conant, 1994).

> As various proposals are reviewed to link Russian-controlled oil and gas pipelines to East Asia, the web of pipelines now under consideration for moving supplies

eastward suggests a renewed Russian influence across EurAsia, long a goal of the previous Soviet Union. Moreover, the question of transporting oil and gas from the southern republics of the former Soviet Union through Iran and/or Turkey is patently of long-standing security and political importance to Russia.

Oil and gas from the former Soviet Union is also of singular importance to Europe, despite Russia's current difficulties in maintaining production and the attendant risk that exports could yet be curtailed. Some countries—notably the United States— once anticipated that a growing European dependence on Soviet exports could give rise to serious security risks. Yet, in less than a decade, the industrial importing nations seek ways to shore up Russian production *and* exports. And there are serious difficulties in that respect. Robert Ebel warns:

> A weakened Russian oil industry cannot begin to offer any alternative to Middle East oil. Nor can it lead to economic reform in that country. Economic rejuvenation generally is not thought likely unless and until the health of the oil sector has been reasonably restored. A time of trouble would await if Russia, by virtue of continued oil production declines, would be forced to cut back on exports to hard currency markets. Not only would it be deprived of its leading source of hard currency earnings, but more importantly the loss of a major world oil supplier, as Russia is and has been, carries political and economic implications for all.

As for China, the oil potential said to underlie the South China Sea could likely be of increasing importance in a future conflict with Vietnam. (The latter has already made clear that its claim to these prospective reserves is "non negotiable.") Or will the Tarim Basin of western China prove to be hugely prolific? It is too soon to count on this new source of urgently needed oil but its location along inner-Asian frontiers will be of special geopolitical importance to Russia and China alike.

The geopolitical implications of Russia's oil situation loom very large, and have significant historic precedence. During World War II, oil geopolitics quickly became a major force behind German moves into southern Russia, as it did in Russian determination to keep German forces out of the Caucasus. Scarcely had that war ended when Russia moved to solidify control over Azerbaijan. Russian forces on the Iranian border threatened incursions from the north toward the oil wealth of Iran and the Gulf. US action was the key factor in limiting Russia's moves southward.

Until the 1980s, Russia had no need for access to Middle East oil, though it did develop tactics designed to destabilize relations between oil producers and importers, and in particular with the United States, against a background of historic interest in securing access to the Gulf and the Indian Ocean. Countering US influence in the region, the Russians turned Iraq, a leading oil exporter, into their ally in the Gulf.

Changes in the top leadership in both countries in the late 1980s enabled the United States and the then-Soviet Union to reach a private understanding that neither of the superpowers would challenge the other's vital interests in the Middle East. For a time at least, access to Gulf oil was not at risk. While Russia has continued to observe that understanding, political change within the Kremlin could alter its policies toward the Gulf and the United States. Moreover, oil importing nations are

> currently watching Russian moves toward former Soviet republics whose geographical location and expectations of oil and gas reserves are clearly of interest to the Kremlin, and several of these new republics will have contacts in the Gulf.
>
> Realistically there is for the near-term little prospect that Russia will have the military capabilities to threaten an industrial oil importer's access to Middle East oil. However, Russian forces could again impress upon the Caucasus and Central Asia its historic imperative to be in control of these borderlands. Russian tactics in the Middle East may again be troubling to the United States and other key importers. In April of this year, for example, Russia concluded "defensive" arms deal with Syria citing the arms deliveries of the United States to Israel. The geopolitics of the Gulf are like a shadowy presence in world affairs, never absent.
>
> If the Europe United States were to move more actively to develop oil sources to replace its dependence on Russia and the Gulf, Venezuela and Canada would be the leading candidates. These countries' increasing extraction of unconventional crudes for export to the United States as well as to Europe and relationship with either producer to the Far East (in the case of Venezuela) could make a crucial difference. The United States has for years avoided any clear special largely because it saw no need to tie itself to "preferential" sources and partly, at least in Canada's case, because the United States has assumed their conventional and unconventional crudes may have no other market. On the other hand, Japan has shown interest in both Canadian and Venezuelan unconventional crudes as a potentially important further diversification of its crude supplies.

Remarkably, 25 years after this was written, Russian ambitions in Europe and the Gulf remain intact, once again casting a specter over global energy politics.

Disclaimer

This book presents a variety of ideas and perspectives on the future research agenda for energy politics. Some are complimentary, others perhaps in opposition to mainstream economic and political thought. The views expressed in this document do not necessarily reflect the views of the Editors. Where the text refers to statements made by third parties, every effort has been made to provide a fair representation of their views and opinions, but the ultimate responsibility for the interpretation lies with the authors. The views presented in this book are not attributable to any specific participant, even those within specific chapters with joint authorship.

Source: Greg Stoicoiu (2021).

Figure I.1 Russian Roulette

Notes

1. Melvin A. Conant worked for Standard Oil (Exxon Corporation) from 1961 to 1973 as a regional political adviser for the firm's interests in East Africa, Asia, the Far East, and Australia. He later served as a senior government relations counselor for Europe, the Middle East, and Asia. He was a US oil adviser at the Law of the Sea Conferences in 1972, 1973, and 1977 and, subsequently, helped found the Council on Ocean Law. In 1973, Mel Conant was invited to help create the International Energy Affairs branch of the Federal Energy Administration (FEA). He was nominated by President Ford to be Assistant Administrator of the International Energy Affairs branch of the FEA. From 1976 until his death on December 11, 2003, he served as President and Director of Conant and Associates, Ltd. In that role he advised government and industry on the political aspects of international energy issues and was editor and publisher of the monthly international report "Geopolitics of Energy." Mel Conant also served as executive staff member of the Council on Foreign Relations and was Professor of International Security Affairs at the National War College. He was a member of the Institute for Strategic Studies, the Royal United Services Institution for Defense Studies in London, the Council on Foreign Relations, and the Harvard University Visiting Committee

for Astronomy and Astrophysics. He was Chairman of the Advisory Committee of the School of Advanced International Studies International Energy Program at the Johns Hopkins University. Melvin A. Conant was an Honorary Trustee of the Woods Hole Oceanographic Institute.

2. Mr Ebel—a leading oil analyst of the former Soviet Union and Russia—was a frequent contributor to the "Geopolitics of Energy." Paragraph extracted from his manuscript entitled "Energy Choices in the Soviet Successor States," to be published in the summer of 1994 by the Center for Strategic and International Studies, Washington, DC. Subsequently published. Robert E. Ebel, Russi-King of the Oil Hill, CSIS, July 21, 2004.

References

Conant, Melvin A. ,The Geopolitics of Oil, Geopolitics of Energy, Volume 16, Number 7, July 1, 1994, Washington DC, © Copyright 1994 Canadian Energy Research Institute.

Considine, Jennifer I., and Keun-wook Paik, eds. *Handbook of Energy Politics*. Cheltenham, UK ; Northampton, MA, USA: Edward Elgar Pub, 2018.

Ebel, Robert E., Russi-King of the Oil Hill, CSIS, July 21, 2004.

PART I

Navigating emerging geopolitical risks: politics, economics, and business in a new world (dis) order

1 The stability of world oil markets and the potential for oil shocks[1]

Jennifer I. Considine, Douglas Cooke, Geoffrey Wood, Sylvain Cote, and Abdullah Aldayel

Introduction: What are the main sources of uncertainty reigning over world oil markets?

Despite a colorful and well-documented history—numerous journal articles, forecasting models, and books—very little is known about the actual quantitative value, or cost to society, of oil shocks (Joëts and Raza, 2014). The potential consequences of any specific political or economic disturbance are unclear and would appear to depend on the market conditions existing at the time of forecast and the exact nature of the shock (Kilian, 2016; Smith, 2020; Board of Governors of the Federal Reserve System, 2020).

In fact, there are many sources of uncertainty for world oil markets. These can be classified into two main categories: short-term risks that pose an immediate risk to the stability of oil prices and long-term risks that will come into play at some time in the future. Short-term risks include geopolitical disruptions to supply, demand, OPEC (Organization of the Petroleum Exporting Countries) spare capacity, inventories, and refining and transportation networks (Till, 2020). Long-term risks represent disruptions that are more enduring to the stability of world oil markets and can be attributed to changes in petroleum fiscal regimes and international energy governance and to permanent changes in consumer income levels and consumption patterns (Xu et al., 2021).

In the long-run, the major sources of structural and institutional risks for global oil markets fall into five major categories: enduring demand destruction from the Russia–Ukraine conflict, coronavirus, the proposed EU "border adjustment" for the carbon content of imports,[2] the lack of an institutional framework for the protection of "post-transition" energy networks, and a longer-term gradual transition to alternative fuels (Wheeler, 2020).

Source: Greg Stoicoiu (2021).

Figure 1.1 Oil Embargo

This chapter is divided into the following sections. Section 1 considers the prospects for a rapid transition to renewable energy and alternatives to hydrocarbons. Section 2 proposes the consideration of a new, adaptive energy policy and a more flexible approach toward well-functioning markets. Finally, the conclusion provides a summary of new challenges facing researchers and policy makers in a world oil market facing the unprecedented challenges of war in Europe, COVID, and climate change.

Renewable energy and alternatives to hydrocarbons

How long are hydrocarbons here to stay? This is a question that has been asked repeatedly since the first of the oil shocks in the 1970s. And, until very recently, virtually every industry analyst and many academics and others would answer the same way: Hydrocarbons are here to stay for quite some time. Some, in fact, going as far as to say for the foreseeable future. The *Palgrave Handbook of Managing Fossil Fuels and Energy Transitions* (Wood and Baker, 2020) was a comprehensive and nuanced attempt to answer three key questions that highlight the complexity of the issue: (1) Can hydrocarbons be replaced by renewable energy sources? (2) How long will this transition take? (3) Can we manage the transition in an orderly fashion? This section will look at each of these three questions in turn.

Can hydrocarbons be replaced by renewable energy sources?

All energy sources can, of course, be at least partially replaced, as shown via historical energy transitions, including the switch from biomass to coal, which powered the Industrial Revolution. In recent history, notable examples include the substitution of coal with nuclear via government state ownership (e.g., France) and coal with gas, largely driven by the privatization of national energy markets in the 1980s and 1990s (e.g., the United Kingdom). The change that is particularly clear in most people's minds today is the energy transition toward modern renewable energy sources (e.g., wind, solar, geothermal), electric vehicles, batteries (and other forms of storage), and hydrogen.

Notably, not all hydrocarbon alternatives are technologically or commercially available, including hydrogen, carbon capture and storage, wave power, or for aviation/shipping purposes, and so on. For example, while there is a whole new generation of new electric battery technology, it is not expected to be commercially available for the next ten or so years. The hydrogen side is very interesting. This is being led by Japan, where Honda, Toyota, and Hyundai have launched the first mass-produced hydrogen fuel cell vehicles. Their fuel cells, moreover, now heat 225,000 homes. Early-mover companies, notably in Japan, are beginning to see lucrative export opportunities (Dundonald, 2020). A few such initiatives led by corporations and governments specifically focus on hydrogen produced from gas—in other words, from hydrocarbons—but, in an increasingly zero-carbon world, green hydrogen (from renewable sources) must be the focus and not just another hydrocarbon-based energy source to be replaced at some undefined 'later' date. There are also supply chain concerns. All nations have at least some renewable energy resources, but the materials for building the infrastructure are not so geographically dispersed. Are we, then, prepared to turn over the energy supply chain to the countries that have the highest reserves, including of rare earth metal resources and lithium and cobalt?[3]

Over the years, many groups have taken the position that there are geopolitical, economic, environmental, social, and moral reasons for replacing hydrocarbon-based energy sources. Climate change has been cited as a compelling reason. The publication in April 2022 of the *Sixth Assessment Report* of the Intergovernmental Panel on Climate Change (IPCC, 2022) warns in unequivocal terms that it is now or never if we want to limit global warming to 1.5°C. The invasion of Ukraine by Russia has been identified as another reason, showcasing that democracies run the risk of supporting the very same regimes they stand against in their inability to wean themselves from fossil fuels. Others have argued that there is also a strong economic rationale, with the majority of new renewable energy technologies plummeting—indeed, onshore wind and solar photovoltaic are now cheaper than gas—while oil and gas prices soar on the back of instability, pandemic, and war (IRENA, 2021). Based on these reasons, energy transition could offer the opportunity to move away from centralized energy systems dominated by a few large-scale powerful companies to a more inclusive distributed system that facilitates democratic and just participation involving engagement by communities and people (Wood, 2016).

There has also been a push to develop green and blue hydrogen in recent years. Whereas green hydrogen is when the energy used to power electrolysis comes from renewable sources like wind, water, or solar, blue hydrogen is hydrogen produced from natural gas through a process of steam methane reforming. The International Energy Agency reported that there are at least 50 blue hydrogen projects under development globally, and capacity is set to increase more than tenfold by 2030[4] (15/02/2022). The European Union's hydrogen strategy, published in 2020, says that "renewable and low-carbon hydrogen can contribute to reduce greenhouse gas emissions ahead of 2030." By 2050, the global trade in hydrogen is expected to be worth more than the global trade in oil, according to the International Renewable Energy Agency. Europe[5] and East Asia are likely to need more hydrogen than they can produce, while the Gulf nations are well-placed geographically to export through ships or pipelines. With its abundant gas reserves and sunshine, Saudi Arabia's ambition is to produce both blue and green hydrogen cheaply. Massive blue hydrogen investments are also planned in North America, particularly in Alberta and North Dakota. Both aim to create low-carbon hydrogen from natural gas. However, this raises the specter of the continued use of fossil fuels under the false guise of 'low carbon.' Termed the 'definitional problem,' Wood (2018: 429) highlighted concerns regarding the way in which we define renewable and low-carbon energy sources:

> Establishing ambiguous and non-legally binding definitions creates politically convenient flexibility in what technologies can be included within the protected domain of state support and promotion, leading to generous subsidy regimes for mature technologies (nuclear) and other options that are not truly renewable or low carbon but could help meet demanding… objectives (certain biomass, CCS).

The argument for the inclusion of blue hydrogen into low-carbon energy taxonomies would clearly add to the definitional problem because, as a fossil fuel–based energy source, it is not low carbon. As such, it does not address anthropogenic climate change.

In addition to the potential growing demand for this new energy source, another consequence of this development is the emergence of new trade flows to enable demand centers with resource-rich regions. Regions with cost-optimal production in renewable energy or natural gas could become major hydrogen export hubs with a certain advantage in terms of trade. In turn, countries with decarbonization ambitions, but without the resources to produce hydrogen, such as Japan, South Korea, and parts of Europe, would turn to imports.

The energy transition is not, and never has been, an issue of simply unplugging one source of energy and plugging in another source (high-carbon to low-carbon infrastructure). Indeed, history has shown that new energy sources have been complementary to one another. Over time, no energy source has been completely displaced in favor of a new one.

How long will this transition take?

The simple answer to this question is that we do not know. There are a number of reasons for this uncertainty. First, it will largely depend on political will. Many countries around the world are deploying increasing amounts of renewable energy technologies and have signed up to international and domestic climate change law (Muinzer, 2022; United Nations, 2022), with some also declaring climate emergencies and passing legally binding zero-carbon targets. Yet, the share of hydrocarbon-based energy sources remains resistant to change, still accounting for 80% of total global energy consumption and around 72% of global power consumption (REN21, 2021). Put simply, "the world is still addicted to and heavily dependent on fossil fuels for the power, heating/cooling and transport sectors" (Wood, 2020a: 611). And greenhouse gas emissions continue to climb. Indeed, projections show that if all currently operating climate change policies are successful, the global temperature rise will reach 3.7°C, way beyond the 1.5°C target.[6]

The question, then, is whether governments are willing to truly accept the reality of anthropocentric climate change and act at the level required. Yet, research has highlighted existing long-term interdependencies between government and the fossil fuel sector in terms of taxes and other revenues and the power of lobbying by incumbents and nongovernmental actors (Wood and Baker, 2020). Government responses to the COVID-19 pandemic also cast doubt on any meaningful action toward climate change. In the same way that many governments abdicated responsibility for continuing measures to control the COVID-19 pandemic, there are fears that slogans will replace meaningful action—'Learn to live with climate change'—as governments and corporations offload responsibility to the individual and continue to exploit and use fossil fuels, on the basis of insufficient concerted action to address climate change and external system shocks like the war in Ukraine. According to Wood (2020b), another century of fossil fuels would, however, be disastrous for the planet and particularly for human social, economic, and political systems—indeed for human civilization as we know it. Paradoxically, some are pointing out that decarbonization might be a slow painful process, a 'long goodbye to fossil fuels' despite repeated warnings of the need for urgent action now (Whitton and Charnley-Parry, 2020). This is supported by the speed with which many nations rushed to develop domestic shale gas sectors over the last decade or so and the continued race to find and exploit new hydrocarbon sources, notably in the Arctic.

Second, not all nations are equal in terms of the capacity and level of responsibility for addressing climate change. In particular, the Global South does not have the luxury of established and stable sustainable energy frameworks or access to the required technology, expertise, labor, and finance that the West enjoys. This has led to arguments that the replacement of hydrocarbons with renewable sources will require at least a dual-track energy transition: one that takes into consideration the developmental needs of many countries in the Global South but should not be abused for purely economic gain (Wood, 2020b). Such arguments are strengthened by the fact that hundreds of millions of people still lack access to modern capacity and historical responsibilities for climate change, leaving 'space' for the Global South to utilize their hydrocarbon reserves to develop and modernize their economies while participating in low-carbon energy transition, again with financial and technological support from the West. This would also mitigate against what some might call the Western-centric approach to energy transition, which envisages a one-size-fits-all approach based on Western notions of what is the best way to decarbonize and fails to understand that nuance and context are important here.

Further complicating the matter is that not everyone agrees on the contribution of new energy sources. The war in Ukraine and the energy disruption it has brought have created tension over whether the development of fossil fuel and its access, particularly gas, should be furthered or whether the crisis will instead accelerate the uptake of clean energy. But even the latter has not forged a consensus yet. Although hydrogen has often been deemed as the fuel of the future, blue hydrogen, more specifically, has been alleged to pollute more than traditional fossil fuels under some conditions.[7] Definitely fuel for thought and a promising subject for future research.

Can we manage the transition in an orderly fashion?

Answering this question depends on the response to the first two questions. Managing the decline of fossil fuels in the energy transition can be done in an orderly fashion—meaning that we do not leave billions of dollars of stranded assets, millions unemployed, communities ravaged, nations lacking the ability to develop, and so on—but only if we accept that fossil fuels can be replaced by existing sources such as renewables (and future energy technologies/ sources) in conjunction with the necessary political will, that governments will act meaningfully. Recognition that we might need a dual-track transition that respects the context of the Global South and the responsibilities of the Global North will help ensure a fair, just, democratic, and equitable transition based on renewables. Only this will result in a route map that offers milestones of certainty toward decarbonization for governments, industry, developers, investors, communities, and citizens. But one question remains: Is there sufficient time left to do so within the urgent timeframe that we as a species have set for ourselves?

Adaptive Energy Policy: A more flexible approach toward well-functioning markets?

A challenge facing policies revolves around the need to capture the complexity and constraints facing energy and its different sources. While some may be complementary, others may compete with one another. The present geopolitical situation has exacerbated those tensions. At the same time, a continuation of global economic growth and development is crucial for the fair and equitable advancement of human welfare as expressed in the United Nations Sustainability Goals. This, in turn, is fundamentally dependent on maintaining and extending access to affordable and reliable modern energy services.

However, given the potential for modern economic development to generate high levels of carbon emissions, which could create climatic conditions that will jeopardize future growth and prosperity, the key challenge remains to provide affordable and reliable energy services in an environmentally sustainable and responsible manner.

Governments have a leading role to play to support an efficient, innovative, timely, and least cost response that balances these goals. But how should governments respond to the challenge?

Experience shows that centrally planned approaches based on 'thin simplifications' and delivered through narrow, prescriptive, and poorly integrated policy and regulatory interventions tend to be unduly expensive and ridged, generate a host of unintended distortions, and do not provide a robust foundation for flexible and adaptable policy responses. Nor do they provide an effective foundation for timely, innovative, and cost-effective commercially driven outcomes.

Nowhere is this more clearly seen than in the mass deployment of renewable generation through production subsidies like feed-in-tariffs. Such programs have successfully supported early adoption but have proven too expensive to fund large-scale deployment globally. For example, in 2015 the German government spent around Euro 22.3 billion on renewable energy subsidies at an average cost of around Euro 140 per MWh produced.[8] In 2020, the German government allocated approximately US$46 billion to sustainable investments in renewables and electric vehicles, including a US$9 billion boost to green hydrogen (Kretchmer, 2020). Ongoing expenditures of this magnitude would be considered unaffordable in many other jurisdictions, especially among developing nations with more limited capacity to pay.

In addition, these subsidy schemes typically have led to renewable generation being poorly integrated into power systems and markets, especially in energy-only power markets. This has created substantial distortions that are threatening power system flexibility and reliability in some cases and have the potential to jeopardize a timely and affordable transition.

In particular, the economics of flexible, mid-merit generators has been eroded by the fundamental distortion of efficient price formation in energy-only wholesale electricity spot markets resulting from out-of-market dispatch of renewable generation combined with policies that have brought forward more variable renewable generation than is needed to meet incremental growth in demand and capacity retirements. This is creating a serious problem for the transition as these are the very plants needed to provide cost-effective backup for the large-scale deployment of variable renewables at this time. Without them, the transition will be slower, riskier, and costlier.

At the same time, the market returns for variable renewable generators are systemically lower due to their mandated reliance on falling spot revenues, which reinforces their ongoing dependence on public subsidies.[9]

These developments have led to calls for a range of narrow and prescriptive interventions, such as capacity mechanisms, that address the symptoms and not the causes of the problem. Such forms of centrally planned intervention are more likely to introduce a host of distortions, leading to pressure for more government intervention while extending and entrenching expensive ongoing subsidies. Ultimately, such policies are unlikely to deliver an efficient, innovative, or commercially sustainable transition globally.

Key features of an adaptable energy policy

The 'wicked' nature of the climate change challenge, combined with our limited understanding of its likely impacts, suggests the need for a flexible and adaptable policy approach that can rapidly respond to an evolving understanding of the science, to technological advances, changes in costs and market-based innovation, and evolving community expectations.

Experience suggests that the most effective policy frameworks are holistic, objective, adaptable, and comprehensive. They are holistic in that they consider technological development in its entirety and seek to provide an interrelated set of targeted stimuli that complement and reinforce incentives for efficient, innovative, and timely development and deployment. Holistic policy frameworks help to avoid unintended consequences that have the potential to derail or fundamentally distort timely and effective technological development and deployment.

They are objective in that they establish clear, outcome-based policy objectives. They are not bound by timetables or timelines, recognizing that technological development is inherently uncertain and rarely proceeds according to a predetermined administrative program in practice. And they do not prescribe how a policy goal is to be achieved. Instead, they seek to create and reinforce incentives to encourage participants to work out the most timely and innovative ways to meet the objective using whatever cost-effective combinations of technologies and commercial arrangements that are available.

Most importantly, effective policy frameworks are adaptable. They can change the range and combination of policies, or moderate policy priorities, quickly and effectively to ensure that the policy framework remains relevant and effective in response to changing technological developments, commercial innovation, relative costs, unanticipated developments, and evolving policy priorities.

In practice, adaptability can be built into the policy process through regular policy evaluation and review based on operational evidence and other information gathered, among other things, from the incremental implementation of support programs.

Three-to-five-year timeframes are probably appropriate in this context. They would provide sufficient time to test and assess policy interventions while enabling timely responses to changing circumstances that avoid potentially harmful 'policy lock-in.' A five-year timeframe would also be consistent with the review period proposed under the Paris Agreement.

A critical enabler for an adaptable energy policy: A Crucial Response to Uncertain Times

Rather than emphasizing central planning, the overall effectiveness of an adaptable energy policy could be greatly enhanced by harnessing the power of independent, decentralized decision-making to drive experimentation, learning, innovation, and the timely development and deployment of solutions to advance the transition at least cost.

And the most practical, proven, and effective means available to help realize this potential are well-functioning markets. Such markets operate within the boundaries set by governments through effective laws, regulations, and market rules.[10] They are inherently dynamic, evolving over time in response to changes in technologies, market innovations, customer tastes, and public policy requirements. This inherent flexibility and adaptability enable the markets to continue to function effectively in the midst of uncertainty and rapid change. As a result, they are better able to adapt to the challenges and inherent uncertainties associated with the transition toward a zero-carbon economy and to do so in an efficient, timely, and least cost manner.

In addition, a market-oriented environment provides scope for governments to create property rights for carbon pollution, which, in turn, can be used to drive the formation of efficient price signals to provide individual buyers and sellers with strong incentives to develop the most efficient and innovative ways to meet climate change goals at least cost. They also provide clear price signals for efficient energy investment, operation, and end-use, which is a fundamental requirement for continuing to deliver access to reliable and affordable energy services during the transition.

In this way, market-leaning approaches provide the basis for the use of more flexible and adaptable policies. They create a robust incentive structure for more predictable commercial behavior, which is a crucial precondition for applying a more incremental and adaptive policy approach as envisaged in the Paris Agreement. If governments can be confident that market participants will respond to price incentives in a predictable way, then they can have greater confidence about how policies might affect behavior and, hence, the outcomes that policy intervention could bring.

As a result, a well-functioning market that fully integrates renewable energy and incorporates effective carbon pricing signals would permit a more integrated and strategic approach to policy—one that relies on fewer, more holistic, and objective-based responses rather than a myriad of narrow, prescriptive, and overly codified interventions.

Where to now?

World oil market conditions are highly variable and change significantly over time, so projections made at any given time may be subject to significant revision. In the future, we are anticipating several drastic events with the potential to result in the tightening of markets, with the risk of extreme downward price shocks. These include the following largest risks stated in sequential order:

- War risk: risk of a continuation or proliferation of war between Russia and the Ukraine and disrupted trade flows
- Sanctions risk: risk renegotiating Russian/Iranian/Venezuelan sanctions and of oil volumes coming back or leaving world oil markets
- Venezuela's political and economic instability could halt in the event of regime change
- COVID risk: Oil markets were balanced heading into 2020; however, there is still considerable uncertainty concerning the sixth wave of COVID-19 and its implications for global oil demand and OECD (Organisation for Economic Co-operation and Development) oil inventories
- OPEC may be unable to react to major events, such as a sixth wave variant COVID-19 outbreak or sanctions on Russian oil and gas, and the resulting demand destruction could be devastating to world energy markets

We believe global oil supply and demand, as well as volatility, have reached unparalleled distortion levels. Markets will continue to struggle with periods of volatility as demand returns to normal levels and a material portion of world oil supply capacity is taken offline indefinitely (Hunter, 2020). This unprecedented situation in global oil markets is summarized by Goldman Sachs as follows: "Not only is this the largest economic shock of our lifetimes, but carbon-based industries like oil sit in the cross-hairs as they have historically served as the cornerstone of social interactions and globalization, the prevention of which are the main defense against the virus."

Source: Greg Stoicoiu (2021).

Figure 1.2 OPEC and COVID-19

In an increasingly complex world of big data, the human factor must also be taken into consideration. As a general rule, people tend to be risk averse and more concerned about losing money and resources than gaining profits. As a result, trading decisions are often impaired by cognitive error, including belief preservation errors, information processing errors, emotional errors, overconfidence, and self-control bias. To address this situation, trading companies and policy makers alike have developed advanced predictive analytics and proprietary digital intelligence to counter the effects of cognitive error in decision-making.

In short, the role of policy makers has changed considerably over the past decade. Policy prescriptions that worked well in tight market conditions can have unintended consequences in loose markets, and in some cases, consequences that undermine the original policy goals when markets are oversupplied. In other words, policy can become maladaptive and suboptimal. The situation is complicated by issues concerning cybersecurity and the geopolitics of new transitional fuels, rare earth metals, lithium, and cobalt. To further complicate matters, there are 'dark' and even 'black' holes in the data available to policy makers and world oil analysts. It can be extremely difficult to access data on non-OECD inventories, but the availability and transparency of this data is essential for the smooth working of critical supply chains (JODI, 2020). Policy makers can lead by example by providing timely and complete energy data, with an emphasis on critical inventory levels.

Notes

1. This chapter is based, in part, on presentations delivered at the private workshop "The Stability of World Oil Markets and the Potential for Oil Shocks," King Abdullah Petroleum Studies and Research Center, Riyadh, Saudi Arabia, February 27, 2020.
2. Similar carbon pricing initiatives are envisioned for Canada, the United States, Mexico, Africa, and parts of Asia and outlined in considerable detail on the World Bank Carbon Pricing Dashboard (World Bank, 2021).
3. Lithium and cobalt are not rare earth metals; however, their use in electric vehicle lithium-ion battery packs is well documented (Goldman, 2017).
4. IEA (2021), Global Hydrogen Review 2021.
5. See the European Union's hydrogen strategy, published in 2020.
6. Looking at a global temperature rise of 3.7°C from another perspective, scientists have estimated that a decrease of 2–4°C from average sent the planet into an ice age that lasted over 100 000 years (Williams et al., 2020).7. A recent study has concluded that blue hydrogen has a 20 percent larger carbon footprint than natural gas and coal when used for heat (Howarth and Jacobson, 2021).
8. See the German energy regulator's *Energy Sector Monitoring Report 2016* for further details. This figure excludes the related and growing cost of managing intermittency. Substantial legacy expenditure on these production subsidy programs is expected to continue well beyond the 2020s.
9. Governments typically mandate that variable renewable generators receive priority dispatch and are price takers in electricity spot markets. Spot revenues are declining as larger volumes of out-of-market variable renewable generation are deployed, which displaces more expensive mid-merit plants that would otherwise set the system marginal price. This phenomenon, commonly referred to as the 'merit-order effect,' is resulting in a range of market distortions, including dwindling revenues for variable renewable generators.

10. Key requirements for a well-functioning market include aligning accountability and responsibility with role and function, such that the party (or parties) best able to manage a particular matter has clear incentive and legal authority to do so in a timely and effective manner at least cost; establishing effective physical and financial markets that facilitate efficient price formation and risk management; establishing an effective market structure that promotes transparency and encourages efficient, competitive behaviors; implementing effective economic and competition regulation, especially for network services; and ensuring access to timely and accurate information to help inform effective decision-making. Governments have a crucial role in establishing the legal, regulatory, and market framework that creates the boundaries for a well-functioning market and to make sure that this framework is amended as required to keep pace with technological, commercial, and public policy advances so that it doesn't become a barrier to efficient and innovative energy sector operation and development.

References

Board of Governors of the Federal Reserve System. 2020. "The Fed - FRB/US Model." March 2020. https://www.federalreserve.gov/econres/us-models-about.htm.

Bragoli, Daniela and Modugno, Michele. "A Nowcasting Model for Canada: Do U.S. Variables Matter?" Board of Governors of the Federal Reserve System, Finance and Economics Discussion Series 2016, no. 36 (April 2016): 1–33. https://doi.org/10.17016/FEDS.2016.036.

Borenstein, Severin, and Ryan Kellogg. "The Incidence of an Oil Glut: Who Benefits from Cheap Crude Oil in the Midwest?" Working Paper. National Bureau of Economic Research, June 2012. https://doi.org/10.3386/w18127.

Camargo, Oscar, "Sources of Uncertainty reigns over oil markets: Predictable or unpredictable behavior?" (presentation, The Stability of World Oil Markets, and the Potential For Oil Shocks, KAPSARC, February 27, 2020). https://www.kapsarc.org/events/the-stability-of-world-oil-markets-and-the-potential-for-oil-shocks/.

CFA Institute. "ESG Investing and Analysis," 2020. https://www.cfainstitute.org/en/research/esg-investing.

Chicago Booth School of Business. "Richard H Thaler." The University of Chicago Booth School of Business, 2017. http://www.chicagobooth.edu/faculty/directory/t/richard-h-thaler.

Chudik, Alexander, and M. Hashem Pesaran. "Theory and Practice of Gvar Modelling." Journal of Economic Surveys 30, no. 1 (2016): 165–97. https://doi.org/10.1111/joes.12095.

Considine, Jennifer, and Abdullah Aldayel. "Balancing World Oil Markets and Understanding Contango and Inventories: The Changing Nature of World Oil Markets." King Abdullah Petroleum Studies and Research Center, July 6, 2020. https://doi.org/10.30573/KS--2020-DP15.

Considine, Jennifer, and Abdullah Aldayel. "The Stability of World Oil Markets, and the Potential for Oil Shocks." KAPSARC, 2020. https://www.kapsarc.org/events/the-stability-of-world-oil-markets-and-the-potential-for-oil-shocks/.

Considine, Jennifer, Philipp Galkin, and Abdullah Al Dayel. "Market Structure, Inventories and Oil Prices: An Empirical Analysis." King Abdullah Petroleum

Studies and Research Center, February 24, 2020. https://doi.org/10.30573/KS--2020-DP02.

Cordesman, Anthony. 2006. "The Global Oil Market." March 1, 2006. https://www.csis.org/analysis/global-oil-market.

Criqui, Patrick. "After the Gulf Crisis: The Third Oil Shock Is Yet to Come." Energy Studies Review 3, no. 3 (December 31, 1991). https://doi.org/10.15173/esr.v3i3.248.

Dundonald, Douglas, "Oil shocks—Is the past a guide to the future?" (presentation The Stability of World Oil Markets, and the Potential For Oil Shocks, KAPSARC, February 27, 2020).

Economou, Andreas, Paolo Agnolucci, and Vencenzo De Lipsis. 2017. "A Structural Model of the World Oil Market: The Role of Investment Dynamics and Capacity Constraints in Explaining the Evolution of the Real Price of Oil." OIES Working Paper, no. WPM 75 (December). The Oxford Institute for Energy Studies. https://doi.org/10.26889/9781784670979.

EIA. 2014. "Behavioral Economics Applied to Energy Demand Analysis: A Foundation." Independent Statistics and Analysis. Washington DC: Energy Information Administration, U.S. Department of Energy. https://www.eia.gov/analysis/studies/demand/economicbehavior/pdf/behavioraleconomics.pdf.

EIA. 2021. "What Drives Crude Oil Prices?." 2021. https:// www .eia .gov/ finance/ markets/ crudeoil/ spot _prices .php; https:// ec .europa .eu/ environment/ strategy/ circular-economy-action-plan_en.

European Commission. "Circular Economy Action Plan," March 2020.

European Commission and Directorate-General for Economic and Financial Affairs. European Economic Forecast: Spring 2021., 2021. https://ec.europa.eu/info/sites/default/files/economy-finance/ip149_en.pdf.

El Wardany, Salma. "Libya Oil Production at 1.1 Million Barrels a Day," November 11, 2020. https://www.rigzone.com/news/wire/libya_oil_production_at_11_million_barrels_a_day-11-nov-2020-163821-article/.

European Parliament. "Legislative Train Schedule." European Parliament, November 10, 2020. https://www.europarl.europa.eu/legislative-train.

Filatochev, Igor, and Roy Bradshaw. 1992a. "EconPapers: The Soviet Hyperinflation: Its Origins and Impact throughout the Former Republics." Europe-Asia Studies, 44 (5): 739–59.

Filatochev, Igor, and Roy Bradshaw. 1992b. "The Soviet Hyperinflation: Its Origins and Impact throughout the Former Republics." Europe-Asia Studies 44 (5): 739–59.

Fouquet, Roger. 2013. Handbook on Energy and Climate Change. Edward Elgar Publishing. https://doi.org/10.4337/9780857933690.

Future of Life. "AI Policy - Russia." Future of Life Institute, 2020. https://futureoflife.org/ai-policy-russia/.

Global Petrol Prices. "Oil Prices Historical Chart | GlobalPetrolPrices.Com." Global Petrol Prices, June 22, 2015. https://www.globalpetrolprices.com/articles/28/.

Goldman. 2017. "Electric Vehicles, Batteries, Cobalt, and Rare Earth Metals." Electric Vehicles, Batteries, Cobalt, and Rare Earth Metals. The Equation. October 25, 2017. https:// blog .ucsusa .org/ josh -goldman/ electric -vehicles -batteries -cobalt -and -rare -earth-metals/.

Hatipoglu, Emre, "KAPSARC Global Oil Model – A Global VAR Analysis" (presentation The Stability of World Oil Markets, and the Potential For Oil Shocks, KAPSARC, February 27, 2020). https:// www .kapsarc .org/ events/ the -stability -of -world-oil-markets-and-the-potential-for-oil-shocks/.

Hashimzade, Nigar, and Michael Thornton. "Handbook of Research Methods and Applications in Empirical Macroeconomics." Books. Edward Elgar Publishing, 2013. https://econpapers.repec.org/bookchap/elgeebook/14327.htm.

Howarth, Robert W. and Mark Z. Jacobson (2021), "How green is blue hydrogen?" *Energy Science & Engineering*, Volume 9, Issue 10 pp. 1676-1687. https://doi.org/10.1002/ese3.956.

Hunter, Brian, "Defining a Price Shock" (presentation The Stability of World Oil Markets, and the Potential For Oil Shocks, KAPSARC, February 27, 2020). https://www.kapsarc.org/events/the-stability-of-world-oil-markets-and-the-potential-for-oil-shocks/.

IEA. "Key Findings – World Energy Investment 2020 – Analysis." IEA. Accessed March 3, 2021. https://www.iea.org/reports/world-energy-investment-2020/key-findings.

IPCC. "Sixth Assessment Report, Climate Change 2022" (IPCC, 2022) <https://www.ipcc.ch/report/sixth-assessment-report-working-group-3/> accessed 12 April 2022.

IRENA. "Majority of New Renewables Undercut Cheapest Fossil Fuel on Cost" (IRENA, 22 June 2021) accessed 13 April 2022, based on the following report: <https://www.irena.org/news/pressreleases/2021/Jun/Majority-of-New-Renewables-Undercut-Cheapest-Fossil-Fuel-on-Cost#:~:text=Abu%20Dhabi%2C%20United%20Arab%20Emirates%2C%20June%2022%2C%202021,costs%20than%20the%20cheapest%20new%20fossil%20fuel%20option>.

JODI. "History of the Joint Organisations Data Initiative | JODI." Joint Organisations Data Initiative (JODI), 2020. https://www.jodidata.org/about-jodi/history.aspx.

Joëts, Marc, and Tovonony Raza. "What Is the Welfare Social Cost of Oil Price?" IAEE Energy Forum Q3 2014 (September 2014).

Kilian, Lutz. "Energy Price Shocks." In *The New Palgrave Dictionary of Economics*, 1–12. London: Palgrave Macmillan UK, 2016. https://doi.org/10.1057/978-1-349-95121-5_3008-1.

Kretchmer, Harry. "Billions for Sustainable Investments – Germany's Plan for a Green Recovery." World Economic Forum, July 2020. https://www.weforum.org/agenda/2020/07/germany-green-recovery-billions-sustainable-investments/.

Mauro, Filippo di, and Hashem Pesaran. "The GVAR Handbook: Structure and Applications of a Macro Model of the Global ... - Google Books," 2013.

Muinzer, Thomas, "National Climate Change Acts: The Emergence, Form and Nature of National Climate Legislation" (Bloomsbury Publishing PLC, 19 May 2022). https://books.google.ca/books/about/The_GVAR_Handbook.html?id=nmzyxQEACAAJ&redir_esc=y.

Oberholzer, Basil. Monetary Policy and Crude Oil: Prices, Production and Consumption. Edward Elgar Publishing, 2017.

Pollitt, Michael G., and Irina Shaorshadze. 2011. "The Role of Behavioural Economics in Energy and Climate Policy." Working Paper. Faculty of Economics. https://doi.org/10.17863/CAM.5237.

REN21. "Renewables 2021: Global Status Report" (REN21, June 2021) <https://www.ren21.net/wp-content/uploads/2019/05/GSR2021_Full_Report.pdf> accessed 13 April 2022.

Smith, Vanessa. "Global VAR Modelling," 2020. https://sites.google.com/site/gvarmodelling/.

Smith, Vanessa. "The Global VAR Model and (De)stabilizing Shocks" (presentation The Stability of World Oil Markets, and the Potential For Oil Shocks, KAPSARC, February 27, 2020). https://www.kapsarc.org/events/the-stability-of-world-oil-markets-and-the-potential-for-oil-shocks/.

Stoicoiu, Greg. 2021. Artist, Calgary, Alberta, Canada.

Till, Hilary. 2020. "When Has OPEC Spare Capacity Mattered for Oil Prices?" EDHEC-Risk Institute Working Paper (November): 9.

Turak, Natasha. "Oil and Gas Companies Set to Lose $1 Trillion in Revenues This Year." CNBC, April 30, 2020. https://www.cnbc.com/2020/04/30/coronavirus-creating-1-trillion-revenue-loss-for-oil-and-gas-companies.html.

United Nations. 'United Nations Climate Change' (United Nations, 2022) <https://www.un.org/en/climatechange> accessed 13 April 2022.

Wheeler, Richard, "Producers' Oil Market Risks: viruses, trade rules, and evolving institutional frameworks" (presentation, The Stability of World Oil Markets, and the Potential For Oil Shocks, KAPSARC, February 27, 2020). https://www.kapsarc.org/events/the-stability-of-world-oil-markets-and-the-potential-for-oil-shocks/.

Whitton, J. and I. Charnley-Parry, "The Long Hello: Energy Governance, Public participation and 'Fracking'." In Geoffrey Wood and Keith Baker (Eds.), "The Palgrave Handbook of Managing Fossil Fuels and Energy Transitions" (Palgrave Macmillan, 2020b) pp.405-425.

Williams, A. Park, E. R. Cook, J. E. Smerdon, B. I. Cook, J. T. Abatzoglou, K. Bolles, S. H. Baek, A. M. Badger, and B. Livneh (2020). "Large contribution from anthropogenic warming to an emerging North American megadrought." Science 370 (6516): DOI: 10.1126/science.abf3676.

Wood, Geoffrey, 'A systemic approach to renewable electricity technology deployment: The "missing link" in optimizing policy delivery in the UK?' In Raphael J. Heffron and Gavin F.M. Little (Eds.), Delivering Energy Law and Policy in the EU and the US: A reader (Edinburgh University Press, 2016).

Wood, Geoffrey, 'Policy Risk, Politics and Low Carbon Energy'. In Jennifer I. Considine and Keun-Wook Paik (Eds.), 'Handbook of Energy Politics' (Edward Elgar Publishing, 2018) pp.405-434.

Wood, Geoffrey, 'Fossil Fuels in a Carbon-Constrained World'. In Geoffrey Wood and Keith Baker (Eds.), 'The Palgrave Handbook of Managing Fossil Fuels and Energy Transitions' (Palgrave Macmillan, 2020a) pp.3-23.

Wood, Geoffrey, 'Managing the Decline of Fossil Fuels: A long Goodbye?' In Geoffrey Wood and Keith Baker (Eds.), 'The Palgrave Handbook of Managing Fossil Fuels and Energy Transitions' (Palgrave Macmillan, 2020b) pp.611-615.

Wood, Geoffrey, and Keith Baker (Eds.), 'The Palgrave Handbook of Managing Fossil Fuels and Energy Transitions' (Palgrave Macmillan, 2020)

World Bank. 2021. "Carbon Pricing Dashboard | Up-to-Date Overview of Carbon Pricing Initiatives." October 2021. https://carbonpricingdashboard.worldbank.org/map_data.

Xu, Bing, Rong Fu, and Chi Keung Marco Lau. 2021. "Energy Market Uncertainty and the Impact on the Crude Oil Prices." Journal of Environmental Management 298 (November): 113403. https://doi.org/10.1016/j.jenvman.2021.113403.

2 Geopolitics and energy security issues in India

Jitendra Roychoudhury

Introduction: What Drives Indian Energy Geopolitics

> "We have no eternal allies, and we have no perpetual enemies. Our interests are eternal and perpetual, and those interests, it is our duty to follow" — Lord Palmerston

India, as a country, represents the last of the large high-growth fossil fuel energy markets with the potential to grow over the coming decades. Low Indian per capita energy consumption (currently about 0.6 tonnes of oil equivalent (toe), which is half of the Asian average and a third of the global average), a fast-growing economy (8.2 percent for the current 2021 fiscal), favorable population demographics (1.3 billion people with an average age of 29), and a rising per capita income, all indicate the potential for future growth (Ministry of External Affairs 2022; Economic Survey 2019).

The Indian economy has grown and benefited immensely because of globalization and has become a part of the global supply chain across goods and services. In 1991, when India started liberalizing its economy, merchandise trade was about 14.1 percent of a US$ 270 billion GDP. By 2020, it had grown to 24.4 percent of a US$ 2.6 trillion GDP (World Bank 2022). As a result of globalization, India is now much more dependent economically and networked within the global economy (S. Menon 2019). The export growth has primarily been from petroleum products, which is noteworthy given that India imports almost 80 percent of its crude requirements. Indian imports of other fossil fuels like coal and gas have also increased over the past decade.

The growth in consumption of fossil fuels in India has meant that annual Indian greenhouse gas (GHG) emissions put it among the world's top emitters in the aggregate (Ritchie and Roser 2020). India has tried to manage the externalities of its fossil fuel economy by adding significant nonfossil sources to its energy mix, ranging from renewables to nuclear (Ministry of New and Renewable Energy 2022). Issues like climate change and GHG emissions for energy and resource-poor India amount to policy makers' complicated trade-offs. While the country must find ways to deal with the constant international pressure to reduce its carbon emissions, it must also meet its needs for improved energy access and sustained economic growth.

Indian per capita energy consumption is expected to quadruple to meet a middle-income country's demand and reach a level of 0.8 in the Human Development Index (Bhaskar 2019). India's significant import dependence on energy sources and the related capital expenditures—for example, fertilizers, power generation, and transmission equipment—pose profound implications for its overall physical and economic security. With these implications in mind, the Indian geopolitical focus has been on managing the external global environment through the Five Cs—communication, coordination, collaboration, cooperation, and coercion—to ensure energy security and access to critical resources are met to support economic growth.

To secure its legitimate economic and security interests, India has been increasingly engaging with global regimes to ensure that its interests help shape the frameworks that are developed to meet energy and climate challenges. This increase in engagement can be seen in the greater involvement that India has exhibited in climate negotiations such as the Conference of the Parties (COP) or as a member of multilateral export control regimes such as the Australia Group and the Wassenaar Arrangement (Jha 2018).

This chapter intends to focus on some of India's current and future challenges in the energy domain and be aligned with the book's objectives to look at these emerging issues through an energy security lens. The chapter also suggests new grounds for future research.

India's Energy Security and the Indian Ocean

"Capacity defines intentions"—Anon

Energy import dependency has meant that the Indian geopolitical focus has been on securing and maintaining the sea lanes of communication. Indian energy needs have primarily focused on the Indian Ocean Region (IOR is the region between the Straits of Malacca in the east and the Suez Canal in the west and extends down to Antarctica), with most crude sourcing coming from the Middle East (Saudi Arabia, Iraq, United Arab Emirates, and Oman). Imports from Qatar, Indonesia, Australia, and South Africa meet energy requirements in terms of gas and coal. The IOR is also crucial for the transit of Indian exports, and its criticality has helped shape many Indian geopolitical approaches to the region. These have been strategic partnerships with key energy suppliers, development of and investment in strategic petroleum reserves with ADNOC (Verma 2020), international investments in offshore oil and gas assets with the United Arab Emirates (Press Information Bureau 2018), and military interactions in the form of military cooperation with the Gulf (Ghosh 2020). India has also attempted to manage the developing security situation in the IOR by focusing on the seven logistics choke points: the Malacca Straits (near Singapore), Strait of Hormuz (in the Arabian Gulf), Mozambique Channel, Suez Canal, Sunda, and Lombok Straits (in Indonesia). These efforts have concentrated on the twin aspects of developing closer relationships with the respective nations and activating or developing military bases near them (Stimson Center 2012). The intention and focus had progressed even before the 2020 Galwan skirmish with China in the high Himalayas.

As risks and vulnerability to energy supply chains have increased, India has focused its strategy on enhancing energy resource security through efficient and assured logistics access, domestic energy distribution, and supply infrastructure. It has built coastal oil refineries and power plants to access energy sources and has diversified its energy sourcing and cooperation to ensure a stable supply. The development of port infrastructure has helped improve efficiencies and ensure that trade and commerce are facilitated.

The IOR will gradually be a contested space with perceptible shifts in the balance of power. As strategic competition and rivalry between the United States and China intensify, the IOR is expected to be an area of intense maneuvering. The development of agreements and alliances in the shape of QUAD[1] and AUKUS[2] point toward that scenario development (Chatterjee 2021). Such strategic competition will have immense energy and trade security implications for India's stable and secure access to energy supplies. Asian powers have a strategic interest in ensuring that the sea lanes are maintained for trade and communication. This interest could shape the formation of coalitions of the willing to balance security interests and protect commercial interests.

The rise of competing powers in the IOR would also mean that external interests could attempt to shape Indian geopolitical actions, either in the form of Indian geopolitical reaction to perceived threats or by the interests directly or indirectly. This was visible during the current conflict in Europe, where Western interests tried to shape Indian energy procurement, going against Indian interests (S. Menon 2022). Indian buying of discounted volumes of Russian crude was sought to be portrayed as India busting the sanctions against Russia imposed by the United States. India was primarily trying to ensure that its domestic economy was shielded from the high energy prices (Schmall and Reed 2022).

As the Ukrainian conflict has shown, energy can be politicized quite easily. Late in 2021, India faced opprobrium for shaping the final summit communique at the COP26, working with China to change the language on coal (Doshi and Roychoudhury 2021). This was despite India pledging to obtain 50 percent of its energy requirements from renewable energy by 2030 and achieve the target of net-zero emissions by 2070 (Press Information Bureau 2022a).

The Continuing Reign of (abated) King Coal?

"Coal is King In India—and will likely remain so" —Samantha Gross, Brookings, 2019

India is the world's second-largest coal producer and the fifth largest in terms of domestic coal deposits (Press Information Bureau 2020). India has depended on coal to fuel the energy needs of its economy. Despite ambitious renewable plans, coal still accounts for 55 percent of India's energy needs (Economic Survey 2022). Coal is used to generate electricity (51.1 percent of installed capacity and almost 77 percent of overall generation), iron and steel production, cement production, and fertilizer production. This dependency on coal is a critical aspect of India's energy security and one that has attracted a lot of attention from external political forces and special interest groups, which have aligned to stymie Indian investments in coal, both domestically and internationally (Patil 2015; Parkin 2021). Fossil fuels also significantly contribute to Indian GHG emissions, and as a result, coal usage has attracted a lot of attention from a decarbonization perspective. Coal markets in India are faced with increasing international pressure about GHG emissions. Policy makers have struggled to obtain an optimum energy mix that both provides the economic benefits of cheap coal and helps them adhere to increasingly stringent climate accords and emission norms. Disruptions from fast-growing renewables capacity expansion have brought further policy challenges in managing intermittency and grid integration (Tata Cleantech Capital Limited 2020). With a low-carbon future becoming a priority, policy makers face complex decisions regarding investments in cleaner fuels and renewables, while at the same time facing more practical challenges such as integrating renewables into their legacy electricity grids. Policy-driven renewable energy incentives (direct incentives such as monetary or indirect incentives such as priority transmission access) threaten commercially viable coal markets. If it were to happen, this would result in declining investments in coal supply, thus raising questions about the associated supply reliability. Supply disruptions in coal would increase price volatility, with highly inflationary impacts on the domestic economy. This is significant as coal demand is expected to double to almost 1.3–1.5 billion tons by 2030, and imports will continue to play an essential role in meeting demand (Economic Survey 2022).

Coal has been a critical enabler of India's drive to ensure universal energy access to its 1.3 billion population. In turn, lack of energy access can significantly impact multiple indicators of suitable living standards, including health, education, food security, and well-being. Coal usage plays a significant role in eradicating poverty. Its easy domestic availability and cost competitiveness compared with other imported fuels facilitates the welfare economics that has helped the political class immensely. For a large developing country like India, coal thus becomes an essential enabler of development and progress, even when accounting for its externalities. Increased coal usage has imposed costs on India regarding environmental pollution and associated deaths, often leading to conflict in coal mining areas and near power plants (Barrows, Garg and Jha 2019). Coal has also brought India to the center stage in the global climate dialogue as one of the world's largest emitters of GHGs. While climate change cannot be divorced from India's energy security, both are integral to its economic and social development. India has tried to manage the energy demands of its economy while being conscious of its international climate obligations. In 2010, India imposed a cess[3] on domestically produced and imported coal to help fund the National Clean Energy and Environment Fund (Garg 2018). This cess has functioned as an enabler for financing the renewable expansion in India. India has also focused on gradually upgrading its boiler fleet to supercritical and ultra-supercritical technology standards and on clean coal technologies to reduce overall emissions from the power sector.

Coal also feeds into a substantial political economy that supports coal's entire rentier value chain—mining, transport, and other ancillary activities. The states of east and central India, where coal mining is most prevalent, are endemically poor, and coal mining provides a source of revenue for the state exchequer as well as employment. Disrupting this political economy by increasing renewable capacity and bringing in storage to manage intermittency is not viable. The country's political leadership is aware of the potential social impacts of such a disruption. The legacy infrastructure built around coal is also a considerable impediment to transition to a cleaner energy future. Understanding the humungous challenges associated with the energy transition is critical to understanding why Prime Minister Modi announced India's net-zero achievement ambition to be by 2070. How the net-zero ambitions will play out over and above the compulsions of Indian energy security and the growing needs of a resource-hungry economy will be crucial to understand. Increasing coal usage could potentially impact the rural–urban divide in India. There is already an increasing focus on urban air quality issues, and the benefits of renewables as a clean energy source have started to trickle into communities.

Net Zero: A Just Transition to Carbon Management

> "Climate justice demands that the little carbon space we still have, developing countries should have enough room to grow"—Narendra Modi

India's pledge at the COP26 underlined its climate ambitions and seriousness toward its obligations. However, India also expected that the rich, developed countries would honor their climate finance promises and help finance and support India's energy transition. India has already requested financial support of US$1 trillion for its own energy transition needs, over and above the annual US$100 billion that was promised to developing nations (Doshi and Roychoudhury 2021).

As part of its 2015 Nationally Determined Contributions commitments in the Paris Agreement, India had committed to achieve emissions intensity reductions of 33–35 percent by 2030, compared with 2005 levels. India is already on its way to meeting these commitments, having achieved an emissions reduction of 28 percent over 2005 levels in 2021. India had also committed that, by 2030, 40 percent of all-electric power will come from renewable energy sources and that it aims to plant enough trees to be able to increase its forest cover to a third of its land by 2030. The goal is to absorb about 2.5–3 billion tons of carbon dioxide from the atmosphere through these carbon sinks (Press Information Bureau 2022a).

Prime Minister Modi's announcement of the 500 GW target at COP26 is incremental over the 450 GW of renewable energy electricity generation capacity by 2030 that he had earlier announced at the 2019 United Nations Climate Action Summit in New York. At COP26, Prime Minister Modi modified the announcement to include nonfossil fuel generation capacity, including hydro. Indian renewable energy generation and generation capacity have been increasing annually at 18percent and 22percent, respectively, so meeting the 500 GW non-fossil fuel target is within the realm of possibility (Deb and Agrawal 2021). A target of 500 GW in eight years (by 2030) would require significant investments to raise the current nonfossil fuel capacity and upgrade the grid to absorb that much renewable energy. This is where the current bankrupt nature of the country's electricity distribution sector might pose a significant challenge.

Distribution companies (discoms) that buy renewable energy from the generators have had to use generation curtailment to reduce their commercial losses as they continue to be bankrupt because of the continued use of the electricity sector to parcel out patronage to vested groups in the form of highly subsidized or free electricity. Discoms have also attempted to renegotiate signed power purchase agreements to try and secure the lowest-possible tariffs. This has increased risks for the renewable energy sector and has impacted growth rates and project execution. An increase in targets for the renewable energy sector without tackling the electricity sector's persistent issues would mean increased challenges, reduced investor appetite, and missed targets. Renewable energy developers face issues related to grid access and congestion, land availability, payments, supply chain, and investor confidence (Singh 2019).

For the projected COP26 targets that Prime Minister Modi has spelled out to crystalize, India needs a massive injection of funds to modernize its transmission grids to cater to the additional variable renewable energy (VRE) demands. The first phase of the Green Energy Corridor (GEC), targeting 32.7 GW and part-funded by the German development bank KfW, has been commissioned, and now, the second phase of the GEC, targeting 20 GW of solar energy transmission, is being planned (Renewable Watch 2020). Many transmission projects will need to be designed, built, and commissioned in line with the targeted VRE capacity expansion. Additional support mechanisms, such as the development of ancillary service/spinning reserve markets and sophisticated forecasting mechanisms, management of the demand side, and integration of storage systems, will need to be expedited (Tata Cleantech Capital Limited 2020). All of these will require massive funding, without which the net-zero pledge will not be successful at all.

India has also engaged with and started working on the Circular Carbon Economy (CCE)[4] framework proposed during its 2020 presidency of the G20 by Saudi Arabia (Saudi Arabia G20 2020). After the G20 leaders endorsed the CCE framework in November 2020, India has been one of the many countries focusing on developing pilots around the framework in its economy. India has been encouraging the circular economy, which Prime Minister Modi highlighted during his address at the G20 Summit Side Event in November 2020 (Ministry of External Affairs 2020). For India, the CCE framework is an essential part of a low-carbon development pathway and helps to ensure that its developmental progress is not hampered.

Along with the Carbon Capture Innovation Challenge under Mission Innovation (a clean energy–focused global innovation initiative launched during the 2015 COP21 in Paris), the CCE framework is enabling India to ensure that the benefits of the clean energy push, defined by its focus on renewables and its existing fossil fuel–based legacy energy infrastructure, are utilized optimally to ensure that the energy transition is just and equitable (Ankur Malyan 2021). The application of the CCE framework also enables multiple global entities to collaborate to provide sustainable solutions in line with climate goals and objectives (U.S. Trade and Development Agency 2020).

Nuclear: adding diversity to the energy mix

While renewables have brought India massive gains in emissions reductions, nuclear is another non-fossil fuel source that India seeks to develop. After the 2005 US–India Civil Nuclear Agreement, access to nuclear fuel and power plant technology has helped India increase its overall utilization of existing nuclear power plants and expand capacity by planning new ones (Ministry of External Affairs 2005). Currently, nuclear power plants comprise 22 operational reactors (approximately 6.7 GW), with the proposed expansion expected to take the capacity to 22.4 GW by 2031 (Press Information Bureau 2022b). Nuclear provides the advantage of generating clean baseload power and would thus help India achieve its clean energy transition ambitions. However, given the long timelines that nuclear takes to be constructed and commissioned, renewables—especially solar—have proved to be much easier to execute with shorter timelines, cheaper levelized cost of electricity, low decommissioning costs, and more efficient deployment of and critically, attractive to foreign capital. The critical aspect of India's growth in nuclear energy will be the politics surrounding India's access to nuclear technology and acceptance into the Nuclear Suppliers Group.

India has developed its own three-stage nuclear power plan with an emphasis on using indigenous reserves of thorium-232. The first stage involves using pressurized heavy water reactors, generating uranium electricity, and producing plutonium-239. The plutonium thus produced would feed into the second stage involving domestically designed fast breeder reactors to generate electricity and additional plutonium. The third and final stage would involve the plutonium combined with thorium-232 to produce energy and uranium-233.

The uranium thus produced would feed the first stage, thus completing the cycle (Tagotra 2020). The cycle remains to be completed, with delays and cost overruns impacting the second stage. However, successful completion and operation of the cycle would support Indian aspirations toward ensuring energy security.

Conclusion: India's Five-C approach toward ensuring energy security

Renewables, including hydro, solar, and wind, account for only about 3 percent of the primary energy supply (IEA-India 2019). The energy transition that is underway globally will accelerate as storage prices decline and renewable technologies become more efficient. The push for energy consumption from a growing population in India will impose a severe stress on existing energy frameworks. An in-depth understanding of the penetration of coal in energy systems across value chains in diverse energy sectors would be of significant help. Low-carbon pathways have been drawn and are helpful, but there is a severe lack of research regarding consumption patterns and changes occurring in these consumption patterns. Fossil fuel, the energy mainstay of all economies globally, is facing its biggest challenge yet as more stringent emission regulations, carbon taxes, and ever-cheaper renewables are rolled out. Over the past few years, robust growth in renewables, especially wind and solar, and regulatory and environmental headwinds have pointed toward a change in the energy status quo, which is already starting to manifest. These changes reflect the growing concerns of policy makers as they try to find meaningful solutions to the challenges of energy affordability, accessibility, and sustainability while striving to meet climate change obligations.

Net-zero pledges complicate the inherent challenges of managing an energy transition from a fossil fuel–dominated economy to one based on clean energy sources. This was visible during the COP26 communique, when India pushed for "phasing down" instead of "phasing out" when referring to coal. Coal will continue to be the mainstay of the Indian economy for the near and medium term, and this will bring increasing international pressure to manage GHG emissions. Indian energy demand is expected to grow exponentially in the decades to come. As India seeks out energy sources globally to meet its needs, its geopolitical footprint will increasingly play a vital role in managing international relations and ensuring its energy security. The past decade has illustrated that globalization has meant that India's dependence on the world for its economic growth has resulted in greater mutual engagement by India. India's role in climate negotiations has evolved tremendously over the past decade, and it is now much more confident in assuming and delivering on international commitments. It will be essential for future research to understand how India navigates the geopolitics of energy toward ensuring its energy security, managing an energy transition for a fossil fuel–based economy, and the implications of its energy partnerships and agreements on global energy markets.

Notes

1. QUAD, the colloquial form of the Quadrilateral Security Dialogue is an informal alliance between United States of America, Australia, India, and Japan, ostensibly focused on regional issues in the Indo-Pacific (Smith 2021).
2. AUKUS, is the trilateral security partnership between United States of America, Australia, and United Kingdom, again focused primarily on the Indo-Pacific (The White House 2021).
3. Clean energy cess is a form of carbon tax levied in India on coal, lignite, and petcoke. It was renamed as Clean Environment Cess in 2016.
4. For a more detailed background on the CCE concept, please visit: https://www.cceguide.org/guide/

References

Ankur Malyan, Vaibhav Chaturvedi. 2021. *Scaling up CCUS to Power Low-Carbon Transitions: India's Progress and the Way Forward.* Accessed January 15, 2022. https://www.ceew.in/blogs/strategy-for-carbon-capture-utilisation-storage-and-current-progress-in-india.

Barrows, Geoffrey, Teevrat Garg, and Akshaya Jha. 2019. *The Health Costs of Coal-Fired Power Plants in India.* Accessed May 19, 2022. https://ideas.repec.org/p/iza/izadps/dp12838.html.

Bhaskar, Utpal. 2019. *Economic Survey sees big gains from higher energy consumption.* July 04. Accessed May 18, 2022. https://www.livemint.com/budget/economic-survey/economic-survey-sees-big-gains-from-higher-energy-consumption-1562228637348.html.

Chatterjee, Manjari Miller. 2021. *The Quad, AUKUS, and India's Dilemmas.* October 13. Accessed May 18, 2022. https://www.cfr.org/article/quad-aukus-and-indias-dilemmas.

Deb, Kaushik, and Mahak Agrawal. 2021. *Evaluating India's COP26 Climate Commitments.* November 17. Accessed May 18, 2022. https://www.energypolicy.columbia.edu/research/interview/evaluating-india-s-cop26-climate-commitments-qa-dr-kaushik-deb-and-mahak-agrawal.

Doshi, Tilak K., and Jitendra Roychoudhury. 2021. *India's Net Zero Pledge: What Does It Really Mean?* November 29. Accessed May 18, 2022. https://www.realclearenergy

.org/ articles/ 2021/ 11/ 29/ indias _net _zero _pledge _what _does _it _really _mean _805606.html.

Doyle, Alister. 2015. *18 climate change quotes from world leaders.* December 01. Accessed May 18, 2022. https://www.weforum.org/agenda/2015/12/18-quotes-from-world-leaders-on-climate-change/.

Economic Survey. 2019. *Ministry of Finance, Government of India.* February. Accessed May 20, 2022. https:// www .indiabudget .gov .in/ budget2019 -20/ economicsurvey/ index.php.

Economic Survey. 2022. "Ministry of Finance, Government of India, Department of Economic Affairs, Economic Division." *Economic Survey.* January. Accessed May 18, 2022. https://www.indiabudget.gov.in/economicsurvey/.

Garg, Vibhuti. 2018. *The Evolution of the Clean Energy Cess on Coal Production in India.* Accessed May 18, 2022. https://www.iisd.org/system/files/publications/stories-g20-india-en.pdf.

Ghosh, Priyanjoli. 2020. *India's Indian Ocean Region Strategy.* Accessed May 18, 2022. https://media.defense.gov/2020/Aug/31/2002488089/-1/-1/1/GHOSH.PDF.

Gross, Samantha. 2019. *Coal is king in India—and will likely remain so.* March 08. Accessed May 18, 2022. https://www.brookings.edu/blog/planetpolicy/2019/03/08/coal-is-king-in-india-and-will-likely-remain-so/.

IEA-India. 2019. *IEA: India Country Profile.* Accessed May 19, 2022. https://www.iea.org/countries/india.

Jha, Martand. 2018. *India and the Wassenaar Arrangement.* February 05. Accessed May 18, 2022. https:// www .livemint .com/ Sundayapp/ AET So9p0H9Dii 7ou9WRvrO/ India-and-the-Wassenaar-Arrangement.html.

Menon, Shivshankar. 2019. *The New Asian Geopolitics.* Vienna: Institute for Human Sciences (IWM), April 29. Accessed 2022. https:// www .youtube .com/ watch ?v = m7B5WgYDEu8.

Menon, Shruti. 2022. *Ukraine crisis: Why India is buying more Russian oil.* April 26. Accessed May 18, 2022. https://www.bbc.com/news/world-asia-india-60783874.

Ministry of External Affairs. 2005. *India-US Agreement for Cooperation concerning peaceful uses of nuclear energy.* Accessed May 18, 2022. https://mea.gov.in/Uploads/PublicationDocs/19149_Frequently_Asked_Questions_01-11-2008.pdf.

Ministry of External Affairs. 2020. *Prime Minister's address at the G-20 Summit Side Event: 'Safeguarding the Planet - The Circular Carbon Economy Approach'.* Accessed January 15, 2022. https:// mea .gov .in/ Speeches -Statements .htm ?dtl/ 33228/ Prime _Ministers_address_at_the_G20_Summit_Side_Event_Safeguarding_the_Planet_ _The_Circular_Carbon_Economy_Approach.

Ministry of External Affairs. 2022. *One of The Youngest Populations in the World – India's Most Valuable Asset.* Accessed May 20, 2022. https://indbiz.gov.in/one-of-the-youngest-populations-in-the-world-indias-most-valuable-asset/.

Ministry of New and Renewable Energy. 2022. *Solar Energy.* https://mnre.gov.in/solar/current-status/.

Parkin, Benjamin. 2021. *India's Adani Group to start exports from controversial Australian coal mine.* December 27. Accessed May 18, 2022. https:// www .ft .com/ content/8670daea-0fe8-43b2-bd98-e6278ccb64c1.

Patil, Mukta. 2015. *India stops fund flow to NGOs working on impact of coal projects.* January 08. Accessed May 18, 2022. https:// www .downtoearth .org .in/ news/ india -stops-fund-flow-to-ngos-working-on-impact-of-coal-projects-48134.

Press Information Bureau. 2018. *India – UAE bilateral investments.* February 13. Accessed May 19, 2022. https:// pib .gov .in/ Pr essRelease IframePage .aspx ?PRID = 1520423.

Press Information Bureau. 2020. *Year End Review 2020- Ministry of Coal.* December 31. Accessed May 18, 2022. https://pib.gov.in/Pressreleaseshare.aspx?PRID=1685058.

Press Information Bureau. 2022a. *India's Stand at COP-26.* February 03. Accessed May 18, 2022. https://www.pib.gov.in/PressReleasePage.aspx?PRID=1795071.

Press Information Bureau. 2022b. *Use of Nuclear Energy for Power Generation.* March 24. Accessed May 18, 2022. https://pib.gov.in/PressReleseDetail.aspx?PRID =1809285.

Renewable Watch. 2020. *Transmission Troubles: Gree Energy Corridors project faces delays in commissioning.* December 03. Accessed May 18, 2022. https:// renewablewatch.in/2020/12/03/transmission-troubles/.

Ritchie, Hannah, and Max Roser. 2020. *India: CO2 Country Profile.* Accessed May 18, 2022. https://ourworldindata.org/co2/country/india.

Saudi Arabia G20. 2020. *G20 Saudi Arabia 2020 Leaders' Declaration.* Accessed April 11, 2022. http:// www .g20 .utoronto .ca/ 2020/ 2020 -g20 -leaders -declaration -1121 .html.

Schmall, Emily, and Stanley Reed. 2022. *India Finds Russian Oil an Irresistible Deal, No Matter the Diplomatic Pressure.* May 04. Accessed May 19, 2022. https:// www .nytimes.com/2022/05/04/world/asia/india-russia-oil.html.

Singh, Mandvi. 2019. *PM Modi's ambition for 450 GW renewable energy comes amidst slowdown.* September 26. Accessed May 18, 2022. https:// www .downtoearth .org .in/blog/energy/pm-modi-s-ambition-for-450-gw-renewable-energy-comes-amidst -slowdown-66961.

Smith, Sheila A. 2021. *The Quad in the Indo-Pacific: What to Know.* May 27. Accessed May 19, 2022. https://www.cfr.org/in-brief/quad-indo-pacific-what-know.

Stimson Center. 2012. "Indian Ocean Rising." *Stimson Center.* July. Accessed May 19, 2022. https://www.stimson.org/wp-content/files/file-attachments/IOR_chapter1_1 .pdf.

Tagotra, Niharika. 2020. *India's Ambitious Nuclear Power Plan – And What's Getting in Its Way.* September 09. Accessed May 19, 2022. https://thediplomat.com/2020/09/ indias-ambitious-nuclear-power-plan-and-whats-getting-in-its-way/.

Tata Cleantech Capital Limited. 2020. *Renewable Integration and Curtailment: Causes, Solutions and Impact on Project Bankability.* November. Accessed May 18, 2022. https://img.saurenergy.com/2020/12/renewable-integration-and-curtailment.pdf.

Temple, Henry John. 1848. *Oxford Essential Quotations.* Edited by Susan Ratcliffe. March 01. Accessed May 15, 2022. https://www.oxfordreference.com/view/10.1093/ acref/9780191826719.001.0001/q-oro-ed4-00008130.

The White House. 2021. *Joint Leaders Statement on AUKUS* . September 15. Accessed May 19, 2022. https:// www .whitehouse .gov/ briefing -room/ statements -releases/ 2021/09/15/joint-leaders-statement-on-aukus/.

U.S. Trade and Development Agency. 2020. *USTDA Supports India's First Refinery Carbon Capture Project.* Accessed January 15, 2022. https://ustda.gov/ustda-supports -indias-first-refinery-carbon-capture-project/.

Verma, Nidhi. 2020. *India allows UAE's ADNOC to export oil from strategic reserve.* October 14. Accessed May 19, 2022. https:// www .reuters .com/ article/ india -oil -adnoc-idUSKBN26Z1KN.

Washington, George. 1796. "Washington's Farewell Address 1796 ." *The Avalon Project - Documents in Law, History and Diplomacy.* Accessed May 15, 2022. https://avalon.law.yale.edu/18th_century/washing.asp.

World Bank. 2022. *GDP (Current US$).* https://data.worldbank.org/indicator/NY.GDP.MKTP.CD?locations=IN.

3 Renewables and hydrocarbon price climbing: implications for Latin America and the world

Alberto Cisneros Lavaller

The implications of renewable energy policy and elevated hydrocarbon prices for Latin American and the world constitute a complex subject. We begin with a review of several issues:(i) the Geoenergy Policy (what has been done, its pitfalls, and the like), (ii) the decarbonization process and how it has impacted Latin America, and, (iii) the factors confronting key regional actors such as Colombia, Venezuela, and Argentina on their path to a successful energy transition. We conclude with some suggestions for a future research agenda, a roadmap for the future.

Geoenergy policy: a move in the right direction...

What they have done....

To begin, we define some key concepts that are critical to the analysis of the energy transition. Geoenergy is a notion that encompasses not only oil but also other energy sources. This is of particular relevance to most hydrocarbons, including gas (the queen of hydrocarbons because it is less pollutant), coal, nuclear, and power (as it is nonindependent and stems from number of sources, including oil products, gas, hydro, and wind).

In the context of this analysis, geoenergy can be interpreted as referring to the global politics of energy at work. Lately, global policy has emphasized that energy consumption needs to shy away from hydrocarbon-based sources (non-renewables) in favor of renewables. The case for this is clearly stated in

COP26 proceedings, along with other efforts to diminish the carbon footprint on the planet.

The prominence of a renewable-led energy transition has indeed emerged with considerable force in many policy circles. Beginning in the developed world, strategies based on renewables soon shifted to the less developed world, particularly to Latin America. Until now, the fuel of choice to 'walk through' the transition has been natural gas. Or, at least, this is what has been emphasized by a host of experts and scholars during various climate summits and webinars. At one point, the conveyed idea had become so convincing that it made many believe as if we were going to wake up 'tomorrow' in a brand new world free of CO_2.

The energy transition has been described as the path to achieving a total transformation of the global energy sector from one that is based on the use of fossil energy to another that aims to emit zero CO_2 into the atmosphere, by the second half of this century. The process of de-carbonizing the energy sector, however, requires urgent action on a global scale. Although the global energy transition is underway, supplementary actions will be needed to reduce carbon emissions and mitigate the effects of climate change. According to the International Renewable Energy Agency (IRENA), renewable energy, in addition to more energy-efficient measures, can achieve about 90 percent of the required carbon reductions (International Renewable Energy Agency (IRENA), 2021).

While this new approach manifests itself through concrete policy actions, it is impinging on the behavior of major oil companies as well, notably BP, Chevron, TotalEnergie, ExxonMobil, Shell, and 'avant-garde' NOCs, such as Saudi Aramco and ADNOC.

BP, for instance, has adopted a policy to reduce its carbon footprint by 50 percent in 30 years (2050). Chevron also followed suit, reducing emissions on its end- products. Total changed its name to TotalEnergie as an endorsement of its new corporate branding (becoming an energy company instead of merely an oil company). The latter's motto is now "towards cleaner energy." Last but not least, the most conservative of the oil majors, Exxon-Mobil, has incorporated new 'Green Directors' onto its Board of Directors, making emission reductions a top priority.

This new tendency has been picked up by other important players. The case of OXY, under a new Chairman (Vicki Hollub), will be discussed in the Latin American section of this chapter. Oxy is devising an innovative method to protect the environment during its extraction, production, and processing of hydrocarbon. A new division has been created within the corporate headquarters to implement the new policies.

Chevron Corporation, on the other hand, is focusing on renewable energy. The company has acquired a 28 percent stake in the nuclear-powered carbon-capture startup Nucarb. The technology is a variation of direct air capture, which uses powerful fans to suck CO_2 from the air. The fans are powered by an experimental small modular nuclear reactor. The first Nucarb pilot may be operational by 2032, depending on the time it takes to permit and build new nuclear plants in the United States. At US$120 M, the investment is substantially less than the cost to capture emissions at the source or move the company away from its core business of extracting, refining, and selling fossil fuels.

In other areas of the world, there are some astonishing movements toward net zero. This can be seen in the Middle East, a region rich in hydrocarbons and oil exports. A few months ago, the Saudi Oil Minister, Abdulaziz bin Salman (one of the oldest sons of King Salman), made an astounding announcement: By 2030/40, power in the kingdom will be supplied by solar energy. The peninsula is dry and without water, but the sun shines almost 365 days a year. Incredible as it might seem, this fact was 'overlooked' until the Prince said Eureka!

Moreover, a few years ago, the Saudi Crown Prince, Mohammed bin Salman, one of the youngest sons of King Salman (half-brother of Abdulaziz), disclosed the kingdom's long-term plans for hydrocarbons. In a comprehensive study, he assessed a window of opportunity for the kingdom to maximize oil production by 2030/40. After that, the competition from other energy sources (renewables, among others) was expected to be fierce, reducing the market share of oil significantly.

In the same geographic area, the UAE Minister of Oil & Energy stated a similar energy policy in November 2021. The Emirates power and electricity sectors will be supplied by solar energy in the mid- to long-term future. The Minister emphasized that it will be necessary to maintain a balance between supply and demand in oil and gas markets. Thus, the UAE will continue its investments in the sector to meet the growing demand for oil and gas and ensure the stability of global markets throughout the transition.

Geoenergy policy: a move in the right direction?

The Mirage...

Upstream capital expenditure (CapEx) on hydrocarbons (inspired by the aforementioned views) has fallen to low levels. This can be seen in the recent financial reports from some major oil companies. The companies' emphasis on the environment and social responsibility, coupled with shareholders' pressure for financial returns, has resulted in lower investment in exploration and production (E&P).

This is quite possibly the result of oil companies leaning toward renewable energy policies that have already been drafted by governments. They forgot about the transition period, in which the world will still largely be dependent on hydrocarbons. At the same time, several institutions have been advocating for the need to adopt renewables as part of their energy matrix. This, in turn, has generated imbalances between post-Covid demand recovery and lower than anticipated new hydrocarbon supplies. Consequently, oil prices jumped up. This presents a quandary, especially if world hydrocarbon prices remain high for a prolonged period. It is worth noting though, as a contrasting trend, that despite that lower investment in CapEx, rig productivity has increased. Is this the harbinger of a new 'high oil price era'?

CapEx is used by companies to secure physical assets or upgrade current assets. A key aspect of CapEx for the oil and gas sector is how companies manage their cash flow. After the collapse of prices due to Covid, many energy companies exerted financial discipline to reduce debt. In other cases, excess cash was redirected to reduce debt and strengthen shareholder returns.

Global investments in CapEx have been falling since 2015 (see Figure 3.1), as have industry concerns of a new high-price regime for oil and gas. The demand for hydrocarbons, on the other hand, is expected to come back once the pandemic recession period subsides. Consulting companies, such as Wood Mackenzie and others, foresee a mid-term lag between the time new investments can result in incremental production (Pugliaresi, 2021).

In a similar vein, Prince Abdul Aziz bin Salman (the Saudi Oil Minister), addressing a forum in mid-December 2021, warned that reduced investment in oil production will be dangerous for the world. According to him, "We are set for a period that could be dangerous. If there isn't more spending on investments to preserve production capacity and to increase it when necessary,

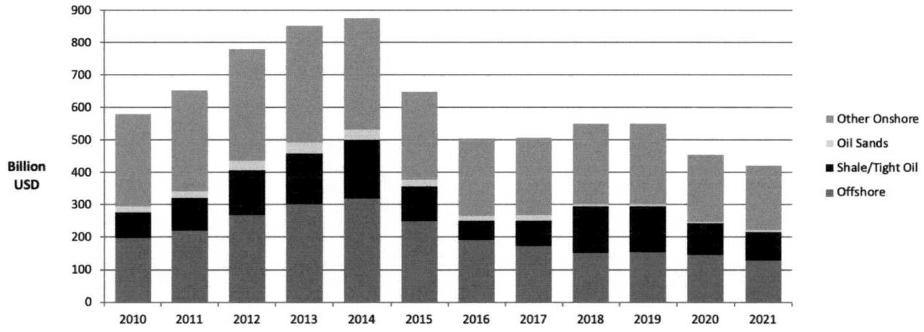

Source: Global Business Consultants, Rystad, 2022.

Figure 3.1 Global E&P Investments by supply

an energy crisis is coming to the world." "In one way or another, I am not predicting, but I am warning that *spare production capacity* will disappear" (Ghantous, 2021).

While warning against the depletion of unused production capacity at the global level, the Minister stressed that "despite a global push to decarbonize, oil will still account for 28% of energy demand until at least 2045, up from 30% in 2020" (Ghantous, 2021).

Within OPEC, Saudi Arabia, as well as some other Gulf countries—such as the UAE and Kuwait—are concerned and investing in hydrocarbons to maintain production levels and even increase them. At the other end of the spectrum, some OPEC African members, such as Nigeria and Angola, are underperformers.

Staged in such a way, the geopolitics of energy might see some unintended consequences. It is worth mentioning the potential consequences of higher oil prices to renewables (with Brent crude rising to US$89/b in mid-January 2022 from US$28/b at the beginning of 2016). Higher oil prices will inevitably result in increased competition from renewables, which are usually costlier to develop. The higher costs might be attributed to the costs of development technology and the high cost of storage of renewables (particularly from 'brand new' sources such as green and blue hydrogen). However, the trend is that these technologies are becoming competitive even at lower oil prices (see Figure 3.2). Thus, higher oil prices are quite likely to reinforce the competitiveness of renewables, resulting in incremental supplies. The geopolitics of energy could come back like a boomerang. This is why we posed a question mark at the beginning of this section and to consider it 'Like a mirage?' Eventually, time will tell.

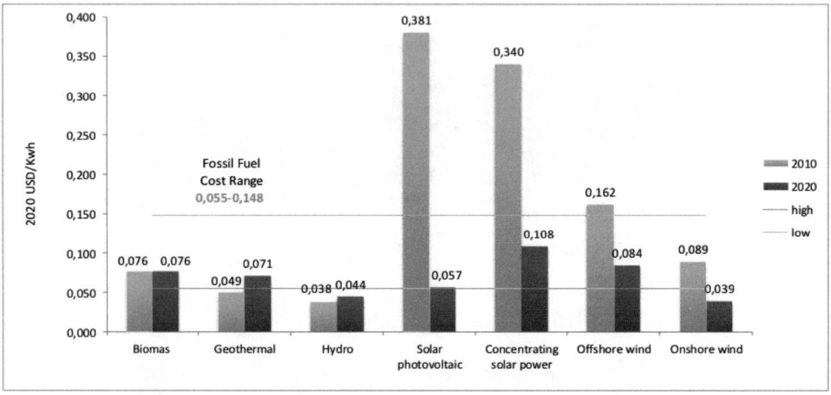

Source: IRENA, Renewable Power Generation Costs in 2020, Global Business Consultants, 2022.

Figure 3.2 The falling costs of renewables

Particular mention should be made of the Russian War in Ukraine. In principle, the conflict has put the hydrocarbon paradigm back to the forefront of headline news. Fossil fuels represent about 80 percent of the current energy matrix, and conventional warfare is highly dependent upon oil and its products (e.g. diesel). All fossil fuels have established logistics for delivery, and some of them are interchangeable—fuel and diesel vis-à-vis gas in power generation. The war guarantees the delivery of energy products for their own special ends. In this regard, the green paradigm appears to be facing a temporary setback (Montamat, 2022).

The war also poses formidable challenges to gas consumption in Argentina and Colombia. It has raised LNG prices globally, and particularly in Europe, which is dependent on Russian gas. Argentina will see LNG imported prices for the winter season boosted as well. The competing prices for exports in other destinations will affect their seasonal prices. On the Colombian side, LNG imports will likely be threatened by incremental US exports to Europe. Thus, this situation is likely to jeopardize the supply of LNG from Sabine Pass and Louisiana (United States) to the Colombian Caribbean coast (Cartagena). Colombian LNG imports from Trinidad and Tobago (T&T) will similarly be affected. Europeans tend to believe that under the war circumstances T&T

has the capacity to become an additional supplier of LNG to their shores. However, T&T might also be tempted to increase its shipments to the United States because of higher gas prices due to the incremental US cargoes destined for Europe. Lastly, as far as prices are concerned, the war shock has resulted in higher global LNG prices, with the capacity to affect regional prices in the Caribbean basin as well.

On the bright side, we do not see US$200/b oil on a sustained basis despite the fact that the war may become a prolonged conflict. There remains a likelihood, however, that hydrocarbon prices could rise significantly—although not at skyrocketing levels—due to other factors. For instance, oil price markers have risen to US$130/b due to the existence of a large geopolitical risk premium. At the same time, Omicron, and strict isolation in certain regions of China, portend a retreat to US$100/b.

What are the implications for Argentina to import LNG prices? And what about the import prices for Colombian LNG? Being a large seasonal importer, the impact of high oil and gas prices on Argentina could be significant. As Colombia is an occasional importer—,not on a regular and frequent basis and only to supplement its domestic production—the impact of the war on domestic prices might be less of a concern.

Hafner and Tagliapietra (2020) present an interesting perspective on how the energy transition might play out among global trading blocks. From a geopolitical/geoeconomics viewpoint, they analyze how the transition might affect or be affected by global governance in different trading regions. They argue that four main drivers will impact the global energy system. On the one hand, the factors, including rising demand in Asia and beyond, could delay decarbonization policies contributing to a better climate. On the other, digitalization could help foster different, more decentralized energy systems. Finally, technological creativity could lead to a more amicable climate policy, including renewables, low carbon transportation, and unconventional hydrocarbons (Hafner & Tagliapietra, 2020).

The global backdrop and its impact on Latin America

The Global Decarbonization Process and Immediate Transfer to Latin America

A high-speed decarbonization process is taking place in the world. This can clearly be seen in Europe, the United States, and other developed economies, where the race to global decarbonization is taking over. Years ago, it seemed that the decarbonization process was destined to be carried out by our children or grandchildren. Nevertheless, today it is an ever-present trend, more real now than ever before.

To review this new shift to decarbonization, Occidental now has the technology able to extract and produce hydrocarbons with no CO2 discharges into the atmosphere. The decarbonization process has been so strong that OXY's current President, Vicki Hollub, has even created within the corporation a full division in charge of the transition. She has reinforced her approach by stating, "What I think that people don't understand is we should not be talking about eliminating fossil fuels. What we really need to be talking about is eliminating emissions and if we can provide and we will. Net carbon zero oil, that is what the world needs, and the world cannot achieve the goals ... of the Paris accord without the oil industry helping with that. We can be leaders in that" (Kimani, 2021).

An excellent example like this is likely to be followed by other major oil companies. When a breakthrough technology pops up, it is integrated quickly into the public domain, and 'copied' (adopted) by the competition eager to escape the damaging label of 'polluters.'

Turning our sights to Europe, international organizations such as the Geneva-based Global Gas Center (GGC) (along with other international bodies) are advancing the notion that natural gas is the preferred fuel for the energy transition rather than renewables. The GGC is taking a lead in the decarbonization process and the use of front-end technologies running on green or blue hydrogen. While there are many more cases to show from the developed world, these examples are sufficient to make the point.

The Process in Latin America

The geopolitics of energy routinely scores high on the critical uncertainty list, but this year, it is substantially higher than even the Covid outbreak of 2020.

This high-impact score is a result of tensions among the big energy players: the United States, China, and Russia. It has been amplified by the countries' energy interdependence and trade tensions, despite record growth in renewable capacity. Lurking in the background, the pressures placed on global leaders by the pandemic promise to keep geopolitics firmly at the head of the global uncertainty agenda (World Energy Issues Monitor, 2022).

Years ago, long-established trends in the developed world were more advanced than those seen in Latin America (at a much later stage). This is the case with LNG contracts, and pricing, where Europe was far ahead of Latin America. There was a well-defined lead time before identical policies were adopted in Latin America.

In contrast, the decarbonization process and the use of front-end technologies—such as those running on green or blue hydrogen— are being discussed in Latin America at almost the same time as they are being examined in Europe and the developed world. This is especially evident in Colombia, Chile, and Uruguay.

Terrapas believes that there are two interpretations to decarbonization. One relates to systems producing CO2 and other greenhouse gases, while the other removes carbon accumulation and deposits from combustion engines. Both processes handle the output (carbon) in a different manner. Decarbonization policies shift energy systems to stop emissions and prevent the release of carbon into the atmosphere. The process will require carbon sequestration to achieve net-zero emissions and to facilitate the move toward a carbon-neutral global economy (Terrapas, 2021).

It is important to notice a few defining ideas. Green hydrogen is the least polluting when compared with its blue, brown, gray, and black counterparts. Green hydrogen comes out from biogas and biomass or water electrolysis. Blue hydrogen is a byproduct of natural gas or refinery production. Lastly, brown, gray, and black hydrogen come from fossil fuels and are, therefore, more polluting than the other types described.

Hydrogen technology has the potential to be so clean that, when applied to car engines, it would only leave water in the atmosphere (through automobile pipes and mufflers). However, there are several problems confronting hydrogen development. The difficulties stem from the physical and chemical properties of hydrogen itself. While hydrogen is a fuel with a large energy density per mass unit, it exhibits very low energy density per volume unit (in liquid as well as solid state). The properties of hydrogen also include undesirable factors such as large diffusivity and permeability, meaning it can go through solids.

That means there can be volume losses from hydrogen that is not adequately stored, which go to the atmosphere. This property reveals the fragility of metals (steel) with which tankers are built. Future research is needed to solve these technological problems, among others, confronting the use of hydrogen in the green transition.

Hydrogen is the highest clean energy source that can be used in most energy applications, including generating electricity and in transportation. Hydrogen fuel energy is expected to be the largest source of clean energy in the future. It can be used in transportation and in long-time storage with low environmental impact (Mostafa & Shinji, 2019).

In other developments, strict Covid lockdown measures have impinged upon the global renewable energy supply chain. It can be broken down into five phases: procurement, generation, transmission, distribution, and demand. These phases cover all processes along the renewable energy supply chain, from raw materials to end product (Engelken, Römer, Drescher, Welpe & Picot, 2016).

Latin America is not exempt from supply chain disruptions. In the solar photovoltaic sector, high transportation costs and maritime delays stem from the high demand for containers—particularly those ordered by China—destined for Latin American harbors. Freight costs have risen significantly. Transportation costs for a large container with the capacity to transport about 650 solar modules of 60 cells each had increased from US$2500 each to about US$15 000 by the end of 2021 for Mexican harbors as the destination (Ortiz D. Carlos. Greenergy Director). In the case of freights destined for Buenaventura, Colombian Pacific harbor (Ardila, 2021), costs had risen from US$2000 up to US$17 000 (with a maximum of US$20 000). Shipments sailing to Chile experienced a significant increase in costs from US$1400 before COVID to approximately US$20 000, leaning toward US$15 500) by the end of 2021 (Sobarzo, 2020).

The year 2022 does not look promising in terms of transportation supply chains costs, which are critical for this type of renewables. Mexico, for instance, is expecting costs of approximately US$14 000 per large container and about US$15 000 for shipments destined for Chilean ports.

The other variable in the transportation supply chain, harbor delays, does not look any better. Origin harbors, such as Shanghai, and destination harbors—Buenos Aires (for Argentina), Valparaiso (Chile), Buenaventura (Colombia), or Manzanillo (Mexico)—are all overloaded. There are other difficulties as well plaguing the transportation supply chains of renewables: Trans-shipments may not have balanced return loads—for instance, some cargoes destined for Buenos Aires. Thus, they may be tempted to unload their cargoes in Santos (southern Brazil) with the expectation that other ships in destination to Buenos Aires may take the cargo to its final destination.

Therefore, countries and companies hoping to import solar panels continue to experience high costs and volume and time delays. Finally, increasing customs fees can be added as a material cost contributing to the burden on the industry.

Quandaries in Key Latin American Countries

There are a number of key countries in Latin America that are worth mentioning and will be the focus of analysis. They include Colombia, Venezuela (on the Northern Node of South America), and Argentina (in the Southern Cone).

Colombia: The troubles of YNC; what about Conventionals YTF?

President Duque's recent hydrogen energy and renewable energy policy has made Colombia one of the pioneers in Latin America. Renewables account for approximately 1 percent of the Colombian energy mix and have the potential to account for 5 percent of the energy mix in the medium term.

Nevertheless, the country continues to take steps in advancing the transition of its energy matrix, incorporating alternative renewable energy sources like solar, wind, and natural gas. In the coming months, Colombia will have seven new large-scale renewable energy plants (three wind complexes, three solar, and a thermal natural gas plant) that will provide more than 1000 MW of installed capacity.

The first project, a wind farm Guajira developed by Isagén, was expected to become operational between January and February 2022. It has an installed capacity of 20 MW. The Guajira wind farm will be followed by the complex solar Plains (in Cordoba and Carthage) developed by the multinational Matrix Renewables. The solar Plains project was expected to become operational in March 2022 with an installed capacity of 100 MW.

The Tesorito Thermal Power Plant was to begin operations between February and May 2022. It is a natural gas power generation project developed jointly by Canacol and Celsia with an installed capacity of 150 MW. Finally, there are the Alpha and Beta wind complexes, of 200 MW and 350 MW of installed capacity, respectively. These will be built by the Portuguese multinational EDP Renováveis and are estimated to become operational in June 2023.

High oil prices, as discussed ut supra, will have an impact on the development of renewable energy supplies, and needless to say, on hydrocarbon supplies. High oil prices will favor renewables development and make them more competitive to conventional hydrocarbon supplies. This will be the case despite technological problems such as storage difficulties facing hydrogen and solar energy projects. So, in a sense, current oil E&P divestments can actually enhance or accelerate the substitution with renewables.

There is a problem though with the sequence of events in the energy transition. Renewables still account for a low share of the global energy mix. Yet, they are being called upon to replace a large percentage of the energy mix currently held by hydrocarbons. Hence, during the energy transition, industry participants will have to rely on hydrocarbons for at least a decade or more to supply Colombian, regional, and global energy demands. In this regard, Ecopetrol has set an example for Latin America by shipping its first cargo of crude with carbon footprint compensation to China in January 2022. The crude oil shipment contained 1 M/b of Castilla blend (heavy crudes from Rubiales, Castilla, and Chichimene fields) sold to Petrochina. The carbon emissions for the cargo, estimated at 32 000 tons of CO2, were counterbalanced with carbon credits of the best quality to benefit a renewable energy project located in Northwest Colombia. The equalizer covers production, dilution, and transportation to Covenas (Caribbean harbor), the full value chain for that crude.

As might have been expected, the high oil prices also impinged upon hydrocarbon production, and Colombia is no exception in this regard. The problem stemmed from a lack of investment in E&P. During the previous administration, no blocks were awarded. It was tantamount to the global E&P disinvestment process. The investment paralysis was inexplicable when viewed in the context of the strategy followed by Colombia during the previous price shock (2008–2009). At that time, the country initiated a steep increase in production, reaching a maximum of approximately 1 Mb/d. The underlying question that remains unanswered is this: If the 2008–2009 strategy was successful, then why has it not been adopted till now—in addition to having been adjusted to new realities—to surmount the 2015–2016 crisis?

Under President Duque, 69 blocks were awarded, with 39 of them being assigned during the bidding round 2020. However, some blocks were returned to ANH (the regulatory body). During the 2021 bidding round, less than half of this figure—only 30 blocks—were awarded (November 2021) within the so-called Yet-Non-Developed (YND) small fields. They represent an incremental future production of about 300 Kb/d. The investment in the awards is approximately US$150M for exploration YND fields. It is striking that a single private operator (Parex Resources) got 18 fields—close to the locations where it has previous wells—and plans to invest about US$ 100 M. The national oil company (Ecopetrol) will invest only US$ 18 M.

The events that occurred as early as 2015, during the last oil crisis, and the conclusions that were drawn from an analysis of the events are worth remembering:

> The Dilemma currently confronting the Colombian Petroleum Oil Industry is invest or divest under a relatively low prices environment. Within that investment dimension it should be distinguished that, although it seems adequate that corporations operating on the oil business could reduce drastically their OPEX investments, it remains questionable to do the same with capital investment. That is so because when CAPEX is dramatically reduced, they jeopardize future production. This requires a delicate balance that is not fully understood by some operators active on the current Colombian oil sector.
>
> What are the implications for Colombian Oil in 2016 and on forward? If there are no major investments on exploration nor an increase in the recovery factor, unfortunately there is not going to be new reserves. That is if as of today Colombian reserves are about 2.4 B barrels, they would last approximately 7 years at current production levels (around 1.0 Mb/d. In the next few years that R/P ratio would decline significantly. In other words, we would be translating current crisis into the future (Cisneros Lavaller & Universidad Sergio Arboleda, 2015).

During 2015–16, it was difficult to discover an oil giant in Colombia. However, it was also true that several small discoveries (labeled 'gnomons' by us) could compensate for a missing Giant. The last round (2021) has the potential to provide an extra 300 Kb/d.

Finally, a word on nonconventional oil developments. There are four pilot projects for nonconventional oil where fracking will be required to produce crude oil flows. However, those nonconventionals are just beginning, and therefore, represent a very long-term project. More conventional oil rounds are badly needed, particularly those related to minor and mature fields, as well as those for undeveloped fields (similar to the 2021 round).

Colombia has shale reserves of 55 TCF. When translated into billon barrels, this is approximately 2.0 B barrels of P3 type of reserves. While these are not to be neglected, they will have to be combined with the development of new conventional undeveloped reservoirs. We should not overlook the problems that their development could bring to relations with Colombian communities.

Issues are liable to the environmental impact that will inevitably accompany the development of shale reserves. Players on both sides of the debate will have to be educated, and a war against those that intend to damage shale developments will inevitably be fought. The process will require time and money to demystify the potential implications in a sensitive country like Colombia, and is suggested as a subject for future research.

Argentina: Renewables and Vaca Muerta with Gas and Oil developments. Imports until when!

Clean energy projects in Argentina had a boom year in 2021. In November, they generated 1600 GW/h. Green energy projects contributed a total of 1000 MW to the nation's electricity grid in 2021.

Solar farms, for instance, had their own record-breaking year, generating 280 GW/h. In November 2021, generation rose by 5 percent over October output, according to official figures from the Administrative Company for the Wholesale Power Market (CAMMESA). Argentinian photovoltaic farms are consolidating, as the second-most important renewable technology after wind power ventures. Wind farms generated about 1 100 GW/h in November 2021.

During the first quarter of 2022, it was expected that three new projects for 40 MW of installed power capacity will be developed by Argentinian photovoltaic farms in the provinces of Mendoza, Cordoba, and Catamarca.

Hydroelectric projects, on the other hand, are beginning to gain ground. They generated 112 GW/h in November 2021. Finally, bioenergy projects are starting to gain ground, with biogas at 37 GW/h and biomass at approximately 68 GW/h in 2021.

The main reason for the incremental renewable energy generation in Argentina is an increase in installed capacity in 2021. According to CAMMESA, the total renewable power installed capacity for the country reached levels as high as 5 095 MW, 64 percent of which belonged to wind farms. Out of that total, almost 1 000 MW were due to green projects from bidding rounds awarded under the former (Macri) administration. The top three regions in the country advancing those endeavors were Patagonic, NorthEast, and Cuyo—Western Provinces—accounting for 90 percent of new renewable installed capacity.

YPF LUZ (a branch of YPF, a state commercial oil company) started its third wind farm at Santa Cruz Province, in Southern Argentina, with 123 MW of installed capacity. Investment costs reached US$180 M for supplying residential homes (about 1 50 000) as well as industries in that area. This project will reduce C02 emissions by 312 ton/year. With the launch of this project, YPF will create almost 400 MW of capacity, becoming the second renewable generator in the country after Genneia. In addition, YPF owns Manantiales Behr in Chubut Province and Los Teros in Buenos Aires Province.

Nevertheless, it is not unrealistic to identify Argentina as a natural gas country, while Venezuela and Colombia can be considered oil countries.

Under such a proviso, it is worth discussing the situation in the Southern Cone of Latin America. At first sight, under the official prism, Argentina has become isolated and shielded by Plan Gas Argentina. As a result, the consumers, or end users (final consumer), have become protected from high tariffs. This is not the case in Europe, the Far East, and other world regions. In fact, Argentinian customers are paying prices as low as about US$2/MBtu.

This is another mirage that needs to be demystified—a process that can be accomplished by a thorough examination of the timing and costs of subsidies. The Argentina Gas Plan sets up a 'convenient' price after public bidding of about US$3.5– 4.5 MBtu. This is a price that the government is paying to operators. But the real price at the end of the line is subsidized by the government, so the end consumer pays an extremely low price. The final end-use price of US$2 MBtu is one of the lowest, not only in Latin America, but also in the world (Markous, 2021).

The demystification process has two stages: timing and cost.

- The timing: When the incumbent government launched the Gas Plan, the situation in Europe and Asia was not the same as far as production cost was concerned. At the time of writing, the region was being confronted with an extremely cold boreal winter.
- The subsidies cost: The government compensation price reached levels as high as US$ 11 B per year, the equivalent of over 2 percent of the GDP. On top of that, Argentinian gas markets have a serious seasonality problem. During the summer months, Argentina becomes an occasional exporter (to Chile), while during the winter, the country imports LNG from Bahia Blanca (a southern harbor in Buenos Aires Province). As a result, the Argentinian government is considering using gas oil and fuel oil (heavy pollutants) during the next winter, because the expected price for LNG by mid-year 2022 could reach about US$24 M/Btu.

Thus, an early interpretation suggests that the subsidies are an extremely costly program and do not tackle the original problem. With a heavily subsidized system—as has been the case during about 15 years of Kirchner-type governments—no stockholder is likely to be willing to invest in Argentina. This is because the 'political prices' for gas are so different from international prices. The next 'interpretative' conclusion stems from the poor compliance with non-contaminants and renewables. This has been 'forced' by the economic environment in which consumer gas prices are kept unrealistically low. The policy of low domestic prices at any cost entices consumers to use gas oil and fuel oil at the expense of alternatives, a vicious cycle.

This raises an important question: How long will Argentina continue to import LNG? There are two sides of a coin in answering this question.

1. From the exporters' side, accelerate imports (Aguilar, 2021). This is much more economical than having to use gas oil or fuel oil. According to them, there could be savings of about US$ 1 B per year just by using the regasification ship during the winter months in Bahia Blanca.
2. From the producers' side, there is a need for ample development—commensurate with a huge reservoir like Vaca Muerta—to guarantee that Argentina becomes a net gas exporter in the years to come. However, there are political constraints as far as the provision of clear incentives for investors is concerned. So far, there are no clear rules of the game to entice international capital to Argentinian shores. It is not clear that it will even be possible to repatriate capital and reverse capital flight. The independence of Argentinian judiciary is at fault, and so on. The money requirements are insurmountable, in the range of several billion dollars per year to fully develop these reservoirs on time.

On the other hand, the window of opportunity is shrinking. Investments can become fruitful only several years down the road. The possibility of renewables dislodging hydrocarbons from the energy matrix is coming ever closer following COP26 and the global drive to net zero. Chances are that, if those monies do not arrive in Argentina in due course (sooner rather than later), Vaca Muerta—or chunks of it—may honor her name and could become 'dead,' remaining in the subsoil evermore.

Several programs for developing renewables that were fostered under the previous administration (President Macri) have been paramount. The incumbent government (President A. Fernandez) is trying to offset those contracts under the former Plan AR because of lack of investment. The lack of available funding has led to noncompliance with contractual financial commitments. Private companies attempting to develop solar, wind, and the like are resisting the battle with the government, appealing to the courts to keep their projects alive.

The fact of the matter is that, during the Macri administration, it was projected that renewables would supply both the CAMMESA (official distributor and transportation outfit) and private demand (the spot market). Instead, the current administration is pressuring the renewables contract holders to return their contracts (approximately 40 percent of the total contracts) because they lack financial support. From 2018 onward, the devaluation of the dollar forced several guarantees for those projects to be withdrawn and/or they expired. As a result, the project owners lack financial backing. The current administration has signaled the need to get rid of those projects because existing transportation and distribution networks are needed for those players who are operative now.

So, as it can be seen, the Argentinian government is not helping the initiatives that the renewables enjoyed previously, to the detriment of a country that has traditionally been blessed with a thriving agribusiness.

A final remark goes to the power and electricity industry, which faces similar quandaries to those of gas. In some European countries, like Germany, the wholesale price has risen to US$289 per KW/h. By comparison, the price in Argentina is only US$70 per KW/h, with heavy government subsidies. End users paid US$25 per KW/h of the total invoice, equivalent to 35 percent, while the remainder 65 percent was paid by the National Treasury (Markous, 2021). In a situation like this, the country is prolonging a disinvestment process in the sector. No private capital would come to Argentina if it were expected to work at a loss.

If Argentina were to modernize its financial sector, there are financial instruments available that can be used on a cooperative basis to 'protect' the final consumer and gradually increase end-use invoices to reflect international prices in a more realistic way. If the intent is to protect those in need, several mechanisms can be used. It would be possible to inversely raise fares to those who can pay, thereby helping those who are in difficulty and cannot afford it. In other words, segmenting tariffs according to social strata.

Venezuela: New Opening. For Whom? And Politics?

Venezuela is predominantly an oil country. When analyzing the Venezuelan energy matrix in this context, renewables represent a very poor fraction of the whole energy spectrum. In fact, a mere 0.13 percent of the energy mix is generated by renewables. That is equivalent to 450 MTPE (million tons petroleum equivalent) (Hernández, 2022).

Out of that total, solar holds 228 MTPE, hydro 94, wind 70, sea power 26, bio energy 17, geothermal 8, and the remainder 7 goes to mini hydro plants. Compared with the hydrocarbon base of 52,161 TPE, renewables have very little impact and are equivalent to less than 1 percent of the total.

The energy transition is a global process based on several international accords. Among them, and one of the most recent, is the Climate Change Agreement inked in Paris in 2015. If Venezuela becomes a signatory, the country will not be exempt from its obligations. The main goal is to control emissions sent into the atmosphere and to reduce the rate of increases in global temperatures.

At the same time, the Venezuelan economy is largely dependent on oil and product exports. These exports will have to dwindle over time as the global demand for hydrocarbons falls. The implications of this are an unavoidable effect of the green energy transition.

In the short run, revamping of the Venezuelan oil industry must be given top priority. It will be a difficult task to raise the industry from a state of almost total paralysis that exists right now. There is a window of opportunity of no more than 20 years while the energy transition takes place. To that effect, large and significant domestic and international investments are urgently needed. This would be hailed as 'a new beginning for the Venezuelan Oil Industry.' However, to launch and sustain such a process, dramatic political change will be required to encourage confidence-building measures for investors and operators alike.

Given the geopolitical dynamics of the energy transition over the long haul, Venezuela will have to adopt a new energy matrix for its existing and new sources of energy supplies, as well as forge new uses from domestic customers. In this regard, an excellent first phase (according to Grupo Orinoco recommendations (Grupo-Orinoco, 2021) would be to encourage fuel substitution. That is, replace diesel and gas oil consumption with gas at industrial as well as residential levels. At the same time, the power sector can be encouraged to rehabilitate thermal plants, such as the conclusion of the Tacoma hydro project. This would also require the restoration of several dams and power generation projects on the Caroni River.

In the second stage, cogeneration plans can be launched and executed along with the generation of clean energy from renewables. This would require leveraging production, storage, distribution, control, and the consumption of energy renewables—mainly solar and wind—coupled with an incremental energy efficiency in the transportation, manufacturing, and construction sectors.

In other words, Venezuela will have to significantly decouple energy intensity used per unit of GDP. The state of Venezuela must shoulder the burden for changing according to new times and the times to come. The government must guide and nurture new customs for the benefit of society as a whole and to honor the intent and purpose of the global energy transition—a far cry from what the incumbent government has done so far. Quite possibly, it will be a task for a new democratic government that will emerge in the future.

Last but not least, new avenues will open up on the investigative horizon. In this regard, further research is needed to monitor the evolution of hydrocarbon prices. Energy prices coupled with new technological developments will determine the pace of the transition to renewables within the energy matrix. This is not only true at the global level, but also in the case of Latin America. Argentina, Colombia, and Venezuela are all facing difficult political transitions, although at different degrees of difficulty. The differences are due to a variety of factors, including incumbent party confrontation (Argentina), new presidential election (Colombia), and the need for eventual regime change (Venezuela) to surpass its current stagnation. The solutions, as diverse as the difficulties, remain a subject for future research.

References

Aguilar, G. (2021). ARPEL Webinar, 2021. Latin Energy Group. Retrieved from https://www.lenergygroup.com/g.

Ardila N., M. (2021). Solar Sales Manager for Latin America & Caribbean, Colombia. Retrieved from https://www.energiaestrategica.com/.

Cisneros Lavaller, A., & Universidad Sergio Arboleda, I. o. (2015). Plan Saudita de Largo Plazo – Impacto En El Mercado Internacional Ramificaciones para Nuestros Productores Latinoamericanos. BrújulaEnergética.

Council., W. E. (2022). World Energy Council. Retrieved 2022, from https://www.worldenergy.org

Engelken, M., Römer, B., Drescher, M., Welpe, I., & Picot, A. (2016, July). Comparing drivers, barriers, and opportunities of business models for renewable energies: A review. (Elsevier, Ed.) Renewable and Sustainable Energy Reviews, 60, 795-809.

Ghantous, Ghaida (2021). "Lower Energy Investment Could Spark Supply Crisis -Saudi Minister." Financial Post, December 13. https://financialpost.com/pmn/business-pmn/lower-energy-investment-could-spark-supply-crisis-saudi-minister.

Grupo-Orinoco. (2021). La Transición Energética: implicaciones y compromisos para Venezuela. Retrieved 2022, from https://grupoorinoco.org/2021/07/13/la-transicion-energetica-implicaciones-y-compromisos-para-venezuela/.
Hafner, M., & Tagliapietra, S. (2020). The Geopolitics of the Global Energy Transition. Lecture Notes in Energy. Springer Open.
Hernández, N. (2022). Venezuela y su potencial energético. Retrieved 2022, from https:// www .costadelsolfm .org/ 2022/ 06/ 07/ nelson -hernandez -venezuela -y -su -potencial-energetico/.
International Renewable Energy Agency (IRENA) (2021). Retrieved 2022, from https:// www.irena.org/energytransition.
Kimani, Alex (2021). "Climate Activism Is Great News For Saudi Arabia And Russia." OilPrice.com, June. https:// oilprice .com/ Energy/ Crude -Oil/ Climate -Activism -Is -Great-News-For-Saudi-Arabia-And-Russia.html.
Markous, Ricardo; Tecpetrol Argentina (2021). Oil & Gas Conference, CARI Argentina, 2021. Buenos Aires.
Montamat, D. (2022, March 26). Otra Vez la energía pone en Jaque a la economía Argentina. La Nación.
Mostafa, E.-S., & Shinji, K. Y. (2019). Hydrogen Production Technologies Overview. Journal of Power and Energy Engineering (7), 107-154.
Ortiz, D. Carlos, Greenergy Director (n.d.). Tendencias de Mercado y Precio en módulos fotovoltaicos. Retrieved 2022, from https://greenergy.com.mx/blogs/noticias.
Pugliaresi, L. (2021, November 3). Energy Policy Research Foundation inc. EPRINC Re-Release of NOPEC Article. Retrieved 2022, from https://eprinc.org/2022/05/the-low-carbon-energy-transition-by-ivan-sandrea-and-lucian-pugliaresi/.
Sobarzo, A. V. (2020). Solar Energy . https://www.jemaenergy.com/es/calidad-de-red-y-bess/entrevista-a-victor-leon-business-development-manager-en-jema-mexico/.
Terrapas (2021, June). Decarbonization 101: What It Is and Why It matters? Retrieved 2022, from https://terrapass.com/blog/decarbonization-101-what-it-is.
World Energy Issues Monitor (2022). *World Energy Council* (WEC). Retrieved from https://www.worldenergy.org.

PART II

Financing the transformation: mobilizing capital in a competitive landscape

4 Russia–EU energy relations: Most recent stages of long-term fluctuations and future research agenda

Andrey A. Konoplyanik[1]

A journey from the establishment of supply chains between the EU and the USSR—to the rise and fall of interdependent energy relations within "Broader Energy Europe"—to the current period of sanctions and proposed political refusal of (total break with) Russian energy supplies—to the new future EU–Russia energy cooperation within "new realities" based on "new normalcies" and economic pragmatism?

Introduction

The European Union (EU) and its internal energy market have evolved over a period of more than 70 years. The EU's evolving history can be traced back to the European Coal & Steel Community (1951) and the Treaty of Rome (1957). Its internal market development went through with the First (1996/1998), Second (2003), and Third (2009) EU Energy Packages and Network Codes to the latter (2010–2016). This was followed by the draft Fourth EU Energy Package (Quo Vadis project 2017–2018), which has been transformed into the EU New Green Deal (2019). And through much of this time, it was accompanied by increasing energy cooperation with the USSR, and later Russia, since the first Soviet gas and oil arrived in Western Europe. This cooperation cannot be characterized as a linear, steady growth across the whole period. Instead, it can be described as, or illustrated by, a generalized 'peak curve' that has clear phases: periods of steady expansion and then of slowing growth, then of fluctuations with a declining trend motivated by both sides, and thereafter a rather sharp decrease, politically motivated by the EU, with a declared abrupt full cancellation by the EU in a few coming years.

While acknowledging that energy cooperation between the EU and the USSR/Russia dates back to the 1950s, this chapter focuses on the post-2014 period and its subsequent shifts. To do so, the author identifies three distinct periods within this time frame, with specific attention to gas:

(1) Between 2014 and 2018, the EU reconsidered its energy reliance on Russia following the Crimean and Ukrainian Donbass/Lugansk events. The latter left the EU and Russia with only one informal channel of professional communication on energy.
(2) Between 2018 and 2022, there was gradual reopening of professional Russia–EU communication on energy on decarbonization agenda.
(3) From February 2022 onward, energy cooperation was suspended by the EU following the Russian special military operation (SMO) in Ukraine.

Whether and when Russia–EU energy cooperation will resume as a result of 'new realities' and 'new normalcies' is still an open question and maybe the key issue of the research agenda for energy politics. As political developments between Russia and the West, including on energy, have evolved from bad to worse, very few experts (this author among them) consider the possibility of new modes and models of cooperation between them in the future.

Will this turned-over U-type of evolutionary development bring to an end the current cycle representing the past and recent modern history of Soviet/Russia–EU energy relations? Or, after this current, long-term cycle is over, will there be a new life cycle of similar or totally new relations? This topic is examined in this chapter. The chapter represents the author's personal views based on his academic and practical knowledge and experience, including his involvement in different capacities during his professional career in many of the developments explained in this chapter.[2]

The chapter presents the author's analysis of Russia–EU energy cooperative trends in their post-peak development phases, that is, from 2014—when the first anti-Russian sanctions, including on energy, were implemented by some Western economies—to date. The key substantial events of each period are discussed, which reflect key elements in the research agenda of Russia–EU energy politics, and doing so will enable us to make enlightened conclusions about the future of Russia–EU energy developments—away from the current sharp language and definitive statements from the EU political leadership on a total breakup with Russia in relation to energy and its future.

From the first sanctions to the current period

The 2014–2018 period: multiple game changers and US LNG as a key one

Since 2014, formal cooperation between Russia and the EU further slowed down after introduction of the first group of Western anti-Russian sanctions—the US and EU financial and technological packages. They related to the March 2014 referendums in Crimea and Eastern Ukraine in response to the February 2014 anti-constitutional coup in Kiev.

WS2 GAC: regulatory agenda

Nevertheless, at the same time, GAC WS2[3] [1] continued to work as an instrument of strong interaction and even cooperative activities between Russia and the EU, first and foremost in relation to the development of the EU Gas Target Model and Network Codes to the Third Energy Package (2010–2016), especially the Codes on Transportation Tariffs and Incremental Capacities.[4] This was because of the direct influence of EU regulation on Russian gas supplies to the EU, since after the EU's enlargement between 2004 and 2007 a part of Russian gas supply chains downstream to the historical DPs of Russian LTCs lies within the EU. Moreover, two WS2 GAC members from the Russian side (Alex Barnes, GMT, and this author) were included in the short-listed ENTSOG group of experts, the so-called prime movers, who prepared Incremental Proposal for NC CAM INC with the aim that justified concerns of long-term shippers/promoters of new capacity are to be taken into account, and were among most active participants due to the above reasons [2–5]. That was really a revolutionary breakthrough in East–West relations because, as a rule, since the beginning of post–Soviet Russia relations with the West, it was Western experts who were involved in drafting legislative acts and regulatory rules for the domestic Russian market and not vice versa, as in the given case. The debates were rather sharp since the dominant view at that time among EU energy regulators was that the EU did not need any more major incremental infrastructure additions since the utilization rate of the existing infrastructure was considered to be about 70 percent, which served as proof for the EU regulators of its already excessive volumes.

Quo Vadis

At the end of 2016, DG ENERGY introduced its Quo Vadis project—"A study of the gas market regulatory framework"—with the proclaimed aim of providing a quantitative assessment of the EU welfare growth arising from the newly developed regulatory structure of the EU internal gas market based on the Third EU Energy Package and its Network Codes. But in the process of Quo Vadis development (2017–2018, and WS2 GAC was actively involved in the debate on it through the whole period [1]), in this author's view, it turned to present a set of scenarios with radical changes of this regulatory system, which was perceived by many as having a clear anti-Russian bias. In fact, Quo Vadis has been developing what can be called a draft Fourth EU Energy Package with its regulatory structure clearly discriminative toward the external gas suppliers to the EU from the East.[5] One can treat Quo Vadis as the then proposed action plan for the next (post-2018) Commission (although that next Commission has preferred to put on its flag the New Green Deal).

Quo Vadis appeared to erect barriers on the path of Russian pipeline gas to the EU, making things easier for the more expensive US LNG. Quo Vadis ideas correlated well with the content of the then expanded anti-Russian US Congressional sanctions—signed by President Donald Trump—first of all, the well-known CAATSA law of August 2, 2017 [6]. And it would have led, most probably, to the reduction of EU welfare since five scenarios of Quo Vadis presented an integrated program of substitution of less costly Russian gas in the EU, at least in its Eastern part, by more costly US LNG [7–12].

An inter-related system of actions was proposed to push out Russian gas from the EU, where its DPs are historically located, to the eastern periphery of the zone where the EU energy acquis is implemented and to create economic barriers for its entry into the EU. The program also proposed the creation of gas transportation/transmission infrastructure from regasification facilities/LNG import terminals on the EU coastline to the traditional delivery points of Russian gas inside the EU, from where it should be pushed out by imported LNG to the Russia–Ukraine border; transit business of Russian gas from its 'new' DPs through Ukraine and other East European states to its 'old' DPs deep inside the EU to be transferred to the EU companies—buyers of Russian gas; and its supply volumes may be diminished through the de-facto proposed system of artificial measures [7–12].

It seems that the Quo Vadis scenarios were constructed not in the interests of the EU, but of the United States, and, thus, were aimed to diminish EU competitiveness in the global context. However, through intensive discussions and with the strong involvement of the WS2 GAC in the public debate on Quo Vadis, DG ENERGY's tutor of Quo Vadis project finally called it just an "intellectual exercise," and its proposals did not make their way into the Fourth EU Energy Package.

Two supply rings for the EU

In this author's view, the Quo Vadis exercise can be considered as a reflection of opening competition between two concepts of dominant gas supplies to the EU(i) continuation of Russian pipeline gas supplies with evolving export infrastructure and (ii) development of LNG supplies, first and most US LNG. The author sees the first as a transition from the historical Soviet and immediate post–Soviet Russia's system of linear supply corridors to the EU to the current linear–circular system of Russian gas supplies to the EU within two current rings of competitive gas supplies being formed. One is an 'integral'—with internal backup and crossovers—ring of permanent Russian pipeline gas supplies fixed to the EU market within the radial-circle gas infrastructure system. The second is a 'disruptive' ring of global LNG supplies, which are flexible within the global market and not fixed to the EU.

In the past, the Central transit—Ukrainian, Polish, and Balkan—corridors for Russian gas were the only, and/or key, transit routes to the EU. Now, with the construction of much more modern Northern and Southern semirings, these were to take the key Russian flows to the EU, while the Central corridors were to work as balancing ones, especially the Ukrainian route with its underground gas storages (UGS), which is nor less important task though with different regime of operations.

The Northern corridor (semiring) for major flows consists of offshore Nord Stream-1—plus its onshore continuations OPAL and Gazelle to the south and NEL to the west—and offshore Nordstearm-2, with its onshore continuation Eugal to the south. There is no transit chain at this semiring between Russia and the EU. The Southern corridor (semiring) for major flows consists of the offshore Turkish stream, plus its onshore prolongation Balkan stream. There is a transit chain at this semiring, which means that it presents substitution of Ukrainian transit risks with Turkish transit risks.[6] It is important to note that the semirings end at the same historical DPs of Russian gas to the EU located at the end of the radial corridors.

In this author's view, two different tasks are to be performed by these two loops. The supply ring based on Russian pipeline gas is aimed to close the supply loop in the West, enabling increased security of supplies. The supply ring based on LNG, especially from the United States, is aimed at closing the loop in the East with the key political task of displacing Russian gas from Eastern Europe. In this competition for the EU market, Europe for Russian pipeline gas supplies is the target market. In contrast, Europe for LNG supplies, including US LNG, is the closing (bridge) market within global arbitrage deals. But, especially for US LNG, Eastern Europe is a target market with the aim 'to kill the competitor'—Russian gas, as the cheapest and abundant—since it prevents US LNG from being sold in the EU 'in the money.' The instrument for this is the US-sponsored creation of the vertical North–South gas corridor in Eastern Europe connected through Ukrainian UGS under the Three Seas Initiative.

US LNG into Europe: why not from the West?

To conquer Continental Europe's gas market, US LNG faces a 'paradox barrier': the problem of entering this market from the West, which means through the nearest to the US entry points, via regas LNG terminals located in the Iberian Peninsula (Spain, Portugal), in the United Kingdom, in Northwestern Europe (Netherlands, Belgium, France), and in Southern Europe (France, Italy). Further transportation of the already regasified LNG pipeline gas from the Iberian Peninsula is impossible as pipeline infrastructure is unavailable. The United Kingdom is connected to Continental Europe through two pipelines: Interconnector and BBL. But since gas production in the UKNS has been falling since the edge of the century, these pipelines work much of the time from continent to the island. To supply regasified LNG from the Northwest and/or South Europe coast to the middle of the continent where the DPs of Russian gas are located, the EU has been lacking incremental volumes of adequate pipeline infrastructure—either vertical/longitudinal (North–South and/or South–North bound) or West–East bound. This is because, historically, gas supplies in the Central part of Europe were developed (and delivery infrastructure as well) in the opposite horizontal/latitudinal (i.e., East–West) direction. The EU Commission evaluated in its Quo Vadis project that all EU regas LNG terminals can supply only one-quarter of their regazified gas to Central Europe (where Russian DPs are located) due to the lack of necessary pipeline infrastructure [7–12]. That said, in November 2019, the EIB approved a policy prohibiting any investment in new oil and gas infrastructure from the beginning of 2022 [14], which means that the aforementioned pipeline gap will continue to exist. That is why this decision was immediately criticized by some prominent experts as "irrational" [15], an assessment that this author shares.

From Intermarium to the Three Seas Initiative

US LNG exports to the EU started in February 2016. This converted into practice the US LNG involvement in Russia–EU relations. And, just prior to this, in 2015, the Three Seas Initiative of 12 Central and Eastern European member states of the EU was launched by the Presidents of Croatia and

Poland with an overarching goal to develop a North–South infrastructure corridor in the region (both countries/initiators have LNG regas projects and plans to become entry points for imported, first and foremost US, LNG to Europe), with the strong backing of the US government. Moreover, this was a US initiative: attention was drawn to Europe's disparity in development in 2014 by a US think tank (the Atlantic Council) close to the US government in a report entitled "Completing Europe," which inspired the two aforementioned Presidents to launch this initiative [16]). In November 2020, the US House of Representatives passed a bipartisan resolution "expressing support of the Three Seas Initiative in its efforts to increase energy independence and infrastructure connectivity thereby strengthening the United States and European national security" [17]. This Three Seas Initiative is the de facto reincarnation of the project Intermarium proposed by Pilsudski a century ago. The aim is to cut-off Russia from Europe. In relation to the energy sphere this means forming a vertical corridor in Eastern Europe, from sea to sea, to intersect the radial-circle Russian gas supply system to Europe at its critical point—where the Ukrainian UGS are located.

The Three Seas Initiative is aimed at de facto development of the North–South vertical gas supply corridor in the Eastern part of the EU. It should connect LNG regas terminals in the North (Poland, Lithuania) and South (Greece, Croatia, Turkey) by expansion of throughput capacities of the gas supply system and pipeline interconnectors with physical reverse capacities at the border points of the member states of the Initiative. The aim is to connect the North-bound and South-bound routes at the UGS in Western Ukraine. This is the largest UGS system in Europe, equal to 25 BCM (billion cu meters, 3/4 of 32 BCM of total Ukraine UGS capacity), which has been working since 2017 as a customs storage warehouse. This idea is supported and promoted by Ukraine itself.

The final aim is to substitute Russian gas in the EU with US LNG coming from the east of Europe by entering the historical Russian transit corridor to the EU in Western Ukraine and using it westward from the Western Ukrainian UGS with the help of such EU regulatory rules as the MTPA (Mandatory Third-Party Access) and UIOLI (use-it-or-lose-it) [47–49].

Why are Western Ukrainian UGS needed for US LNG?

And here is the key element of the US idea, as I see it. If/when regasified US LNG comes to the Western Ukrainian UGS and rips into the middle of the Ukrainian transit corridor of Russian gas, then it can go further to the West, to the middle of Europe, by using the already existing gas pipelines that were built during Soviet times. I mean the part located in the former CMEA countries and further westward [47–49]. But to escape the Ukrainian part of this Russian export corridor (GTS upstream of UGS in Western Ukraine), which has been severely underfinanced by Ukraine in post-Soviet times. This has resulted in a high accident rate, which, according to KPMG, in Ukrainian GTS is nine times higher that in the EU as a whole and ten times higher than that in Germany [73].

And the one who controls the Ukrainian UGS controls the state of the market in Central Europe—at the CEGH in Baumgarten. This is historically one of the key DPs of Russian LTCs, from where one of the gas flows is southbound to Italy, while the other is further westbound, through the Czech Republic to Germany and other countries of Northwestern Europe.

The International Energy Agency (IEA) proposed to cut-off Russian gas supplies from Europe too (in its ten-point program of March 3, 2022 [18]), as did the Commission (in its REPowerEU plan of March 8, 2022 [19, 44], updated on May 18, 2022 [45–46]). This is why, in my view, Poland and Bulgaria—the northern and southern entry points of the vertical corridor within the Three Seas Initiative—were the first to refuse shifting to the new payment procedure for Russian gas. It was established on April 1, 2022, by Russian Presidential Decree #172 of March 31, 2022 [20], in response to anti-Russian sanctions and de facto expropriation of US$300 billion of Russian international liquidity reserves. These two countries have de facto stopped in advance their contractual purchases of Russian gas, which were to end in end 2022 (10 BCM LTC with Poland and 3 BCM LTC with Bulgaria).

Poland and Bulgaria would like to become regional gas hubs for the EU in the northeast and southeast of Europe (they have multiply proclaimed such endeavors) to accumulate and then redistribute non-Russian gas flows for Europe (i.e., LNG, first and foremost US LNG, and non-Russian pipeline gas), including for Ukraine. In 2015, Ukraine stopped direct purchases of Russian gas from the East and since then has been receiving all its import supplies from the West. Nevertheless, these have mostly been the same gas of Russian origin, now coming to Ukraine through the longer route and through the chain of intermediaries (thus becoming more costlier than the direct purchases of Russian gas). But this has proved the validity of buying in the future more costlier US LNG as well from the North and the South and, thus, stimulating the use of underground gas storages in Western Ukraine not only and/or not so much for seasonal adjustments of Russian gas supplies to the EU (direct gas transit flows from the East to the West), but also for using these UGS as an instrument of influence on the state of the market in Central Europe, first and most, with US LNG supplies (thus for both direct and reverse gas flows to and through West Ukraine which enables the use of Ukrainian UGS, first and most of West Ukraine, in customs warehouse regime).

The use of huge Western Ukrainian UGS is vitally needed for US LNG to compensate the discrete character of LNG supplies within the implemented Three Seas Initiative attempts to substitute Russian gas supplies to the EU with US LNG coming from the East of Europe [47–49].

The 2018–2022 period: decarbonization tops the agenda

EU Green Deal

In 2019, the new European Commission commenced its life cycle. Compared with its predecessor, it has rather radically different priorities. The 2011–2014 Commission had announced at the end of its term that the basics for internal EU gas markets were developed and it could be considered to be liquid now since churn rates (a number of trades of the given traded product at the hub during trade day—the key indicator of market liquidity) of the major EU gas hubs had exceeded the benchmark limit established by the EU Gas Target Model. EU officials had, however, preferred not to mention that this benchmark GTM churn rate equal to 8 was administratively established at a much lower level than the churn level equal to 15 generally accepted by businesses as the floor for considering this or that marketplace to be liquid. This artificial bureaucratic diminishment of churn from 15 to 8 enabled the Commission to report a success in creating the basics of a liquid EU gas market, since, at that time, two key EU gas hubs—NBP (UK) and TTF (Netherlands)—had their churn rates at about 10–12.

After the 2015 Paris Agreement (COP21), the climate agenda began to grow in importance in the EU. This is why the 2015–2018 Commission concentrated both on the finalization of development of the internal EU energy market and on the climate agenda. The 2019–2022 Commission has put climate agenda on the very top of its agenda. The EU Green Deal [21] was aimed at climate protection, but also, which is not less important, at the development of low-emission technologies to put forward EU to new technological levels and, thus, motivate economic growth. The key breakthrough technological avenues for this, inter alia, were multidimensional energy efficiency and combination of renewables (RES) and renewable hydrogen (RenH2) produced with this renewable electricity. In July 2020, the EU Hydrogen strategy was adopted, which is based on a combination of RES and RenH2 as a breakthrough development path. By 2030, 40 GW of electrolyzers (to produce RenH2) are to be built in the EU and another 40 GW beyond the EU in the neighboring states from which produced H2 shall be transported to the EU by different means [22].

There were multiple aims, direct and indirect, of such vision and prospective development of the EU H2 Strategy beyond the climate agenda. The key one, in my view, is to create a global H2 market based on the Euro. This is mentioned, although not yet articulated in the front pages of the Strategy. But it is this real aim that the EU has been trying to develop using the window of opportunities that was presented by the then US President's (Donald Trump) withdrawal of the United States from COP21. That US decision provided an opportunity for the EU to start creating a new H2 global market that would not be based on the US dollar. This would have diminished the competitive position of the United States in the global commodities markets and would have increased such a role of the EU. However, I disagree with the vision that it might have been possible to create a global H2 market as a commodity market similar to oil and/or gas or other commodities. H2 is not and will not be a globally tradable good; it will not enable arbitrage deals, although some trade flows of H2 in the pure form (gaseous and/or liquid) or in the fixed form (e.g., methanol, ammonia) will be developed between individual markets, mostly 'energy islands,' such as between Australia and Japan. But the global market of H2-related equipment, first and foremost for RenH2 production (electrolyzers, etc.), will definitely be developed. And it was the EU's intention to establish it and to continue with its 'organic growth' to expand the EU's shrinking market niche in the global economy, non-dependent current de-globalization trends, by expanding Euro-priced equipment with 'Made in the EU' logo. In my view, this clear understanding of the potential threat for the United States from such EU developments if the former will continue to stay outside COP21 motivated President Joe Biden to sign back to COP21 on the first day after his election.

Another aim, although not well articulated by the EU at the beginning but clear from the very start, was the intention to substitute dirty, imported molecules with clean, domestically produced electrons. Since the 2006–2009 Russia–Ukraine gas transit crises, the EU has paid greater attention to diversifying its gas supply sources, routes, and suppliers with the aim of diminishing Russian/Gazprom's share in the EU gas market. Forced RES development based on huge state subsidies (I will put aside their correlation with the WTO rules) was aimed, inter alia, at diminishing Russia's role in the EU energy supplies much before the 2022 Ukrainian crisis. So, until January 2018, the dominant EU vision of its energy future was based on the formula that it will be "digital, electrical, renewable," which means 100 percent electrification based on RES-electricity.

WS2 GAC: gas decarbonization as a new common denominator

In 2018, a new window of opportunities for Russia–EU informal cooperation opened. In January 2018, the EU Commission updated its vision for the EU energy future to "renewable electricity plus decarbonized gases." I call it the 'Borchardt turn,' since it was voiced by Klaus-Dieter Borchardt, the then Deputy Director General of DG ENERGY of the Commission responsible for the external energy dimension and the EU co-chair of GAC [23]. It was then that the topic of decarbonization emerged on top of the WS2 agenda, displacing the previous, mostly regulatory, topics. One of the key debated issues referred to the role of H2 in Russia–EU cooperation in the decarbonization area, which was considered then by the parties as another unification avenue, although both parties had different decarbonization priorities.

The EU has a clear preference for RenH2 ("green" H2 in EU terminology) while accepting for the transition period the role of "blue" H2 with obligatory CCS (produced by MSR from natural gas). Russia, for clear reasons, prefers H2 from natural gas produced by pyrolysis technologies with no direct emissions of CO2 ("turquoise" H2). Russia's (and this author's [24–30]) vision has been to use the existing gas transportation grid within the Broader Energy Europe to supply natural gas to the EU where to produce turquoise H2 within Continental Europe and blue H2 in the coastal areas where it will be needed (within so-called hydrogen valleys—the areas of concentrated demand for H2) on the basis of modular pyrolysis plants with their capacities needed for this or that particular H2 valley.

The EU has preferred, and has presented this in its 2020 Hydrogen Strategy [22], to produce half of the H2 needed in the EU, first and mostly green H2. The other half is to be produced beyond the EU and imported, by preference, through the existing and modernized and/or newly built gas transportation grid either as pure H2 or as MHM. For Russia, the EU proposed to produce green H2 at the not fully utilized capacities of hydro and nuclear power stations spread across the country and blue H2 at production sites in Western Siberia and Yamal and from there to transport H2 in the form of MHM to the EU. The major objections from the Russian side were that transportation of MHM with any concentration of H2 in the mix would kill the existing Russian GTS, since the metal of the pipes was not designed for the presence of H2 molecules, in any concentration, in the transported gas. This was nondependent on whether the older (Ukrainian or Polish corridors) or newer (such as Nord Stream 1 or 2 or Turkstream) pipelines were considered. H2 would destroy the pipes (embrittlement problem). And since nuclear and hydro power stations were spread across Russian territory, such proposal, if implemented, would kill the whole GTS, not just one or two pipes [24–30]. Unfortunately, this debate and the whole WS2 process, which had been quite constructive, were stopped in March 2022 by a letter of the Commission, which informed the participants that "EU's engagement under GAC WS2 is suspended for a non-determined period of time" [1].

EU and ECT: 'killing gap' once again?

The post-COP21 developments have intensified the public climate-related debate, which had been increasingly converted, first by different NGOs and 'greens,' into a campaign in favor of RES and against traditional energy companies, which were accused of being the key polluters. That is why any supportive instruments for the multibillion oil and gas industry, like investment protection tools such as the ECT, diminishing its objective risks (the highest among other industries), were proclaimed as climate damaging and, thus, socially harmful. And a campaign against them began, including against the ECT, by using the ongoing process of modernization of this multilateral legal instrument [31]. In the EU, rather radical proposals were voiced by politicians to adapt the multilateral ECT to the EU's current political agenda [32]. This meant to straightforwardly interpret the values of the Green Deal, as if it only favored RES, while all other energies needed to be "positively discriminated" with the aim to totally ban the use of fossil fuels. But a similar dichotomy happened already in the past when EU acquis deviated from ECT rules post-2003 with the adoption of the EU Second Energy Package. It was proposed by the then EU politicians to adapt the broader-than-the-EU multilateral ECT standards, unanimously agreed by this broader community with the EU participation, to the evolving EU views, policies, rules. In this case, that ECT provisions should be adapted to the new values of the EU Green Deal [32]. Now it seems that climate issues can act as another 'killing gap' between EU acquis or, more likely, EU political aspirations and the ECT.

Since 2003 (when adoption of the Second EU Energy Package created a gap between the ECT and EU acquis rules) the EU has de facto disliked the ECT since it has been considered as a less 'liberal' piece of legislation compared with the evolving EU energy acquis. But at that time it was Russia who more actively and publicly disliked the ECT post-2003 and, especially, post-2004 (Yukos case), and even more so after January 2006 and the January 2009 Russia–Ukraine gas crises. But, finally, with adoption of the EU Green Deal, the EU's unhappiness with the ECT came to surface. In my view, there were two main reasons for this. Both related, directly or indirectly, to ECT Article 26, which has long been considered one of the key legal novelties of the ECT.

ECT Article 26: from legal novelty to legal obstacle

First, there was an increasing number of investment claims in international arbitration courts of investors of the EU member states against the EU and/or EU member states based on ECT Article 26.

It is well known that EU member states have signed the ECT in two capacities: as individual sovereign states and as the EU as a whole. From this standpoint, the ECT dominates over the EU acquis, since for the EU as a whole, its acquis is a 'domestic' law while the ECT is an 'international' law. This opens the door for ECT Article 26 arbitrations. When the ECT was negotiated, this legal novelty was introduced with the perception that it would protect Western (EU) investments in the East—in the NIS of the FSU. It was not perceived in the early 1990s that this clause could work the other way round—that is, against the EU and/or its member states—which is happening now. As of December 1, 2021, 92 of 145 ECT arbitrations referred to intra-REIO cases, which means the claims of investors from EU member states against the EU and/or EU member states. Those were mostly RES-related claims that referred to the public–private partnership contracts with a guaranteed reasonable rate of return (RROR), which were unilaterally withdrawn by the state before expiration of the initially agreed terms. As of December 1, 2021, 91 of 145 investment cases based on the ECT referred to RES, with total damages claimed equal to €23 billion, which represented 57 percent of total claims (if Yukos claims are excluded) [33]. Most of the RES-related claims refer to Spain and Italy. This, in my view, is the key reason why Italy withdrew from the ECT in 2016, with the nondependent sunset clause on ECT investment provisions staying in force for 20 years after termination from the Treaty. Spain, in contrast, agreed to chair the ECT modernization process.

The legal conflict between national and international laws was similarly settled in 2019 both in Russia and the EU by the decisions of the National Supreme/Constitutional Courts that now national legislation dominates over international laws. This de facto marked the end of the globalization process with the intended dominance of commonly accepted international rules fixed in international law, which, thus, should dominate over national ones.

Second, the EU Green Deal. The whole campaign was organized against the ECT in the EU, first and mostly by NGOs and greens, as if the Treaty is the legal barrier for the implementation of the EU Green Deal by preventing 'positive discrimination' of fossil fuel companies with their 'climate-dirty' businesses by protecting their investment with ECT Article 26 [32]. This was presented as if the ECT was now an obsolete Treaty, since it appeared to discriminate against

RES by providing investment protection for oil–gas–coal companies as RES competitors (as demonstrated earlier, considering ECT-based international arbitration statistics, this is just not true! [33]). Thus, the ECT should be considered as a barrier to speeding up decarbonization of the EU economy, and either its overall investment protection measures should be deleted from the Treaty or selective implementation of investment protection measures should be allowed in the course of ECT modernization—to allow investment protection of only such investments that are considered politically acceptable, appropriate. For instance, to allow only those investments that politicians (and/or civil society in the face of NGOs) consider climate friendly.

From now into the future

Europe's current energy crisis: who is responsible?

Today, many Western observers (according to the mainstream Western media) consider Russia's actions and, especially, the current situation in Ukraine as the real origin of the ongoing energy crisis in Europe. Although even some political leaders of leading economies tend to consider Russia and President Putin as being responsible for all current global troubles, in this author's view, the effects of these circumstances have just aggravated the energy crisis in Europe, which began in mid-2021, that is, much before the current developments in Ukraine started in February 2022. This crisis is the result of much earlier handmade undertakings by European authorities that have created the current architecture of EU energy markets, which very nervously reacts to any changes in the spot markets, especially with regard to the competition between Europe and Asia for flexible LNG (mostly US LNG) supplies. Sanctions against Russia, with their direct and returnable effects, have redoubled—and will continue doing so—negative consequences for Europe itself.

This author is convinced that Russia and Europe have been strongly interdependent through the centuries because of common historical (although sometimes with differing memories), both cultural and economic, ties and, in relation to energy (especially through the last 50-plus years), also because of common cross-border, immobile capital-intensive large-scale infrastructure that has created a Broader Energy Europe. Some may even remember the long-debated 'common economic space from Lisbon to Vladivostok' years ago.

So, it is in the mutual benefit of the two parties to continue cooperation, in energy in particular, which will lead, inter alia, to the growth of welfare of

European citizens and improve Europe's competitive position in the global markets. Of course, the 'new normal,' when reestablished after the end of the current political turbulences, will differ from the past energy relations. This will open up new opportunities for both Russia and Europe. And I am quite consciously stating this at the current time, when the new wave of antagonism toward Russia in the political circles of Europe has reached one of its biggest historical extremums, at least during the post-Second World War period. And at a time when the EU has been considering one-by-one new sanction packages against Russia: As of July 27, 2022, the EU has introduced 1351 anti-Russian sanctions since 2014, including 1103 since February 22, 2022 [34].

Hand-homemade market structure

The top–bottom regulatory reform of EU energy, which started with the First EU Energy Package of 1996 (electricity) and 1998 (gas), continued by the Second (2003) and finalized by the Third (2009) and its Network Codes (2010–2016), has created a new architecture of the internal EU gas market. Vertically integrated energy companies (VIOCs, like BP, Shell) were unbundled, that is, not allowed to be present simultaneously in all segments of EU energy value chains, although it were the VIOCs, with their huge capital investments and Groningen-type long-term (supply) contracts (LTCs) that have provided pay-back of those investments and have developed the EU gas market since the early 1960s to the point of its current diversified infrastructure—the backbone of the energy business.

Production (upstream) and energy processing and end use (downstream), as competitive businesses, are now legally separated from the midstream (transmission), as natural monopoly business. MTPA to energy infrastructure is now legally binding (since 2003). The internal EU gas market today consists of a number of gas market zones united by pipeline interconnectors (a sort of 'pool' system); each zone has a virtual trading point (gas hub) where the price is established. All this was aimed to provide uninterruptible flows of gas within the EU from the low-price, oversupplied zones to high-price undersupplied zones.

Contractually, the EU gas market consists of two segments: about 70 percent of supplies are covered by LTCs with indexation formulas and the rest by spot deals. Spot and futures gas prices are defined at the hubs by market players based on perceptions of supply and demand. The hubs are to be liquid to provide clear and undistorted price signals, but only three in Europe today correspond (two of those three, marginally) to the criterion of liquidity established by the EU Gas Target Model (churn rate to be above eight)—

Dutch TTF (churn 2020–2021 approximately 130), UK NBP (8–12), Austrian CEGH (10–11). Contractual gas prices in LTCs have been historically linked by pricing formulas in Europe to petroleum product prices with a time-lag effect of six to nine months and now they are linked mostly (by 80 percent in Russian gas LTCs) to spot and forward hub (TTF) quotations as a result of the European Commission's (DG COMP) case against Gazprom 2012–2018 [35].

So, when the gas market is in oversupply, spot and forward prices go down and stay below contractual prices, and when the market is in undersupply, spot prices go up above contractual prices—and can go well above them if/when concerns of/uncertainties for market players are unpredictably high. This is because spot and futures prices are driven by market players' perceptions of future developments, not by physical energy balance. This is the case currently, when prices are being pushed further upward as a result of speculations that Russian military actions in Ukraine can/will destroy the Ukrainian gas transportation system and thus disturb or even stop gas transit through Ukraine equal to 40 BCM, from the total 155 BCM Russian gas exports to Europe, according to the IEA, in 2021.

Despite the fact that around 70 percent of gas volumes to the EU are supplied under LTCs with currently moderate prices (three to four times or even lower than spot quotations because of the rocket-style increase of the latter) due to the time lag in their pricing formulas, it is sky-rocketed spot price quotations that are on the front pages of the newspapers. Spot deals cover only 30 percent of gas supplies, but they are transferred into LTC by indexation formulas. The two-segment gas market structure activates the multiplier effect of spot price, which strengthens the influence of market dis-balances on the prices, especially when the stock levels are low. This has been the case in the EU since 2021.

The takeoff of spot and futures hub-based prices is based also on perceptions that Russia will stop its energy supplies to the EU, using its energy resources as an 'energy weapon.' But it has been multiply stated, including at the highest political level in Russia, that the country has been following and will follow all its contractual obligations in full. At least, until they are accurately paid for, and until they are limited/cutoff by the EU partners (buyers and/or transitters) themselves.

Russia would not like to lose (give up to the competitors as a result of unfair competition) the EU gas market since both Russia and the EU are technically and contractually (some LTCs to last into the 2040s) interconnected and, thus, interdependent. The nondependent phraseology of the current EU political leadership as if the EU would cutoff Russian energy supplies to the EU by 2027 is not in the interests of both parties.

And how it has worked today

In mid-2021, post-Covid recovery and weather conditions increased EU gas demand. Low-wind summer 2021 diminished the production of renewable electricity, while hot weather increased electricity demand for air conditioning. To cover this gap, gas and coal generation capacities (which are backups to RES) were to increase production instead, which led to demand growth for these fossil fuels. The incremental demand for coal was covered mostly by increase of its import from Russia. The growing gas demand was not covered in full, although import supplies increased, as well as withdrawals from UGS, while domestic production has been falling in Europe.

- **UGS:** Usually from spring to autumn, energy companies inject gas into UGS in preparation for next winter heating season. In mid-2021, traders instead preferred not to buy high-priced gas for injection but to offtake gas from UGS, where it was injected much earlier when it was bought at the cheaper gas prices, to cover the high-priced increase of market demand and to earn on this price gap. This has diminished filling level of European UGS since mid-2021 below its average range for 2015–2020, and the gap has been increasing. This has increased nervousness of the market and further pushed spot and forward prices up. In spring 2022, the filling level of EU UGC was at its lowest historical levels.
- **Production:** The Dutch Groningen field is to be shut down soon, although it was this former giant (discovered in 1959) that has pushed forward development of the EU gas market and gave its name to the Groningen-type LTC—the contractual basis of this development. UK production has for long been on a decline, and Norway's is on a plateau. Northern Africa is facing problems with incremental export, both technical limitations and transit (Algeria–Morocco) issues.
- **LNG:** European LNG regas capacities stood half empty for two years, since global LNG (whose market is yet constrained) went to Asia due to the higher Asian price premium. Only since mid-December 2021 has flexible LNG reversed to Europe—after the Asian market reached some level of saturation and the European market became the premium one. But the price of this 'victory' has been excessive: once TTF gas prices almost reached US$4000 per thousand cu meters.
- **Gazprom:** Russian Gazprom slightly diminished its spot supplies to Europe in the second half of 2021, but was strictly fulfilling its long-term contractual obligations, in line with nominations of the customers. Gazprom was

> not covering incremental gas demand above contractual volumes by spot deals, which enabled IEA Director General Fatih Birol, in the *Financial Times* of January 12 [36], to accuse Gazprom of creating a gas crisis in Europe (although a week later, another not less competent professional, Professor Jonathan Stern, OIES and EU co-speaker of GAC during 2011–2016, publicly disagreed with Birol on this, also in the *Financial Times* [37]). No such accusations were addressed to LNG exporters, which preferred to supply their LNG to Asia rather than Europe to earn extra on the Asian price premium.

But, first, Gazprom has the right (but not an obligation) to supply such volumes, since it has, as a state company, its primary obligation by the Russian law on gas supply to deliver gas at first to its domestic customers in Russia and inject into Russian domestic UGS in preparation for the winter. It has the right (but not an obligation) to supply gas to its European customers above its LTC volumes.

Second, it would have been strange to expect Russia and Gazprom to conduct in a unilateral manner such a 'goodwill' behavior (to supply Europe in quantities above strictly legally binding contractual obligations) in the long-lasting situation of direct unilateral political discrimination by the EU of the Nord Stream-2 (NS-2) and OPAL (onshore prolongation of offshore Nord Stream-1) gas pipeline projects.

And, third, the EU Commission has for long been developing the 'security of supply' concept, not in terms of guaranteed passing of the winter peak demand (it is only now that it has returned to this issue by proposing to safeguard annually obligatory UGS filling rates by the beginning of the winter heating season—80 percent this year and 90 further on), but in terms of diminishing dependence on Russian gas supplies (which it has further enhanced by its action plan REPowerEU of March 8, 2022 [19]).

In 2019, the Amendments to the Third EU Gas Directive [38] were adopted, aimed at discrimination of the de facto single NS-2. Then, the EU joined the United States in the sanctions on this project, established by US CAATSA law of August 2, 2017 [6], which decelerated by two years NS-2 construction. Finally, German energy regulator BNetzA first slowed down the NS-2 certification procedure, then delayed it, and, finally, fully stopped it in end February. This means that the pipeline already built and filled with gas has been laying idle at the sea bottom ready to solve all EU gas deficit problems at once. NS-2 volumes, when contracted by the EU customers and certification procedure is timely over, would have been very helpful in the given crisis to provide additional supplies, calm down the market, and push prices down.

But, in the given circumstances, by taking current Russian actions in Ukraine as the pretext, it is to advantage of those who have created this crisis by developing the corresponding EU gas market structure (aimed not at physical gas deliveries, but at gas trades at the virtual hubs) to show that it is Russia that has created this crisis and, thus, to appeal to abandon Russian energy supplies.

Or to provoke nonpayment for Russian gas, neglecting its new payment procedure, which was established in response to the precedent of freezing Russian international liquidity reserves and anti-Russian sanctions on purchases of import goods while these purchases were made from bank accounts abroad where payment for gas arrived.

New payment procedure for Russian gas: pay or lose

A few contractual supplies of Russian gas were cancelled in April–May 2022 (Poland and Bulgaria on April 27 and Finland on May 21) because the governments of these states gave orders to their state companies (PGNiG, Bulgargaz, and Gasum, correspondingly) to refuse to shift to the new procedure of payments for gas established since April 1, 2022, by Russian Presidential Order #172 of March 31, 2022 [20]. This is important to be underlined: These were political decisions that were taken by the three governments and translated for economic execution to their state companies. Under the new procedure, payments in the contractual currency (Euros or USD) should be made to the Russian Gazprombank at special K-accounts (currency and rouble accounts) in Russian jurisdiction and are considered to be executed in full when the payments in currency of the contract are converted into roubles and the latter transferred to Gazprom's bank account in the same GPB. This new procedure is aimed at diminishing risk for both contractual parties of nonpayments for Russian gas due to the possible actions of third party(ies)—the Western states that can again freeze Russian hard currency (gas payment received) in the bank accounts in foreign banks abroad, as was done (and, thus, the precedent was created) with US$300 billion of Russian international liquidity reserves. This new payment procedure creates two safety perimeters for both the seller and the buyer of pipeline gas. The first safety contour is created because payment transactions are moved to Russian jurisdiction, which excludes the risk of another Western expropriation(s) of payments for gas. The second safety contour is established because all aspects of the new procedure are carried out within one financial institution, so transaction costs are minimized and transaction risks are zeroed out [39–40].

There were a number of statements from European politicians that this action was an ineligible action of the Russian state, that is, the principle of 'sanctity of contracts' had been violated by the unilateral intervention of the Russian state. But any sovereign state has a 'right to regulate.' There is an internationally accepted 'doctrine of state enforcement.' And the Presidential Decree obliged Gazprom as a state-controlled company (and that acts as an economic agent of its sovereign state) to act according to such state enforcement. Moreover, I recall that the EU Commission has, more than once in the past, used the same 'doctrine of state enforcement' in its relations with Gazprom, and in a more radical form. Here are two well-known examples of DG COMP claims on Gazprom reflecting the same doctrine:

As of 2012, as if Gazprom violates competition rules in East Europe by using petroleum products indexation formulas in its LTCs (this means, by using pricing formulas of the Groningen-type LTCs). As a result of long case examination (2012–2018) pricing formulas were adapted and spot quotations were added dominating in the formulas [35].

As of 2003, after the Second EU Energy Package was adopted, that as if destination clauses, presented in Gazprom's LTCs, violates new legal rules established by the new energy package. The EU Commission stated that destination clauses prohibit free reselling within the EU of Russian gas purchased at the DPs at the EU border. They limit its sales only to the destined area, mentioned in the contract, which violates the 'free movements of goods' principle established in the EU. Such destination clauses (also the key element of Groningen-type LTC) were protecting producers' resource rent: They prohibit the buyers of Russian gas destined for more distant markets than the DP, thus being sold at the lower contractual price, to resell it at the nearest market to this DP for which market contractual price at this same DP would be higher (due to net-back replacement value pricing principle) [41]. Nevertheless, destination clauses were eliminated from acting Gazprom's LTCs by trilateral agreements, first the Gazprom–ENI-Commission, then the Gazprom–Ruhrgas-Commission, and so on [42].

So, the Russian state had similar rights to act on the basis of the doctrine of state enforcement to update the payment procedure for Russian pipeline gas, especially since it was aimed at diminishing the currency risks for both parties in the unpredictable Western sanctions environment [39–40]. And most of the buyers of Russian gas have agreed to shift to the new payment procedure. Among 54 companies buying Russian pipeline gas (according to Alexander Novak, Deputy Prime Minister of Russia [43]), only 6 companies from five so-called unfriendly states have refused to move to the new payment scheme: 5 of these companies (PGNiG, Poland; Bulgargas, Bulgaria; Gasum, Finland; Orsted, Denmark; Gas Terra, the Netherlands) are state owned or state controlled, while the sixth is Shell Germany (the parent company being Royal Dutch Shell, registered since 2005 in the Netherlands, one of the most active countries in anti-Russian sanctions. So the refusal was purely based on politically motivated decisions of these EU national states (within their sovereign 'right to regulate' and their 'state–agent' relations) deliberately aimed at reaching the predetermined result of such actions—cancellation of supplies as a consequence of Order #172 [20]—in line with the stated REPowerEU aim to nullify Russian energy imports [19, 44–46] first by 2030, then updated by 2027.

IEA and the European Commission's questionable plans

The IEA on March 3, 2022, in its ten-point plan [18] and the European Commission on March 8, 2022, in its REPowerEU program [19, 44], updated on May 18, 2022 [45–46], have presented their proposals on how to reduce EU dependence on Russian gas by 2022 year end by one-third and two-third, respectively. Compared with 155 BCM of Russian gas exports to the EU in 2021, according to the IEA, this means by 50 BCM and 100 BCM within the nine months to year end.

EU leaders plan to become totally independent from Russian energy supplies before 2027, while today EU gas consumption depends 90 percent on imports, of which 45 percent is covered by Russia (figures differ across a broad range for different EU states). Russia provided a quarter of oil and 45 percent of coal EU imports. On April 11, 2022, the EU introduced its fifth sanctions package, which includes the EU embargo on import of Russian coal to the EU. And, on June 3, 2022, the EU introduced the sixth sanctions package, with a partial oil embargo.

In my view, the proposed measures, both by the IEA and especially by the Commission, are unrealistic within the stated time frame, more so before 2022 year end.

Practically all these measures to substitute Russian supplies have either a capital-intensive investment and, thus, a long-term character (renewables, hydrogen, energy efficiency) or are based on a distorted understanding by the authors of such proposals of today's market realities (like proposed substitution of contractually guaranteed deliveries by LTC with TOP provisions through the fixed Russia–EU gas pipeline infrastructure to the EU as a target market for Russian gas by flexible LNG supplies, much of those on spot basis, aimed at arbitrage operations within the global market). Such proposals seem to look more like propaganda aimed at unenlightened inhabitants, such as demonstration to the EU electorate of 'must-to-be-done' immediate political reaction.

What is crystal clear is that all these measures on the supply side, based on alternative energy supplies, will be much costlier for the EU compared with Russian energy supplies and, thus, will decrease the global competitiveness of the EU business due to increase of energy costs of EU goods and services. On the demand side, administrative energy demand restrictions, such as the most recent voluntary (which may and/or most probably will become obligatory) 15 percent gas savings, adopted by EU Energy Ministers, from August 1, 2022, until March 31, 2023 [51], will lead to the worsening of life quality and diminishment of welfare of EU citizens. The beneficiary of both types of measures will be, first and foremost, the United States, which will be given incremental market share in the EU gas market by direct restrictions of Russian gas in favor of US LNG and which will earn from the EU handmade worsening of the global competitiveness of EU business and from the growing social tensions within the EU.

"Clever mechanism" of sanctions and permanent sovereignty on natural resources

According to Ursula von der Leyen, the EU was working on "clever mechanisms" of oil sanctions. "What should not happen is that (Russian President Vladimir) Putin collects even higher prices on other markets for supplies that would otherwise go to the EU," she was quoted as saying. "The top priority is to shrink Putin's revenues" [50]. The EU political leadership has been considering putting in place a price cap on Russian oil as one of the key instruments for reaching this goal. Although it seems that this idea of a price cap was not the EU's, but a US, invention, simply cutting off exports of Russian oil to the West could backfire with an immediate price rise.

Former US Ambassador to Moscow McFaul was the first to propose, on March 22, 2022, a 'clever formula' for Russian oil—to take deliveries but pay only after the SMO in Ukraine and, in the meanwhile, to put Russian oil revenues in the escrow accounts without access to them by the Russian side [52]. Then US Treasury Secretary, Janet Yellen, gathered some the world's most powerful financial leaders together for a private dinner in Washington on the night of April 21, 2022, to discuss mechanisms of G7 restrictions on Russian oil export; they began to be worked out within the G7 after this meeting [53].

G7 leaders discussed at their summit in Schloss Elmau, Bavarian Alps, Germany, on June 28, 2022, how best to establish a price cap on Russian oil traded internationally. They agreed to explore imposing a ban on transporting Russian oil that has been sold above a certain price. The idea behind the cap is to tie financial services, insurance, and the shipping of oil cargoes to a price ceiling. A shipper or an importer could only get these if they committed to a set maximum price for Russian oil [54]. European officials discussed targeting the insurance firms that underwrite tankers hauling Russian oil, the vast majority of which are British or in the EU, as they began to work toward a sixth sanctions package this spring [53]. The G7 was also exploring the possibility of a gas price cap, a move pushed for especially by Italy. France meanwhile called for price caps on all energy sales [54].

The ceiling is to be established at the price level, which covers cost of production and transportation of Russian oil to the market, including RROR. The balancing revenue (difference between the price and the costs plus RROR) is either to be compulsorily withdrawn from Russia by the third states through different instruments or they will not allow Russia to sell its oil at the price above the level established by these third states.

The current international debate primarily revolves around quantitative parameters of this artificial ceiling—whether it will be US$40–60 per barrel. Some Russian commentators argue that production costs (lifting costs?) at some Russian fields are US$15 per barrel or less, so this artificial ceiling established by a few third states will still leave Russian oil trade 'in the money.' Even the Russian Deputy Prime Minister responsible for energy, Alexander Novak, has paid attention only to the quantitative side of the oil price cap story by stating that Russia will not sell its oil internationally if the oil price cap will not cover the production costs of Russian oil, that is, Russia will not sell its oil at a loss [55].

I for one would like to refer to the qualitative side of the oil price cap G7 proposal/intention. All these proposals, debated within official circles and/or voiced in international media, do not address the fact that all of them discuss ways and means of extraction of the natural resource rent (at the stage of monetization of oil produced by the nonmarket instruments) from the sovereign state by the third states to whom this natural resource rent does not belong by international law.

The difference between the price and the costs, including RROR, is the natural resource rent. It belongs to national sovereign states—the owners of the subsoil natural resources (except in two cases—the United States and Canada—where the oil in place can belong to the private landowners). UN GA Resolution 1803 of December 14,1962, established, after a decade of intensive debates [56], permanent sovereignty over natural resources [57]. The G7 proposal de facto aims to refuse from this principle, without proclaiming this straightforwardly. We can interpret this proposal as an intention to return to 'resource colonialism' times, when management of natural resources of the host states was in the hands of third states. This is clearly the issue for the research agenda for energy politics.

Questionable diversification

Here is just one example that will raise questions about the validity of the whole plan of Europe becoming independent from Russia in terms of energy. Both the ten points of the IEA [18] and the REPowerEU plan [19, 44–46] propose to substitute, as if unreliable, 'autocratic' molecules of Russian pipeline gas by, first of all, LNG (which should thus be considered to be more reliable?), including 'molecules of freedom' of US LNG.

But according to Spencer Dale, Chief Economist of BP, who has multiply repeated this in different capitals, Gazprom has won its market share in the EU gas (about one-third before politically motivated artificial diminishment of its import to the EU began in early March 2022) in global competition, including with global LNG. This means that the proposal is to substitute a more competitive gas (less costly Russian pipeline gas) with a less competitive one (the costlier US LNG, since it can be 'in the money' at the EU market only under higher gas prices).

The IEA plan proposes no new gas supply contracts with Russia and to replace Russian supplies with gas from alternative sources. Expiring LTCs with Russia (although none of those expire before year-end 2022) will reduce, according to the IEA, the contractual minimum TOP levels for gas imports from Russia and enable greater diversity of supply. The IEA proposes to obtain around 30 BCM in additional gas supply from non-Russian sources.

REPowerEU went further by proposing under non-Russia diversification measures—up to end 2022—to replace Russian gas with 50 BCM of LNG diversification and 10 BCM pipeline import diversification. This means, in total, to substitute 60 BCM of existing Russian gas import supplies, twice as much as the IEA proposes, by 2022 year end.

On the one hand, this is just technically impossible—no Gazprom's LTC expires before year end.

Poland has for long declared that it will not renew its LTC with Gazprom (10 BCM, expires year-end 2022, but the Polish government announced on May 23 that it was unilaterally breaking the intergovernmental gas agreement with Russia of 1993 with immediate effect, which meant that the contract that was to expire in year-end 2022 was cancelled seven months before its expiration date). Instead, Poland aimed at US LNG. But it was clearly stated, by the then US President, Donald Trump, to Polish President Duda during their meeting in Warsaw in July 2017 that it would be a costlier option [58]. And Poland also aims at pipeline gas from Norway delivered through the newly built Baltic pipe, which means on the basis of the Norwegian–Polish LTC with TOP provisions, which were needed as an investment tool for construction of the Baltic pipe to secure payback for its investments. So, this will be de facto 'exchange' of Russian TOP for Norwegian TOP, but the TOP provision will remain.

Bulgaria, for the first time, said in mid-March 2022 that instead of renewing its LTC with Gazprom (3 BCM, expires year-end 2022), it plans to buy Azery pipeline gas (originates from the Caspian offshore Shah-Deniz field) and US LNG. But to substitute gas from the Russian diversified gas pipeline system—loop-backed with shunt pipes and fueled from many, including mega-sized, fields—with supplies from one single field through one single pipe of the Southern Gas Corridor means to increase geological and technical risks that are mitigated up to zero level when gas is supplied from a pool-like gas system like Russia's.

On the other hand, to increase supply 'diversity' through flexible LNG means to diminish supply 'security,' since LNG supplies, similar to renewables, are unpredictable: They go not to where they are most needed by politicians, say to Europe, but to where the price is highest, and this is Asia most of the time. This is contrary to pipeline gas, whose supplies to the customer are guaranteed by the TOP provisions of LTCs.

The European Commission and renewables, hydrogen, and efficiency

The EU Commission mentioned three avenues to become independent from Russian energy: renewables (RES), hydrogen, energy efficiency [19, 44–46]. The three are presented as universal solutions for the EU to "become truly independent from Russian oil, coal and gas" [44]. Instead, this author sees that at least the last two avenues present good opportunities for cooperation between Russia and the EU for the mutual benefit of the parties when the current 'war of sanctions' comes to an end and a 'new normality' is developed by all parties involved within a 'new reality.'

Hydrogen

In its 2020 Hydrogen Strategy [22], the EU defined renewable hydrogen (renH2 or 'green' H2) as the preselected final choice among other technologies of H2 production with low and/or zero CO2 emissions, like steam reforming with CO2 capture and sequestration (SMR+CCS, 'blue' H2) and/or methane pyrolysis ('turquoise' H2). RenH2 was three times costlier than blue H2 before the 2021 price rise. Now their cost correlations might change in favor of green H2. But there is not enough capacity in the EU (including available territories for placing RES and water resources to 'feed' electrolyzers) for production of all RenH2 needed for it. And there are a lot of other fundamental physical and chemical, technical and economic obstacles [59–61] that inspired Samuel Furfari, former chemical and energy professional from the EU Commission with 36 years in this field, to call it just "The hydrogen illusion" [60]. The Commission plans to install 40GW of electrolyzers in the EU and 40GW abroad (Northern Africa, Western Balkans, Ukraine) and to import RenH2 from there to the EU. This means that new pipeline transmission systems especially designed for H2 would need to be built, since the existing gas pipelines are not suited for H2 transportation, neither as pure H2 nor as MHM with any concentration of H2 in the mix. The so-called hydrogen embrittlement will destroy the existing metal pipes that were designed for transportation of methane with zero content of H2—its molecules being very small and flexible will easily penetrate into the metal of long-distant gas transmission pipelines in their stringer beads, which are not protected by coating from inside the pipe.

And the perception of green H2 as being a 'clean' one, without CO2 emissions, as defined in the EU H2 Strategy, is correct only in regard to direct CO2 emissions in the course of RES electricity production and RenH2 production. This means if only Scope 1 & 2 emissions are considered. But if Scope 3 emissions are to be considered, which means the emissions in the course of equipment production aimed at production of RES electricity and renewable H2, then those emissions are much higher than in the corresponding manufacturing value chains of equipment for electricity production based on NRES. It is proven, say by Olivier Vidal in his fundamental research [62], that material intensity measured for six fossil fuel–based and seven RES-based power generation technologies through four key structural materials used to manufacture different power generation infrastructure (concrete, steel, aluminum, copper), both per unit of installed capacity and/or per unit of electricity generation, differs greatly in favor of fossil fuel–based power generation. This means that the material intensity of manufacturing RES-based power generation technologies is much higher, and so are the energy use and corresponding emissions. As Daniel Yergin, Pulitzer Prize winner for *The Prize,* at the presentation of his new book, *The New Map*, very correctly and cleverly stated, "New supply chains for net-zero carbon requires carbon!!! … They require diesel to operate shuttle in mining…" [63].

The best is to produce H2 close to end use, in the places of concentration of it users, in the so-called EU Hydrogen valleys. In my view, the mutually beneficial scenario for Europe is to use the existing cross-border diversified Russia–EU gas pipeline infrastructure for continued supplies of natural gas, now also as a feedstock for H2 production close to or within EU Hydrogen valleys with pyrolysis technologies [24–30]. They do not emit CO2; instead, per ton of H2, three tons of black carbon are produced, which is climate neutral, can be used in many existing and new industries, and is easily stockpiled. Joint commercialization of pyrolysis technologies is a good avenue for Russia–EU technological cooperation in low-emission energy development in a post-sanctions period of reestablishment of EU–Russia energy relations within a 'new normality.' This has been one of the key topics of discussions within WS2 GAC in 2020–2021 [64–67].

Energy efficiency

This is the best way to diminish the energy cost burden on states, industries, households. Technological improvements decrease unit energy consumption and, thus, demand for end-use and primary energy. This might change the supply–demand balance and can lead to oversupply, which will move prices down. In importing countries, this can reduce the import bill for energy; in producing states, this will downgrade their capital spending on exploration and production of primary energy because of increased energy output–capital ratio.

Among the most prospective areas for energy efficiency measures in the EU is the current housing stock, especially multistory buildings and especially in Eastern Europe. This area is also a good avenue for Russia–EU technological cooperation since most of the housing stock in Eastern Europe (in the former COMECON states) was built on the basis of former Soviet low–energy efficiency standards from the times when domestic energy prices there were supported at socially affordable low levels, which did not create stimuli to improve energy efficiency. There have also been big energy losses in the heating systems connecting cogeneration power plants with multistory buildings in the cities. So, energy efficiency of the housing stock and heating systems both in Russia and Eastern Europe provides good prospects for mutually beneficial energy cooperation between Russia and the EU. And it was penciled as provisional topic for the next WS2 GAC meeting that was planned for early spring 2022, and both parties demonstrated their practical interest in this topic, but this meeting did not occur due to the March 2022 decision of the Commission that "EU's engagement under GAC WS2 is suspended for a non-determined period of time" [1].

Expansion of cooperation into the energy-efficiency area, with its huge domino effects in reducing emissions, would be a much more preferable alternative compared with the ill-omened attempts of the EU leaders to break historical and mutually beneficial interdependence between Russia and the EU and to substitute it with energy dependence (of the import-dependent EU) on third states with costlier (US LNG or domestic RES) and less reliable (LNG in general and domestic RES) and/or more risky (alternative pipeline supplies and domestic RES) energy supplies.

Sanctions: direct and reverse, and domino effects

Both the IEA ten-point plan [18] and the REPOwerEU program [19, 44–46] propose de facto a 'buyer's embargo' on Russian gas/energy supplies. This will support nervousness in the EU gas/energy market and, under its existing architecture, will inevitably continue to support high energy prices.

Many foreign companies have withheld or fully stopped their activities in Russia since end-February 2022, and some of them (like Shell and BP) have decided to leave the country with immediate effect. Together with the effects of negative sanctions on Russia (the most significant among them and yet unprecedented was the freeze of first-line reserves of the Russian Central Bank worth US$300 billion—this is de facto real expropriation), this will have (and has had already) a direct reverse effect on the sanctioning states, will lead (and has led already) to countersanctions, and will worsen (and has worsened already) the multiple negative effects of the energy crisis mostly for Europe, not so much for other Western states. Thus, sanctioning Russia will be first and foremost at European's cost.

Russian foreign trade turnover with the countries that have supported anti-Russian sanctions equals 54 percent of its total. Most of those are European states, since Europe in aggregate has a much higher share in foreign trade turnover with Russia than other sanctioning states [68].

Unilateral closure of the Russian market for EU goods and services, introduced by the EU sanctions, means that corresponding revenues are lost (not received) by EU business in Russia, while the corresponding costs already undertaken (both in Russia and abroad) are not compensated.

Western sanctions on Russian goods have already caused domino effects for global food and raw material industries since both lie in the fundament of deeply internationalized value chains. The sustainability, security, and affordability of global material supplies have already been influenced since Russia, inter alia, is one of the raw material centers for the world.

Due to rising energy costs, production costs in many, especially energy-intensive, industries in Europe will continue to grow. This has already led to either diminishing of their competitive position or full closures of their production facilities. This has covered a broad range of European industries. To change the flows logistics, to find alternatives suppliers (if any), to organize new supply chains will all take time, increase the costs, and diminish the competitiveness of those who introduce sanctions. Europe will face it first—and has been facing it already. Sanctions always hurt those who introduce them.

Is it in European interests to abandon Russian energy supplies?

This time will pass; the conflict in Ukraine will come to its end, hopefully, sooner the better, and inevitable sobriety and understanding of the choice will come back to Europe.

Whether Europe will continue to follow trans-Atlantic solidarity and anti-Russian sanctions and, thus, take on the burden of related incremental costs (first in energy), which will decrease the welfare of EU citizens and the EU's competitive position in the global markets is the key question. This is because all alternatives to Russian energy supplies are costlier or less reliable from a geological, technical, and/or economic standpoint. Or will Europe continue mutually beneficial cooperation with Russia—though, as mentioned, based on new conditions, within a new reality and new normality—since Europe and Russia have been inseparably linked (inter alia, by the immobile cross-border capital intensive-energy infrastructure) and, thus, have been interdependent through half a century in terms of energy and, for many centuries, culturally and historically? In this second scenario, political emotions are to diminish, and sanctions inevitably will begin to erode.

So, the pledge for European prosperity lies in continuing mutually beneficial interaction with Russia. This is what the United States is afraid of, and this is why it has been trying for long to disunite Russia and Europe, since Europe in cooperation with Russia becomes a strong competitor for the United States in the global economy, where energy ties are the basis for mutually beneficial cooperation between Russia and the EU.

Today's development of RES, H2, and energy efficiency, in my view, should be undertaken not with the specific aim to substitute Russian energy supplies in Europe but as a natural step forward to the new technological mode of low-emission economic development from its currently high-emission character—similar to how it happened in the past, after the energy crises of the 1970s, when the world began its move from energy-wasteful to energy-efficient type of economy [69–71]. Joint development toward the low-emission energy future will create a new competitive medium where both economic and ecological considerations will play their role. With fair and reasonable involvement, the host states will use their 'right to regulate' to decide on the 'rules of the game,' providing a fair play. And the open market, without unilateral sanctions, will decide which technological solutions for sustainable, affordable, and secure energy supplies will work best for all the citizens of the countries within the interdependent Broader Energy Europe and beyond it.

Notes

1. Disclaimer: The views expressed in this chapter do not necessarily reflect and/or coincide with the official position of the Russian government and/or of the Gazprom Group (including Gazprom JSC and/or Gazprom Export LLC), its stockholders, and/or persons affiliated with it/them or any Russian official authority and fall within the full personal responsibility of the author of this chapter.
2. Many of the views and arguments were examined in detail and explained by this author in his publications, presentations, interviews which are all placed at his website www.konoplyanik.ru.
3. Work Stream 2 Internal Markets of the Russia–EU Gas Advisory Council; the latter was established in 2011 and was working intensively till Spring 2022. In March 2022 the EU side suspended its activity in WS2 GAC for an indefinite period of time [1].
4. This can be seen from the agendas of the WS2 GAC meetings of that time [1].
5. This author has researched this issue in details in his publications and presentations through 2017-2018.
6. The transit risk pyramid was explained by this author in his publications and presentations [12, 13, etc.].

References

All publications and presentations of this author, mentioned in this reference list, are available from his website at www.konoplyanik.ru.

[1] Website of the Russian Ministry of Energy => Activity => International cooperation => Russia-EU Energy Dialogue => GAC => WS2 GAC (https://minenergo.gov.ru/node/14646)

[2] A.Barnes, A.Konoplyanik. Prime Movers' comments on draft CAM amendment for Incremental Capacity (6th SJWS on ENTSOG "Incremental Proposal" (CAM NC amendment), Brussels, ENTSOG, 24th June 2014)

[3] A.Barnes, A.Konoplyanik. Prime Movers' vision on intermediate results of ENTSOG "Incremental Proposal" (why justified concerns of long-term shippers / promoters of new capacity are not yet taken into account?) (5th SJWS on ENTSOG "Incremental Proposal" (CAM NC amendment), Brussels, ENTSOG, 08 April 2014)

[4] A.Barnes, A.Konoplyanik. Draft RF/GG vision of "Coordinated Open Season" for "New Capacity" within ENTSOG "Incremental Proposal" (2nd JSWS on ENTSOG "Incremental Proposal" (CAM NC amendment), Brussels, ENTSOG, 26 February 2014)

[5] A.Barnes, A.Konoplyanik. Remarks on ENTSOG Preliminary View on Incremental Proposal as of 14.01.2014 within the framework of Acer Guidance to ENTSOG as of 29.11.2013 (19th round of Informal Russia-EU Consultations on EU Regulatory Topics & 12th meeting of the EU-Russia Gas Advisory Council's Work Stream on Internal Market Issues (WS2 GAC) combined with ENTSOG Workshop on "Incremental Proposal" (CAM NC amendment), Vienna, E-Control, 31 January 2014)

[6] COUNTERING AMERICA'S ADVERSARIES THROUGH SANCTIONS ACT. PUBLIC LAW 115–44—AUG. 2, 2017 (https:// www .govinfo .gov/ content/ pkg/ PLAW-115publ44/pdf/PLAW-115publ44.pdf)

[7] A.Konoplyanik. EU Quo Vadis: a theoretical exercise with an anti-Russian Flavour? ("Global Gas Perspectives", 19 October 2017)

[8] A.Konoplyanik. Quo Vadis: оценка эффективности Третьего энергопакета ЕС или подготовка новой «линии Керзона»? («Нефть, газ и право», 2017, №4, с. 42–53; №5, с.47–56; №6, с. 51–59)

[9] A.Konoplyanik. Оценка эффективности применения Третьего энергопакета Евросоюза и проект Еврокомиссии Quo Vadis. («Газовая промышленность», спецвыпуск №4 (75), 2017, с. 36–46)

[10] A.Konoplyanik. EU's fourth energy package. Gazprom in Europe: what to prepare for. ("Oil and Gas Vertical", May 2018, No.2 (433), p.16–25)

[11] The EU, Russia and the Fair Gas Trade debate (introductory article and conversation of A.Konoplyanik with K.D.Borchardt) ("Global Gas Perspectives", 06.07.2018) (www.naturalgasworld.com/ggp-62532/)

[12] А.Конопляник. Как США и ФРГ собираются поддерживать Украину. И какой сценарий перехода от конфронтации к сотрудничеству может предложить Россия. (Корпоративный журнал «Газпром», сентябрь 2021 г. (№9), с. 24–34)

[13] А.Конопляник. Экономическая подоплека газовых проблем в треугольнике Россия-ЕС-Украина и возможные пути их решения. (ИНП РАН, Открытый семинар «Экономика энергетики (семинар А.С.Некрасова)», 152-е заседание от 21 октября 2014 г. – Москва, Изд-во ИНП РАН, 2014 г., 132 с.)

[14] EU Bank launches ambitious new climate strategy and Energy Lending Policy, 14.11.2019 (https:// www .eib .org/ en/ press/ all/ 2019–313 -eu -bank -launches -ambitious-new-climate-strategy-and-energy-lending-policy)

[15] Costis Stambolis. EIB's Decision to Suspend Funding for Fossil Fuels Projects Can Only be Described as Irrational. (IENE Comment No22, December 5, 2019)

[16] Three Seas Story. (https://3seas.eu/about/threeseasstory)

[17] The Three Seas Initiative. (In Focus – Congressional Research Service, IF 1 1547, 26/04/2021) (https://sgp.fas.org/crs/row/IF11547.pdf)
[18] A 10-Point Plan to Reduce the European Union's Reliance on Russian Natural Gas. (IEA, 3 March 2022) (https://www.iea.org/reports/a-10-point-plan-to-reduce-the-european-unions-reliance-on-russian-natural-gas)
[19] COMMUNICATION FROM THE COMMISSION TO THE EUROPEAN PARLIAMENT, THE EUROPEAN COUNCIL, THE COUNCIL, THE EUROPEAN ECONOMIC AND SOCIAL COMMITTEE AND THE COMMITTEE OF THE REGIONS. REPowerEU: Joint European Action for more affordable, secure and sustainable energy. (European Commission, Strasbourg, 8.3.2022 COM(2022) 108 final) (https:// eur -lex .europa .eu/ resource .html ?uri = cellar: 71767319–9f0a -11ec -83e1–01aa75ed71a1.0001.02/DOC_1&format=PDF)
[20] Указ Президента Российской Федерации от 31.03.2022 г. № 172 «О специальном порядке исполнения иностранными покупателями обязательств перед российскими поставщиками природного газа» (В редакции Указа Президента Российской Федерации от 04.05.2022 № 254) (http://www.kremlin.ru/acts/bank/47699)
[21] European Commission. A European Green Deal: Striving to be the first climate-neutral continent. (https:// commission .europa .eu/ strategy -and -policy/ priorities-2019–2024/european-green-deal_en)
[22] COMMUNICATION FROM THE COMMISSION TO THE EUROPEAN PARLIAMENT, THE COUNCIL, THE EUROPEAN ECONOMIC AND SOCIAL COMMITTEE AND THE COMMITTEE OF THE REGIONS. A hydrogen strategy for a climate-neutral Europe. (European Commission, Brussels, 8.7.2020 COM(2020) 301 final) (https:// eur -lex .europa .eu/ legal -content/ EN/ TXT/ ?uri = CELEX:52020DC0301)
[23] All you need to know on the EU energy market in 2018–2019… in one interview! (exclusive interview to Klaus-Dieter Borchardt (Director, DG ENER), by Ilaria Conti (Head of FSR Gas Area) – recorded in Brussels on 9th January, 2018 – on the future of the EU energy market.) (https://fsr.eui.eu/need-know-eu-energy-market-2018–2019-one-interview/)
[24] A.Konoplyanik. Decarbonising European Gas: A New EU-Russia Partnership? ("Global Gas Perspectives", 07 July 2020) (https:// www .naturalgasworld .com/ gas -decarbonisation-in-europe-80282)
[25] А.Конопляник. Декарбонизация газовой отрасли в Европе и перспективы для России. Чистый водород из природного газа как новая основа для взаимовыгодного сотрудничества РФ и ЕС в газовой сфере. («Нефтегазовая Вертикаль», 2020, №16, с. 30–41 (часть 1); №17, с. 29–38 (часть 2); №18, с. 50–56 (часть 3); № 19, с. 66–74 (часть 4); № 20, с. 39–45 (часть 5))
[26] A.Konoplyanik. Gas Decarbonisation in Europe: Clean Hydrogen as the New Prospective Area for Russia-EU Cooperation. (OGEL Special Issue on "The Hydrogen Economy", OGEL, February 2021, Vol. 19 - issue 2)
[27] А.Конопляник. Водородная энергетика России: альтернативный внешнеэкономический сценарий. («Энергетическая политика», 2021, № 3 (157), с. 20–33)
[28] А.Конопляник. Водородный раскол мнений: новый виток противостояния. («Нефтегазовая вертикаль», январь 2022, №1 (494), с. 58–68 (часть 1); февраль 2022, №2 (495), с. 66–81)

[29] A.Konoplyanik. Energy transition and green energy: the struggle for climate and for a new redivision of the world—and the proposal for a balanced Russia–EU solution. ("The Journal of World Energy Law & Business (JWEL&B)", jwab031) (https://doi.org/10.1093/jwelb/jwab031)

[30] A.Konoplyanik. Challenges and potential solutions for Russia during global gas transformation and "Green Revolution". ("Energy Policy", Volume 164, May 2022, 112870) (https://doi.org/10.1016/j.enpol.2022.112870)

[31] International Energy Charter. Modernization of the Treaty. (https:// www.energychartertreaty.org/modernisation-of-the-treaty/)

[32] A.Konoplyanik. EU Climate Change Politics should not be Based on Deliberate Mistakes. // "Natural Gas World/Global Gas Perspectives", 16.09.2020 (https:// www.naturalgasworld.com/eu-climate-change-politics-should-not-be-based-on-deliberate-mistakes-81897)

[33] International Energy Charter. Cases/Statistics (https://www.energychartertreaty.org/cases/statistics/)

[34] Russia Sanctions Dashboard. Current as of 27 July, 2022 (https://www.castellum.ai/russia-sanctions-dashboard)

[35] CASE AT.39816 – Upstream gas supplies in Central and Eastern Europe. ANTITRUST PROCEDURE Council Regulation (EC) 1/2003. Article 9 Regulation (EC) 1/2003. Date: 24/05/2018 (https://ec.europa.eu/competition/antitrust/cases/dec_docs/39816/39816_10148_3.pdf)

[36] IEA chief accuses Russia of worsening Europe's gas crisis. Fatih Birol says low supplies coincide with 'heightened geopolitical tensions over Ukraine' // "Financial Times", 12.01.2022 (https://www.ft.com/content/668a846e-d589–4810-a390–6d7ff281054a)

[37] Letter: Europe's energy crisis should not be blamed on Gazprom. From Professor Jonathan Stern, Distinguished Research Fellow, Oxford Institute for Energy Studies, EU Speaker for the EU-Russia Gas Advisory Council 2011–15. // "Financial Times", 17.01.2022 (https://www.ft.com/content/e447ae74–7e93–4b5c-9952–0e570507d671)

[38] DIRECTIVE (EU) 2019/692 OF THE EUROPEAN PARLIAMENT AND OF THE COUNCIL of 17 April 2019 amending Directive 2009/73/EC concerning common rules for the internal market in natural gas (Official Journal of the European Union, 3.5.2019, L 117/1) (https://eur-lex.europa.eu/legal-content/EN/TXT/PDF/?uri=CELEX:32019L0692&from=EN)

[39] А.Конопляник. «Карибский газовый кризис» Европы. Политические лидеры Европы ведут ее к саморазрушению своим намерением отказаться от российского энергоимпорта. // «Нефтегазовая Вертикаль», 2022, №4, с.60–69 (часть 1); №5, с.72–89 (часть 2)

[40] A.Konoplyanik. Explaining Putin's Rubles-For-Gas Decree. Russia's decree on new procedure for gas payments reduces risks for both buyer and supplier. // *"Natural Gas World – Global Gas Perspectives"*, 01.06.2022 (https:// www.naturalgasworld.com/explaining-putins-rubles-for-gas-decree-98578)

[41] A.Konoplyanik. Russian Gas to Europe: From Long-Term Contracts, On-Border Trade, Destination Clauses and Major Role of Transit to …? ("Journal of Energy and Natural Resources Law", 2005, vol.23, N 3, p. 282–307)

[42] А.Конопляник. «Правовые аспекты процедуры недискриминационного конкурентного доступа к свободным мощностям транспортировки (ДЭХ, TAG и ЕСГ)», с.142–156. – в кн.: Нефтегаз, энергетика и законодательство (выпуск 8/2009). (Информационно-правовое издание

топливно-энергетического комплекса России и стран СНГ (ежегодник). – Москва, «Нестор Экономик Паблишерз», 2009, 160 с.)
[43] Новак сообщил, что половина из 54 покупателей газа открыла счета в рублях. // РБК, 19.05.2022 (https:// www.rbc.ru/ economics/ 19/ 05/ 2022/ 6285 f6f79a7947c424f5dfa4)
[44] REPowerEU: Joint European action for more affordable, secure and sustainable energy. // European Commission – Press Release, Strasbourg, 8 March 2022 (https:// safety4sea.com/wp-content/uploads/2022/03/EU-Joint-European-action-for-more -affordable-secure-and-sustainable-energy-2022_03.pdf)
[45] COMMUNICATION FROM THE COMMISSION TO THE EUROPEAN PARLIAMENT, THE EUROPEAN COUNCIL, THE COUNCIL, THE EUROPEAN ECONOMIC AND SOCIAL COMMITTEE AND THE COMMITTEE OF THE REGIONS. REPowerEU Plan {SWD(2022) 230 final} // Brussels, 18.5.2022, COM(2022) 230 final (https://eur-lex.europa.eu/resource.html?uri=cellar:fc930f14 -d7ae-11ec-a95f-01aa75ed71a1.0001.02/DOC_1&format=PDF)
[46] REPowerEU: A plan to rapidly reduce dependence on Russian fossil fuels and fast forward the green transition. // European Commission, Press-Release, 18 May 2022, Brussels (https://ec.europa.eu/commission/presscorner/detail/en/ip_22_3131)
[47] А.Конопляник. Американский газ в степях Украины. // «Эксперт», 6–12.06.2022, с.48–51 (https:// expert .ru/ expert/ 2022/ 23/ amerikanskiy -gaz -v -stepyakh-ukrainy/)
[48] А.Конопляник. Как США продвигают свой СПГ в ЕС против России и самой Европы. Украинские подземные хранилища – американский ключ к газовому сердцу континента. // «Независимая газета - ежемесячное приложение «НГ-Энергия»», 13.06.2022, с.11 (https://www.ng.ru/ng_energiya/ 2022–06–13/11_8459_usa.html)
[49] А.Конопляник. Американский СПГ в ЕС против России и самой Европы. // «Энергетическая политика», №7(173), июль 2022, с. 26–39 (https:// energypolicy.ru/ amerikanskij-spg-v-es-protiv-rossii-i-samoj-evropy/ gaz/ 2022/18/18/), (анонс статьи: https://t.me/energopolee/1467)
[50] New EU sanctions on Russia to target Sberbank, Commission head tells paper. // Reuters, 17.04.2022 (https://www.reuters.com/business/finance/new-eu-sanctions -russia-target-sberbank-commission-head-tells-paper-2022–04–16/?utm_source= Sailthru&utm_medium=newsletter&utm_campaign=global-investor&utm_term= Reuters%20Global%20Investor%20-%202021%20-%20Master%20List)
[51] Save Gas for a Safe Winter: Commission proposes gas demand reduction plan to prepare EU for supply cuts. Press release, 20 July 2022, Brussels (https:// ec.europa .eu/commission/presscorner/detail/en/IP_22_4608)
[52] McFaul formula for Russian oil – take deliveries but pay only after special operations in Ukraine. // Frontier India, 22.03.23 (https:// frontierindia .com/ mcfaul -formula-for-russian-oil-take-deliveries-but-pay-only-after-special-operations-in -ukraine/)
[53] Janet Yellen's global campaign to defund Russia's war machine. The U.S. is pushing leaders around the world to buy oil from Russia only at heavily discounted prices. Obstacles loom. // The Washington Post, 14.07.2022 (https://www.washingtonpost .com/us-policy/2022/07/14/yellen-putin-oil-price-russia/)
[54] G7 agrees to explore cap on Russian oil price. // Reuters, June 28, 2022 (https:// www.reuters.com/ business/ energy/ g7-leaders-agree-study-russian-energy-price -caps-officials-2022–06–28/)

[55] Новак: Россия перестанет поставлять нефть за рубеж, если цена на нее будет ниже затрат на добычу. // Коммерсантъ, 20.07.2022 (https://www.kommersant.ru/doc/5470883)

[56] Permanent Sovereignty over Natural Resources General Assembly resolution 1803 (XVII), New York, 14 December 1962. Procedural History (https://legal.un.org/avl/ha/ga_1803/ga_1803.html)

[57] United Nations General Assembly resolution 1803 (XVII) of 14 December 1962, "Permanent Sovereignty over Natural Resources" (https://legal.un.org/avl/ha/ga_1803/ga_1803.html)

[58] Трамп сулит Европе газ: цены немного подрастут, но это ничего (https://smotrim.ru/video/1687354)

[59] С. С. Белобородов, Е. Г. Гашо, А. В. Ненашев. Возобновляемые источники энергии и водород в энергосистеме: проблемы и преимущества. (Санкт-Петербург, Наукоемкие технологии, 2021, 151 с.)

[60] Samuel Furfari. The Hydrogen Illusion. (Amazon Fulfillment, Poland, Wroclaw, 09.09.2020)

[61] Litvinenko V.S., Tsvetkov P.S., Dvoynikov M.V., Buslaev G.V., Eichlseder W. Barriers to implementation of hydrogen initiatives in the context of global energy sustainable development. (Journal of Mining Institute. 2020. Vol. 244, p. 428–438. DOl: 10.31897/PMI.2020.4.5)

[62] Olivier Vidal. Mineral Resources and Energy. Future Stakes in Energy Transition. // ISTE Press Ltd - Elsevier Ltd, UK-US, 2018, 156 pp. (Figure 5.2./p. 72; Figure 5.3./p. 74)

[63] A conversation with Pulitzer Prize winner and energy expert Daniel Yergin, Atlantic Council, 25.09.2020 (https://www.youtube.com/watch?v=hWMOU8IjRhI)

[64] Discussion on potential joint research on key decarbonization issues of mutual interest, Leaded by Co-chairs Work Stream 2 "Internal Markets", Russia-EU Gas Advisory Council. (29th meeting of the EU-Russia Gas Advisory Council's Work Stream on Internal markets Issues (GAC WS2), Berlin, Germany, 21 October 2019) (https://minenergo.gov.ru/node/14646)

[65] A.Konoplyanik. A "Clean Hydrogen from Natural Gas Alliance" Proposal – why it is in mutual benefit for the EU and Russia; proposal for creation of the platform. (Presentation at the 31-th meeting of WS2 GAC, online, 18.09.2020) (https://minenergo.gov.ru/node/14646)

[66] A.Konoplyanik. Russia's Hydrogen Strategy in the making & prospects for effective Russia-EU cooperation in this field: different aspects for WS2 GAC discussions. (Presentation at the 32-th meeting of WS2 GAC, online, 13.11.2020) (https://minenergo.gov.ru/node/14646)

[67] A.Konoplyanik. Russian hydrogen development strategy: key provisions and some critical comments in comparison with the EU (a follow-up of presentation on Russia's H2 Strategy in the making & prospects of effective RF-EU cooperation, 32d WS2 GAC, 13.11.2020). (Presentation at the 36th meeting of the Work Stream 2 "Internal Markets", Russia-EU Gas Advisory Council, 22.10.2021, online) (https://minenergo.gov.ru/node/14646)

[68] Доли основных стран во внешней торговле России с 2015 по 2021 г. (Статистика внешней торговли России. Анализ онлайн) (https://statimex.ru/strany/)

[69] А.Конопляник. Россия на формирующемся Евроазиатском энергетическом пространстве: проблемы конкурентоспособности. (М.: «Нестор Академик Паблишерз», 2004, 655 с.)

[70] A.Konoplyanik. Key Aspects of the Seventh Energy Transition And Its Point of Divergence and Mutually Acceptable International Economic Solutions For Russia. ("Energy Systems Research", Vol. 4, No. 4, 2021, p.30–45) (http:// dx .doi .org/ 10 .38028/esr.2021.04.0004)

[71] А.Конопляник. О новой парадигме развития мировой энергетики, рисках и вызовах для России и мира. (Москва, Институт народнохозяйственного прогнозирования РАН, 2019 г., 116 с.) (https:// ecfor .ru/ publication/ o -novoj -paradigme -razvitiya -mirovoj -energetiki -riskah -i -vyzovah-dlya-rossii-i-mira/)

[72] A.Konoplyanik. On the New Paradigm of International Energy Development: Risks and Challenges for Russia and the World on the Way to the Low-Carbon Future (pp. 287–339). – chapter 11 in: "The Palgrave Handbook of Managing Fossil Fuels and Energy Transitions", (Geoffrey Wood and Keith Baker (Editors), Palgrave Macmillan, xxxiii+637 pp., published 26 November 2019) (ISBN 978-3-030-28076-5))

[73] Situation of the Ukrainian natural gas market and transit system. Market Study. (KPMG, 10.04.2017, p.37–38)

5 China's energy investment through the lens of the Belt and Road Initiative

Dongmei Chen and Philipp Galkin

The Belt and Road Initiative (BRI): Progress Amid Controversies

Overview of the BRI

President Xi Jinping announced the BRI in 2013 during his official visits to Kazakhstan and Indonesia. The vision for a Silk Road Economic Belt connecting Central Asia and Europe was outlined in his speech in Kazakhstan, and the roadmap for a Maritime Silk Road linking the two continents was described in his speech in Indonesia (SCIO 2016). In the eight years since its inauguration, the initiative has evolved, simultaneously shaping the global political economy.

The geographical scope of the initiative has gradually transformed from a general concept to a structured plan. Several versions of the BRI routes and maps have been discussed since the initiative was launched. The first roadmap with an official stamp became available only in 2015, when the National Development and Reform Commission, the Ministry of Foreign Affairs, and the Ministry of Commerce released the vision and action plan for the BRI (State Council of China 2015).

In the action plan, the Silk Road Economic Belt focuses on three routes: through Central Asia and Russia to Europe (the Baltic); through Central Asia, West Asia, and the Persian Gulf to the Mediterranean Sea; and through Southeastern Asia and South Asia to the Indian Ocean. As shown in Figure 5.1, one route of the 21st-Century Maritime Silk Road is designed to link China's coast to Europe through the South China Sea and the Indian Ocean, and the other is meant to connect China's coast to the South Pacific through the South China Sea.

However, continued development of partnerships has extended the BRI map far beyond its 2015 plan. As of February 2022, 148 countries and 32 international organizations had joined the BRI by signing memorandums of understanding (MOUs) with China (Belt and Road Portal 2022). This includes 51 countries in Africa, 27 in Europe, 38 in Asia, 11 in the Pacific, 12 in North America, and 9 in South America and is in line with China's stance that the BRI is an open arrangement that welcomes the participation of all countries.

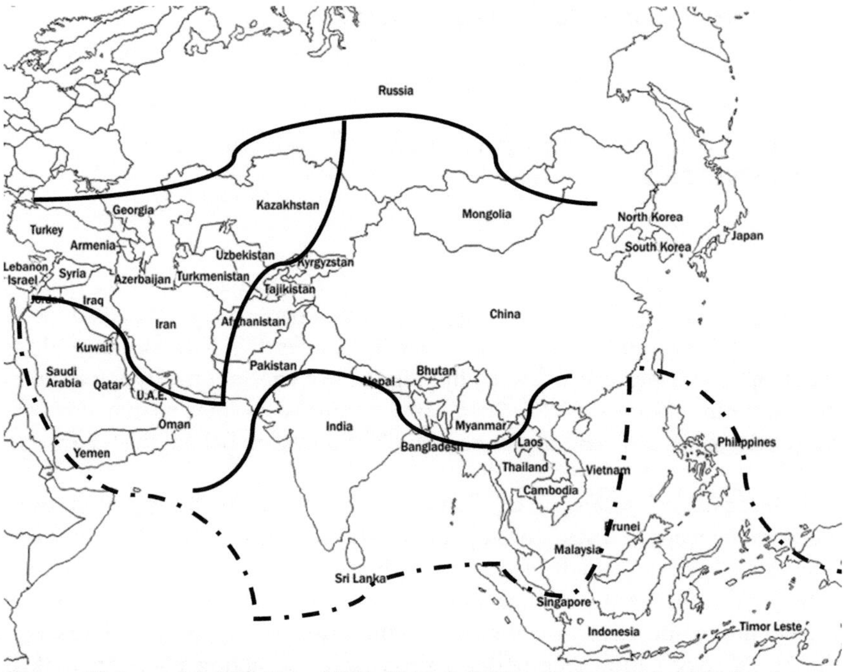

Notes: Vision and Action Plan of BRI, 2015. Solid line represents the Silk Road Economic Belt. Dashed line represents the New Maritime Silk Road.
Source: KAPSARC, based on State Council of China (2015).

Figure 5.1 Geographical scope of the BRI.

The initiative has also expanded its scope of cooperation. Five thematic areas—policy coordination, facilities connectivity, unimpeded trade, financial integration, and people-to-people bonds—were proposed under the initial BRI framework (SCIO 2016). Over the years, several new elements have been added. The first is the Digital Silk Road (DSR), which was announced in 2015. The DSR focuses on financing and technical cooperation with regard to digital connectivity, including telecommunications networks, cloud computing, and e-commerce. A total of 16 countries had signed agreements on DSR cooperation with China as of 2019 (MFA 2019). The second is industrial capacity cooperation, which has been developed as a relatively independent component rather than being embedded within the theme of unimpeded trade. As of 2019, 40 countries have signed industrial cooperation agreements with China (MFA 2019). The third is the Health Silk Road, which emerged in 2016 in President Xi Jinping's speech to Uzbekistan's legislature of. It emphasizes the importance of improving public health infrastructure under the BRI framework and gained prominence during the coronavirus (COVID-19) outbreak.

China has expressed its long-term commitment toward BRI. In October 2017, the BRI was included as a key component in the revision to the Constitution of the Chinese Communist Party. The initiative has quickly become synonymous with China's outward investment strategy and broader foreign policy over the past years. In 2021, despite the Covid-19 outbreak, more than 15,000 trains traveled between China and Europe, delivering more than US$75 billion in commodities (Belt and Road Portal 2022). By the end of 2020, more than 11,000 overseas enterprises had been established along the BRI countries, and China's outward direct investment (ODI) to BRI countries totaled to approximately US$140 billion (MOFCOM, NBS, and SAFE 2021). In total, approximately US$1.38 trillion of Chinese ODI and financing have been provided for more than 2500 projects under BRI (Silk Road Think Tank Network 2020). These projects have strengthened hard infrastructure, with new roads, railways, and ports; soft infrastructure, with trade and investment agreements; and even cultural ties, with university scholarships and people-to-people exchanges.

Moreover, China has shown its willingness to adapt to change through learning-by-doing feedback. The initiative has been undergoing a process of recalibration and adjustment. The clearest example is the so-called BRI 2.0, which was manifested at the Second BRI Forum in Beijing in May 2019. This forum was widely seen as China's effort to reboot the initiative and show its willingness to adopt a more inclusive, transparent, and sustainable approach to BRI projects (Economist Corporate Network 2019).

China is taking steps to restructure its approach to BRI projects, including adopting formal lending rules similar to those of multilateral development banks (MDBs) and shifting toward a more multilateral architecture for financing and project implementation. The multilateral financing institutions constituted for the BRI represent one example. China established the Multilateral Cooperation Center for Development Finance (MCDF) explicitly for the BRI in 2017, with support from its Ministry of Finance and eight MDBs. A new fund was launched in 2020 under the MCDF with contributions from Egypt,

Saudi Arabia, Hungary, Cambodia, and the Philippines. This is the third multilateral institution initiated by China after the New Development Bank (NDB) and Asian Infrastructure Investment Bank (AIIB).

Although China has made significant efforts to diversify capital resources and extend cooperation with MDBs, the questions of how to operate these funding institutions and what standards to follow in practice continue to be focal points for external observers.

Geopolitics Around the BRI

Politically, the momentum driving the BRI remains firm on China's side. However, international responses to the BRI have evolved and split further.

A BRI that succeeds on China's terms was seen as a major challenge to the US-centered global trade and financial system, posing risks to supply chains, international currency, and technical standards (Hillman 2018). In a bid to strengthen connectivity in Southeast Asia, the United States consolidated its Overseas Private Investment Corporation and other development finance programs into a new International Development Finance Corporation in October 2018 (OPIC 2018).

The cooperation between China and Central and Eastern European countries under the BRI framework caused concern within the European Union (EU) that this mechanism could undermine EU unity on policies toward China. The EU unveiled its strategy for connecting Asia and Europe in 2018, primarily emphasizing networks that bring people, places, and opportunities closer together, with a particular focus on transportation, energy, digital, and human dimensions (European Commission 2018). Later, in 2021, the EU elevated its global connectivity efforts, directing its attention toward Africa and Latin America as well (Widmann 2021).

China's growing influence and the BRI's continued expansion have also led to intensified competition in the Indo-Pacific region. The region's growing economic, demographic, and political weight makes it a key player in shaping the international order and addressing global challenges.

The United States published its first "Strategic Framework for the Indo-Pacific" through the National Security Council in February 2018. In the "Indo-Pacific Strategy of the United States" (US White House 2022), the United States further stated its long-term position on and commitment to the Indo-Pacific. The Quadrilateral Security Dialogue (Quad), a framework for security cooperation between the United States, India, Japan, and Australia, is shaping up to be a 'minilateral' mechanism in the Indo-Pacific aimed at countering China's growing influence in international fora. The Quad leaders' first joint statement, "The Spirit of the Quad," issued after the inaugural summit in March 2021, pledged to strengthen cooperation in areas including climate change, critical technologies, quality infrastructure investment, health security, and maritime domains (US White House 2021).

The EU adopted a common position on its Indo-Pacific strategy in April 2021, after France, Germany, and the Netherlands first announced their national-level policies on the Indo-Pacific. On September 16, 2021, a Joint Communication was subsequently presented by the European Commission and the High Representative of the EU for Foreign Affairs and Security Policy, providing a further rationale for the EU's approach and strategy (European Commission 2021). This has paved the way for the EU to step up its strategic engagement with this region in seven prioritized areas, including green transition, connectivity, digital governance, and security and defense. Evidently, the EU does not intend to join a US-led containment strategy directed against China, nor does it exhibit any zero-sum mentality when it comes to the Indo-Pacific construct (Lin 2021). In fact, the EU intends to encourage China to play a constructive role in the Indo-Pacific region.

The Association of Southeast Asian Nations (ASEAN) also realized the importance of setting an agenda for cooperation that emphasizes its centrality, neutrality, and leadership in the Indo-Pacific. In this context, ASEAN announced its Outlook on the Indo-Pacific at its June 2019 summit. The Outlook highlights the importance of maritime cooperation in areas such as the peaceful settlement of disputes, maritime environment and pollution, exploitation of marine resources, and maritime connectivity. The Outlook also aims to ensure that connectivity initiatives in the Indo-Pacific region complement and support the existing Master Plan on ASEAN Connectivity 2025 (ASEAN 2019).

In addition, several major players, including Japan and India, have proposed their own connectivity strategies that run parallel to the BRI's in terms of infrastructure investment and construction.

These recent developments have given rise to intense geopolitical competition, contributing to increasing trade and supply chain tensions. In their responses to the BRI, both the United States and the EU have focused on fostering a rule-based international order, a level playing field, and an open and fair environment for trade and investment. Most of the debates center on three issues: the motivation behind the BRI, financial sustainability for recipient economies, and the role of China's state-owned enterprises (SOEs) in BRI financing and project implementation.

Geoeconomics or Geopolitics?

The Chinese leadership has repeatedly asserted that in pursuing the BRI, China will not resort to outdated geopolitical maneuvering or interfere in other countries' internal affairs. Instead, the goal is to explore a new model of win–win cooperation for economic and social development with the partner economies (Xinhua 2017).

China's approach to international development echoes the basis of its own economic boom: heavy investment in infrastructure along with the expansion of foreign trade and investment. Beijing focuses on tangible development projects and does not attach overtly economic or political terms, contrary to the conventional approach adopted by Western economies and development institutions.

This challenges the institutional architecture, central principles, and underlying values of the established system (Baltensperger and Dadush 2019; Federation of German Industries 2019; Renwick, Gu, and Gong 2018). Such foundational differences have led to debate over Beijing's motivations for the BRI in particular and international development in general.

One view holds that the BRI's economic goals are primarily a means to achieve greater geopolitical hegemony. Therefore, the initiative is driven by China's ambitions to break the existing US alliance structure in the Asia–Pacific region and expand its global influence (Miller 2017; Mitchell 2018; Tellis 2017; US Department of Defense 2018). By enhancing connectivity across Eurasia and beyond, China increases its ability to project economic and military power and reshape geopolitical dynamics.

An alternative perspective emphasizes the economic benefits of establishing such a network for China, stating that any geopolitical gains are of secondary importance (Cai 2017; Djankov and Miner 2016). The BRI is a logical result of China's economic context, particularly its excess industrial production capacity and imbalances between its coastal and interior provinces. The initiative aims to build strategic connections with BRI countries for joint development, rather than replacing or competing with established frameworks or the geopolitical status quo.

The third point of view argues that that the BRI is meant to achieve both economic growth and increased political influence (Baruah 2018; Clarke 2017; Fukuyama 2016; Fulton 2017; Hillman 2018; Hurley, Morris, and Portelance 2018; Saalman and Dethlefsen 2017). The initiative helps China consolidate its own political, economic, and social model, which is characterized by substantial state control and systemic competition with liberal market economies. By reshaping the international economic order and political balance through the BRI, China can entrench its model globally.

State-dominated Financing?

China's SOEs are the central pillars of its domestic economy and lead the implementation of the BRI. Several projects under the BRI framework are high risk with uncertain returns. Disputed elections, corruption, unclear land and property rights, and other political and legal risks can threaten an investment's viability and financial performance. Funding risks also arise from the capital-intensive nature of infrastructure projects, long repayment schedules, and macroeconomic challenges endemic to developing economies (Wijeratne et al. 2017). Compared with private enterprises, SOEs have a higher risk-taking capacity because of their greater scale of operations and ability to leverage resources. Although SOEs may not always operate at the efficiency frontier, they are crucial for large-scale infrastructure projects with long-term investment horizons in difficult environments.

While the technological progress and increasing international competitiveness of leading Chinese companies cannot be attributed solely to state support, there is a growing concern that China's state-dominated economic system is incompatible with the liberal market paradigm. Critics allege that Chinese companies enjoy unfair advantages over their competitors from other countries because of favorable financing conditions from state-affiliated banks and other direct and indirect subsidies (Federation of German Industries 2019; Hillman 2018).

This perspective leads to further questioning about the operation of SOEs. Chinese SOEs may act in a coordinated manner at the behest of the central government. This implies that national interest, for example, access to raw materials and energy, trade relations, and job creation, may carry greater weight than commercial and financial viability in SOE project assessments for investment (Baltensperger and Dadush 2019). In addition, Chinese SOEs can present a unified front when dealing with a recipient country, integrating many elements and stakeholders in a single deal. This has given Chinese SOEs unique advantages in comparison with their Western peers.

Another view argues that cultural differences lead to divergence between Chinese and Western approaches to infrastructure project development. The Western approach is transactional: Projects are rigorously evaluated for their financial viability and value according to a risk–reward assessment. China's approach, on the other hand, is relational and follows the philosophy of 'support first, profit later.' Project assessments initially focus on their long-term macroeconomic benefits, and their risks are addressed with partners throughout their development (Bennon 2017; Renwick, Gu, and Gong 2018).

Debt Trap for Distressed Economies?

Infrastructure building and upgrading in developing countries constitute a considerable financial burden. Developing Asia will need to invest US$26 trillion from 2016 to 2030, or US$1.7 trillion per year, if the region is to maintain its growth momentum, eradicate poverty, and respond to climate change. Currently, this region has an estimated investment gap of US$819 billion annually for infrastructure (ADB 2017). African infrastructure needs amount to US$130–US$170 billion a year, with a financing gap in the range US$68–US$108 billion (AfDB 2018).

Consortiums of banks and funds led by China have accumulated significant capital for BRI investment in recipient countries' infrastructure across many sectors, including power, water, transportation, and communications. The initiative also aims to link local industries with the global market, improve trade logistics, and increase the knowledge and skills of local entrepreneurs.

Several new organizations have been established, adding to the existing Chinese institutions—such as the China Development Bank (CDB) and Export–Import Bank of China (CEXIM—that were already financing overseas investments prior to the BRI. These new organizations include the AIIB (founded with US$100 billion of capital), the BRICS NDB (US$10 billion), the Silk Road Fund (US$40 billion), and 14 bilateral investment funds with partner countries that have already secured over US$100 billion in funding for BRI projects.

Debate on debt sustainability in BRI investment has emerged owing to the economic and political instability encountered by projects in some investment-recipient countries.

China has been accused of using 'debtbook diplomacy' to advance its strategic goals in the region. Critics holding this view argue that this is why Beijing funds projects with questionable financial viability that profit-motivated companies would be unlikely to sponsor (Mundy and Hille 2019; Parker and Chefitz 2018; Zhang and Miller 2017).

Other analysts conclude that the BRI is unlikely to cause a systemic debt problem, especially at the global level. Among the 68 BRI countries, Hurley, Morris, and Portelance (2018) identify only 8 that may face a debt sustainability issue: Djibouti, Kyrgyzstan, Laos, Maldives, Mongolia, Montenegro, Tajikistan, and Pakistan. Moreover, the foreign debt in these countries was not necessarily induced by loans from BRI institutions but rather had accumulated over several decades (Askary and Ross 2018; Feng and Liang 2018; Zhao 2018). As a latecomer to the global capital market, China has not yet made a significant impact on its partners' debt levels in percentage terms.

Energy at the Core of the BRI Landscape

The Belt and Road countries possess over 50 percent of the remaining proven reserves of crude oil and over 70 percent of natural gas reserves. They are projected to dominate global exports of these commodities in the medium term. Some of the most resource-rich economies, including Russia and Kazakhstan, share a border with China, as do key transit countries (e.g., Myanmar).

China has focused attention on energy security since it became a net oil importer in 1993 and has rapidly increased its reliance on oil and gas imports. This has led to continuing efforts to build strategic energy import routes and create interconnected oil and gas channels linked to China's domestic energy market. As shown in Figure 5.2, four energy import channels are taking shape: the Northeast channel (crude oil and planned gas pipelines from Russia), Northwest channel (crude oil and natural gas pipelines from Central Asia), South channel (crude oil and gas pipelines through Myanmar), and East channel (maritime oil and liquefied natural gas [LNG] import facilities). These can be viewed as precursors of the BRI economic corridors, most of which have been laid out along these energy import routes.

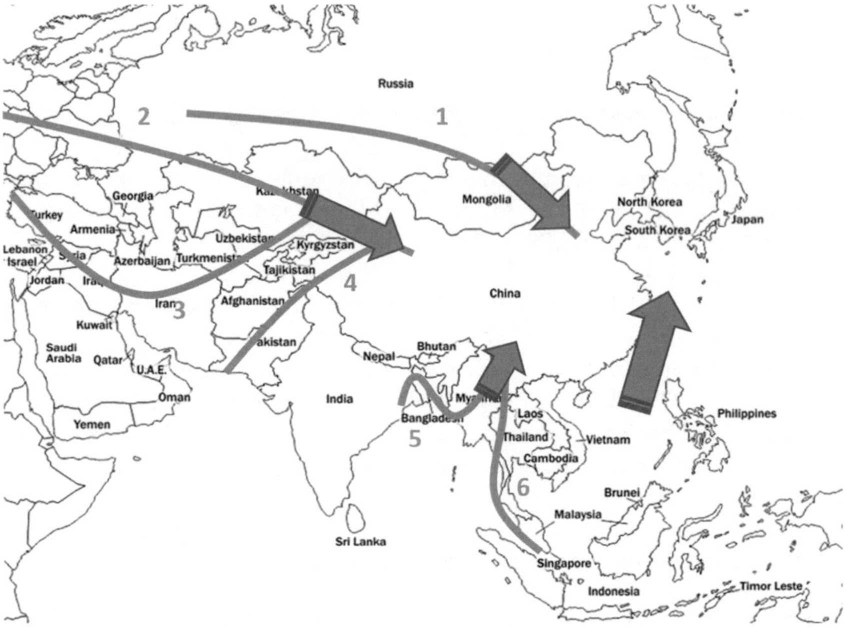

Notes: The blue arrows indicate four energy import channels. 1. The China-Mongolia-Russia economic corridor; 2. The New Eurasian Land Bridge economic corridor; 3. The China-Central Asia-West Asia economic corridor; 4. The China-Pakistan economic corridor; 5. The Bangladesh-China-India-Myanmar economic corridor; 6. The China-Indochina Peninsula economic corridor.
Source: KAPSARC, based on Belt and Road Portal (2018) and General Office of the State Council (2013).

Figure 5.2 Strategic energy import channels for China.

Since the launch of the BRI, China has invested in several large gas and LNG projects, including in the Russian Arctic, Pakistan, and Malaysia. However, most of China's overseas oil and gas pipeline projects were approved and financed prior to the BRI's official launch. Some projects take more than a decade to go through the business and political decision process. Infrastructure construction for these energy import channels may require many deals, involving a variety of elements, for example, financing, trading, upstreaming oil and gas field investment, downstream refining, and industrial cooperation. The interconnection between energy and non-energy-related activities is further strengthened under the BRI.

China's overseas energy activity has been shaped by national policies and foreign relations strategies. With the BRI becoming synonymous with China's outward investment strategy and broader foreign policy, its development will definitely impact the priorities and approach of China's overseas energy investments. This provides an interesting angle to analyze the changes in the drivers of China's overseas energy investment before and after the inception of the BRI. The role of state financing and the debt sustainability issue under the BRI would also be worth investigating. This would shed light on the debates centered around the BRI as mentioned in the previous section.

Change of Drivers for China's Overseas Energy Investment

Before the BRI

China's dependence on oil imports has grown rapidly since it became a net oil importer in 1993. This has been further fueled by the economic boom after China joined the World Trade Organization in 2001. China imported 59 percent of its oil demand in 2013, and 52 percent of that oil was imported from the Middle East (Jiang and Ding 2014).

The growing reliance on imported energy has exposed China to a variety of risks that could undermine continued energy supply. These include instability in producer countries, military clashes along supply routes, threats of supply cut-offs, and financial sanctions and export controls imposed by the United States (Meidan 2021). China has made considerable demand-side and supply-side efforts to mitigate these risks. Reducing the reliance on oil in domestic consumption, transitioning toward renewable energy development, and improving energy productivity in major economic sectors have been the main domestic policy responses. On the supply side, the country's policy and actions have largely focused on diversifying oil supply and transportation and building stronger relationships with oil-rich states.

Concerns about the security of the energy transportation route, which often refers to the key maritime chokepoint in the Strait of Malacca, have created a need for China to invest in countries that can transport oil and gas through overland pipelines or alternate shipping routes across the Pacific Ocean. As of 2013, China had three oil pipelines and four cross-border gas pipelines constructed in three major energy channels. Most projects operating after 2013 (Table 5.1) were either approved and financed prior to the BRI's inception or have continued construction following the original plan. The Sino–Kazakhstan oil pipeline is China's first oil import pipeline. With two spur lines connected to the Russian Eastern Siberia–Pacific Ocean (ESPO) oil pipeline and three Central Asia–China gas pipelines becoming operational, China's anxiety over avoiding a Malacca dilemma has somewhat diminished. Although the Sino–Myanmar oil pipeline will not transport locally produced oil, it has created an option to transport some of China's imports from the Middle East and Africa bypassing the Strait of Malacca. Similarly, Chinese investment in South America, for example, in Venezuela, Brazil, and Ecuador, may also yield promises to ship oil to China via an alternate supply route across the Pacific Ocean.

The global financial crisis of 2008–2009 also lent impetus to increase the allocation of Chinese capital to ODI. This is because of concerns about the performance of dollar-denominated assets—particularly US government debt—which comprise a significant portion of Chinese foreign investments. Tight capital and exchange rate control have caused foreign exchange reserves to rise exponentially, creating a capital surplus that could be partially allocated to foreign markets and investment projects. China has thus directed a significant share of its capital to the foreign energy sector, primarily upstream oil and gas projects and midstream infrastructure. This is aimed at alleviating the country's energy security concerns by obtaining control over energy supply assets abroad. However, when it comes to investment activities by Chinese national oil companies (NOCs) related to upstream oil and gas projects, commercial motives have played a primary role.

In 1992, the China National Petroleum Corporation (CNPC) invested US$6.5 million in Canada's oil sands development project (Oil and Gas Journal 1992). This marked the first of China's overseas oil and gas investments. In view of the stagnation in domestic oil supplies and soaring energy demands, Chinese NOCs have become more active in overseas investment since 2000. This may involve purchasing exploration and drilling rights, securing a guaranteed percentage of production from the host country, constructing energy-related infrastructure in the host country, or acquiring foreign energy companies (Wolfe and Tessman 2012).

As relative newcomers on the global energy market, Chinese NOCs faced a steep learning curve on many fronts. Directing investment toward economically and politically unstable countries allowed them to gain experience with a low level of international competition (Kennedy 2010; Meidan 2014; Wolfe and Tessman 2012; Zhang 2012). Through a trial-and-error process, the NOCs gradually gained confidence and know-how about risk management, technical operations, and financing in the international energy market. In this process,

Table 5.1 China's cross-border oil and gas pipelines.

From	Pipeline	Status	Year start construction	Year start operation	Capacity
Russia	Eastern Siberia-Pacific Ocean (ESPO) oil pipelines	Operational	2009	2011, 2018	30 (million tonnes/year)
	Power of Siberia 1 gas pipeline	Operational	2014	2019	38 (bcm/year)
	Far East gas pipeline	Planning			10 (bcm/year)
	Power of Siberia 2 gas pipeline (via Mongolia)	Planning			50 (bcm/year)
	Power of Siberia 1 expansion	Planning			6 (bcm/year)
Kazakhstan	China-Kazakhstan oil pipeline	Operational	2004	2006	20 (million tonnes/year)
Turkmenistan Uzbekistan Kazakhstan	Central Asia-China Pipeline A	Operational	2007	2009	15 (bcm/year)
	Central Asia-China Pipeline B	Operational	2007	2010	15 (bcm/year)
	Central Asia-China Pipeline C	Operational	2012	2014	25 (bcm/year)
	Central Asia-China Pipeline D	Under construction	2014		30 (bcm/year)
Myanmar	China-Myanmar oil pipeline	Operational	2010	2017	22 (million tonnes/year)
	China-Myanmar gas pipeline	Operational	2010	2013	12 (bcm/year)

Source: KAPSARC, based on Chen (2021) and Xiong (2022).

the NOCs exhibited independent behavior rather than coordinated actions under governmental direction (Jiang and Ding 2014).

Chinese NOCs experienced huge losses in the early stages of investing abroad. China's big three oil corporations (CNPC, Sinopec, and China National Offshore Oil Company) had invested in approximately 144 overseas projects totaling US$70 billion by the end of 2010, but two-thirds of these overseas investments suffered losses (Oxford Analytica 2011). In a financial analysis of 28 Chinese loan-for-oil deals, Gholz, Awan, and Ronn (2017) found only one project that was profitable for China.

Arguably, economic rationales are secondary if the NOCs' oil production outside China can help improve China's energy security. However, China can only meet a relatively modest fraction of its import needs through investment in direct access or ownership of oil reserves. Acquisition through overseas energy investments cannot guarantee China an oil supply that is more reliable and less expensive than the international market supply (Jiang and Sinton 2011; Leung 2011; Zhang 2012). Most oil produced through acquisition of overseas oil fields and equity oil production by Chinese NOCs was sold in the international market. This increased the supply of oil in the global market but not specifically for Chinese consumers. Neither pipeline construction nor alternative transportation routes would make China immune to US influence should a blockade occur (Gholz, Awan, and Ronn 2017; Zhang 2012). Thus, the actual contribution of Chinese overseas energy investment in securing energy supply to China is limited. China's energy security dependence on global oil market stability has been on the rise (Jiang and Ding 2014; Leung 2011; Zhang 2012).

More reasonably, Chinese overseas energy investment activities can be interpreted as driven by corporate interest, with gradually growing comfort with the global market economy. Additionally, the political and financial support that the NOCs receive from the Chinese government have increased their risk-taking capabilities. Events since the beginning of 2011—such as the Arab Spring uprisings that swept through North Africa and the Middle East, sanctions imposed on Iran, and fighting since South Sudan's independence—as well as security concerns in countries like Nigeria seriously threatened the NOCs' activities (Jiang and Sinton 2011). Consequently, the NOCs started relying more heavily on the Chinese government's diplomatic and financial support to minimize their risks and losses in these countries.

New Impetus Under the BRI

Energy has long played a central role in China's overseas investment. However, in recent years, its energy ODI has decreased in absolute terms and fallen as a portion of its global ODI from a peak of 66 percent in 2005 to below 30 percent in 2021 (Figure 3). Although BRI regions attracted more than 50 percent of Chinese energy investment from 2013 to 2021, the share of energy in the BRI ODI flow dropped from a high of 55 percent in 2013 to 30 percent in 2021. This structural shift in BRI investment can be explained by China's increasing diversification across sectors and its emphasis on manufacturing and infrastructure projects. This is particularly the case as China's energy security considerations give way to other BRI priorities, such as capacity transfer and the internationalization of Chinese industrial companies.

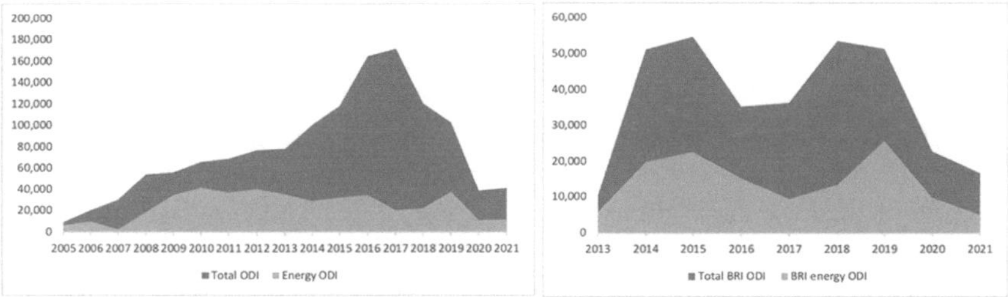

Source: American Enterprise Institute (2022).

Figure 5.3 Chinese energy ODI in the BRI countries and all countries and their share of total Chinese ODI.

BRI energy investment also shows a change in China's energy security strategy, moving away from oil and gas field acquisitions to a focus on transit routes. China's overseas investment in coal, oil, and natural gas has decreased since 2015, with growing concentration in mid- and downstream petrochemical product manufacturing and processing (Ma, Springer, and Shao 2022). Most oil- and gas-related investments and financing through the BRI have focused on energy import channels, which include increasing oil and gas pipeline connections with Russia, piloting the Arctic LNG route, and exploring a potential fifth energy channel through Pakistan.

After the Power of Siberia 1 gas pipeline became operational in 2019, China and Russia agreed on a new deal in February 2022 to add 10 bcm of natural gas supply to northeast China via a new line from Russia's Far East region (Chen 2022). Theoretically, the oil and gas flow from Russia to China may increase, as the EU has decided to reduce the reliance on Russian energy imports in response to the Russia–Ukraine war. However, in this case, China will have to face unprecedented geopolitical pressure. Moreover, the increase would come at the cost of intensified relations with major developed economies, which may impact cooperation on non-energy elements under the BRI framework.

The China–Pakistan Economic Corridor (CPEC), which could potentially provide China with an alternative and shorter route for energy imports from the Middle East and Africa, has received significant attention in the BRI. Financing of energy projects from two Chinese policy banks to CPEC reached US$20 billion during 2014–2020, ten times the pre-BRI levels (Chen 2021). However, given the challenging geographical and geopolitical conditions in the China–Pakistan border area, it is still questionable as to when this strategic channel will begin to play a meaningful role and at what cost.

The change in China's energy security strategy is connected to its domestic energy infrastructure investment. The up and running LNG infrastructure along the coastline—referred to as the East channel—has improved the balance between land and sea route transportation. It has also reduced the reliance on shipments through the Strait of Malacca. As of 2019, 23 LNG regasification terminals with a combined capacity of 113 bcm/year were in operation. Another 84 bcm/year of capacity will be online in the next two to three years. At the end of 2013, China had only nine LNG terminals in operation, with a total receiving capacity of 38 bcm/year (Chen 2021). Increasing volumes of LNG are being shipped to northern ports without transiting through the Strait of Malacca and South China Sea.

The rise of climate change on the global agenda and accelerated energy transition have provided an opportunity for China to strengthen its leadership on clean energy. As of February 2022, more than 83 countries had announced mid-century net-zero targets, accounting for 74 percent of global emissions. This has brought about unprecedented changes in policy regulations, business strategies, and investment flows worldwide. As reflected in Boston University's data tracking, Chinese energy investment has targeted transmission and distribution more than power generation since 2019, and greenfield investment in the electricity sector is increasingly oriented toward alternative and renewable energy (Ma, Springer, and Shao 2022).

As the world's largest producer of wind and solar energy, China is well positioned to capture the market arising from the global energy transition. Seven of the top-ten solar panel manufacturers and six of the top-ten wind turbine makers by global market share were based in China in 2020. Large-scale deployment in the domestic market has strongly supported China's renewable technology development and industrial supply chain expansion. This has generated a dramatic reduction in global costs and advanced the deployment of renewable energy in the BRI countries.

Meanwhile, the BRI, prominently characterized by green energy, also faces the challenges arising from growing concerns about the resilience and reliability of supply chains for clean energy.

The quantity of minerals required for clean energy is much higher than that for traditional energy. A typical electric car requires six times the mineral inputs of a conventional car, and an onshore wind plant requires nine times more mineral resources than a gas-fired plant (IEA 2022). The extraction and refining of many energy transition minerals is more concentrated than that for oil or natural gas. For example, the Democratic Republic of the Congo and China were responsible for approximately 70 percent and 60 percent of the global production of cobalt and rare earth elements, respectively, in 2019. The level of concentration is even higher for processing operations: China's share of refining is approximately 35 percent for nickel, 50– 70 percent for lithium and cobalt, and approximately 90 percent for rare earth elements (IEA 2022). With a growing number of countries attempting to develop domestic clean energy capabilities, the competition for critical materials will intensify. Political decisions will play a much more significant role in supply chains going forward, particularly as governments make decisions about strategic resources and securing their competitive advantage (IHS Markit 2022). This, in turn, is likely to sharpen political scrutiny of the affected sectors and could limit China's outbound cleantech investments.

Furthermore, the energy transition could also result in potential risks for BRI investment. China's commitment toward attaining carbon neutrality by 2060 will reduce the demand for oil, which could significantly reduce the importance of energy transit as a BRI consideration. The loss of oil and gas revenues could create political instability in producer countries, leading some of China's overseas investments to become stranded assets. Producer countries' loss of revenue or output could also inhibit their ability to repay loans issued by China (Meidan 2021).

China's domestic regulatory changes continue to directly impact its overseas investments. Slower economic growth and emerging overcapacity problems in major domestic industries have lent impetus to seeking overseas investment opportunities, especially since the BRI became a new strategic focus in 2013. China was increasingly willing to fund these opportunities, as its foreign exchange reserves peaked in 2014 at US$4 trillion. Restrictions on China's ODI flows in late 2016 to mitigate risks to the Chinese financial system were a crucial factor in the drop of BRI investment in 2016–2017 (Figure 5.3). Loosened capital controls and an incipient renminbi devaluation trend have, since 2018, led to the reversal of this brief decline in BRI investment. In contrast, China's outbound global investments have declined continuously since the 2016 regulatory changes. Throughout this period, China has faced currency depreciation, corruption, domestic real estate bubbles, and changing global investment and trade environments.

Financing System for China's Overseas Energy Investment

Financing Mechanisms Under the BRI Framework

The prior analysis of China's energy ODI and allocation of government loan support to BRI projects shows that the country's energy investment strategies are increasingly defined by China's wider geopolitical ambitions and global macroeconomic factors rather than by energy/supply security. As the BRI continues to expand in strategic and geographical scope, it is essential to view Chinese energy ODI in the context of the broader BRI priorities. By extension, it is critical to examine how bilateral and multilateral energy projects can support or connect the initiative's overarching goals.

Energy ODI can facilitate the financial integration priorities outlined in the policy document of the National Development and Reform Commission (NDRC 2015) ---: "Vision and Actions on Jointly Building Silk Road Economic Belt and 21st-Century Maritime Silk Road." These include developing the regional bond market, establishing bilateral currency swap facilities, ensuring a greater role for regional development financial institutions, and collaborating in the financial risk management and mitigation domains. The National Energy Administration (NEA 2017) emphasizes the development of all vehicles of energy investment, including mergers and acquisitions, public–private partnerships, and industry plus finance cooperation. The expansion of Chinese energy investment in the BRI regions also promotes other strategic goals not explicitly mentioned in the BRI policy documents. This includes internationalization of the renminbi, expanding Chinese financial institutions, and reshaping global energy and commodity markets through the establishment of new trade hubs and rerouting of global energy trade flows.

The BRI regions have enormous energy investment potential. According to Asian Development Bank (ADB 2017) estimates, developing countries in Asia will require US$11.7 trillion of investment (US$14.7 trillion adjusted for climate mitigation measures) in the power sector alone from 2016 to 2030—amounting to over 2.5 percent of their gross domestic product. The utilization of investment vehicles deployed under the BRI can help bridge this investment gap.

ODI and Chinese development finance are the two main channels for financing BRI projects (Dollar 2017). In addition to utilizing their own funds (in the case of private financial institutions and companies) and sourcing funds from capital markets, Chinese companies involved in the BRI, especially SOEs, obtain substantial funding from the Chinese government (Kong and Gallagher

2016). Chinese and international financial institutions can directly invest in BRI projects and provide indirect financial support, for example, through loans and guarantees.

Direct Financing of BRI Projects

The direct financing of BRI investment projects, including those in the energy sector, is conducted through ODI by Chinese and foreign investors. These include Chinese SOEs and private companies as well as state-owned, private, or foreign funds and investment management companies.

In late 2014, the Chinese government established the Silk Road Fund, a sovereign wealth fund with a mandate to finance BRI projects, with capital from the China Investment Corporation and the State Administration of Foreign Exchange (SAFE). The fund has directly invested a total of US$1.65 billion in BRI projects along the CPEC (Xinhua 2015). Chinese state-owned investment management companies have also established funds that directly invest in the BRI. For example, the China International Trust Investment Corporation launched a dedicated US$113 billion fund in 2015 to finance over 300 projects in BRI countries from Singapore to Turkmenistan (Reuters 2015).

The Chinese government advises private Chinese firms on policy-driven investment project participation. In such cases, the companies usually commit to BRI-related investment, attempting to balance national interests with commercial benefits while ensuring compatibility with their expertise and existing portfolios. Thus, their investments tend to be more focused. For example, the China Minsheng Investment Group (CMIG) and the Green Ecological Silk Road Investment Fund (established by private Chinese enterprises) limit their BRI exposure to solar energy and sustainable energy solutions.

Compared with their Chinese counterparts, the direct participation of foreign funds in BRI energy projects remains limited, primarily because of administrative barriers and competitive disadvantages. Portfolio investors can invest in the BRI through the Hong Kong and Shanghai stock markets as well as by purchasing US dollar–denominated bonds. Potential direct investors, however, face greater difficulty because China is keen to retain control over BRI projects. Foreign funds lack the key advantages enjoyed by Chinese government–backed investors, such as lower insurance rates and preferential access to the most lucrative projects. One of the few examples of a successfully implemented public–private partnership scheme with foreign investor participation is the construction of a thermal power plant in Port Qasim, Pakistan, under the CPEC framework. Qatar's Al-Mirqab Capital obtained a 49 percent share in the project through a partnership with the Chinese SOE Sinohydro Resources. This arrangement, facilitated by Sinosure, covered a wide range of project- and country-related risks. In most cases, however, the direct involvement of foreign firms in BRI energy projects is limited to subcontracting with Chinese lead investors.

In addition to the inherent political and financial risks in some BRI-participating countries, potential investors from China and their foreign joint venture partners must also deal with China's domestic regulations. These regulations have led Chinese companies participating in the BRI to develop specific corporate structures and project-financing strategies. According to China's Ministry of Commerce (MOFCOM 2017), more than half of the country's ODI goes to Hong Kong. The Cayman Islands and British Virgin Islands also appear among the top destinations. These jurisdictions act as financial hubs from which Chinese companies engage in overseas financial activities. Chinese companies also tend to use their own international subsidiaries, rather than the parent companies in mainland China, as contractual entities with foreign counterparts. For example, the CMIG established CMI International, a subsidiary in Singapore, to implement the group's BRI agenda.

Chinese parties in joint investment funds also tend to prefer incorporating in traditional offshore centers, such as Hong Kong in the case of the China–ASEAN Investment Cooperation Fund and Luxembourg for the China–Central and Eastern Europe Investment Cooperation Fund. ODI constitutes a primary financing mechanism for Chinese overseas investments, including those under the BRI framework. However, the top–down data, such as total ODI or capital outflows from mainland China, does not provide an adequate representation of capital flows. A preferred approach would be to track BRI investments and their sources on a project basis.

Chinese investors structure overseas investments in the aforementioned ways because of four reasons:

- Tax advantages: The taxation regime in preferred overseas jurisdictions is less burdensome and simpler than that in mainland China. The overall level of corporate income tax in Hong Kong is 16.5 percent, compared with 25 percent in mainland China (KPMG 2019). Other offshore hubs have even lower (or no) corporate tax (e.g., the Cayman Islands or British Virgin Islands).
- Better regulation and supervision: For Chinese companies involved in ODI, investing through overseas jurisdictions can significantly reduce regulatory burdens. Despite prioritizing the BRI, Beijing has not yet eased

the approval procedures for mainland firms to invest abroad. Moreover, the ODI of mainland companies is subject to frequent reviews and heavy reporting requirements from the China Banking Regulatory Commission, SAFE, People's Bank of China, and other authorities.

- Cross-border capital mobility: China imposes strict regulations on outbound currency transfers. This involves long and stringent ODI approval procedures imposed by parent companies in China. In contrast, overseas companies can obtain financing from Chinese financial institutions more easily. Thus, most Chinese companies tend to apply for credit financing through their overseas subsidiaries and reinvest the returns using them.
- Confidence in law and arbitration: Foreign partners prefer other jurisdictions, such as Hong Kong or Singapore, over mainland China for contractual relations and joint ventures. These jurisdictions offer well-established law and arbitration systems and greater judicial transparency than China, especially when dealing with Chinese SOEs and other powerful Chinese firms.

Aiming to improve China's commercial dispute resolution, Beijing established two special courts in 2018 for international commercial cases and BRI-related disputes. Located in Xi'an and Shenzhen, these courts are supported by mediation centers with international expert committees and a think tank. The rules and procedures for BRI-related disputes were developed collectively with the Singapore International Mediation Centre and the China Council for the Promotion of International Trade. Although several high-profile cases have already been accepted, it remains to be seen whether these courts become trusted jurisdictions for Chinese and international firms.

Indirect Financing Mechanisms

Two state-owned policy banks, the CEXIM and CDB, play key roles in the indirect financing of the BRI by providing loans and issuing credit guarantees. According to Gallagher and Irwin (2014), China issued outward foreign direct investment (FDI) loans totaling over US$144 billion between 2002 and 2012, 88 percent of which came from the CEXIM and CDB.

South Asia and Russia have been the primary destinations for CEXIM and CDB energy loans among the BRI-65 participants (see Table 5.2). The regional distribution of BRI policy loans to energy projects is different from that of China's energy ODI. Government-backed financial support is primarily required for investments in countries that are viewed as highly financially or politically risky, especially for capital-intensive projects. Conversely, in jurisdictions with well-functioning capital and financial markets, lower political

Table 5.2 Energy ODI and CDB and CEXIM loans to the BRI-65 countries by region (2014–2018).

Region	Energy ODI, US$ million	CDB / CEXIM Bank loans, US$ million	Loans / ODI, %
Africa	2,030		0.0%
Central Asia	6,030	2,851	47.3%
East Asia	2,000		0.0%
Europe	6,880	1,645	23.9%
Gulf Cooperation Council	26,010		0.0%
Middle East and North Africa	21,640	5,347	24.7%
Russia	15,760	15,700	99.6%
Southeast Asia	50,890	11,262	22.1%
South Asia	41,730	27,615	66.2%

Source: American Enterprise Institute (2022); Boston University (2019).

risks, and a strong presence of Chinese businesses, such as most Southeast Asian countries, energy financing is dominated by private capital without the support of Chinese government institutions.

Four state-owned commercial banks—the Bank of China (BOC), China Construction Bank (CCB), Agricultural Bank of China, and Industrial and Commercial Bank of China (ICBC)—also play major roles in financing the BRI in general and energy projects in particular. In addition to providing loans, they help participating firms issue corporate bonds overseas, a common fundraising approach for Chinese energy companies. Three Chinese national oil majors—CNPC, SINOPEC, and CNOOC—issued US$7.6 billion and US$9.5 billion of bonds in 2012 and 2013, respectively, whereas the State Grid Corporation issued a total of US$5.5 billion of bonds in 2013 (Kong and Gallagher 2016). The state-owned banks have also been actively forging partnerships with foreign state-owned financial entities. For example, the ICBC, CCB, and BOC signed MOUs with Investment Enterprise Singapore in 2016 to facilitate the participation of Singaporean companies in the BRI (Sejko 2017).

MDBs are also expected to contribute to the financing of BRI energy projects. Since the BRI announcement, two development banks (both headquartered in China) have been established. The AIIB was launched in 2015 with US$100 billion in capital; China holds 26.6 percent of the voting rights, thus possessing an effective veto power. The NDB, formerly referred to as the BRICS Development Bank, was created by a 2014 treaty among the five BRICS countries—Brazil, Russia, India, China, and South Africa—which hold equal shares and voting rights. The two development banks are not exclusively focused on financing BRI-related projects, and the AIIB includes member countries, such as Australia and Canada, that are not formal BRI participants. However, these banks have already developed a portfolio of projects in BRI-participating countries. In the energy domain, the NDB is primarily focused on renewable energy and energy conservation, whereas the AIIB has a broader energy portfolio, ranging from power generation to natural gas infrastructure projects.

The AIIB and NDB also attract funding from and develop in collaboration with other multinational development banks, such as the ADB, World Bank (WB), and European Bank for Reconstruction and Development (EBRD). While the AIIB has already approved funding for several joint projects, including a combined-cycle gas-turbine power plant in Myanmar (with the International Finance Corporation) and the Trans-Anatolian Natural Gas Pipeline project (with the WB), the NDB has provided a loan to the Eurasian Development Bank and the International Investment Bank to finance the Nord-Hydro project in Russia. Such partnerships can help source additional financing for BRI energy projects, spread financing risks, and enhance China's global role in development financing for energy and other projects.

Chinese insurance companies play another important part in financing BRI projects. As of 2017, China's insurers collectively managed assets of RMB 14.2 trillion, including RMB 2.3 trillion in bank deposits. The China Insurance Regulatory Commission (CIRC) has been encouraging insurance companies to mobilize their funds into BRI-related areas, such as bond investment. The BRI engagement strategies of the insurance sector differ among the SOEs, private Chinese companies, and foreign enterprises.

China's state-owned insurance companies have been the most responsive to the CIRC's call, providing insurance coverage for BRI projects that private and international insurers may perceive as financially or politically risky. They also help finance some projects either directly (as shareholders) or indirectly (e.g., through bond investment). A variety of state-owned and private insurers, including the China Pacific Insurance Company (CPIC), the People's Insurance Company of China, China Reinsurance, and Ping An Insurance, have financed BRI projects through joint investments. For instance, CPIC has a joint BRI fund with the CCB.

Private insurance companies, however, seem to take a more calculated approach to their participation in the BRI, focusing on countries with stable political and economic environments, such as Singapore and other East Asian economies, or charging extra premiums at market rates in other cases.

Debt Sustainability in China's Overseas Energy Investment

Debt sustainability is a growing concern for certain BRI-participating countries. According to the Heritage Foundation (2019), the fiscal health scores of Pakistan, Laos, Sri Lanka, Tajikistan, Venezuela, and Vietnam indicate potential macroeconomic instability and uncertainty. The additional debt burden accumulated from BRI projects could further worsen the financial stability of the recipient countries and jeopardize project economics.

Some analysts argue that, for most participating countries, debt from the BRI projects is insignificant relative to the total government debt. Thus, the BRI is unlikely to fundamentally change the financial health of these countries and the wider regions. Moreover, the recipient country's government is often not the only borrower and may not be involved at all. National energy companies and the private sector (sometimes including foreign investors) account for a sizable proportion of BRI loans. Table 5.3 shows the share of CDB and CEXIM energy project loans obtained via government borrowing between 2014 and 2018, along with the fiscal health ratings and total foreign debt levels for selected 'problematic' BRI countries.

The indicators listed in Table 5.3 reflect the different approaches to managing energy loans, and foreign debt in general, among BRI participants. Out of the initial BRI-65 countries, only Pakistan and Laos may risk significant fiscal consequences from BRI energy loans. They are the only two countries that meet three criteria: low fiscal health ratings, high rates of government borrowing, and energy loans that amount to a significant share of their foreign public debt. Although Sri Lanka and Tajikistan are in similar positions, energy loans comprise only a small percentage of their total debt, limiting their potential fiscal impact. Venezuela and Vietnam, in contrast, structure their borrowing through government-owned or private companies. In these countries, energy loans do not directly impact the state of public finances. However, Chinese investors and loan providers face an increased risk in all these countries.

Table 5.3 Recipients of the BRI energy project loans and their fiscal conditions.

BRI country	Total CDB and CEXIM loans (2014–2018), US$ million	CDB and CEXIM loans borrowed by governments (2014–2018), US$ million	Percentage of loans borrowed by governments	Fiscal health rating	Total foreign government debt, US$ million
Angola	8,900	0	0%	58.2	
Argentina	5,542	5,542	100%	33	277,921
Bangladesh	3,745	1,203	32%	77.6	
Bolivia	1,000	0	0%	17.6	
Bosnia and Herzegovina	782	0	0%	17.6	
Brazil	28,150	0	0%	5.9	
Cambodia	100	100	100%	89.1	
Cameroon	142	142	100%	59.7	8,238
Dominican Republic	600	600	100%	89.9	
Ecuador	759	759	100%	32.1	44,822
Egypt	757	0	0%	0	
Ethiopia	333	250	75%	83.3	
Guinea	1,200	1,200	100%	87.2	
Indonesia	3,039	1,200	39%	88.1	
Iran	3,000	0	0%	89.5	
Jordan	1,590	0	0%	60.6	
Kenya	398	264	66%	13.8	27,030
Laos	1,776	1,207	68%	66.5	9,762
Malaysia	1,100	1,100	100%	82.4	
Morocco	300	0	0%	66.9	
Nepal	1,516	0	0%	98.5	
Nigeria	500	500	100%	68.2	
Pakistan	21,206	17,082	81%	49.2	95,108

BRI country	Total CDB and CEXIM loans (2014–2018), US$ million	CDB and CEXIM loans borrowed by governments (2014–2018), US$ million	Percentage of loans borrowed by governments	Fiscal health rating	Total foreign government debt, US$ million
Papua New Guinea	260	0	0%	75.2	
Russia	15,700	0	0%	86.6	
Serbia	863	608	70%	90.1	
Somalia	257	257	100%	N/A	
South Africa	4,500	0	0%	62.6	
South Sudan	1,900	1,900	100%	62.6	1,925
Sri Lanka	1,148	1,148	100%	30.4	52,310
Tajikistan	411	79	19%	60.3	2,274
Uganda	483	483	100%	68.6	7,163
United Kingdom	7,800	0	0%	68.6	
Uzbekistan	2,440	1,240	51%	98.7	
Venezuela	2,200	0	0%	17.6	
Vietnam	5,247	0	0%	40.7	
Zambia	1,741	1,741	100%	12.3	10,050
Zimbabwe	1,000	0	0%	23.7	
Total	**132,384**	**38604**	**29%**		

Source: Boston University (2019); CEIC (2019); Heritage Foundation (2019); Trading Economics (2019).

Chinese policy makers are aware that this problem will become even more pressing as more countries with shaky public finances in Africa (e.g., Cameroon, Zambia, and Zimbabwe) and Latin America (e.g., Argentina and Ecuador) join the BRI. The recent "Debt Sustainability Framework for Participating Countries of the Belt and Road Initiative" issued by China's Ministry of Finance (2019) outlines risk assessment and management processes for financing BRI projects.

Notably, economies with problematic macroeconomic and/or political risk profiles are limited in their development financing options. Major non-Chinese international development institutions, such as the WB, ADB, or EBRD, have

Table 5.4 Sources of financing for energy projects in Pakistan between 2000 and 2018

Source	Energy FDI/loans, US$ million	Including coal, US$ million
World Bank	5,944.2	0
Asian Development Bank	10,877.9	750.6
European Investment Bank	282.5	0
International Finance Corporation	571.9	0
Islamic Development Bank	1,105.1	200.0
Agence Française de Développement	293.4	0
KfW Development Bank	233.6	0
USAID	187.7	0
Japan International Cooperation Agency	467.7	0
China Development Bank	10,370.0	4,270.0
Export-Import Bank of China	14,406.0	2,506.0

Source: World Bank (2022); Asian Development Bank (2022); European Investment Bank (2022); International Finance Corporation (2022); Islamic Development Bank (2022); Boston University (2019); CEIC (2019).

strict, formal project risk assessment procedures that limit their operations in such economies. International Monetary Fund loans, on the other hand, are usually bundled with economic policy conditions, some of which (e.g., austerity measures) may not be conducive to economic development (Dreher 2004; Stubbs et al. 2018). This often leaves China-led financing as the best or only option for such economies.

This premise is illustrated using the case of Pakistan, as shown in Table 5.4. The two Chinese policy banks have captured a majority of Pakistan's energy FDI financing requirement since 2000. Moreover, coal-related projects have been exclusively financed by Chinese investors, apart from a few projects financed by the ADB and Islamic Development Bank. This echoes China's wider dominance in foreign investment into Pakistan: In 2018, China accounted for 58 percent of the total annual FDI into the country. For some developing BRI economies with poor fiscal health, this figure can exceed 85 percent in certain years, as in the case of Laos (CEIC 2019).

Conclusions

The analysis of China's energy investment in BRI projects shows that the country's strategies are increasingly defined by its wider geopolitical ambitions and global macroeconomic factors, rather than by considerations of energy supply security. China's commitment toward attaining carbon neutrality by 2060 will further reduce the importance of energy security as a BRI consideration. As the BRI continues to expand in strategic and geographical scope, it is essential to view Chinese energy investment in the context of broader BRI priorities. The evolving domestic economy, the formation of regional trade and investment markets, and the progress of internationalization of the renminbi will shape the approach and priority of China's future investment.

The rise of climate change on the global agenda and the accelerated global energy transition have provided an opportunity for China to strengthen its leadership on green energy. China-based production networks of renewable energy have made significant contributions to continued cost reduction and technology deployment in the last decade. China pledged in 2021 that it would not build new coal-fired power plants abroad and would step up its support for developing green and low-carbon energy in developing countries. This sends a clear signal to financial institutions, investors, and companies to prioritize investment in green and renewable energy projects under the BRI.

However, China's outbound cleantech investments will have to face challenges arising from growing political scrutiny for investment and trade activities. The shift to a clean energy system requires strong growth of strategic minerals and components that are critical for renewable energy products. To build competitive advantage for green industries and alleviate the risks that could arise from physical disruption, trade restrictions, or other developments in major producing countries, a growing number of countries have announced plans to invest in and develop their domestic capabilities. This may lead to increased barriers and intensified competition in strategic areas.

Given the changes arising from the energy transition and the increasing tensions in global trade and investment, the following questions arise with regard to China's energy geopolitics:

- What is China's strategy to balance its economic growth, energy security, and carbon neutrality?
- What are the impacts of China's domestic energy policy on international energy geopolitics?

- Will the establishment of China's energy trading centers change the global energy and commodity markets?
- What are the geopolitical implications for the shift of Chinese overseas investment to green energy?
- What role could the regional cooperation mechanism play in aligning China's investment with that of other major players in decarbonizing energy infrastructure?

References

African Development Bank (AfDB). 2018. "African Economic Outlook 2018." https:// www .afdb .org/ fileadmin/ uploads/ afdb/ Documents/ Publications/ African _Economic_Outlook_2018_-_EN.pdf.

American Enterprise Institute. 2022. "China Global Investment Tracker." Accessed February 20, 2022. http://www.aei.org/china-global-investment-tracker.

Asian Development Bank (ADB). 2017. "Meeting Asia's Infrastructure Needs." https:// www .adb .org/ sites/ default/ files/ publication/ 227496/ special -report -infrastructure .pdf.

Asian Development Bank (ADB). 2022, "Asian Development Bank," Accessed May 20, 2022. https://www.adb.org/

Association of Southeast Asian Nations (ASEAN). 2019. "ASEAN Outlook On the Indo-Pacific." https:// asean .org/ asean2020/ wp -content/ uploads/ 2021/ 01/ ASEAN -Outlook-on-the-Indo-Pacific_FINAL_22062019.pdf

Askary, Hussein, and Janson Ross. 2018. "Why China's 'Debtbook Diplomacy' is a Hoax." *International Schiller Institute*, August 30. https://schillerinstitute.com/why -chinas-debtbook-diplomacy-is-a-hoax/.

Baltensperger, Michael, and Uri Dadush. 2019. "The Belt and Road Turns Five." *Bruegel Policy Contribution* 1(January). http://bruegel.org/wp-content/uploads/2019/01/PC -01_2019_.pdf.

Baruah, Darshana M. 2018. "India's Answer to the Belt and Road: A Road Map for South Asia." *Carnegie India*, August. https:// carnegieendowment.org/ files/ WP _Darshana_Baruah_Belt_Road_FINAL.pdf.

Belt and Road Portal. 2018. "Six Economic Corridors." Accessed February 20, 2022. https://www.yidaiyilu.gov.cn/zchj/rcjd/60644.html

Belt and Road Portal. 2022. "List of Countries Who Have Signed BRI Cooperation Agreement with China." Accessed February 20, 2022. https://eng.yidaiyilu.gov.cn

Bennon, Michael. 2017. "Western and Chinese Infrastructure Development Abroad." Presented at the CSIS-Stanford Joint Seminar, Washington, D.C., December 18. https:// www .csis .org/ events/ western -and -chinese -infrastructure -development -abroad.

Boston University. 2019. "China's Global Energy Finance." *BU Global Energy Finance Center*. Accessed April 11, 2019. https://www.bu.edu/cgef/#/2017/Country

Cai, Peter. 2017. "Understanding China's Belt and Road Initiative." *Lowy Institute Analysis*, March. https:// www .lowyinstitute .org/ publications/ understanding -belt -and-road-initiative.

CEIC. 2019. "Global Database." Accessed April 30, 2019. https://insights.ceicdata.com.
Chen, Dongmei. 2021. "China's Belt and Road Initiative: Changing Investment Priorities in Pursuit of Energy Security and Carbon Neutrality." *Oxford Energy Forum* 126:15–18. https://a9w7k6q9.stackpathcdn.com/wpcms/wp-content/uploads/2021/02/OEF-126.pdf
Chen, Aizhu. 2022. "Russia, China Agree 30-year Gas Deal via New Pipeline, to Settle in Euros." *Reuters*, February 4. https://www.reuters.com/world/asia-pacific/exclusive-russia-china-agree-30-year-gas-deal-using-new-pipeline-source-2022-02-04/.
Clarke, Michael. 2017. "The Belt and Road Initiative: China's New Grand Strategy?" *Asia Policy* 24:71–79. DOI:10.1353/asp.2017.0023.
Djankov, Simeon, and Sean Miner. 2016. "China's Belt and Road Initiative: Motives, Scope, and Challenge." Briefing 16-2. *Peterson Institute for International Economics*, March. https://piie.com/publications/piie-briefings/chinas-belt-and-road-initiative-motives-scope-and-challenges.
Dollar, David. 2017. "Is China's Development Finance a Challenge to the International Order?" Presented at the Japan Center for Economic Research, Tokyo, October.
Dreher, Axel. 2004. "IMF and Economic Growth: The Effects of Programs, Loans, and Compliance with Conditionality." Research Paper Series No. 1/November, Thurgauer Wirtschaftsinstitut (TWI) and University of Konstanz, Kreuzlingen, Switzerland. https://www.twi-kreuzlingen.ch/wp-content/uploads/2017/12/twi-rps-001-dreher-2004-11.pdf.
The Economist Corporate Network. 2019. "BRI Beyond 2020: Embracing New Routes and Opportunities Along the Belt and Road." Accessed February 20, 2022. https://www.bakermckenzie.com/-/media/files/insight/publications/2019/11/bri-beyond-2020.pdf?la=en.
European Commission and High Representative of the Union for Foreign Affairs and Security Policy. 2018. "Joint Communication to The European Parliament, The Council, The European Economic and Social Committee, The Committee of the Regions and The European Investment Bank: Connecting Europe and Asia - Building blocks for an EU Strategy." September 19. https://www.eeas.europa.eu/sites/default/files/joint_communication_-_connecting_europe_and_asia_-_building_blocks_for_an_eu_strategy_2018-09-19.pdf.
European Commission and High Representative of the Union for Foreign Affairs and Security Policy. 2021. "Joint Communication to The European Parliament and The Council: The EU strategy for Cooperation in The Indo-Pacific." January 24. https://eeas.europa.eu/sites/default/files/jointcommunication_2021_24_1_en.pdf.
European Investment Bank. 2022 "European Investment Bank," Accessed May 20, 2022. https://www.eib.org/en/index.htm.
Federation of German Industries (BDI). 2019. "Partner and Systemic Competitor—How Do We Deal with China's State-Controlled Economy?" January. https://english.bdi.eu/publication/news/china-partner-and-systemic-competitor.
Feng, Da Hsuan, and Haiming Liang. 2018. "Is BRI Road to a 'Debt Trap'? The Numbers Say No." *Global Times*, November 21. http://www.globaltimes.cn/content/1128434.shtml.
Fukuyama, Francis. 2016. "One Belt, One Road: Exporting the Chinese Model to Eurasia." *The Australian*, January 4. https://www.theaustralian.com.au/news/world/one-belt-one-road-exporting-the-chinese-model-to-eurasia/news-story/269016e0dd63ccca4da306b5869b9e1c.
Fulton, Jonathan. 2017. "The G.C.C. Countries and China's Belt and Road Initiative (BRI): Curbing Their Enthusiasm?" *Middle East Institute*, October 17. https://

www.mei.edu/publications/gcc-countries-and-chinas-belt-and-road-initiative-bri-curbing-their-enthusiasm.

Gallagher, Kevin P., and Amos Irwin. 2014. "Exporting National Champions: China's Outward Foreign Direct Investment Finance in Comparative Perspective." *China and World Economy* 22(6):1–21.

DOI:10.1111/cwe.12089.

General Office of the State Council. 2013. "12th Five Year Plan for Energy Development." January 23. http://www.gov.cn/zwgk/2013-01/23/content_2318554.htm.

Gholz, Eugene, Umul Awan, and Ehud Ronn. 2017. "Financial and Energy Security Analysis of China's Loan-for-oil Deals." *Energy Research & Social Science* 24:42–50. DOI:10.1016/j.erss.2016.12.021

Heritage Foundation. 2019. "2019 Index of Economic Freedom." Accessed April 24, 2019. https://www.heritage.org/index/explore.

Hillman, Jonathan E. 2018. "China's Belt and Road Initiative: Five Years Later." Testimony before the U.S.-China Economic and Security Review Commission, Center for Strategic & International Studies (CSIS), Washington, D.C., January 25. https://www.csis.org/analysis/chinas-belt-and-road-initiative-five-years-later-0.

Hurley, John, Scott Morris, and Gailyn Portelance. 2018. "Examining the Debt Implications of the Belt and Road Initiative from a Policy Perspective." *Center for Global Development* (CGD), March. https://www.cgdev.org/sites/default/files/examining-debt-implications-belt-and-road-initiative-policy-perspective.pdf.

IHS Markit. 2022. "The Great Supply Chain Disruption: Why it Continues in 2022." January. https://ihsmarkit.com/info/0122/great-supply-chain-disruption.html.

International Energy Agency (IEA). 2022. "The Role of Critical World Energy Outlook Special Report Minerals in Clean Energy Transitions." March. https://www.iea.org/reports/the-role-of-critical-minerals-in-clean-energy-transitions.

International Finance Corporation, May 20, 2022. https:// www .ifc .org/ wps/ wcm/ connect/ CORP _EXT _Content/ IFC _External _Corporate _Site/ Home/ HomePageDefaultContent.

Islamic Development Bank, 2022. https://www.isdb.org.

Jiang, Julie and Jonathan Sinton. 2011. "Overseas Investments By Chinese National Oil Companies: Assessing the Drivers and Impacts." February. IEA Report. https://iea.blob.core.windows.net/assets/9763ca18-32be-4e05-9c10-57322d016715/overseas_china.pdf.

Jiang, Julie, and Chen Ding. 2014. "Update on Overseas Investments by China's National Oil Companies Achievements and Challenges since 2011." IEA report. https://iea.blob.core.windows.net/assets/900e23de-e76a-43ca-82fb-7dd6e70f11f9/PartnerCountryS eriesUpdat eonOversea sInvestmen tsbyChinas NationalOi lCompanies.pdf

Kennedy, Andrew. 2010. "China's New Energy-Security Debate." *Survival* 52(3):137–58. DOI:10.1080/00396338.2010.494881.

Klynveld Peat Marwick Goerdeler (KPMG). 2019. "Corporate Tax Rates Table." Accessed April 30, 2019. https://home.kpmg/vg/en/home/services/tax1/tax-tools-and-resources/tax-rates-online/corporate-tax-rates-table.html.

Kong, Bo, and Kevin P. Gallagher. 2016. "The Globalization of Chinese Energy Companies." *Global Economic Governance Initiative, Boston University. Accessed February 20, 2022.* https://www.bu.edu/pardeeschool/files/2016/06/Globalization.Final_.pdf.

Leung, Guy C.K. 2011. "China's Energy Security: Perception and Reality." *Energy Policy* 39:1330–37. DOI: 10.1016/j.enpol.2010.12.005.

Lin, Joanne. 2021. "The EU in the Indo-Pacific: A New Strategy with Implications For ASEAN." *ISEAS Perspective,* September. https://www.iseas.edu.sg/media/op-eds/the-eu-in-the-indo-pacific-a-new-strategy-with-implications-for-asean-op-ed-by-joanne-lin-in-think-china/.

Ma, Xinyue, Cecilia Han Springer, and Honest Shao. 2022. "Outlier or New Normal? Trends in China's Global Energy Finance." *Global Development Policy Center, Boston University*, March 11. https://www.bu.edu/gdp/2022/03/11/outlier-or-new-normal-trends-in-chinas-global-energy-finance-2/.

Meidan, Michael. 2014. "The Implications of China's Energy-Import Boom." *Survival* 56(3):179-200. DOI:10.1080/00396338.2014.920147

Meidan, Michael. 2021. "China's Emergence as A Powerful Player in the Old and New Geopolitics of Energy." *Oxford Energy Forum* 126:12–15. https://a9w7k6q9.stackpathcdn.com/wpcms/wp-content/uploads/2021/02/OEF-126.pdf.

Miller, Tom. 2017. *China's Asian Dream: Empire Building Along the New Silk Road.* London: Zed Books.

Ministry of Commerce of the People's Republic of China (MOFCOM). 2017. "2016 China Foreign Direct Investment Statistics Bulletin." http://fec.mofcom.gov.cn/article/tjsj/tjgb/201709/20170902653690.shtml.

Ministry of Commerce (MOFCOM), National Bureau of Statistics (NBS), and State Administration of Foreign Exchange (SAFE), China. 2021. "2020 Statistical Bulletin of China's Outward Foreign Direct Investment." September. http://www.gov.cn/xinwen/2021-09/29/5639984/files/a3015be4dc1f45458513ab39691d37dd.pdf.

Ministry of Finance, China. 2019. "Debt Sustainability Framework for Participating Countries of the Belt and Road Initiative." http://m.mof.gov.cn/czxw/201904/P020190425513990982189.pdf.

Ministry of Foreign Affairs of China (MFA). 2019. "BRI: Progress, Contribute and Prospect." July 26. https://www.mfa.gov.cn/ce/cgpenang/chn/zt/yidaiyilu/t1683609.htm.

Mitchell, Tom. 2018. "Beijing Insists BRI is no Marshall Plan." *The Financial Times,* September 26. https://www.ft.com/content/48f21df8-9c9b-11e8-88de-49c908b1f264.

Mundy, Simon, and Kathrin Hille. 2019. "The Maldives Counts the Cost of its Debts to China." *The Financial Times*, February 11. https://www.ft.com/content/c8da1c8a-2a19-11e9-88a4-c32129756dd8.

National Development and Reform Commission (NDRC). 2015. "Vision and Actions on Jointly Building Silk Road Economic Belt and 21st-Century Maritime Silk Road." http://en.ndrc.gov.cn/newsrelease/201503/t20150330_669367.html.

National Energy Administration (NEA). 2017. "Vision and Actions on Energy Cooperation in Jointly Building Silk Road Economic Belt and 21st-Century Maritime Silk Road." https://eng.yidaiyilu.gov.cn/qwyw/qwfb/1084.htm.

Oil and Gas Journal. 1992. "China Joins Alberta Oil Sands Research." *Oil and Gas Journal* 108(12):42. https://www.ogj.com/general-interest/companies/article/17219855/china-joins-alberta-oilsands-research.

Overseas Private Investment Corporation (OPIC). 2018. "OPIC Statement on the Inclusion of a New Development Finance Institute in the U.S. Government's Reform and Reorganization Plan." June 21. https://www.opic.gov/press-releases/2018/opic-statement-inclusion-new-development-finance-institution-us-governments-reform-and-reorganization-plan.

Oxford Analytica. 2011. "China: State Firms Face Scrutiny for Overseas Losses." *Oxford Analytica Daily Brief*, October 20. https://dailybrief.oxan.com/Analysis/DB171451/Chinas-state-firms-face-scrutiny-for-overseas-losses.

Parker, Sam, and Gabrielle Chefitz. 2018. "Debtbook Diplomacy: China's Strategic Leveraging of its Newfound Economic Influence and the Consequences for U.S. Foreign Policy." *Harvard Kennedy School*, May.https://www.belfercenter.org/sites/default/files/files/publication/Debtbook%20Diplomacy%20PDF.pdf

Renwick, Neil, Jing Gu, and Sen Gong. 2018. "The Impact of BRI Investment in Infrastructure on Achieving the Sustainable Development Goals." K4D Emerging Issues Report, Institute of Development Studies, Brighton, United Kingdom. https://assets.publishing.service.gov.uk/media/5be9560ced915d6a166edb35/K4D_Helpdesk_BRI_REPORT_2018_final.pdf.

Reuters. 2015. "China's CITIC to Invest $113 Billion for 'Silk Road' Investments." June 24. https://www.reuters.com/article/china-citic-investments-idUSL3N0ZA3AH20150624

Sejko, Dini. 2017. "Financing the Belt and Road Initiative: MDBs, SWFs, SOEs and the Long Wait for Private Investors." *APEC Currents* 2017 (11).

Saalman, Lora, and Knut Dethlefsen. 2017. "Following the Forum-China's Belt and Road Initiative and the EU." *Friedrich-Ebert-Stiftung*, July. https://library.fes.de/pdf-files/bueros/singapur/13565.pdf.

Silk Road Think Tank Network. 2020. "Belt and Road Projects Database Summary." *Internal Information Sharing.*

State Council of China. 2015. "Action plan on the Belt and Road Initiative." http://english.gov.cn/archive/publications/2015/03/30/content_281475080249035.htm.

State Council Information Office of China (SCIO). 2016. "Review of Xi's Speech on the Belt and Road Initiative." http://www.scio.gov.cn/m/31773/35507/gcyl35511/Document/1529099/1529099.htm.

Stubbs, Thomas, Bernhard Reinsberg, Alexander Kentikelenis, and Lawrence King. 2018. "How to Evaluate the Effects of IMF Conditionality." *The Review of International Organizations* 15:29–73. DOI:10.1007/s11558-018-9332-5.

Tellis, Ashley J. 2017. "Protecting American Primacy in the Indo-Pacific." *Testimony before the U.S. Armed Service Committee,* April 25. https://carnegieendowment.org/2017/04/25/protecting-american-primacy-in-indo-pacific-pub-68754.

Trading Economics. 2019. "Government Debt." https://tradingeconomics.com/country-list/government-debt.

U.S. Department of Defense. 2018. "Summary of the 2018 National Defense Strategy of the United States of America." January 19. https://dod.defense.gov/Portals/1/Documents/pubs/2018-National-Defense-Strategy-Summary.pdf.

U.S. White House. 2021. "Quad Leaders' Joint Statement: The Spirit of the Quad." March. https://www.whitehouse.gov/briefing-room/statements-releases/2021/03/12/quad-leaders-joint-statement-the-spirit-of-the-quad/.

U.S. White House. 2022. "Indo-Pacific Strategy of the United States." February. https://www.whitehouse.gov/wp-content/uploads/2022/02/U.S.-Indo-Pacific-Strategy.pdf.

Widmann, Manuel. 2021. "The EU Connectivity Strategy: Putting Words into Action." *EIAS Briefing Paper,* August. https://eias.org/wp-content/uploads/2021/08/The-EU-Connectivity-Strategy-.pdf.

Wijeratne, David, Joshua Yau, Gabriel Wong, Mark Rathbone, Neu Boon Ling, and Stella Lau. 2017. "Repaving the Ancient Silk Roads." *PricewaterhouseCoopers Analysis,* May. https://www.pwc.com/gx/en/growth-markets-centre/assets/pdf/pwc-gmc-repaving-the-ancient-silk-routes-web.pdf.

Wolfe, Wojtek M., and Brock F. Tessman. 2012. "China's Global Equity Oil Investments: Economic and Geopolitical Influences." *Journal of Strategic Studies* 35(2):175–96. DOI:10.1080/01402390.2011.635467.

World Bank. 2022. "World Bank Open Data" The World Bank, Accessed May 20, 2022. https://data.worldbank.org/.

Xiong, Wei. 2022. "Could China Take All of Europe's Gas Volumes from Russia?" *Rystad Energy Gas Market Analytics,* March 14.

Xinhua. 2015. "Commentary: Silk Road Fund's 1st Investment Makes China's Words into Practice." Accessed April 4, 2019. http://www.xinhuanet.com/english/2015-04/21/c_134170737.htm.

_____. 2017. "Work Together to Build the Silk Road Economic Belt and the 21st Century Maritime Silk Road." *President Xi's Speech at Opening of Belt and Road Forum,* May 14. http://www.xinhuanet.com/english/2017-05/14/c_136282982.htm.

Zhang, Zhongxiang. 2012. "The Overseas Acquisitions and Equity Oil Shares of Chinese National Oil Companies: A Threat to The West but a Boost to China's Energy Security?" *Energy Policy* 48:698–701. DOI: 10.1016/j.enpol.2012.05.077

Zhang, Shu, and Matthew Miller. 2017. "Behind China's Silk Road Vision: Cheap Funds, Heavy Debt, Growing Risk." *Reuters News*, May 15. https://www.reuters.com/article/us-china-silkroad-finance/behind-chinas-silk-road-vision-cheap-funds-heavy-debt-growing-risk-idUSKCN18B0YS.

Zhao, Minghao. 2018. "Five Years on, BRI Tastes Success on Several Fronts." *Global Times*, August 28. https://www.globaltimes.cn/page/201808/1117400.shtml.

6 From Paris to Glasgow and beyond: what future for clean energy technology deployment under Article 6?

Elizabeth Carey and Xiaoliang Yang

Introduction

What is Article 6, and what was achieved at Glasgow?

At a time when the COVID-19 pandemic and Russia's invasion of Ukraine highlight the importance of global solidarity and multilateral cooperation based on shared principles and common interests, the international climate negotiations that took place in 2021 at COP26 have provided a welcome point of contrast.[1] The successful completion of the rulebook of Article 6 of the Paris Agreement after years of negotiation was, in particular, one of the most highly anticipated outcomes of the COP26 Climate Conference at Glasgow, which concluded in November 2021 with nearly 200 Parties agreeing to the Glasgow Climate Pact (United Nations Climate Change Conference UK 2021).

The latter kept alive the Paris objective of limiting the global temperature increase to 1.5 degrees Celsius compared with the pre-industrial era, while all Parties agreed to revisit and strengthen their national contributions (or Nationally Determined Contributions [NDCs]) in 2022, rather than in 2025, as initially planned (UNFCCC 2015). For the first time, the COP agreed to the phasing out of unabated coal, while it went further than ever before in addressing the issue of loss and damage from the existing impacts of climate change (United Nations Climate Change Conference UK 2021). Negotiations for the rulebook of Article 6 were concluded in parallel following a five-year process, thereby finalizing a global framework for Parties to cooperate in meeting their NDC pledges in a more economically efficient manner while delivering higher levels of mitigation of greenhouse gas (GHG) emissions and sustainable development.[2]

Article 6 recognizes and proposes alternative and complementary approaches to voluntary cooperation between Parties in meeting their climate pledges. It does so in a facilitative rather than a prescriptive way, in line with the spirit of the Paris Agreement. Its market-based approaches include Art. 6.2, with internationally transferred mitigation outcomes (ITMOs), and Art. 6.4, which establishes a new crediting mechanism (A6.4M) for emissions reductions (A6.4ERs). Art. 6.2 covers country to country transactions, while Art.6.4 covers projects and activities undertaken by public and private entities. Art. 6.8 brings in nonmarket approaches to voluntary cooperation as an alternative to the Art. 6.2 and Art. 6.4 market transactions.[3]

The market mechanisms of Article 6 lay the foundations for the development of a global interconnected carbon market that has the potential to deliver lower GHG abatement costs and help accelerate the transition to a net-zero emissions world.[4] It encourages the participation of new entrants thanks to the universal nature of the Agreement and to the space provided for private sector participation.

Four key principles underpin the Article 6 rules: sustainable development, environmental integrity and transparency, robust accounting and the avoidance of double counting, and delivering an overall mitigation in GHG mitigation (the OMGE principle). While negotiations for the Article 6 rulebook were a highly technical and complex process undertaken under the auspices of the Subsidiary Body for Scientific and Technological Advice of the United Nations Framework Convention on Climate Change (UNFCCC), they remained fundamentally a political process aimed at resolving key issues, such as what ITMOs refer to (reduction, removal, or avoidance of GHG emissions) and how to account for them or how to transition away from the Clean Development Mechanism (CDM) of the Kyoto Protocol.[5]

Several 'crunch' issues at the heart of the Article 6 rules were resolved at Glasgow, allowing for negotiations to be finally concluded. New environmental integrity rules were adopted to ensure that all recorded carbon credits use verifiable and comparable accounting systems, building on the San José principles adopted in 2019.[6] Rules to avoid double counting of carbon credits through corresponding adjustments (CAs) were agreed upon, with the host country to decide if it will forgo booking carbon credits within its own NDC or whether it will instead sell them to an international government purchaser.[7] It was decided that the definition of ITMO includes reductions and removals of GHG emissions, with the question of whether it would also cover 'avoidance' of GHG emissions being reserved to a later work program (Marcu 2022).

Other important issues that were resolved at Glasgow include a 5 percent equivalent of the 'share of proceeds' from the new multilateral mechanism set up in Article 6.4 (A6.4M) to go toward a climate adaptation fund for developing countries. Article 6.4 transactions are also to be subject to a 2 percent cancellation fee in order to help ensure a guaranteed net reduction in overall emissions mitigation. In terms of the impact of the Art. 6.2 and Art. 6.4 rules on voluntary commitments by the private sector, it was decided that no CA would be imposed by the UN system, meaning that transfers can take place internationally for use in voluntary markets without Party authorization, if the Party so decides, and without the need for a CA. However, the new rules may, in practice, also guide full private sector voluntary market activities (Marcu 2022).

Together with progress on these issues, a compromise was reached over the legacy of carbon credits from the CDM (Carbon Emissions Reductions or CERs), that is, to what extent these will be carried over into the new Article 6.4 mechanism—with credits generated after 2013 eligible for inclusion in the first tranche of a country's NDC (Marcu 2022). Taking into account the position and interests of countries that host a large number of CDM projects, such as Brazil and India, while creating a new system that takes on board lessons learned from the experience of the CDM, was a key aspect of designing a credible new framework.

How can implementation of the new Article 6 system support the transition to low-carbon energy systems?

While much work remains to be done over the coming years to get the Article 6 mechanisms up and running, the conclusion of the negotiations at Glasgow lends greater credibility to the idea of a global carbon market that can deliver higher levels of sustainable development and accelerate the transition to a carbon-neutral world. While previous areas of research focused on designing an effective set of technical rules under Article 6 that would both allow for a political agreement to be reached and create a credible, functioning framework, the key issue now is that of the implementation of the Article 6 rulebook in the years and decades to come.

One important aspect of the implementation of the new Article 6 system concerns its potential benefits in terms of accelerating the deployment of critical clean energy technologies, such as Carbon Capture Storage (CCS), that are essential to meeting the climate objectives of the Paris Agreement.[8] These types of technologies may come to play an even more important role in the future, in the wake of the COVID-19 pandemic and of the war in Ukraine, with both of these crises, and in particular the latter one, raising fundamental questions that include the structure of energy supply chains and energy security and affordability.

The purpose of this chapter is to map out the following key issues in relation to clean energy technology deployment and the implementation of Article 6 going forward, with a focus on CCUS.

- A first introductory step underlines the key role that clean energy technology deployment must play in helping reduce GHG emissions globally and considers the basic dynamics of clean energy technology deployment.
- A second step considers the nature of Article 6 and the ways in which its implementation can facilitate clean energy technology deployment, such as through tapping into each country's comparative advantage and providing a blueprint that can connect low-carbon policies and mechanisms worldwide.
- A third step considers some of the ways in which CCUS and oil-producing economies could be brought into the global Article 6 system, with a view to accelerating the deployment of this critical technology on a global scale.

In conclusion, ways in which the COVID-19 pandemic and the situation in Ukraine may affect the deployment of clean energy technology and GHG emissions will be considered.

Bridging the emissions gap: the critical role of clean energy technology deployment

The emissions gap and how to close it: the critical role of clean technologies such as CCS

The deployment of clean energy technologies on a global scale is a key part of efforts to close the emissions gap. The latter represents "the difference between projected global greenhouse gas (GHG) emissions assuming full implementation of the mitigation pledges that countries have made for 2030, and emissions under least-cost pathways consistent with the Paris Agreement's long-term goal of limiting global average temperature increase to 'well-below 2°C' and pursuing efforts to limit it to 1.5 degrees, compared with pre-industrial levels" (UNEP 2021, p.29).

As Table 6.1 shows, countries' pledges still fall short of closing the emissions gap. Compared with previous unconditional NDCs, the new pledges for 2030

Table 6.1 Projected global GHG emissions and emissions gap in different scenarios

	Total global GHG emissions in 2030
Year 2010 policies	64 Gt CO2e
Current policies (full implementation of conditional and unconditional NDCs)	55 Gt CO2e
	Emissions gap in 2030
Below 2 degrees scenario with full implementation of unconditional NDCs (updated NDCs and announcements)	13 GtCO2e
Below 2 degrees scenario with full implementation of conditional NDCs (updated NDCs and announcements)	11 GtCO2e
Below 1. 5 degrees scenario with full implementation of unconditional NDCs (updated NDCs and announcements)	28 GtCO2e
Below 1.5 degrees scenario with full implementation of conditional NDCs (updated NDCs and announcements)	25 GtCO2e

Note: The emissions gap for 2030 is defined as the difference between total global GHG emissions from least-cost scenarios that keep global warming to 2 degrees Celsius, 1.8 degrees Celsius, or 1.5 degrees Celsius with varying levels of likelihood and the estimated total global GHG emissions resulting from the full implementation of the NDCs (UNEP 2021 report, p. XXIII).
In the UNEP 2021 report, the NDC scenario includes all the most recent NDCs (new or updated NDCs, if submitted, and previous NDCs otherwise) as well as all officially announced climate change mitigation pledges for 2030 with a cut-off date of August 30, 2021 (UNEP 2021 Report, p. XXIII).
Source: UNEP 2021 Emissions Gap report, p. XXIV.

reduce projected 2030 emissions by only 7.5 percent, whereas 30 percent is needed for 2 degrees Celsius and 55 percent is needed for 1.5 degrees Celsius (UNEP 2021, p.XXIII). Furthermore, estimates of the world's remaining carbon budget from 2018 onward stand at 580 GTCO2 for a 50 percent chance of keeping global warming below 1.5 degrees Celsius, representing less than 15 years of global emissions at current rates (Rogelj, Forster and Piers Forster 2019). Meanwhile, the IEA estimates that only 2 out of 46 critical clean technologies and sectors are on track to meet the IEA's Net Zero Emissions by 2050 Scenario (IEA 2021).

Table 6.2 Required CO2 emissions reductions from CCS in different scenarios studies.

	2020	*2025*	*2030*	*2035*	*2040*		*2045*	*2050*	*2055*	*2060*
IEA-2DS	*0.02*	*0.42*	*1.17*	*2.43*	*3.82*		*5.06*	*5.52*	*5.92*	*6.77*
IEA-B2DS	*0.02*	*0.91*	*2.02*	*3.67*	*5.83*		*7.67*	*8.61*	*9.91*	*11.25*
Shell-Sky	*0.00*	*0.04*	*0.20*	*0.74*	*2.16*		*3.69*	*5.2*	*6.83*	*8.35*

Note: Unit: GtCO2e

While all clean technologies need to be deployed, CCS has a particularly critical role to play in meeting the well- below 2 degrees objective, as illustrated in the IEA's 2DS and Beyond 2DS scenarios and in Shell's Sky Scenario (as shown in Table 6.2), and in bridging the emissions gap (UNEP 2021). By 2030, the latter will be equivalent at best to 11 GtCO2e and at worst to 28 GtCO2e (see Table 6.1).

Deploying critical clean technologies at scale such as CCS is fundamental to reaching carbon neutrality or "a balance between anthropogenic emissions by sources and removals by sinks of greenhouse gases in the second half of this century" (Article 4 of the Paris Agreement), as illustrated in Table 6.2. Reaching carbon neutrality does not imply that all countries do so, but rather that some countries will achieve net-zero emissions earlier than others, while other countries will be unable to ever reach carbon neutrality. Hence, the need for Parties to be able to purchase negative emissions outcomes from host Parties that are endowed with the capacity to deploy critical clean technologies, this being one of the purposes of Article 6.

Prior to considering how Article 6 can provide an effective framework to help accelerate the deployment of clean energy technologies, the nature and dynamics of clean energy technology deployment, including its drivers and inhibitors, will be considered.

Understanding the nature and dynamics of clean technology deployment

Defining clean technology deployment: a complex, context-sensitive process

Technology types and the cycle of innovation

The primary purpose of clean energy technology—that is, based on low-carbon- or zero-carbon-intensive sources of energy—is to mitigate GHG emissions and other air pollutants as well as enhance countries' ability to adapt to the impacts of climate change. Clean energy technology refers to a wide range of low-carbon technologies, including

- electric vehicles,
- energy storage,
- solar photovoltaic (PV),
- onshore wind,
- offshore wind and hydropower,
- energy efficiency,
- carbon capture sequestration and storage (including CCUS), and
- nuclear power (IEA, 2021).

Clean technology deployment refers to the entire clean energy technology process, including research, development, demonstration, market formation, and deployment itself. The cycle of innovation does not follow a linear progression, but rather is characterized by a high level of unpredictability and disorganization (Coninck and Sagar, 2015a). Energy technology in itself is not a single technology, but rather "a complex array of interconnected technologies that pervade the entire economy on both the demand and supply side" (Bonvillian and Weiss, 2009, p. 28). The deployment of clean technology is therefore part of a process of economic development or 'catching-up' for developing countries and of the development of firms and industries worldwide (Watson et al. 2015). Clean technology innovation and deployment depend on a highly complex process that involves multiple actors, stakeholders, connections, and networks and that is closely linked with the innovation cycle (Coninck and Puig, 2015).

A multidimensional, context-sensitive process

Clean technology transfers are a key aspect of the process of technological deployment. While there is no universally accepted definition of what technology transfer actually is, the International Panel on Climate Change (IPCC) defines it as "a broad set of processes covering the flow of know-how, experience and equipment for mitigating and adapting to climate change amongst different stakeholders such as governments, private sector entities, financial institutions, non-governmental organizations and research/education institutions. It comprises the process of learning to understand, utilize and replicate the technology, including the capacity to choose it, adapt it to local conditions, and integrate it with indigenous technologies" (IPCC 2000, p.3).

The IPCC's definition underlines the multidimensional nature of clean technology transfer. The literature on technology tends to focus first on the hardware dimension (i.e., equipment, infrastructure, financing) and second on the software dimension, which represents an equally fundamental aspect of technological deployment. The software dimension includes tacit knowledge, skills, know-hows, human capital, as well as domestic institutional capacities (Coninck and Sagar 2015). A third, but often overlooked, dimension of technology transfer is the orgware. Orgware refers to capacity building by institutional actors and stakeholders that are involved in the adaptation process of a technology (Dobrov 1979). While these three equally important dimensions overlap and are intertwined, technology is essentially knowledge, with technological hardware, in particular, representing the "artifact of applied knowledge" (Ockwell and Byrne 2016, p.15).

Clean energy technology is very different from conventional consumer technologies. First, it involves delivering a public good, over and above achieving commercial value. The primary purpose of clean technology is, in effect, to address environmental and climate change problems. Second, most clean energy technologies, in particular where these involve large-scale clean energy facilities (such as CCS, nuclear or wind and solar farms), have a long lifespan that involves slow capital stock turnover. They, thus, typically involve complex processes and decisions linked to developing viable and effective commercial models. Third, some clean technologies may not benefit readily from public acceptance (such as wind farms close to inhabited areas) or may be rejected for political or ideological reasons (such as civil nuclear power).[9] Taken together, these factors can lead to slower market development and more limited financing opportunities for clean energy technologies compared with conventional consumer technologies, with implications in terms of their global diffusion.

The role of public policy in driving clean energy technology deployment

Clean energy technology has historically relied on public policy support to reach a stage of maturity, both technical and commercial, that enables its deployment. This has been the case for clean technologies such as solar PV and wind power, while other technologies, such as nuclear power, systematically require either direct or indirect state aid as a result of their prohibitively high upfront capital costs.

Governments, thus, play a key role in deploying policy and regulatory tools that support the process of clean energy technology deployment. On the supply side, they establish national support schemes, provide direct and cost-shared R&D funding, as well as tax incentives. On the demand side, governments use public procurement, tax incentives and subsidies, and modify or introduce new regulations and technical standards. These policies are necessary to create the right conditions to reduce risk and uncertainty over the long run for developers and investors in clean technologies.

Public policies can also support investment in clean technologies that deliver additional public goods such as energy security or emissions mitigation, that is, technologies that might not otherwise be invested in or deployed purely on a commercial basis, as in the case of nuclear power or wind and solar, particularly in their initial deployment phases. Crises such as the COVID-19 pandemic and the war in Ukraine can prompt governments to operate U-turns or adapt their energy policies in favor of greater investment in low-carbon technologies that also offer the advantage of increased energy independence and security (Sam Ori 2022). Still other types of clean technologies will need 'clubs' of interested countries (i.e., governments) to provide the political and commercial impetus to otherwise still marginal, yet essential, carbon mitigation technologies, such as CCUS (Heidug and Zakkour 2019).

Innovation in the sphere of public policy is considered to be an integral part of clean technology innovation (Lundvall and Borras 2004). The role of governments and public policy in setting the clean technology agenda has increased over the past two decades as climate and environmental policies have become an increasingly important driver of clean technology innovation, with the pace of innovation accelerating worldwide since 2000. This stands in contrast to estimates for the period 1978–1990, when energy prices were the main driver of clean technology innovation (Dechezleprêtre et al., 2011, p.36).

<u>Clean technology deployment as a function of institutional capacity and trade flows</u>

A country's ability to deploy clean technology is a function of both its institutional capabilities and its level of integration into the world economy. Developed countries that innovate the most have the institutional capability to deploy these technologies, as this goes hand-in-hand with levels of economic development, while less developed countries tend to require capacity building in order to develop the institutional framework that will enable them to benefit from technology transfers. Less developed countries are not as integrated into the world economy as developed or emerging countries, which decreases their ability to absorb, adapt, and develop clean technology transfers.[10]

Technology transfers, including those for clean energy technology, are indeed largely a function of trade flows, with innovative technologies being absorbed by those countries that present attractive investment opportunities. Technology transfers are generally considered to benefit from an open trade regime (Saggi 2002; Dechezleprêtre et al. 2013), which is a function of intergovernmental cooperation under the rules of the World Trade Organization. On the other hand, the absence of intergovernmental cooperation or tensions within the global trade regime will have a detrimental effect on the deployment and transfer of technologies, affecting even the most developed economies, as is apparent in the case of the trade wars between the United States and China (Lockett, FT 2019).

While markets play a key role in the deployment of clean energy technology, governments, thus, also play a fundamental role at all levels by creating and guaranteeing the political, legislative, and regulatory frameworks needed to create these markets and incentivize the deployment of clean energy technology globally. Policy and decision-makers are instrumental in designing new policies and mechanisms in response to changing contexts and priorities, such as a growing awareness of the scale and urgency of the climate problem, or in response to new international frameworks or agreements, such as the Paris Agreement. Governments are, moreover, major investors in clean technologies (see Figure 6.1).

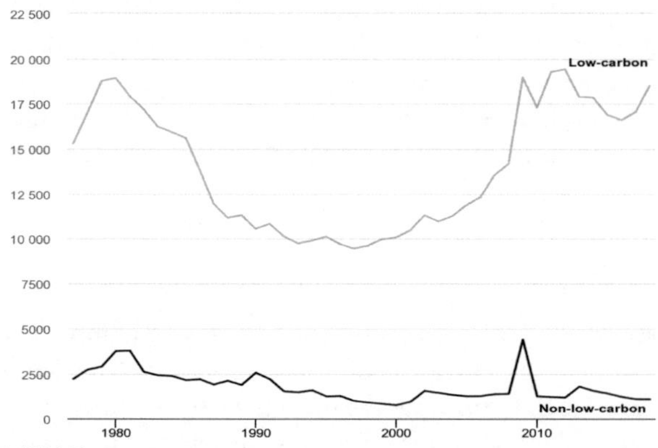

Source: IEA (2019).

Figure 6.1 Public low-carbon energy RD&D budget in IEA member countries, in million US$ (2018 PPP) 1977–2018

Beyond COP26 at Glasgow: How can Article 6 help accelerate the deployment of clean energy technologies?

The nature of Article 6: a complementary and adaptive framework for global cooperation

Article 6 approaches as complementary and mutually reinforcing alternatives for global cooperation

The purpose of Article 6 is to address the global commons problem that is the climate crisis, by creating a system that could help accelerate the deployment of clean technology at scale while supporting low-carbon development at a global level.

The market mechanisms of Article 6, in particular, may be instrumental in achieving this objective. Arts. 6.2 and 6.4 indeed lay the basis for a global carbon market that will be fundamentally different from the one operating under the CDM. While the CDM was reliant on a uniform emissions-based approach for industrialized countries and credited single mitigation projects, the system under the Paris Agreement is more inclusive and decentralized, that is, based on a greater diversity of goals and objectives. This implies rules that mark a significant departure from the rules of the CDM and that create enhanced opportunities for a wider range of technology-neutral mitigation options, in line with the objective of enhancing *"indigenous capacities and endogenous technologies in developing countries"* (Article 4 commitment 5 The Convention 1992).

Moreover, while Article 6 consists of distinct market and nonmarket approaches, it functions as a single, unitary provision with alternative approaches that are both complementary and mutually reinforcing (ADB 2018). In terms of the future development of a global carbon market, both the market and nonmarket provisions of Article 6 have a role to play.

While Art. 6.2 creates a system based on mitigation outcomes that can be internationally transferred (the ITMOs), the mechanism of Art 6.4 is essentially a crediting mechanism that can apply to a project, program of activities, or other type of activity that contributes to the OMGE principle resulting in the issuance of A6.4ERs. Parties that host an emissions reduction activity under Art. 6.4 will have to consider whether to use their mitigation options to meet their NDCs or whether to participate in a mitigation activity that would result in an international transfer to another Party under the Art. 6.4 mechanism. Calculation of the costs of different types of mitigation activities prior to participation in Art. 6.4 activities will likely be an important aspect of this decision (Ellis, Lo Re et al., 2019).

The nonmarket approaches of Arts. 6.8 and 6.9 provide an alternative to Arts. 6.2 and 6.4 for nontransferable joint activities. Nonmarket approaches can apply to developing or least developed countries that do not have the capacity to participate in market mechanisms or to early-stage mitigation technologies that are not sufficiently mature to fall under the market provisions of Art. 6.2 or 6.4. Cooperating in areas such as capacity building, financial and technology transfer could incentivize and enable some developing countries to envisage future participation in the market provisions of Art. 6.

The combination of market and nonmarket approaches reflects the comprehensive approach to international voluntary cooperation envisaged under Art.6.8 as being "*integrated, holistic and balanced.*" The fundamental objectives of all provisions are, thus, identical and aim to create an ecosystem that builds on countries' comparative advantages for higher, more cost-effective ERs while promoting sustainable development and the eradication of poverty.

Article 6 as an adaptive framework that accounts for different types of GHG mitigation goals and outcomes

While Article 6 is to be implemented in the context of the Paris Agreement as a whole, its market-based approaches, in particular, are linked to the Agreement as an adaptive framework that will evolve and broaden out over time (see Figure 6.2). As Parties move forward with implementation of the Agreement and submit successive NDCs that represent a progression over time in terms of both scope and scale, so will Article 6 evolve progressively toward setting the foundations for a functioning international carbon market.

Article 6 connects the NDCs together while helping to progressively widen their scope and promote greater precision and convergence in terms of common metrics and methodologies. Through its adaptive and progressive characteristics and, most importantly, because it is not limited in time and applies to all signatory Parties, the Paris Agreement represents a stronger starting point for the development of an international carbon market than the CDM.

Moreover, Article 6 addresses the fact that the Paris Agreement presents particular challenges with regard to quantifying mitigation goals and outcomes, due to the multiple and diverse types of contributions presented by Parties in their NDCs (Hood et al. 2016). While under the Kyoto Protocol the contributions of Annex I Parties were registered, tracked, and assessed through an integrated accounting framework, with the use of quantified GHG targets relative to a base year, under the Paris Agreement, Parties present multiple and/or overlapping types of GHG mitigation contributions. The latter may, moreover, be either single year or multi-year. These contributions take the form of economy-wide contributions expressed in terms of annual GHG targets relative to a base year; GHG emissions relative to a baseline; or non-GHG goals, such as a policy, a technology, or the use of land.[11]

These diverse types of mitigation goals represent a challenge in terms of defining a common approach based on common metrics and methodologies. Article 6 takes into account a diversity of mitigation activities and outcomes as well as Parties' national circumstances and voluntary cooperation preferences. It allows for different types of accounting methodologies within different settings, thereby facilitating the global deployment and transfer of clean technologies that would be more difficult to effectively quantify otherwise.

The governance of Article 6: key issues for an effective framework

Rethinking the governance framework for international cooperation under the Paris Agreement

The effective deployment of clean energy technology at a global level will also be determined by the governance framework adopted for both the market and nonmarket approaches of Article 6.

The issue of governance, and of the transition away from the mechanisms of the Kyoto Protocol, is particularly central to the design of effective Art. 6.2 cooperative approaches and Art. 6.4 activities. Article 6.2 provides for a decentralized system of governance for the ITMOs, provided that it be "consistent with guidance" adopted by the COP/CMA.[12] Under Art.6.2, Parties have considerable discretion in selecting what metrics to use to measure and account for ITMOs, this being balanced by their obligation to "promote sustainable development and ensure environmental integrity and transparency, including in governance" (Art. 6.2).

Art. 6.4 provides for a comparatively more centralized system of governance. The latter is to be supervised by a body that will be designated by the COP/CMA, in effect establishing a system that will be placed directly under the auspices of the UNFCCC. The metrics and methodologies that apply to Art.6.4 activities are those of the IPCC. The more centralized system of Art.6.4 thereby provides for a greater measure of continuity with the CDM, while also leaving open the possibility of those mitigation activities and outcomes subsequently transitioning to Art. 6.2 as ITMOs.

Arts. 6.2 and 6.4, thus, represent alternative systems of institutional governance, reflecting a need to reframe and diversify international cooperation under the Paris Agreement compared with the Kyoto Protocol. While the latter was characterized by a uniform emissions budget approach standardized across industrialized countries, the Paris Agreement's much broader base, its country-specific approach, and its enhanced focus on collaboration between Parties and stakeholders imply a more diverse and inclusive governance framework.

The concept of 'bounded flexibility,' or choice within limits, is central to the challenge of designing this type of new system. On the one hand, introducing greater flexibility can guarantee maximum Party and stakeholder participation, with this having the ability to create a larger and more liquid market leading to a higher level of cost-effective overall emissions reduction. On the other hand, the absence of sufficiently rigorous safeguards and limits may undermine the creation of an effective global market for mitigation outcomes and activities. Finally, it is also essential that these outcomes and activities be comparable on a global level in order to guarantee their credibility and fungibility as tradable or transferrable assets or units, with this requiring a minimum degree of convergence and uniformity.

Transitioning to an effective global framework: basic principles

In addition, lessons learned from the experience of the CDM, growing recognition of the importance and value of carbon sinks, and the development of carbon markets worldwide provide valuable insights into key principles for an effective transition to new collaborative approaches in the implementation of Article 6.

A first principle is the importance of placing sustainable development on a par with the objective of achieving OMGE. The CDM, primarily designed to help Annex I countries meet their GHG mitigation targets under the Kyoto Protocol more cost-effectively, fell short of delivering on sustainable development (Tsayem Demaze 2013).

An effective transition to a new framework guarantees that technology transfers deliver long-term transformational results, rather than a one-off, one-time transfer. Alongside technology transfer and deployment, the idea of technology diffusion is, thus, also a useful concept to use with regard to Article

6, reflecting as it does the objective of sustainable development for all nations as well as the much more global nature of technology flows.

The Paris Agreement itself provides a positive starting point, with participation in the collaborative approaches of Article 6 being open to signatory Parties in a more holistic, comprehensive, and open-ended manner than under the CDM. The bottom-up nature of the Agreement, based on each Party's national circumstances, provides Parties with a greater degree of discretion in accounting for mitigation outcomes (Art. 6.2) while fostering a sense of ownership favorable to greater participation in voluntary cooperation under Article 6, provided that there is sufficient political will to provide adequate voluntary contributions.

The design of a new framework based on a more inclusive, long-term approach provides the incentive for Parties and stakeholders (with private sector participation being encouraged under Art. 6.8b) to develop technologies, solutions, and partnerships that will enable them to participate in a future global carbon market. In particular, well-designed rules, with consistent metrics and methodologies, may encourage the preservation and development of carbon sinks, both natural and geological, as Parties develop and market their endogenous resources and expertise. Well-designed rules under Article 6 may, thus, help reconcile the tension between sustainable development and GHG emissions reduction that existed under the CDM.

A second principle is to set an ambitious emissions reduction objective that creates value for a future global carbon market and dynamic economic incentives for stakeholders and participants. This represents an essential aspect of the creation of functional market-based approaches, as it creates scarcity and, thus, a market value for tradable emissions reduction activities and outcomes.[13]

The ratchet-up mechanism of the NDCs, whereby Parties are expected to present mitigation objectives and strategies that are progressively more ambitious, can contribute to this, underpinned by a shared sense of the urgency and scale of the climate change problem, including the risks it poses for the stability of financial markets and the global economy.

Designing novel contracts between governments (which hold sole responsibility for meeting their commitments under the NDCs) and the private sector (which, while it may participate in the collaborative approaches of Article 6, is not accountable in the same manner) is one aspect of this, with Article 6 pilots developing new types of public–private contractual arrangements (Greiner et al., 2019). The latter represent an important part of the operationalization of

Article 6 that should also guarantee that any profit from the sale of ITMOs or A64.ERs will be reaped by the hosts of cooperative approaches under Art. 6.2 and Article 6, paragraph 4 activities. This includes local stakeholders and communities, some of which have a fundamental role to play in preserving mankind's natural habitat, as in the case of tropical rainforests.[14]

Finally, the role of Article 6 in incentivizing and creating global linkages between low-carbon policies and strategies and, in particular, between national, regional, and local carbon markets is a fundamental aspect of fully realizing the potential economic value of Article 6 in the context of clear and ambitious emissions reduction objectives. According to research from the Joint Global Change Research Institute at the University of Maryland (Yum Sha Et al. 2018), the emissions trading market value of Article 6 could reach US$222 in 2030, US$572 in 2050, and US$1430 in 2100 (in 2015 US$ billion). Around half of the signatory Parties to the Paris Agreement intend to have a contribution from international market mechanisms to meet their NDC pledges (IETA 2018).

The case of CCUS under Article 6

Bringing a market-based mechanism into policy-driven global technological deployment

Technology lies at the heart of the Paris Agreement's climate objectives. However, it is clear that the global pace of developing and deploying clean energy technology has so far not been fast enough to meet these objectives. Government funding alone is far from sufficient to solve this global challenge. In addition to stable government leadership, a market-based carbon mechanism will be needed to mobilize private investment. Article 6 of the Paris Agreement may initiate a global carbon market that can also be linked to existing national low-carbon mechanisms and policies. A global market–based carbon mechanism can be formed to drive greater technological change.

Governments around the world have provided tremendous support for clean energy technology development. However, clean energy technology policies are not only easily impacted by the global fiscal cycle, but are also inadequate to create a competitive carbon market. For instance, China, one of the largest investors in markets for clean energies, has cut the financial support for renewables and electric vehicles (EVs). EV sales had fallen significantly for half of the year 2019, after the government slashed subsidies, with support for solar technologies facing a similar situation in 2019. Outbreak of the coronavirus pandemic worsened the situation. A carbon market, operating within and driven by global policy, is needed to reverse these trends. Article 6 of the Paris

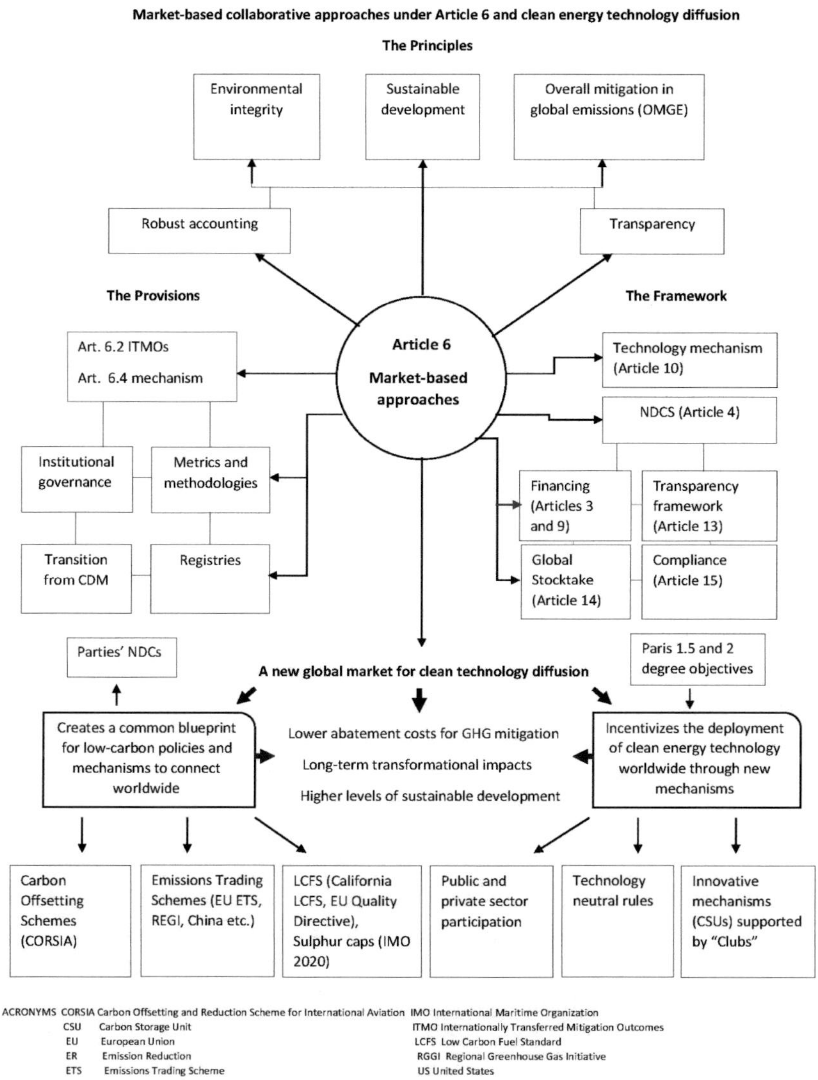

Figure 6.2 Market-based collaborative approaches under Article 6 and clean energy technology diffusion

Agreement may have just offered this opportunity, particularly the deployment of CCS, which cannot be realized without a carbon price.[15]

Article 6: taking CCS development to the next level with existing support

The scale required from CCS cannot simply be achieved through technology-push policies at the domestic level. A well-designed CO2 market that puts competitive prices on CO2 may be the only hope of bringing CCS to the level required in the 2DS (see Table 2). However, so far, only a limited number of market-based emissions reduction programs have incorporated CCS, such as Norway's CO2 tax and California's Low Carbon Fuel Standard (LCFS), even though these are developing, in particular in the United States, which is leading the way in the development of the next wave of CCS technologies (Page 2020).

Importantly, negotiations for the operationalization of the market approaches of Article 6 of the Paris Agreement did involve CCS from the beginning, such as through integrating into the final text the term 'removals.' This leaves open the opportunity for oil-producing countries to develop and market their potential for CCUS in the future (Heidug and Zakkour 2019).

Integrating this type of option into Article 6 helps broaden the support base for CCUS based on 'clubs' of interested Parties (Heidug and Zakkour 2019). So far, at least 20 major economies have been strong champions of CCUS development over the last two decades. Some of them have clearly mentioned CCS in their NDCs, submitted to the Paris Agreement in 2015. In the meantime, there are also some existing multilateral forums or networks that focus on the joint research, development, and deployment of CCS at the governmental level, such as the Carbon Sequestration Leadership Forum, Mission Innovation, and Clean Energy Ministerial. These existing channels provide a solid foundation for discussions linking CCS to a global market among these countries. Several of these have even started their own national or regional carbon markets, such as the United States, Canada, China, and the EU. At the project level, there are 135 commercial CCS facilities globally (27 fully operational), as reported in the 2021 Global CCS Status Report.

Most of these projects are located in countries that have already been a support of CCUS. Many of these projects may have an interest in linking up to a carbon market for revenue. Moreover, the UNFCCC has already had experience in incorporating CCUS into the Clean Development Mechanism in Durban in 2011.

Under the CDM, only those non-Annex 1 countries that have established laws and regulations for CCS projects can host CCS projects. These domestic laws and regulations must address site selection and characterization, access rights to storage sites, financial provisions for each project activity, responsibilities for liability, and responsibilities for the reversal of storage. Before project developers apply for approval by the Executive Board of the CDM (EB), the country's designated operational entity (DOE) needs to validate the project design document. DOEs also need to request registration of a proposed CCS project and to verify emission reduction as a CDM project. Then, DOEs can certify and request the EB to issue CERs accordingly. Article 6 can help bridge the last mile toward a global carbon market, which can encourage both public and private investment in CCUS.

Starting the discussions to link CCS to national and regional carbon markets under Article 6

The Paris Agreement has stimulated a global momentum to deploy market-based policy programs for CO2 emissions reduction. Given its critical role in achieving the well-below 2 degrees goal, now is the best time to begin a policy discussion on how to blend CCS into future carbon markets under the Paris Agreement and what steps can be taken now.

An ideal carbon market would operate at a global scale and offer equal access to all approved emission mitigation approaches. It could, in particular, help connect major regional markets, such as the EU ETS, China's national scheme, RGGI in the United States, which could eventually help accelerate CCUS through dedicated schemes and mechanisms such as NER 300.

Building a market that operates at a global level requires years of stakeholder consultation and needs to be implemented incrementally. This lengthy process well matches the fact that CCS can only be gradually embedded into a global carbon market (Figure 6.2). First, in many countries, CCS is still in the stage of technical demonstration and sector-specific deployment, where technology-push-side policy, government direct support, is more effective. Second, bringing CCS from sectoral demonstration to full economic deployment might take ten years from the perspective of technology innovation. However, it must be clear that CCS is a solution rather than a single technology, which means that certain CCS technologies might enter the commercial stage ahead of others.

At the level of the Paris Agreement, Article 6 could represent an ideal gateway to support the development and deployment at scale of CCS. The inclusion

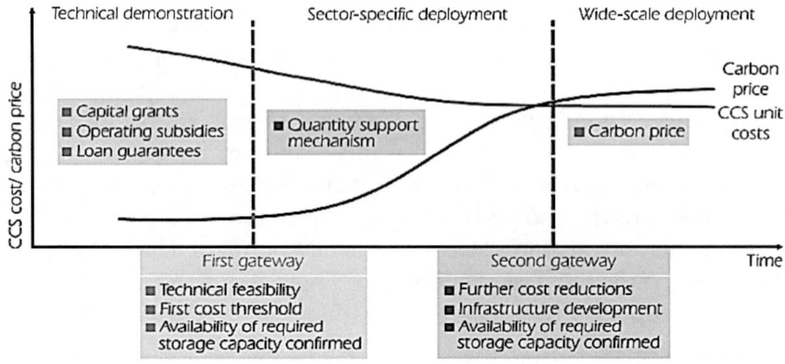

Source: International Energy Agency (IEA), 2012. A policy strategy for carbon capture and storage. Paris: OECD/IEA.

Figure 6.3 Policy Gateways for CCS development

of 'removals' in the final text of the rulebook for Article 6 is fundamental to guaranteeing that CCS and, in particular, CCUS can be developed in the future and traded on international markets as ITMOs.

Meanwhile, standards and schemes operated or to be launched at the national and subnational level offer a great entry point for CCS technologies. These programs include California's LCFS, Oregon's Clean Fuels Program, Canada's Clean Fuel Standard, the EU's Fuel Quality Directive, and IATA's Carbon Offsetting and Reduction Scheme for International Aviation. California's Air Resources Board has included a protocol for CCS in its LCFS, which became effective on January 1, 2019.

Introducing CCS to a CO2 market is highly complicated both from the perspective of technology and from the perspective of the market, not to mention its political feasibility. In general, CCS needs to be recognized in the domestic market first, before being accepted in the global market, just like projects approved under the CDM. Enacting an LCFS requires regulators to make a number of important design decisions, all of which require significant regulatory efforts (Sperling and Yeh, 2010). While LCFS is a very particular type of instrument that is not similar to a broader carbon market, these types of decision-making factors, summarized by Lade and Lawell (2015), could have a profound impact on whether CCS or CCUS can be included in a carbon

Table 6.3 Criteria for including CCS in domestic and international markets

Domestic CO2 Market	International CO2 Market
Legal and policy frameworks Establishment of a legal and regulatory framework for CCS (e.g., liability, environmental integrity) Definition of the CCS value chain in different sectors (e.g., who should be regulated) Establishment of Certified Emission Reduction (e.g., accounting) Establishment of monitoring, reporting, verification guidelines Establishment of CCS tax credits and incentives (e.g., US 45Q) Inclusion of CCS specific mechanisms systematically in emissions trading schemes (e.g., NER 300) Technological requirements Undertaking of environmental impact assessment for CCS projects Addressing the issue of CO2 leakage (e.g. fugitive emission, indirect emissions...) Undertaking of site-characteristics assessment	Article 6 Inclusion of 'removals' in the final text of the Article 6 rulebook Inclusion of provisions to facilitate cross-border transfers Definition of robust carbon accounting rules and measures to quantify ERs accurately and prevent double counting of ERs Creation of a space for policy innovation under Article 6 (e.g., Innovative CCS-specific mechanisms) Definition of links between Art. 6.2 ITMOs, Art. 6.4 activities, and Art.6.8 nonmarket approaches Promotion of cross-jurisdictional linkages of low carbon standards and mechanisms under Article 6, to create a global interconnected market for CCS technology Mobilization of public sector and private sector participation in Article 6 cooperative approaches through adequate national contributions under the Paris Agreement Creation of 'clubs' of interested Parties to support CCS deployment under Article 6

CCUS and oil-producing countries: smart supply-side policies in a future global carbon market

CCS has a critical role in bridging the emissions gap and meeting the climate objectives of the Paris Agreement, as has been highlighted (see Table 6.2). Effective rules under Article 6 are fundamental to setting in place the conditions to incentivize the deployment of CCS globally, building on public policy momentum in countries such as the United States, which is currently the global leader in putting new CCS facilities in place. New market-based global mechanisms under Article 6 need to operate alongside these public policy drivers, connecting emissions trading schemes, tax incentives, LCFS, and international offsetting mechanisms worldwide, thereby creating a global high-value market for CCS and other clean energy technologies.

Designing such a framework under the Paris Agreement can create incentives for the deployment of CCUS in oil-producing countries. The latter are endowed with large-scale capacity to store CO2 in oil reservoirs that can be traded as a mitigation outcome under the market mechanisms of Article 6. Possible mechanisms to connect CCUS to Article 6 include creating a new carbon storage unit that would represent 1 tonne of verified sequestered CO2 tradable as an ITMO (Heidug and Zakkour, 2019).

The Paris Agreement, through its inclusive membership, can thus encourage the development of smart supply-side climate policies that can benefit Parties such as oil-producing countries, while contributing to higher levels of cost-effective global emissions outcomes. These smart or 'progressive' supply-side policies mark a departure from previous policy and seek to mobilize fossil fuel resource holders into taking ambitious and meaningful climate action (Zakkour, Heidug et al, 2020). Against this background, linkages across jurisdictions can incentivize global mitigation outcomes that lie at the intersection of CCS and negative emissions technologies, such as with the deployment of CCUS to deliver carbon-neutral or carbon-negative oil, in line with an increasingly carbon-constrained global policy landscape.

Conclusion

Article 6 implies rethinking international cooperation on a larger scale than under the Kyoto Protocol, based on the universal nature of the Agreement and on its bottom-up emphasis on each country's national circumstances, preferences, and capacities. It represents an opportunity to achieve higher levels of both overall mitigation and sustainable development by facilitating participation from a wider range of Parties and stakeholders, thereby tapping into the comparative advantage of each participating country. A technology-neutral and inclusive approach embedded in the Article 6 rulebook, such as through inclusion of the term 'removals,' enables oil-producing countries to contribute to the carbon-saving effort with critical technologies for which they have the resources and expertise.

Implementing the Article 6 rulebook also requires leaving a space for policy innovation, in order to leverage the opportunities created by the design of a new system and to overcome historical barriers to the deployment of certain types of technology, such as CCUS. Concepts for technology-specific mechanisms that could sit under Article 6 are being developed and could provide the impulse for the creation of more viable business models at an international level, built on 'clubs' of interested Parties and stakeholders (Heidug and Zakkour 2019). Success in the implementation of Article 6 will also be measured by the ability of this new framework to act as a blueprint that could, in time, connect carbon markets worldwide, thereby laying the foundations for a global system operating under a common set of rules.

The COVID-19 crisis underlines the importance of this type of multilateral cooperation to deploy clean energy technology at scale in order to preserve the planet's ecological and environmental stability while promoting sustainable economic recovery and growth. The coronavirus pandemic and its dramatic impacts in terms of public health, livelihoods, and economic outlooks, but also its more positive impacts—such as lower CO2 emissions and the experience of cleaner air in urban areas—highlight more than ever the importance of taking urgent action to address the climate change problem and transition to a carbon-neutral system.

Like COVID-19, climate change is a threat that is difficult to perceive in daily life and is a public goods issue.[16] Some of its impacts are already felt across the globe, such as extreme weather events and rising average temperatures, while future impacts could be akin to those of COVID-19, including the potential appearance of new viruses as a result of global warming. Governments have a particularly central role to play in supporting clean energy innovation in the wake of the COVID-19 pandemic, through the economic recovery packages that are being developed (IEA 2020).

In parallel, the war in Ukraine is already prompting governments— such as EU member states—to profoundly rethink their energy strategies.[17] Investment in clean energy technologies by these governments, such as in nuclear or wind power, is most likely to increase, perhaps dramatically, in order to increase levels of energy independence and security as well as promote regional security among like-minded countries. In this case, GHG emissions may be expected to decrease and the market for carbon credits to grow. The dramatic events in Ukraine may, thus, have as a corollary higher levels of GHG mitigation and more ambitious NDCs, as a result of the synergies that exist between clean energy technologies and energy security.

The impact of the situation in Ukraine on countries' energy and climate policies and the ripple-off effects on the implementation of Article 6 have yet to be fully assessed, with some countries, such as Belgium, already postponing their exit from nuclear energy as a result of Russia's invasion of Ukraine. Both the COVID-19 and Ukraine crises highlight more than ever the importance of international collaboration based on integrated frameworks involving a wide range of countries and stakeholders, such as that represented by the Article 6 system. If implemented effectively, the development of a global carbon market has the potential to bring economic benefits to all signatory Parties to the Agreement, while, at the same time, addressing the climate crisis common to all of humankind and highlighting the value and importance of multilateral cooperation.

Notes

1. For the full text of the Paris Agreement, see https://unfccc.int/sites/default/files/english_paris_agreement.pdf. For the text of the Glasgow Climate Pact, see https://ukcop26.org/wp-content/uploads/2021/11/COP26-Presidency-Outcomes-The-Climate-Pact.pdf
2. In this chapter, the term 'Parties' refers to the signatory Parties to the Paris Agreement, namely, 194 Parties (193 States and the European Union).
3. The Glasgow decision on 6.8 notes that NMAs may include social inclusivity, financial policies and measures, circular economy, blue carbon, just transition of the workforce, and adaptation benefit mechanism. The decision notes that these approaches should involve more than one Party. However, NMAs are not 'transactions' and would not be 'regulated' under the rules of Art. 6.2 and the Art. 6.4 mechanism (Di Leva and Vaughan 2021).
4. However, participation in Article 6 can also be entirely bilateral between two countries, that is, with no participation in a global market, following multilaterally agreed rules.
5. The Clean Development Mechanism (CDM) is one of three flexibility mechanisms under the Kyoto Protocol (adopted in 1997 and entered into force in 2005). Its purpose is to allow Annex I countries (industrialized countries and countries in transition) to finance or develop ER projects in non-Annex I countries (developing countries) as a way of meeting their allocated GHG ER quotas under the Kyoto Protocol. The CDM supports sustainable development and is the de facto vehicle for technology transfer under the Kyoto Protocol (UNFCCC 2022)
6. The San José Principles for High Ambition and Integrity in International Carbon Markets were adopted in December 2019 at COP25 by a group of 31 leading countries. These principles set the basis for a fair and robust global carbon market (Cambio Climate 2019)
7. CA will be required for all carbon credits issued by the host country, regardless of whether they are generated from GHG or sectors covered by its NDC or not, with request for transition by project participants having to take place by 2023 and approval by the Supervisory Board granted by 2025. No temporary or long-term CERs may be used toward NDCs. No CA is required for pre-2020 CERs. (Marcu 2022).
8. Carbon Capture and Storage (CCS) is an ER process designed to prevent large amounts of carbon dioxide (CO2) from being released into the atmosphere. It comprises three stages: capture, transport, and injection for storage. CCUS (Carbon Capture, Utilization, and Storage) is CCS that also enables the 'utilization'

of the CO2. In practice, CCS and CCUS are often used interchangeably. In this chapter, CCUS refers to a subset of CCS technologies.

9. The NIMBY factor—or not-in-my-backyard—has been an obstacle to the deployment of onshore windfarms in countries such as the United Kingdom, while countries such as Germany or Austria have rejected civil nuclear power for historical and ideological reasons.
10. The Convention recognizes the importance of integration into an open economic system, in particular to assist developing country Parties: "The Parties should cooperate to promote a supportive and open international economic system that would lead to sustainable economic growth and development in all Parties, particularly developing country Parties, thus enabling them to better address the problem of climate change (UNFCCC Convention, Article 3 Principles, 5, 1992).
11. Prag, Kimmel, and Hood identify three different types of mitigation goals: Type I or GHG Goals, Type II or non-GHG Goals with short-term impacts on GHG emissions, and Type III or non-GHG Goals with long-term transformational impacts. While the majority of Parties communicate Type I Goals or a combination of Type I and Type II Goals, Type III Goals present challenges in terms of accounting methodologies and, hence, in terms of their potential conversion into tradable units under the market approaches of Article 6. Type III Goals can refer to a policy, a technology, or the use of land, meaning that the impact of these in terms of mitigation outcomes is measurable generally after their implementation or completion (Prag, Kimmel, and Hood 2013)
12. While COP refers to the Conference of the Parties to the Convention, CMA is the Conference of the Parties to the Paris Agreement. 194 out of 198 Parties to the Convention are Parties to the Paris Agreement (https://unfccc.int/process/the-paris-agreement/status-of-ratification).
13. Scarcity is the foundation of the essential problem of economics: the allocation of resources that are limited to needs that are limitless. Smith, Ricarbo, Malthus, and Marx all explored the concept of scarcity. It became widespread as a definition in economics after World War II with Paul Samuelson's classic, *Economics* (published in 1948). Setting ambitious mitigation objectives or targets indicates that only a certain amount of GHG emissions is deemed to be appropriate (e.g., corresponding to the planet's remaining carbon budget or to the Paris Agreement's 1.5/2 degrees objectives). The entitlement to emit, therefore, becomes scarce, and emissions have a cost (even if quotas or entitlements are allocated on a free basis). Reductions, thus, have a value, which creates a functioning carbon market. For more on the design of carbon markets, see Fankhauser and Hepburn, "Designing carbon markets," Parts I and II (Energy Policy 2010).
14. The potential for UNFCCC transfer and crediting mechanisms to contribute to the preservation of rainforests was identified already in the context of the CDM. See "The economic incentives for rain forest conservation across scales" (Kremen et al. 2000).
15. As Schneider underlines, a stable and high carbon price is desirable for the future of technology transfer. See "Understanding the CDM's contribution to Technology Transfer" by Schneider, Malte, Andreas Holzer, and Volker H. Hoffmann (2008).
16. A public good is a good from which no individual may be excluded from using it, and one individual's using it does not decrease its availability to any other individual. It can refer to air, open spaces or public libraries for instance. A public good may give rise to a "free-rider" problem, as in the case of climate change, where

individual users wish or are tempted to make use of the public good while leaving its cost to others.

17. Such is the case of Belgium, which has decided to postpone its exit from nuclear power by ten years and increase its investment in renewables, in the wake of the situation in Ukraine and its implications in terms of prices and national security. https://www.euronews.com/2022/03/19/nuclear-energy-belgium-postpones-phase-out-by-10-years-due-to-ukraine-war

References

Asian Development Bank. 2018. Decoding Article 6 of the Paris Agreement. April. https://www.adb.org/publications/decoding-article-6-paris-agreement

Bonvilian, William and Weiss, Charles. 2009. *Structuring an Energy Technology Revolution.* Chapter 2, p. 28. MIT Press.

Cambio Climate. 2019. https://cambioclimatico.go.cr/press-release-leading-countries-set-benchmark-for-carbon-markets-with-san-jose-principles/

Charles E.Di Leva and Scott Vaughan. 2021 The Paris Agreement's new Article 6 rules https://www.iisd.org/articles/paris-agreement-article-6-rules. 13 December.

Coninck, Heleen de, and Ambuj Sagar. 2015a. "Making Sense of Policy for Climate Technology Development and Transfer." *Climate Policy.* https://doi.org/10.1080/14693062.2014.953909

Coninck, Heleen De, and Ambuj Sagar. 2015b. "Technology in the 2015 Paris Climate Agreement and beyond." *International Centre for Trade and Sustainable Development,* no. 42.

Coninck, Heleen De, and Daniel Puig. 2015. "Assessing climate change mitigation technology interventions by international institutions". *Climatic Change.* Issue 131, 417-422. https://doi.org/10.1007/s10584-015-1344-z

Dechezleprêtre, Antoine, Glachant, Matthieu, Haščič, Ivan, Johnstone, Nick and Ménière, Yann. 2020. Invention and Transfer of Climate Change Mitigation Technologies on a Global Scale: A Study Drawing on Patent Data. January 11. SSRN: https:// ssrn .com/ abstract = 1414227 or http:// dx .doi .org/ 10 .2139/ ssrn .1414227

Dechezleprêtre, A., Glachant, M. & Ménière, Y. What Drives the International Transfer of Climate Change Mitigation Technologies? Empirical Evidence from Patent Data. *Environ Resource Econ* **54,** 161–178 (2013). https://doi.org/10.1007/s10640-012-9592-0

Dobrov, Gennady. 1979. The strategy for organized technology in the light of hard-, soft- and org- ware interaction. Long Range Planning Volume 12 Number 14. International Institute for Applied Systems Analysis. Laxenburg, Austria.

Ellis, Jane, Luca Lo Re, Manasvini Vaidyula and Andrew Prag. 2019. Designing the Article 6.4 mechanism: assessing selected baseline approaches and their implications. Climate Change Expert Group. Paper No. 2019 (5). OECD. November. https://www.oecd.org/environment/cc/Designing-the-Article-6-4-mechanism-assessing-selected-baseline-approaches-and-their-implications.pdf

Greiner, Sandra, Thiago Chagas, Nicole Kramer, Axel Michaelowa, Dario Brescia, Stephan Hoch et al.2019."Moving Towards Next Generation Carbon Markets : Observations from Article 6 pilots". Climate Finance Innovators. Climate Focus and Perspectives ed. https://climatefocus.com/publications/moving-towards-next-generation-carbon-markets-observations-article-6-pilots/

Heidug, Wolfgang and Paul Zakkour. 2019. A Mechanism for CCS in the Post-Paris Era: Piloting Results-Based Finance and Supply Side policy under Article 6. KAPSARC. April.

Hood, Christina et al. 2014. GHG or not GHG: Accounting for diverse mitigation contributions climate framework. Organization for Economic Cooperation and Development (OECD). Environment Directorate and international Energy Agency. Climate Change Expert Group. May.

International Emissions Trading Association (IETA). 2018. Piecing together the future of carbon markets. *IETA Insights Quarterly Report.* No.4. Greenhouse Gas Market Report. November. p.9.

International Energy Agency (IEA), 2012. A policy strategy for carbon capture and storage. Paris: OECD/IEA. https://www.iea.org/reports/a-policy-strategy-for-carbon-capture-and-storage

International Energy Agency (IEA), 2019. Public low-carbon energy RD&D budget in IEA member countries, 1977-2018. Paris: IEA. https://www.iea.org/data-and-statistics/charts/public-low-carbon-energy-rd-and-d-budget-in-iea-member-countries-1977-2018

International Energy Agency (IEA). 2020. Clean Energy Innovation in the Covid-19 Crisis: Investing in Today to Secure a Sustainable Tomorrow. July 7. https://www.iea.org/articles/clean-energy-innovation-in-the-covid-19-crisis

International Energy Agency (IEA). 2021. Tracking Clean Energy Technology Progress. https://www.iea.org/reports/tracking-clean-energy-progress-2021

International Panel on Climate Change. 2000. Special Report on Methodological and Technological Issues on Technology Transfer (SRTT). A Special Report of Working Group III. Summary for Policy Makers, p.3.https://www.ipcc.ch/report/methodological-and-technological-issues-in-technology-transfer/

Kremen C, J. O. Niles, M. G. Dalton, G. C. Daily, P. R. Ehrlich, J. P. Fay, D. Grewak and R. P. Guillery. 2000. "Economic Incentives for Rain Forest Conservation Across Scales." *Science* 288 (5472): 1828–1832. https://doi.org/10.1126/science.288.5472.1828

Lade, Gabriel E. and Lawell, C.-Y. Cynthia Lin, 2015. "The Design and Economics of Low Carbon Fuel Standards." Economics Publications. 99.
https://lib.dr.iastate.edu/econ_las_pubs/99

Locket, Hudson. 2019. "US manufactures hit harder than China's in trade war". Financial Times. 13 November.

Lundvall, Bengt-Åke & Borrás, Susana. 2004. Science, Technology and Innovation Policy. The Oxford Handbook of Innovation. 10.1093/oxfordhb/9780199286805.003.0022.

Marcu, Andrei. 2022. Article 6 Rulebook, a post COP26 assessment. 22 November. https://ercst.org/wp-content/uploads/2021/11/20211122-COP26-Art6-final

Ockwell, David, and Rob Byrne. 2016. *Sustainable Energy for All.* p.15 https://doi.org/10.4324/9781315621623.

Ori, Sam. The Ukraine crisis is a wake-up call for energy security. 2022. March 1. https://www.forbes.com/sites/ucenergy/2022/03/01/the-ukraine-crisis-is-a-wake-up-call-for-energy-security/?sh=670f864c6ba1

Page, Brad. 2020. "US leads new wave of carbon capture storage deployment". May https://thehill.com/opinion/energy-environment/476783-us-leads-new-wave-of-carbon-capture-and-storage-deployment, Accessed May 2020.

Prag, A., M. Kimmel and C. Hood (2013), "A role for more diverse metrics in framing climate commitments?" OECD/IEA CCXG Presentation at COP19 side event, 13 November 2013.

Rogelj, Joeri and Piers Forster. 2019. "A new approach for understanding the remaining carbon budget". Carbon Brief. July. https://www.carbonbrief.org/guest-post-a-new-approach-for-understanding-the-remaining-carbon-budget. Accessed February 2020.

Saggi, K. 2002. "Trade, Foreign Direct Investment, and International Technology Transfer: A Survey." *The World Bank Research Observer* 17 (2): 191–235. https://doi.org/10.1093/wbro/17.2.191.

Schneider, Malte, Andreas Holzer, and Volker H. Hoffmann. 2008. "Understanding the CDM's Contribution to Technology Transfer." *Energy Policy* 36 (8): 2930–38. https://doi.org/10.1016/j.enpol.2008.04.009.

Sperling D. and Yeh S. 2010. Toward a global low carbon fuel standard. Transport Policy. Vol 17 issue 1, 47-49.

Tsayem Demaze, Moïse. 2013. "Les Retombées Du « Mécanisme Pour Un Développement Propre » Pour Les Pays En Développement : Une Faible Réception de Technologie et Un Développement Durable Vague." *Les Cahiers d'Outre-Mer* 66 (262): 247–76. https://doi.org/10.4000/com.6870.

United Nations Climate Change Conference UK 2021. COP26 keeps 1.5C alive and finalizes the Paris Agreement. https://ukcop26.org/cop26-keeps-1-5c-alive-and-finalises-paris-agreement/

United Nations Framework Convention on Climate Change. 2015. Paris Agreement. https://unfccc.int/sites/default/files/english_paris_agreement.pdf

United Nations Framework Convention on Climate Change. Clean Development Mechanism. Accessed 10 April 2022. https://cdm.unfccc.int/

United Nations Framework Convention on Climate Change. 1992. The Convention. https://unfccc.int/files/essential_background/background_publications_htmlpdf/application/pdf/conveng.pdf

United Nations Environment Program (UNEP). 2021. Emissions Gap Report. https://www.unep.org/resources/emissions-gap-report-2021

Watson, Jim, Rob Byrne, David Ockwell, and Michele Stua. 2015. "Lessons from China: Building Technological Capabilities for Low Carbon Technology Transfer and Development." *Climatic Change* 131 (3): 387–99. https://doi.org/10.1007/s10584-014-1124-1.

Yum Sha, Ryna, Gui, Stephanie Waldhoff, Sonny Kim and Jae Edmonds. 2018. The Value of Article 6. University of Maryland joint Global Change Research Institute. Presentation at 18th IEA-IETA-EPRI Annual Workshop on Greenhouse Gas Emissions Trading, 6-7 November, Paris.

Zakkour, Paul, Wolfgang Heidug, Andrew Howard, R. Stuart Haszeldine, Myles R.Allen & David Hone. 2021. "Progessive Supply-Side Policy Under the Paris Agreement to Enhance Geological Carbon Storage." *Climate Policy* 21(1): 63–77. https://doi.org/10.1080/14693062.2020.1803039

PART III

Global scenarios: harnessing the benefits of global geo-economic shifts

7 Big data, black holes, and tapping the value of futures price data

Hilary Till and Joseph Eagleeye

Introduction

This chapter will discuss inferring crude oil market fundamentals through price-relationship data, largely through the perspective of a commodity futures trader. In doing so, the chapter will briefly cover (1) the promise of big data, (2) the reality of data 'black holes,' (3) the wealth of futures price data, (4) what futures prices reveal about petroleum-complex fundamentals, and (5) caveats on the use of price data. The conclusion notes that the most important future research related to the chapter's topic is in the provision of accurate fundamental data, given emerging controversies on this issue.

The Promise of Big Data

After the energy crisis of the 1970s, the United States committed to a very "ambitious and comprehensive effort to collect detailed information on the production, processing, distribution and consumption of energy," as described by Kemp (2015). "The result is [that] the market has [very] good real-time data on what is happening to fuel supply and demand in the United States" via the US Energy Information Administration (EIA), observed Kemp (2015). A further consequence is that there is a great deal of promise for the use of "big data" in the US energy markets, whether it is for (1) algorithmic trading, (2) industry cost reduction, or (3) tapping the value of data embedded in the energy industry, as noted by Anderson (2017a).

Algorithmic Trading

Commodity trading is different from other asset classes in that new fundamental data that seemingly should impact prices (at least of certain tenors) is continuously coming at us, including data on (1) geopolitical developments, (2) the weather, (3) rig counts, (4) gasoline sales, (5) gas storage, (6) crude and product inventory, (7) oil and liquefied natural gas tanker positions, and (8) power plant outages. Perhaps no other asset class consistently receives as much new, material fundamental information into the market that needs to be assimilated. Thus, the 'bigness' of the data involved can potentially dwarf that of other asset classes, and the value of high-tech analytics may hold great potential.

Industry Cost Reduction

Examples of the application of big data in the energy industry include (1) component failure prediction, (2) maintenance optimization, (3) transmission grid infrastructure management, and (4) oil and gas imaging and the prediction of geology and drilling results. Improvements in these areas can have a dramatic impact on industry cost structure, as seen during the shale oil revolution.

Tapping the Value of Data Embedded in Industry

Although a wealth of data is potentially available, it is simply not collected currently. For example, utilities have not historically kept real-time, granular records of electricity consumption. Companies are looking at tapping this information. As a result, energy companies serving retail customers could eventually see themselves, in effect, as data and information companies, in addition to their primary functions.

The Reality of Black Holes

Emerging Markets

Even though there are a number of potential applications for big data in the United States, one should also note the reality of black holes in emerging markets and even in some aspects of the petroleum-complex markets in the United States. As pointed out by Kemp (2015), emerging markets accounted "for more than half of global oil demand for the first time in 2013 and 2014," so now most of the oil market is not transparent. As a result, the head of Citi's commodity research department, Ed Morse, stated in CFTC Talks (2017):

With "emerging markets ... [becoming] increasingly dominant in the international economy, we have more and more 'black holes'" in data coverage. "We know what [the level of crude oil] inventories are ... in OECD countries ... We have a ... decent idea in some other countries; Saudi Arabia is very good, for example, at posting their inventories of products and crude oil, as is Brazil," explained Morse. But "China, which produces a lot of statistics, has a lot of missing barrels, a lot of missing molecules, [and] a lot of missing tons of grains because their inventory [data] is a state secret. ... So [data] black holes are getting larger and larger and impacting our understanding of [commodity] fundamentals."

Some Markets in the United States

But, to be complete, not every physical market location in the United States has immediately available data. The following example is from Martin (2017) of J.P. Morgan Commodities Research. The August and September 2017 hurricanes "hit the Texas refining system hard." The "true impact" of refinery outages could not be directly understood because not all affected markets published data, so Martin (2017) noted that commodity researchers would be looking "at price signals as a guide for the underlying [crude oil and product] market dynamics." And that introduces the central concept of this chapter: how oil market traders and analysts have learned to use price-relationship data, such as examining futures spreads, to infer petroleum-complex fundamentals.

The Wealth of Futures Price Data

The Evolution of Pricing in Oil Markets

Figure 7.1 is a diagram on the evolution of pricing in oil markets since the 1960s, from long-term contracts to more spot-oriented market pricing, which enables us to potentially deduce market fundamentals. This evolution reflected an observation by Morse in CFTC Talks (2017): "The whole framework for commodities changes rapidly. Sometimes more rapidly than [what] you [would] think."

Petroleum-Complex Futures Markets Provide Needed Transparency

Even when fundamental data on oil markets is sparse or opaque, large-scale supply and demand shifts leave footprints in futures price relationships, from which one can potentially infer the market's fundamentals. In the presence of

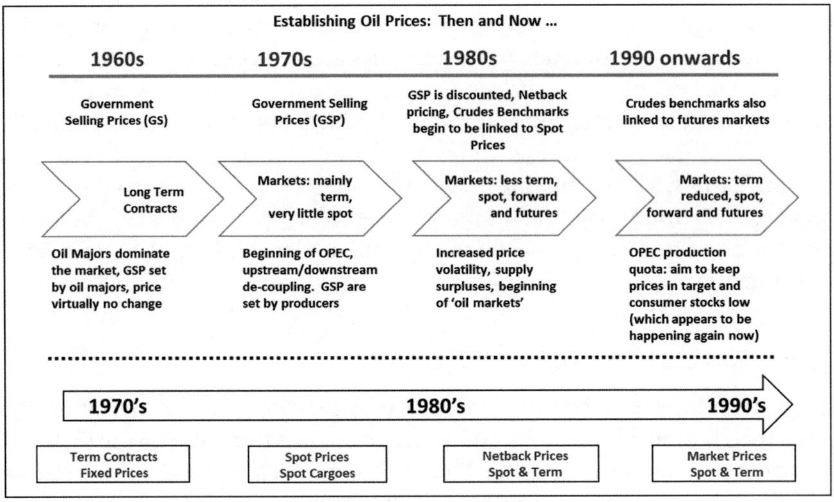

Source: Chart based on Tchilinguirian (2006), Slide 4.

Figure 7.1 Evolution of Pricing in Oil Markets

active futures markets, an observer need not be a member of a cartel or a large corporation to gain insights into oil markets.

What Prices Reveal about Petroleum-Complex Fundamentals

We will now launch into the heart of the chapter, that is, what price data can potentially reveal about petroleum-complex fundamentals. This section discusses how price relationships can (a) incentivize fundamental behavior, (b) drive fundamental behavior, (c) provide proxies for physical market information, (d) furnish an understanding of Chinese demand, (e) signal how well the domestic US crude oil surplus was absorbed, and (f) indicate the market's perception of the marginal cost of production for crude oil.

Incentivizing Fundamental Behavior

A future trader interprets a commodity's price as part of a dynamic process. A commodity's price moves in whatever direction needed in order to elicit a supply or demand response that will balance a commodity market. It may be useful to review the technical aspects of this interplay.

Building Distillate Inventories before Winter

Figure 7.2 shows the typical seasonal pattern of building distillate inventories from April through the fall in the United States. In this graph, distillate inventories are represented as a fraction of the prevailing crude oil inventories. The graph illustrates that once sufficient inventories are built, the winter heating oil crack spread collapses: There is no longer a need to incentivize the production of heating oil. For clarification, the heating oil crack spread is the difference between the price of heating oil and the price of crude oil and provides the profitability of refining crude oil into heating oil.

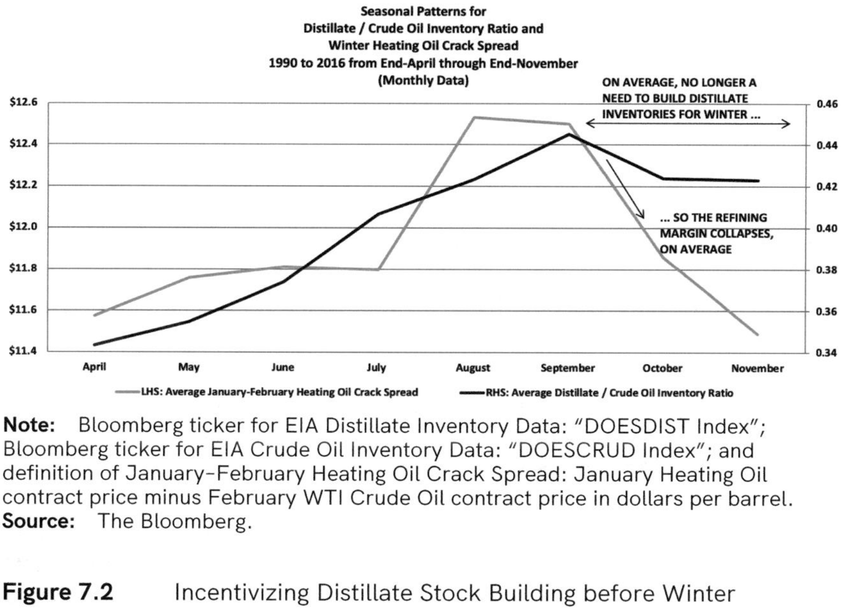

Note: Bloomberg ticker for EIA Distillate Inventory Data: "DOESDIST Index"; Bloomberg ticker for EIA Crude Oil Inventory Data: "DOESCRUD Index"; and definition of January-February Heating Oil Crack Spread: January Heating Oil contract price minus February WTI Crude Oil contract price in dollars per barrel.
Source: The Bloomberg.

Figure 7.2 Incentivizing Distillate Stock Building before Winter

Hurricane Katrina

One can also examine the aftermath of Hurricane Katrina in the United States in 2005 for another good example of the dynamic interplay between an oil product's price and its supply and demand situation. According to a 2005 Dow Jones Newswire report, "[Hurricane] Katrina shut in nearly all of oil and gas production in the Gulf of Mexico. The large-scale supply disruption and fear of an economic shock triggered a massive [domestic and international] government[al] response," including fuel releases from the International Energy Agency (IEA) and crude oil releases from the US Strategic Petroleum Reserve.

The dramatic governmental response caused gasoline prices to decline from their post-Katrina peak.

Further, with that response, fears of an economic slump diminished, which in turn caused deferred interest rate contracts to decline, as the market resumed pricing in the expectation that the Federal Reserve Board could continue tightening interest rates at the time.

Refinery Constraints

Another example of price incentivizing fundamental behavior is from 2007 through mid-2008. At that time, "refiners were using more marginal capacity and could not raise gasoline or diesel output without producing excess fuel oil," explained Ribeiro et al. (2009) of J.P. Morgan Global Asset Allocation & Alternative Investments Research. As the IEA (2006) had earlier noted, "For refiners to run profitably, gasoline and diesel prices ha[d] to rise to offset the discounts needed to clear the fuel oil surplus and to encourage marginal refiners to process additional crude oil." This phenomenon became visible in the 'upgrading spread,' which can be defined as the difference between the maximum price of transportation fuels and the price of fuel oil. When the upgrading spread widened as much as it did from 2007 to mid-2008, analysts inferred that there was "a shortage of refinery capacity" and that there was "insufficient flexibility in the refining system to meet the demand for lighter products" that are used as transportation fuels," as stated in Ribeiro et al. (2009). When markets are tight, prices increase "to provide the right incentives for both current production and future investment," as put forth by the J.P. Morgan researchers. And, in fact, "the first half of 2009 [was to] represent … the first large increase in refinery capacity additions," observed Tchilinguirian (2008), having previously noted that "oil refining capacity [had] peaked in 1981" (2006).

Driving Fundamental Behavior

Arguably, hedging opportunities became much more relevant in the crude oil markets with the shale oil revolution. Regarding shale oil, "from a financing perspective, the great bulk of the positive cash flows occurs early in each project's life. This is preferred from a general risk and discounting perspective, but also figures very importantly … [in] hedging efforts, as the oil [derivatives] market … offers liquidity only out about 2 to 3 years or so. So there's a [good] … match between forward market liquidity and the shale oil production profile," as explained in Till and Jesse (2016). As a result, one can monitor when there is a sharp pick up in hedging activity, which would then be expected to eventually translate into US rig count additions.

Proxying the Physical Market with Futures Spreads

One can also potentially infer aspects of the physical oil market by examining the level of futures calendar spreads. A 'calendar spread' consists of taking offsetting positions during the different delivery months of a particular futures contract. There is a considerable amount of evidence that one can estimate the amount of crude oil commercial inventories, at least in Organisation for Economic Co-operation and Development (OECD) countries, by reference to the level of crude oil futures spreads. As explained by Longson and Volynsky (2015), "Prompt [term] structure can be a good real-time proxy for the physical [oil] market, and the data proves that out."

Caveat: Inventories Are Only Part of the Picture

There are several caveats on the importance of inventory-related data. We had previously noted that there is a contemporaneous relationship between futures spreads and inventory data. The historical relationship of inventory data with the outright price of crude oil is a bit more complicated.

Hicks and Smith (2006) pointed out that the price of oil had been highly negatively correlated to the OECD inventory situation before OPEC (Organization of the Petroleum Exporting Countries) spare capacity started becoming an issue in 2004. At that point, the outright price of oil and oil inventories were not very correlated from mid-2004 through the end of 2005. Their analysis represented the OECD industry oil stocks in terms of the number of days covering forward demand. Once OPEC spare capacity came under pressure, oil prices became highly negatively correlated to spare capacity as a percentage of worldwide demand. Hicks and Smith (2006) showed that inventories are only part of the picture in examining the drivers for the outright price of oil. At least historically, when OPEC spare capacity has become low, inventories alone are not as significant a driver of price, a point covered in Till (2016).

Caveat: Spare Capacity Has Mattered in Interpreting the Oil Futures Curve Shape

Prior to 2004, if there were scarcity in the crude oil market, one could expect two outcomes: (1) increasing spot prices and (2) trading of the front-month price to an ever larger premium to deferred-delivery contracts. In this state of the world, the market would be encouraging the commodity's immediate use rather than its storage. In this case, the outright price of oil and the front-to-back spread were highly positively correlated. During 2004, OPEC's immediately deliverable spare capacity collapsed.

When there has been inadequate spare capacity, the futures curve has provided a return for storage since there would be a pressing need to incentivize precautionary stockholdings in oil. In this state of the world, the prompt futures price has traded at ever more of a discount to provide a sufficient return for storage, and the spot price of oil has increased to encourage consumer conservation. In this case, the outright price of oil and the front-to-back spread have been highly negatively correlated. In the case of 2008, eventually a demand-destroying oil price spike occurred at low levels of OPEC spare capacity, followed by the dramatic drop in the price of oil. With the demand destruction that occurred as a result of the price spike, OPEC spare capacity recovered.

An Additional Caveat on Spare Capacity

One should note that an analyst needs to also include US tight oil excess supply, and not just OPEC spare capacity, in considering spare productive capacity, as explained by Foreman (2017). But again, regarding outright prices, as long as surplus capacity has not been at pinch-point levels, inventories have been an important driver of the price of oil.

Understanding Chinese Demand

In 2005, oil futures traders first became aware of not solely relying on OECD data to make predictions on the direction of oil price relationships. It was at that time that the potential impact of temporarily concentrated Chinese demand started to reveal itself through various futures price relationships. Observers of price action in the commodity markets noted a common waxing and waning of prices in crude oil, soybeans, and copper coincident with the Chinese New Year's holiday in 2005, presumably when Chinese demand was temporarily absent. This factor appeared to overwhelm any other factor in these three markets. Stein (2005) wrote that 2005 marked the "first business cycle where Chinese demand is having a global effect on prices, notably of energy and other raw materials."

Later, in the summer of 2008, the heating oil crack spread indicated an extraordinary demand for middle distillates. There were no severe weather events, supply disruptions, or large-scale trading blowups in the United States or Europe at the time, so it was not immediately apparent why this spread should spike so extraordinarily—that is, except for news from China, including the devastating earthquake in China, which damaged power supply grids, and pre-Olympic stocking of petroleum products in order to ensure that there would be no shortages during the historic Beijing Olympics. These were among the key events in China that drove a spike in diesel and gasoline imports, as illustrated in Figure 7.3.

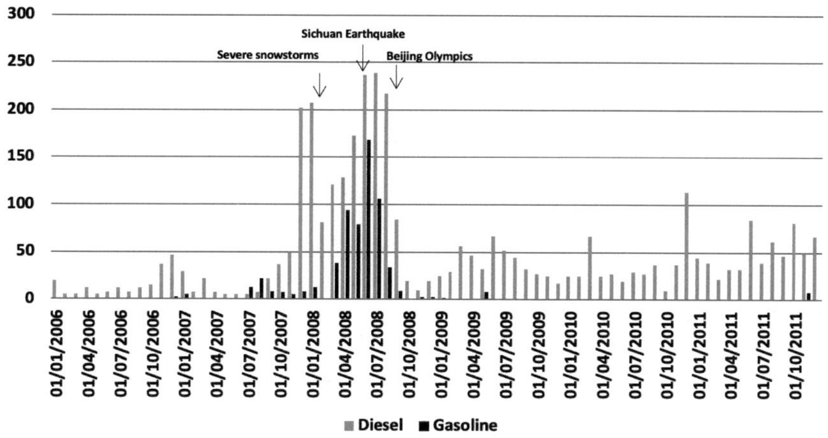

Note: Chart based on Fenton (2012), Slide 24. Bloomberg ticker for Diesel imports: CNIVDF; Bloomberg ticker for Gasoline imports: CNIVGSOL. Bloomberg data was converted from monthly tonnes to barrels per day using the CME Group's Conversion Calculator, which was accessed at: http://www.cmegroup.com/tools-information/calc_refined.html on November 27, 2017.
Source: China Customs General Administration and The Bloomberg.

Figure 7.3 Chinese Gasoline and Diesel Imports Surged in 2008 Due to a Number of Key Events in China (Thousands of Barrels per Day)

As discussed in the Alphaville section of the *Financial Times* (2013), "In oil market analyses, it is essential that refined products are also taken into account, as it is misleading to solely look at crude prices, crude inventory, and crude supply ... in isolation," which we can also conclude from this chapter's earlier section on upgrading spreads.

In understanding past Chinese-related demand through price signals, one can also draw from Kaufmann and Ullman (2009). These researchers investigated "where changes in the price of crude oil originate and how they spread ..." Their paper did so "by examining causal relationships among prices for crude oils from North America, Europe, Africa, and the Middle East." The authors looked into where "innovations in world oil prices enter the market," using price data from a variety of grades of oil from both OPEC and non-OPEC nations from 1987 through March 2008. One of their results was that the spot price for Dubai–Fateh oil had been a "'gateway' for innovations to crude oil prices." "A large fraction of the crude oil shipped to Asian nations from the Middle East (more than 10 ... [million barrels per day]) uses the spot price for Dubai–Fateh as a benchmark ... As such, innovations in the spot price for Dubai–Fateh may [have] reflect[ed] increasing demand [over time] in Asia," they inferred.

Managing the Domestic US Crude Oil Surplus

At the end of 2013, alert futures traders had an early signal that, as phrased by J.P. Commodity Research (2013), "the boom in ... [domestic oil] production ha[d] been well absorbed by existing U.S. infrastructure." Refinery margins no longer needed to consistently rally at the end of each month to provide an extraordinary return for transporting domestic crude oil, in whatever way possible, to US refineries. This observation is illustrated in Figure 7.4, which shows the degradation in performance of a bullish refining-margin trading strategy, starting in late 2013. This graph displays the cumulative performance of entering into futures spread trades that represented near-month refinery margins from the end of 2010 through the end of 2015.

Figure 7.4 specifically shows (a) how the cumulative performance of the bullish refining-margin strategy leveled off at the end of 2013 and (b) how, as of the end of 2013, the rolling t-statistic for this trade began falling off. At that time, the markets no longer needed to incentivize extraordinary profits for transporting and refining burgeoning domestic crude oil supplies.

The Marginal Cost of Production for Crude Oil

As a final note on what futures prices can potentially reveal about petroleum-complex fundamentals, one can examine the five-year-ahead futures price to understand what the market's perception is of the then-current marginal cost of oil production, as explained by Goldman Sachs Economic Research (2015). Anderson (2017b), though, cautions that one should perform a more precise analysis of long-run variable costs than simply inspecting five-year forward market prices.

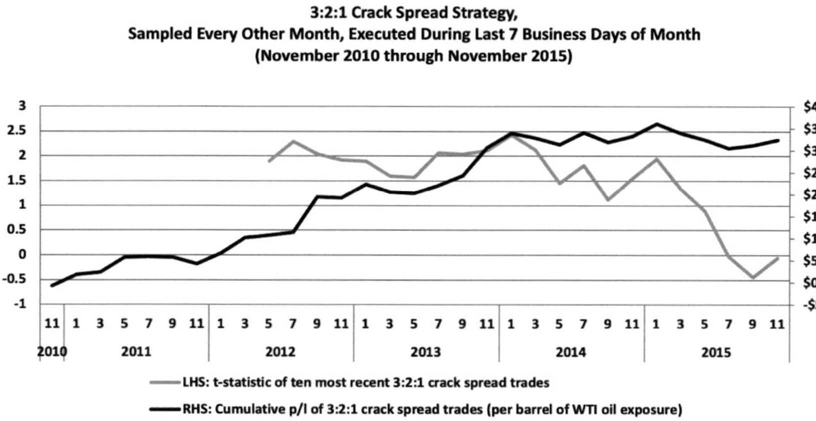

Note: "A 3:2:1 crack spread reflects gasoline and distillate production revenues from the U.S. refining industry, which generally produces roughly 2 barrels of gasoline for every barrel of distillate. The 3:2:1 crack spread is calculated by subtracting the price of 3 barrels of oil from the price of 2 barrels of gasoline and 1 barrel of distillate," as noted in https://www.eia.gov/todayinenergy/detail.php?id=1630, accessed on October 12, 2017. Here, the 3:2:1 crack spread was calculated using these proportions, but then the total was divided by 3, thereby expressing the spread as per one barrel of crude oil. Further, the spread was calculated with the gasoline and heating oil nearby futures contracts and also with the WTI crude oil second nearby futures contract.
Source: The Bloomberg.

Figure 7.4 Degradation in Performance of a Bullish Refining-Margin Trading Strategy, Starting in Late 2013

Caveats on the Use of Price Data

We will now cover some of the caveats on the use of price data, namely, that prices can be driven by purely technical effects and that forward prices are not predictions.

Purely Technical Effects

Dynamic Hedging

One purely technical effect is the temporary impact on futures prices from the hedging of option deals. In the case of oil, Verleger (2007) explained how the activity of traders may have (temporarily) interacted with market fundamentals to magnify the oil price rally during the fall of 2007. Verleger noted how large-scale industrial consumers, such as airlines, had purchased out-of-the-money call options on oil futures contracts to protect against price rises. Obviously, someone had to sell the industrial consumers these options: the money-center banks. As crude oil rose toward the level(s) where there was a concentration of call option strikes, this might have created a cascade of dynamic hedging purchases by bank dealers, who in turn were hedging the options they had written. This might have caused the oil price to (temporarily) rise still further.

In the terminology of derivatives traders, the bank dealers likely had maximum 'negative gamma': Their exposure to being short crude was rising at an accelerating rate, forcing them to purchase crude oil contracts at an accelerating rate, too.

Once market participants became aware of this interaction effect, it has been common since 2008 to note where the concentrations of option strikes are in the crude oil futures market. As the aforementioned example should make clear, futures traders are aware that market microstructure effects may predominate as the driver of price over short timeframes.

Liquidation Pressure

Another purely technical factor is the temporary effect of liquidation pressure. Futures traders are aware that when traders have to liquidate large positions, this can be a temporary, but meaningful, driver of price. A highly leveraged fund can enter into a "critical liquidation cycle," whereby once a fund crosses a threshold of losses, a cycle of investor redemptions can occur and/or the fund's credit providers may demand the reduction of leverage, and the value of the fund's holdings thereby declines precipitously as the fund sells off holdings in a distressed fashion (De Souza and Smirnov, 2014).

Both of the technical factors mentioned in this section can cause a temporary overshooting of prices.

Not Predictions

Finally, a futures market is not a forecasting agency; it facilitates risk sharing and the efficient allocation of resources. To expect futures prices to only reflect predictions of future prices ignores its other functions. Figure 7.5 shows how the "forward curve [for oil has] not [been] a good price predictor, but still functions well for hedging storage costs and requirements," citing, once again, Ed Morse, this time from a Citi presentation at the Center for Strategic and International Studies (CSIS) in 2017.

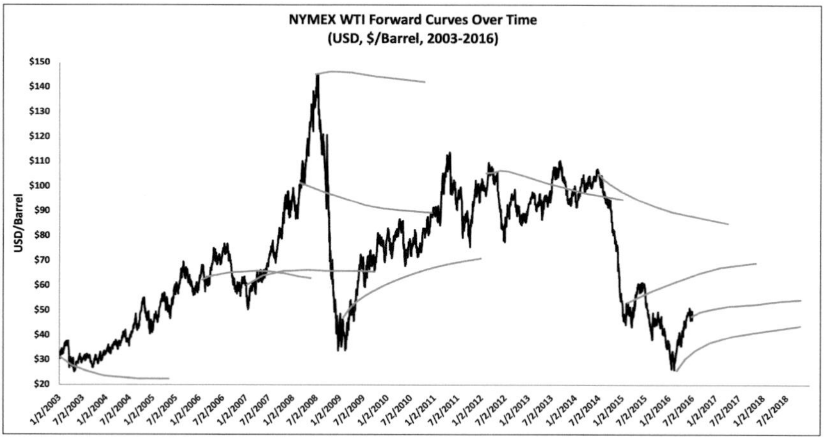

Note: Chart based on CSIS (2017).
Source: The Bloomberg.

Figure 7.5 New York Mercantile Exchange (NYMEX) West Texas Intermediate (WTI) Forward Curves over Time, Overlaid Against Crude Oil Front-Month Futures Price Realizations

A Futures Trader's Conclusion

Instead of asking whether the fundamentals justify the oil price, this chapter adopted the view of a veteran oil futures trader and asked the opposite question: What is the price telling us about the expected value of fundamentals? The reason for this outlook is as follows: The market imposes sufficient discipline to prevent a trader from ignoring price, except for a very short space of time!

Future Research Agenda

This chapter focused on using market signals to infer the fundamentals in the petroleum complex, but that emphasis is not meant to undercut the need for accurate, politically neutral data in these markets. Perhaps somewhat surprisingly, a dispute on this matter flared up at the end of March 2022 with "OPEC+ decid[ing] to stop using the IEA's data, replacing it with reports from consultancies Wood Mackenzie and Rystad Energy. OPEC+ uses the data to assess crude oil production and the conformity of participating countries with agreed output curbs," wrote El Dahan et al. (2022). The IEA responded by noting that "its data and analysis was 'rigorous and objective,'" according to El Dahan et al. (2022). The decision by OPEC+ followed the sharply contrasting analyses by Rystad Energy and the IEA from a year earlier, where Rystad forecasted that "[t]housands of new oil wells and hundreds of new oilfields will be needed to meet global demand even if it falls sharply towards the middle of the century," according to Reuters (2021). Continued Reuters (2021): "The IEA, on the other hand, had concluded that "investors should not fund new oil, gas and coal projects if the world wants to reach net-zero emissions by mid-century." Arguably, accurate oil data and realistic future scenarios are crucial for avoiding a "messy energy transition" and "energy poverty," as covered in Till (2021). After all, without objective information on these crucial markets, there is a risk that policy errors could have meaningful humanitarian consequences. Therefore, the most pressing future research in the oil markets consists of both (a) providing transparent and accurate data on the petroleum complex and (b) carrying out pragmatic forecasts on these crucial markets.

- This chapter draws on insights from Till (2008) and Till and Eagleeye (2017).

References

Anderson, Thorvin [Energy Industry Analytics Professional] (2017a), Private correspondence, 2 July.

Anderson, Thorvin (2017b), Private correspondence, 19 December.

[CFTC] Commodity Futures Trading Commission (2017), 'CFTC Talks: Andrew Busch, Chief Market Advisor, with Edward Morse, Global Head of Commodities Research, Citi', Washington, D.C., 19 September.

[CSIS] Center for Strategic and International Studies (2017), Citi Presentation by Edward Morse, Washington, D.C.

De Souza, C. and M. Smirnov (2004), 'Dynamic Leverage', *Journal of Portfolio Management*, **31** (1), 25-39.

El Dahan, M., Ghaddar, A. and A. Lawler (2022), 'OPEC+ Sticks to Modest Oil Output Rises, Ditches IEA Data', *Reuters*, 31 March.

Dow Jones Newswire (2005), 'Nymex Crude Tumbles as Output Recovers', 6 September.

Fenton, C. (2012), 'On Estimating the Commodity Risk Premium', Slide Presentation, J.P. Morgan Commodities Research, May.

Financial Times (2013), 'The Role of Dark Inventory in the Commodities Bull Run of 2008', Alphaville column by Izabella Kaminska, Comment section, 25 November.

Foreman, R. (2017), 'OPEC Policies, Production and Price Responses', Slide Presentation at the EIA Workshop on 'Economic Activity and Oil Prices,' Washington, D.C., 19 September.

Goldman Sachs Economic Research (2015), 'Commodities and Currencies in the New Oil Order', March 20.

Hicks, B. and E. Smith (2006), 'Trends in Energy and Base Metals - Outlook for 2006', U.S. Global Investors, Inc., Slide Presentation, 26 January.

International Energy Agency (2006), 'Oil Market Report', 12 May.

J.P. Morgan Commodity Research (2013), 'Commodity Markets Outlook and Strategy: 2014 Outlook — And the Walls Come a-Tumblin' Down', 30 December.

Kaufmann, R. and B. Ullman (2009), 'Oil Prices, Speculation, and Fundamentals: Interpreting Causal Relations amongst Spot and Futures Prices', *Energy Economics*, **31** (4), 550–558.

Kemp, J. (2015), 'Data Availability Bias in the Oil Market', *Reuters*, 6 July.

Longson, A. and E. Volynsky (2015), 'Crude Oil: Beyond the S&D', Morgan Stanley Slide Presentation at Independent Petroleum Association of America Conference, 25 June.

Martin, D. (2017), 'Oil Market Weekly: Harvey Hurts WTI, Helps Brent – For Now', J.P. Morgan Commodities Research, 8 September.

Reuters (2021), 'Unlike IEA, Rystad Energy Sees Need for Hundreds of New Oil Fields', 28 May.

Ribeiro, R., L. Eagles and N. von Solodkoff (2009), 'Commodity Prices and Futures Positions', J.P. Morgan Global Asset Allocation & Alternative Investment Research, 16 December.

Stein, G. (2005), 'World Oil Demand Revised Down Again', Lombard Street Research, World Service Daily Note, 9 September.

Tchilinguirian, H. (2006), 'Market Prices: What Do Oil Prices Say about Fundamentals: Presented to the 7th China Oil Traders' Conference', International Energy Agency Slide Presentation, Nanjing, Jiangsu, China, 18 April through 20 April.

Tchilinguirian, H. (2008), 'In Financial Turmoil, What Perspectives for Oil?', *Oil Markets Outlook*, BNP Paribas Corporate and Investment Banking, 26 September.

Till, H. (2008), 'The Oil Markets: Let the Data Speak for Itself', *EDHEC-Risk Institute Publication*, October.

Till, H. (2016), 'When Has OPEC Spare Capacity Mattered for Oil Prices?', *Global Commodities Applied Research Digest*, **1** (1), 47-52.

Till, H. (2021), 'OPEC Spare Capacity and Oil Prices', Slide Presentation at the Workshop on 'The Volatility of Crude Oil Prices, and the Mitigation of Oil Price Risk,' Co-hosted by KAPSARC (KSA), the Oxford Institute for Energy Studies, and the Centre for Energy, Petroleum and Mineral Law and Policy at the University of Dundee, 20 December.

Till, H. and J.-H. Jesse (2016), 'Swing Oil Production and the Role of Credit', *Global Commodities Applied Research Digest*, **1** (2), 70-88.

Till, H. and J. Eagleeye (2017), 'Inferring petroleum-complex fundamentals through price-relationship data', *Global Commodities Applied Research Digest*, **2** (2), 111-133. This article was also published as an *EDHEC-Risk Institute Working Paper*.

Verleger, P. (2007), 'Prepared Testimony', The Permanent Subcommittee on Investigation of the U.S. Senate, Committee on Homeland Security and Governmental Affairs and The Subcommittee on Energy of the U.S. Senate, Committee on Energy and Natural Resources, 11 December.

8 Scenario analysis: imagining the unimaginable!

Richard Wheeler

Introduction

Before starting this forward-looking chapter on future energy scenarios, it is important to define what is and is not intended to be discussed. Many readers will expect to find a forecast of future energy use, with possible scenarios based on multiple variables and data extrapolated from current trends. Such a forecast is not the purpose of this chapter. There are already many comprehensive future energy scenario publications, written by leading organizations that use entire teams of highly qualified people who analyze data to draw their conclusions. Publishing another such forecast would not add significant value to the existing discussion.

Instead, this chapter will demonstrate two possible future scenarios as a thought experiment, in order to stimulate a discussion about how technology advances or policy changes might affect the design of future energy systems and the mix of different fuels used in those systems. These possible scenarios do not necessarily reflect the author's views on how the future of energy should evolve. This chapter's intention is not to promote the use of one fuel over another or to advocate for any specific policies. Instead, it will focus on how a specific technical advance or a shift in regulatory approach—in isolation—might alter the energy landscape, thus influencing the use of specific fuels in national and regional energy systems, how global markets could be affected, and how geopolitics could be altered.

Two specific scenarios will be considered: (1) a technological advance in one specific fuel type and (2) a change in approach toward energy governance and regulation. In the first, this contribution will consider how an unforeseen breakthrough in the use of solar photovoltaics (PV) will influence national and global fuel mixes. No other technological breakthroughs for other fuel types will be envisioned, although gradual improvements on battery economics will be included in this scenario because current forecasts generally agree that battery technology will continue to gradually improve. No specific prices for the production of different types of energy will be provided (with the exception of oil, for illustrative purposes), because energy pricing mechanisms include many variables and constantly change over time and across different markets. The intention was to compare fuels relative to each other rather than starting a discussion about price formation. No regulatory or political governance breakthroughs will be envisioned in this first scenario aside from those that have already been declared and are, therefore, likely to be implemented according to current conventional wisdom. The second scenario will envision greatly enhanced international cooperation on pursuing a shared policy of deep carbonization. Without creating a single global energy-related organization, this scenario will draw upon the existing constellation of multilateral organizations and will especially assume that an intense, although voluntary, cooperation between national and regional energy regulators will be undertaken for the purpose of sharing and implementing best practices in designing energy markets for a swift transition toward deep decarbonization. Unlike the previous scenario, this second scenario will not include any technological breakthroughs, to avoid obscuring the influence of governance and regulatory initiatives on energy markets. General assumptions for both the scenarios include a steady drive by many countries to pursue decarbonization policies and an ongoing battle between different fuel types as well as the countries that are leaders in various fuel sources. Simply put, even a radical change in the global energy mix will not necessarily mean an end to geopolitical competition over fuel sources and energy security, although this competition will likely play out very differently from the current situation.[12] That said, while it is always difficult to forecast the future of energy, technological improvements or changes in energy governance might not occur either at the speed or to the degree as mentioned in the following scenarios.

Scenario 1: Technological breakthrough

Premise of the scenario

In 2005, who would have thought that the combined use of existing and new technologies—hydraulic fracturing and horizontal drilling—would so radically change the global energy landscape ten years later? The shale revolution that resulted led to the United States transforming itself from an energy importer into a net energy exporter by the late 2010s and becoming the world's largest producer of oil and gas. The improved economics of extracting nonconventional and shale oil and gas, as well as enhancements in LNG technology, completely changed the dynamics of both oil and gas trade and even led to adjustments in oil producers' geopolitical approaches, as seen in the

Organization for Petroleum Exporting Countries (OPEC)+ initiatives led by Russia and Saudi Arabia.

It is widely acknowledged that these applied uses of technology, and especially their resulting effects, were unexpected. Considering the current energy landscape, from where is the next technological breakthrough likely to come? Which fuel types will be most affected by this change, and how will it influence future energy trade and geopolitics? Will such changes take place within existing energy types, such as the case with the shale revolution, or will an alternative form of energy become more affordable, thus changing the energy landscape?

Although there are many different sources of energy, end use can be categorized as one of two basic types: electrons or molecules. Electricity consumes electrons, which can be produced from a very wide variety of sources: nuclear, solar, wind, methane, hydrogen, coal, oil, conventional hydro (traditional dams), and alternative hydro (ocean wave turbines). In contrast, molecules—traditionally derived from hydrocarbons such oil and natural gas, or more recently, from hydrogen gas or biogas—can be used to create heat, generate electricity, or power engines. Therefore, when considering which single type of technological breakthrough would best illustrate how resulting changes in the fuel mix could influence energy economics and geopolitics, the most efficient approach was to find a single change that would affect the economics of both electrons and molecules in the fuel mix and could, at the same time, be considered a realistic breakthrough, given the current state of the science of energy production and the possibilities to quickly scale up usage.

Therefore, although more distant technological breakthroughs—such as nuclear fusion or mass capture of renewable electricity by ocean wave technology—could have been used as examples, it was decided to envision a breakthrough in solar PV technology, accompanied by accelerated (but not revolutionary) improvements in battery technology. As will be seen, a breakthrough in solar technology would both transform the electricity mix (electrons) and strongly influence nonelectric fuel usage (molecules) through improved economics for hydrogen gas production. The envisioned steady improvements in battery technology also aid this process in the scenario. Although this breakthrough in technology and its practical application are not beyond the realm of possibility, given current trends in solar PV economics and quantum mechanics research, the timetable has been greatly accelerated from current conventional wisdom in order to deprive other fuel sources time to adjust to the new reality, thus allowing the results of the simulation to fulfill the premise of constructing a currently 'unimaginable' scenario.

The scenario

This future scenario takes place in 2035, by which time electricity produced from PV solar panels has become so cheap that, by a wide margin, solar PV is now the cheapest way to generate electricity. So cheap that, despite its variable nature and lack of dispatchability if not paired with a storage solution, solar PV is now the most widely generated form of electricity in most parts of the world. As already mentioned, battery reliability has also steadily improved. These changes have resulted in an increased electrification of total energy use in most markets. But, perhaps, the most significant change to the energy mix in most countries is not this displacement of other forms of generation from the electricity grid; cheaper electricity meant a significant drop in the cost of producing 'green' hydrogen by electrolysis.[3] More cheaply available hydrogen allowed for the partial displacement of fossil fuels such as natural gas (methane) and oil, where the increased intensity of molecules rather than electrons is needed for the intense heating required for industrial production (e.g., steel and cement) as well as for certain transportation solutions.

How did these technological advances come about? In a word, quantum mechanics research.[4] During the early part of the 21st century, improvements in our understanding of quantum physics resulted in advancements in computing power. Quantum scientific research turned its attention to chemistry, and improvements of nano materials followed.[5] The energy application of microscopic-sized materials—one of the early breakthroughs—was publicized in 2019, when scientists were able to raise the maximum theoretical solar PV efficiency from 29 to 35 percent due to a newfound ability to coax two electrons from a single proton by changing the composition of solar panel materials.[6] Further research in subsequent years led to greater efficiency improvements, and by 2025, electricity generated through utility-scale solar PV panels—in locations with excellent solar irradiation—was twice as cheap as that produced any other method.[7] Thus, mass production of these improved panels commenced. In geographic locations that had poor solar irradiation, utility-scale solar PV during summer months was generally competitive with the other, less expensive fuel sources for electricity production, but was used on a seasonal basis. Better knowledge of nano materials also improved battery technology, although not quite as radically as was the case with PV panels.[8] By 2028, the installation of new PV technology meant that solar PV became the cheapest source of electricity in much of the world.[9] Significantly, in areas blessed with strong solar irradiation, electricity became cheap enough to produce 'green' hydrogen gas, which was price competitive with natural gas (methane) in many parts of the world.[10]

During the late 2020s, national and regional markets for hydrogen began to emerge, with the process accelerating during the early 2030s. The creation of a demand for hydrogen led to a scramble among energy producers to provide hydrogen gas, which was price competitive with natural gas (methane). Given that one of the most important price factors for hydrogen is the cost of electricity, the breakthrough in solar PV efficiency meant that PV producers had a strong 'first mover' advantage. However, other electricity producers—such as those working with other renewable energy sources (e.g., thermal solar, onshore/offshore wind), as well as natural gas and nuclear producers—also tried to find ways to enter the hydrogen market on an economically competitive basis.

Effects on the energy mix

As mentioned, in places blessed with good solar irradiation, PV solar, by a wide margin, became the cheapest source of electricity. Given the improvement in battery technology, the problem of day/night intermittency was mostly solved in these markets for much of the year; however, battery technology had not yet improved to the point that it could provide seasonal storage of variable, non-dispatchable energy sources. This meant that other types of energy—mostly natural gas and hydropower, due to their flexibility and dispatchability—could compete for a share of the electricity generation market as seasonal supply or as a backup for grid stability; however, especially for natural gas, this relegation to seasonal or nighttime use meant a slight deterioration in economic viability for its use in electricity generation.

As mentioned, the creation of viable hydrogen markets and even entire hydrogen economies, facilitated by the arrival of cheap electricity, arguably had an even greater effect on global energy markets than solar power's newfound dominance of many electricity grids. With the advent of a stable demand for hydrogen, economic innovations in electricity pricing became the norm across different fuel sources. In particular, the demand for hydrogen provided a lifeline to some, but not all, nuclear power plants.[11] Those nuclear plants that had already operated long enough for their capital investments to have been fully amortized were able to produce electricity at low cost. In some cases, these nuclear plants were partially subsidized by local or national governments in order to preserve jobs or as part of a strategy to pursue deep decarbonization. In other cases, their position as a provider of baseload electricity was politically protected, even in areas with abundant solar power production, for the same reasons mentioned for justifying subsidies. In all cases, these nuclear plants were able to produce at full capacity, with electricity superfluous to load demands being diverted for hydrogen production through electrolysis.

Full-capacity production thus enhanced the economic profile of these nuclear reactors and resulted in an extension of life spans for some nuclear plants that were not too old to operate safely and economically. Although new-build nuclear power plants were too capital intensive for OECD (Organisation for Economic Co-operation and Development) economies,[12] and therefore not built, countries such as Russia and China were willing to subsidize the construction of new-build nuclear power plants both domestically and abroad for both economic and geopolitical reasons.[13] However, it should be noted that the significant upfront capital required to finance these new-build reactors—when contrasted with the relatively cheap start-up costs of solar PV and other forms of renewable energy that also vied for a place in the green hydrogen market—presented a major budgetary risk for both constructing and recipient countries. The expectation of continuing efficiency gains for renewable forms of electricity also added to this risk.

Solar PV producers did not take this newfound competition lightly. In the same way that natural gas producers were able to provide associated shale gas at very low rates during the previous decade,[14] all producers of variable renewable energy adjusted their operational models to run at full capacity—instead of intermittently, as was previously the case—with electricity not needed for the grid being used for hydrogen production. Project economics for solar PV prior to 2020 was based on using partial production capacity for the electricity grid; all electricity generated for hydrogen production through electrolysis could be considered as very low-cost or cost-free electricity[15] and was strategically priced at a level that would allow the hydrogen produced to be economically competitive against natural gas and other hydrogen producers.[16] Due to land usage issues, given that utility-scale solar power requires a lot of land per megawatt of capacity, solar PV by 2030—despite its cost advantages—was not able to fully supply all global hydrogen demand, thus providing another opportunity for other hydrogen producers, in spite of the risks for nuclear power operators mentioned in the previous paragraph.[17]

In 2027, the European Union (EU), taking advantage of new technology, decided to accelerate its decarbonization drive, reducing its fossil fuel use by 80 percent by 2035 and aiming to be fully carbon neutral by 2040. Similar aggressive deep decarbonization goals were also put into place by many US states and Canadian provinces, despite the fact that no federal policies were enacted in those two countries. As a result of decarbonization strategies in some countries, natural gas demand dropped globally by 2035 by about 30 percent due to losses in market share in power generation and due to newfound competition from hydrogen. However, such losses were cushioned by an ability to win market share from oil, which lost between 30 to 40 percent of its global demand between 2020 and 2030, largely due to a battle in all transportation sectors[18] between electric vehicles, hydrogen fuel cells, and natural gas (remaining demand was buoyed by chemicals and plastics demand).[19] Electricity production from coal was nearly completely phased out in Europe, North and South America, and Africa by 2030; it was likely to be full halted globally by 2040. With the exception of its phasing out of coal production, China pursued an 'all of the above' energy policy to meet its steadily growing demand.

The real transformation of the global energy mix by 2035, which had been unimaginable as recently as 2018, was that renewable sources of energy took not only market share away from fossil fuels but also replaced much of overall fossil fuel consumption in absolute terms.[20] This was a remarkable achievement, given the lack of a globally coordinated decarbonization policy between the major economies.

Geopolitical effects

The main effect of this energy transition was the 'democratization' of energy production. Fuel competition did not completely end, but the importance of oil resource security and gas pipeline politics faded. Fierce competition ensued to become the preferred supplier of molecules. The pursuit of decarbonization policies was more important for some markets than others, which salvaged the competitiveness of natural gas and black/blue hydrogen in some markets.

The main geopolitical result of this sudden energy transition was a broad cleavage between the OECD world and the Eurasian market. The OECD world (which included India for political reasons, and Latin America) promoted renewables, hydrogen and natural gas, with environmental concerns playing an important role; the Eurasian market, centered around China (and included Russia, and Central and Western Asia, specifically Pakistan and Iran for geopolitical reasons), pursued an 'all of the above' approach based primarily on economics and security of supply. Strategically, China endeavored to compete across all fuel sources, except for oil and coal. In addition to pursuing an 'all of the above' energy policy, China also continued its 'go out' policy, building supply chains and energy systems along its Belt and Road Initiative. The 'battleground' markets, where renewables and nuclear battled, were in Africa and Southeast Asia. Saudi Arabia and the Gulf Cooperation Council States saw the wisdom in quickly transitioning to solar/hydrogen production to augment their existing oil- and gas-dependent economies. Putting aside political considerations—due to the high up front capital requirements for building nuclear facilities—the OECD model came to be viewed as economically advantageous under the technological advance of this scenario.

Oil demand became more of a niche market, with an abundance of potential producers. This meant that competition on market share became more important than price competition. Therefore, the most expensive production, such as arctic and deep offshore, ceased. Pleads by oil exporting countries to OECD countries to assist their transition to a decarbonized future fell on deaf ears; OECD markets threatened stiff tariffs for a variety of reasons. The EU countries had already made a strategic decision to pursue deep carbonization; the United States, Canada, and a small number of other countries decided to shelter their domestic production—from what was widely perceived as unfair foreign competition—for energy security reasons and to protect industry jobs.[21] These tariff threats rendered as useless any attempt by OPEC to maximize its short-term cash flow by selling oil at US$15–20 per barrel (in constant 2018 dollars). Therefore, OPEC + cooperation continued, keeping oil prices from dropping below the US$40–45 range. Gas trade remained economically competitive across global markets, especially in LNG, but due to the aforementioned decarbonization policies was in the process of being phased out in Europe and parts of North America.

Scenario 2: Convergence on global energy governance and regulatory frameworks

Premise of the scenario

In 2035, the opening ceremony for the newly created World Energy Agency (WEA) was held. This body, the founding documents of which were drafted using the UN Charter as a template, was invested with extraordinary delegated powers from the world's nations, with broad authority to compel its member states to …

… if this future scenario sounds unimaginable, you are correct that it is unlikely to happen. Some degree of energy governance convergence and cooperation is expected in the coming years if countries are serious about decarbonization. After explaining the reasons that a scenario involving a central energy governance organization is unlikely to happen, this contribution will outline a more plausible scenario for energy governance convergence, one that could result in a policy coordination that, in our current reality, would seem similarly unimaginable.

There has always been a reluctance among nation-states to surrender their authority on energy-related issues. Access to reliable and affordable energy supply is often viewed as a national security issue in the world's capitals, given the importance of energy as an economic input. Regarding 'energy security,' there have been a multitude of definitions over the years.[22] [23] The emphasis on sustainability became increasingly important during the late 2010s, and under the governance scenario that will be outlined in this chapter, by the early 2020s a global consensus on the urgent need to mitigate the worst of the effects of climate change was reached among most leading nations' capitals. In fact, the term 'climate change' in public discourse was increasingly replaced by the term 'climate emergency.'

Given a traditional lack of centralized energy governance, energy issues have been debated and acted upon by a constellation of many different energy-related organizations.[24] Some organizations advocate for energy-consuming countries (IEA), while others advocate for energy-producing countries (OPEC), while yet others deal primarily with specific types of fuel sources (OPEC, IAEA, IRENA, Solar Alliance).[25] Some organizations are more political in nature and mostly serve as platforms for dialogue, while others are very technical oriented. Some generalist organizations, such as the G7, G20, and UN, have been very active on energy issues. Broadly speaking, the broader and larger an organization's constituency, the more difficult it is to gain internal consensus for action.

To best understand the chosen future scenario, I would like to elaborate both the differences and the potential symbiotic relationship between politically oriented organizations and the more technical ones. One the one hand, the political organizations, such as the G7, G20, and UN (United Nations Framework Convention on Climate Change), provide the opportunity to achieve a broad consensus on politically or legally binding agreements, such as the Paris Agreement. I will also explore the potential of technical organizations such as the Energy Community, ACER, ENTSO-E or ENTSOG[26] that deal with the implementation of energy policy at the regional or national level. Implementation of energy policy, for the purposes of this chapter, means establishing regulatory frameworks for energy use and cross-border energy systems. It is in this synergy, between politically agreed policy on the one hand and technical policy implementation on the other, where a possible integration of global energy governance is possible. It should be noted that while steady improvements in technology and economics for certain forms of energy are envisioned in this scenario, there will be none of the sweeping technological breakthroughs envisioned in the previous scenario.

The scenario

In recent years, proposed changes in energy usage and energy systems have resulted from an increasing awareness of the need for a coordinated policy of deep decarbonization, motivated by climate change. It became recognized that a more integrated coordination of energy policy was now necessary, and as mentioned, a stronger link was forged between political platforms for dialogue and organizations dealing with technocratic regulatory frameworks. This was implemented through three main mechanisms: broad political agreement and direction at high-level platforms; an integration of decarbonization into free trade agreements; and, on a volunteer basis, a closer coordination and sharing of best practices on the technical and economic aspects related to the decarbonization of energy systems, grids, and cross-border energy arrangements.

Thus, during the early 2020s this broad global consensus emerged on the necessity to embark upon an aggressive decarbonization campaign. As a result, mechanisms for global energy governance were strengthened, but not in the way that many would think in an 'unimaginable' scenario. As mentioned, no WEA was founded. Instead, broad-based platforms for dialogue, such as the G20 and UN, were used as political platforms for dialogue and general agreement. Although political direction was important for the global decarbonization efforts, practical leadership in energy governance fell to other forums.

Following this logic, in 2025 an additional protocol was attached to the Paris Agreement,[27] which made decarbonization goals binding for the protocol signatories, whereas previously they were voluntary. By making decarbonization goals binding by international law, the protocol created an overall framework, without specifically proscribing exactly how it should be implemented. This allowed each country to pursue its energy policies in a flexible manner, without favoring any specific type of fuel if deep decarbonization was the result. Within that protocol, other energy-related organizations were encouraged to share best practices on agreeing new policy pathways for decarbonization. The protocol also established an annual Review Meeting on Decarbonization and created a framework of committees whereby experts from energy-related international organizations[28] could meet to informally discuss policy pathways. Another significant development was the establishment of an informal mechanism within a new body called the Paris Energy Club.[29]

The Paris Energy Club was an important energy governance innovation. It consisted of several technically themed subcommittees that debated and recommended technical solutions from national DSOs and TSOs on standardization of pipelines,[30] encouragement of "electricity to X"[31] policies, the pursuit of sector coupling,[32] and the prioritization of decarbonized electricity dispatchment over other forms of electricity generation. Testimony from private sector companies on practical technical matters was also taken into consideration, enhancing the public–private nature of the club. These technical recommendations had the effect of easing cross-border trade of hydrogen gas and methane biogas and removing obstacles to cross-border cooperation. As a direct result, leading national and regional regulators started to draft common rules and guidelines in order to ensure interoperability and market access for carbon-free energy sources. These subcommittees, based on the practical experience of their members, also recommended strategic scientific subfields where breakthrough research would assist decarbonization policy. Although the main meetings of its governing board were held in Paris, timed to coincide with the Paris protocol's annual Review Meeting, many of the subcommittee meetings were held outside of Paris. This structured linkage of technically oriented and politically oriented organizations led to formal taskings by the broad political organizations (the UN, G20, G7, EU, and others), so that policy-oriented organizations (IEA, IRENA, Europe's Energy Community, and others) could conduct policy research and propose broader nontechnical regulatory and policy solutions. International organizations such as the IEA, IRENA, and G7 took leading roles in facilitating this policy coordination.[33]

As a result of policy research and coordination, by 2029 many of the leading multilateral trade agreements—North American Free Trade Agreement, Association of Southeast Asian Nations, Asia Pacific Economic Cooperation, Transatlantic Trade and Investment Partnership, Comprehensive Economic and Trade Agreement, EU/Canada—to differing degrees of scope and ambition included different trade-based mechanisms to encourage decarbonization, including the easement of technology transfer for some types of energy production. The agreement reached between the United States and EU in 2026 with regard to harmonizing their approach toward carbon 'border adjustments' was a big step in this direction. Although by 2030 halting steps toward more broadly implementing cross-border versions of carbon taxes, carbon offsets, and emissions trading markets were considered, there was a reluctance by many countries to enshrine these mechanisms into international trade law, as there was great hesitation to impose such sweeping economic models on individual countries through multilateral action, as these models would infringe upon national budget and taxation policies and might have a negative effect on fit-for-purpose national implementations of such financially based approaches.[34] The process of using free trade agreements to encourage decarbonization started in 2019, when an initiative was launched to start negotiations on an Agreement on Climate Change, Trade, and Sustainability

(ACCTS).[35] The ACCTS created binding rules to eliminate fossil fuel subsidies, and the key innovation of this approach was a shift to legally binding obligations, where previously agreements were centered on voluntary commitments. The ACCTS process had a profound effect on how free trade agreements were later restructured.

Effects on the energy mix

The two main results of this policy coordination were deep decarbonization on a global scale and a moderate increase in energy prices. Due to an increase in cataclysmic weather events, an increase in energy production and delivery costs was seen in economic terms—and with a broad general consensus—as a down payment on mitigating the economic and human losses that resulted from these extreme weather events. Compared with the first scenario—where a specific technological breakthrough abruptly lowered the cost of both electrons and molecules and in fact caught many unsuspecting producers of other fuels flat-footed in defending their market shares—the pricing dynamic in this scenario was quite different. Although we will see that the resulting changes in the global energy mix are quite similar in this scenario to that of the previous one (partially to avoid an apples versus oranges complication), using a pathway of coordinated policy rather than sudden market-based changes had noticeable knock-on effects for energy pricing, profound effects on geopolitics, and some subtle effects on the (hypothetically) emerging energy mix.

In order to deeply decarbonize as quickly as possible, there was broad political consensus that any decarbonized form of energy was generally acceptable. Also, despite coordination on infrastructure standards and regulatory frameworks, it was agreed that each country should decide for itself which energy source to emphasize and how to go about implementing its own energy mix. That said, the significant multilateral nature of changes to energy governance and policy coordination had an outsized influence on how individual countries decided to exercise this freedom.

As mentioned, in this scenario the energy mix does not radically differ from that of the previous scenario. Most countries moved to deeply decarbonize their electricity grids through a combination of renewable sources of onshore/offshore wind, PV/thermal solar, different forms of hydropower, and in some cases, nuclear energy. Each national energy mix depended on the resources available to a given country, or to its neighbors, in the case of a broader regional electricity grid. One of the most sharply debated issues centered around the use of natural gas: Although deep decarbonization meant that natural gas was widely considered to be a transition fuel rather than a destination fuel in most circumstances, policy views differed on how quickly this transition should occur. The economic competitiveness of blue hydrogen against green hydrogen also depended on resource availability, as well as the specific mix of financial incentives (carbon trading markets, green certificates, carbon taxes, or mandated levels of decarbonized energy in the grid). Coal was nearly completely phased out in OECD countries by 2030. By 2035, oil lost nearly 40 percent of its global energy demand, as was the case in other scenarios, but natural gas lost 30 percent of global use (also in absolute terms), mainly due to the coordinated transition to decarbonized molecules.

Geopolitical Effects

In contrast with the previous scenario, where the change in fuel usage was initiated due to a technological advance—which in turn sparked a frantic rush by different fuel producers to economically and geopolitically compete with each other in a changed market reality—this scenario envisions much more cooperation between countries. The coordinated effort succeeded in sparing most hydrocarbon producers from financial disaster (Figure 8.1).

Such a coordinated and cooperative approach, although likely in the years leading up to 2050, cannot be assumed as a base case in future energy governance. This scenario assumes an international consensus for prioritizing action to mitigate climate change and its destabilizing effects. However, in recent years, we have seen that energy security and price stability are also a priority for governments. The COVID-19 pandemic resulted in a disruption in global supply chains, and a corresponding collapse in energy demand. These dynamics have resulted in supply/demand imbalances as economies recover from the pandemic, leading to higher energy prices and increased inflationary pressures. Adding to the complexity of the current situation, in the context of Russia's military invasion of Ukraine,[36] and the probable emergence of rival trading and military blocs replacing a fully globalized economy, the OECD world has rediscovered the importance of energy security. Broad global cooperation in pursuing a coordinated decarbonization agenda will likely be affected with the OECD world (on the one hand) pursuing a reduction in fossil fuel use for economic and security reasons in addition to its pursuit of decarbonization and (on the other hand) an emerging 'Eurasian' bloc pursuing its own energy policies.

Returning to this chapter's scenario, leading oil producers such as Saudi Arabia and Russia—but especially countries that had high production costs—pushed to monetize their stranded oil assets, which were likely to be declared as impaired assets due to the sharp drop in oil demand. These producer countries had counted on support from institutional investors, but due to the relatively gradual (over several years) transition from fossil fuels to decarbonized energy sources, the 'smart money' investors had rebalanced their portfolios, thus avoiding systemic risks for the global financial system. OECD countries recognized the risk of oil producers 'dumping' rapidly devaluing oil and gas assets onto global markets at well below the cost of production, so a carrot-and-stick approach was adopted. The 'stick,' as mentioned in the previous scenario, was to include trade tariffs into regional trade agreements on oil and petrochemical products that sank below a certain level. To therefore avoid tariffs, OPEC ++ (with the United States joining as a full-fledged member)[37] agreed on a trading framework with OECD countries to pursue the best price-maximization deal that they could achieve under the circumstances, to maintain the price of oil within a range of US$ 45–55 per barrel, in constant 2018 dollars.[38] The 'carrot,' in order to help alleviate the economic suffering of the oil producers, was to agree to joint financing and scientific research, which would help these countries to transition to a decarbonized world. As a concession to these now-vulnerable oil producers, they were deemed eligible for advantageous project funding in renewable energy by multilateral financing mechanisms. Middle Eastern and other equatorial countries with good solar irradiation were able to transition their electricity grids to renewable energy and were also granted 'green' credits for decarbonizing the footprint of their oil production process for use in emissions trading markets. For Northern countries like Russia, which lacked the solar irradiation necessary to launch large-scale renewable energy projects, joint research with OECD countries was stepped up within the framework of the IAEA, a global nuclear industry plan was agreed, and joint projects for the construction of a modest number of new-build nuclear power plants received taxpayer backing in a broad range of countries. In geopolitical terms, energy cooperation—undertaken due to the common nature of the climate emergency—became a 'confidence-building measure' that enhanced global security.

Conclusion

The goal of this contribution was to 'imagine the unimaginable' about the future of energy. The means for doing so was to provide plausible advances in energy technology and in political will—in separate scenarios—in order to stimulate a discussion on the importance of applied scientific research and policy pathways toward creating an energy future where the energy mix is radically transformed as a result. After all, it would be pointless to talk about flying automated vehicles that are all fueled by incredibly inexpensive mini nuclear fusion reactors or to discuss a single and all-powerful WEA that holds vast political and regulatory authority. . Instead of providing futuristic scenarios

Figure 8.1 Illustration by Greg Stoicoiu 2021.

that are unlikely to become a reality in the coming decades—and, therefore, of little use for policy discussion—the author tried to show how, in isolation, a single narrowly scoped breakthrough in technology or political will might influence other aspects of the future energy mix and energy policy.

Regarding technological advances, for the purpose of this contribution, calibrating the correct scale of advances involved walking a fine line. Too little of an advance, and it becomes no longer unimaginable, and would not add anything meaningful to policy discussions. However, too great a technological advance would have resulted in nearly cost-free solar-generated electricity,[39] batteries that could be used for widespread seasonal electricity storage, and electrolysis-generated hydrogen that would have become so cheap as to obliterate the economic case for using any other type of molecule-based fuel source for most energy needs. This overstep would have also rendered the thought exercise useless.

Admittedly, one of the more 'unimaginable' aspects of the scenarios was the exceptionally fast rate of change that resulted in a speedy and broad transformation of the energy mix and had collateral economic and geopolitical implications. The fast transition in the scenarios was by design. That said, a more conventional view of likely future change would envision technological and political evolution rather than breakthroughs. The resulting effect of a slower rate of change is that natural gas and nuclear, along with other forms of renewable energy, would likely have time to gain a foothold in the market share. Given that the production cost of green hydrogen from renewable-sourced electrolysis is unlikely to decrease as quickly as per the scenario, it also would be reasonable to assume that blue hydrogen from natural gas—or green hydrogen from some nuclear reactors—might be economically competitive in the coming decades, depending on the dynamics of the specific electricity market in question. Therefore, competition between different fuel sources to create hydrogen and the future role of natural gas (methane) will be a key battleground. A secondary battleground could be in calibrating a carbon-free electricity mix—which will differ between national and regional electricity grids due to economic cost, availability of renewable resources, and policy decisions, thus proving to be fit for purpose for each grid's overall energy needs. Policy concepts like sector coupling and 'power to X,' which are currently being actively pursued by the EU, provide a possible glimpse of this secondary battleground's future. Thus, even a wholesale shift from fossil fuels to decarbonized sources of energy will not likely mean the end of competition between different fuel sources, especially if the rate of change is gradual.

As regards a possible relationship between the two scenarios outlined in this chapter, in reality, it is likely that they will unfold simultaneously but at different speeds. It is also entirely possible that a technological advance related to a different type of fuel source might significantly alter the energy mix suggested in the first scenario. The speed of change between the two scenarios matters, because regulatory frameworks and financial incentives are often enacted while considering current and very immediate future technical and economic conditions. In addition, energy infrastructure is usually built to be utilized over a 20–40-year horizon, which means that current fuel sources often enjoy incumbent advantage for years to come. As regards the possibility of technological breakthroughs in other fuel sources, the only significant difference with the scenario outlined would be if the breakthrough is related to molecules rather than electrons. For example, a sudden technological breakthrough in any electricity-producing source—thermal solar, onshore/offshore wind, nuclear fission or fusion, hydropower, and so on—would mean a different source of cheap electricity for hydrogen production by electrolysis, without changing the overall dynamic. In contrast, any changes related to the carbon content or economic cost of molecules—carbon sequestering, gas or oil production, or even hydrogen production directly from fossil fuel sources[40]—would challenge the current assumption that increased electrification of the energy mix is inevitable.[41] Stepping away from this contribution's two scenarios, the author feels that the most interesting and complicated energy sectors over the next two decades will be those that sit at the nexus of the electron–molecule space. The author also believes that the perception of addressing fossil fuel use as a geopolitical security policy will influence governments' openness to decarbonization: If decarbonization is perceived as contributing to energy security and price stability, then it is more likely to be pursued.

Following from this, fuel competition, if anything, is likely to accelerate, with countries and private companies attempting to broaden their participation into an ever-widening range of fuels and to promote the fuel source within which they and their allies excel. Carbon reduction is likely to remain an overall guiding framework in this emerging competition. Some countries will find geopolitical and security advantages in crowding out from markets the fuel sources of their rivals and adversaries. That said, rapid and deep carbonization will only take place if technological advances, energy policy governance, and demand reduction are all considered as part of an interlocking puzzle. For example, wide-ranging decarbonization in global energy systems will not happen without broad policy frameworks and policy pathways. By the same token, improvements in energy governance will require technological advances in order to more quickly deliver on policy objectives. Therefore, if we assume the existence of an emerging consensus about the need to decarbonize the global energy mix, then both basic and applied scientific research across all forms of decarbonized energy should be prioritized. By the same token, regulatory frameworks should be designed so as to allow for such technological advances to be seamlessly utilized for the improvement of future energy systems in a nondiscriminatory manner.

When considering further research on this topic, the author suggests looking at specific decarbonization pathways, such as industrial steelmaking and the potential of green hydrogen in the food–energy nexus. Much attention is already focused on the decarbonization of the electricity grid and of transport systems; increased attention should be paid to the technical viability of renewable hydrogen as a replacement for coal in steelmaking or natural gas in fertilizer (ammonia) production. The interrelation between social sciences and the energy transition is an area that is currently underfunded and relatively less understood. For example, more attention should be paid to the effects of decarbonization efforts on national politics and international diplomacy and to the policy drivers that will lead governments to choose their policy preferences with regard to decarbonization, security of supply, and price considerations.

Notes

1. For an excellent examination of how changes in the energy mix are likely to influence geopolitics, please refer to Van de Graaf, Thijs, "A new world: the geopolitics of the energy transition," Secretariat of the Global Commission on the Geopolitics of Energy Transformation (2019).
2. For more information on energy and geopolitics competition, please see: Laidislaw, Sarah and Nikos Tsafos, "Energy spheres of influence," September 2019, Center for Strategic & International Studies, www.csis.org/analysis/energy-spheres-of-influence, accessed on 15 September 2019.
3. The technical aspects of cost reduction for green hydrogen through electrolysis have been simplified for this scenario in order to concentrate on the policy impacts. Many factors influence the production cost for electrolysis, including electricity price, the cost of electrolysis itself, and transportation costs. IRENA forecasts a possible halving of electrolysis costs by the 2040s. For a more comprehensive view about green hydrogen production costs, please refer to Bellini, Emiliano, "The slow, inexorable rise of green hydrogen" PV Magazine, 26 September 2019, accessed 29 September 2019, www.pv-magazine.com/2019/09/26/the-slow-inexorable-rise-of-green-hydrogen/.
4. For more information about developments in quantum mechanics, please refer to public lectures and publications by the British physicist Dr Jim Al-Khalili.
5. Although scientific disciplines such as physics, chemistry, and biology are indeed separate disciplines, there is much convergence between them at the atomic and subatomic level. Quantum mechanics deals with tiny particles (quarks, leptons, bosons) in the subatomic world. These tiny particles are difficult to observe and measure, and follow counterintuitive but scientifically confirmable behavior when they are in this unmeasurable state.
6. In reality, this laboratory research has already been achieved by MIT researchers. Chandler, David, "New solar cell allows a photon to release two electrons, not just one," July 15, 2019, accessed on August 21, 2019 at energypost.eu/new-solar-cell-allows-a-photon-to-release-two-electrons-not-just-one/.
7. Although more expensive than utility-scale PV production, rooftop solar in sunny climates in this scenario was still slightly cheaper than the other alternatives; however, in this scenario, in cloudy or northern locations, rooftop solar was more expensive than the cheapest alternatives.
8. Solar PV advances were achieved due to the solar panel's improved ability to master the sun's energy, absorbing a greater number of photons when exposed to sunlight (due to an improvement in panel heat management), as well as increasing the panel's ability to coax an increased number of electrons from each photon. Advances in battery performance (as well as in fuel cell engines) resulted in marginal improvements in material conductivity and economy. Although different levels of advancement resulted from the differing nature of PV and battery technology, in this scenario, scientists will continue to search for that ever-elusive breakthrough in battery technology during the 2030s.
9. See map on solar irradiation, https://globalsolaratlas.info, from the Global Solar Atlas 2.0, a free web-based application developed and operated by the company Solargis s.r.o. on behalf of the World Bank Group, utilizing Solargis data, with funding provided by the Energy Sector Management Assistance Program.

10. Hydrogen is currently classified into 'green,' 'blue' and 'gray' categories, depending on the level of carbon required to produce it. Green hydrogen is produced from renewable energy sources and does not involve the use of CO_2; gray hydrogen is produced from a fossil fuel, usually natural gas; blue hydrogen has the same fossil fuel sources as gray hydrogen but sequesters the CO_2 through carbon-capture technologies.
11. For an example of efforts to use hydrogen production as an additional income stream for existing nuclear reactors, kindly refer to: Yurman, Dan, "US nuclear plants to produce carbon-free hydrogen," in EnergyPost, September 17, 2019, at www.energypost.eu/u-s-nuclear-plants-to-produce-carbon-free-hydrogen/, accessed September 20, 2019.
12. For an example of the long lead times, cost overruns, and the significant upfront capital requirement for new-build nuclear reactors, kindly refer to: Cholteeva, Yoana, "Hinkley Point C nuclear project to run 2.9 billion Pounds over budget," in Power Technology, September 27, 2019, at www.power-technology.com/news/hinkley-point-c-nuclear-project-to-run-2-9bn-over-budget/, accessed September 28, 2019.
13. In the case of Russia, relatively weak solar irradiation in most of the country (as per the map on solar irradiation, https://globalsolaratlas.info, referenced in note 9) meant that, in this scenario, green hydrogen for the most part could only be produced in a large scale on an economically competitive basis (against natural gas) by either nuclear-powered electrolysis or from natural gas (blue hydrogen). Due to entrenched infrastructure and the relatively low cost to produce electricity for the Russian domestic market by natural gas, hydropower, and nuclear, there was little incentive in Russia to install large-scale capacity in wind-generated electricity. Both China and Russia undertook an intense marketing campaign to build new nuclear power plants across Africa, West Asia, South Asia, and Southeast Asia.
14. The capital costs (and sometimes a portion of the variable costs) of producing associated shale gas in the Permian and Bakken basins were often assigned to the primary oil production, thus allowing for competitively priced LNG exports from the United States.
15. Renewable energy sources such as solar and wind have no fuel costs and almost negligible operating costs, which are incurred by increasing production from intermittent to full capacity.
16. Depending on the market, in this scenario, the production cost of green hydrogen became either lower or equal to that of blue hydrogen produced from natural gas with accompanying carbon sequestration.
17. In the United States, approximately 12.71 acres of land per megawatt are required, compared with 43.503 acres of land per megawatt produced. For further details, kindly refer to: Stevens, Landon, "The footprint of energy: land use of US electricity production," Strata, June 2017.
18. Including light and heavy transportation on the ground, maritime shipping, and short-haul aviation. In this scenario, experiments in decarbonizing long-haul aviation in a way that would be economically viable were still ongoing in 2030.
19. The cheaper operating and fuel costs of electric vehicles and hydrogen fuel cells resulted in a scramble between manufacturing countries and car makers to win market share in the post-combustion engine market.
20. It should be noted that the goal of decarbonization is to decrease the total amount of carbon emissions, not just have decarbonized energy sources take a growing share of the energy mix. Up to 2017, new forms of energy tended to capture new

energy demand, but use of older energy sources was not reduced in absolute terms. Therefore, under this scenario, the usage reduction in absolute terms for coal and oil is revolutionary. For further details, see chart on cumulative history of energy use on https://ourworldindata.org/grapher/global-primary-energy

21. Under this scenario, given the sharp drop in electricity and mobility costs, consumers in North America did not mind tariff policies to protect the domestic oil industry, the ongoing operation of which also provided a valued source of competitively exportable associated natural gas.
22. It could be argued that Winston Churchill started the energy security discussion early last century when he famously claimed that "Safety and certainty in oil lie in variety and variety alone" (from https://www.brookings.edu/testimonies/oil-diplomacy/). The IEA (International Energy Agency) has defined energy security as "the uninterrupted availability of energy sources at an affordable price" from (IEA official website: http://www.iea.org/topics/energysecurity/).
23. The "Energy Trilemma" has been defined as meaning that energy supplies should be secure, equitable, and environmentally sustainable (from World Energy Council official website: http://www.worldenergy.org/wp-content/uploads/2013/09/Trilemma-original.pdf).
24. Wheeler, Richard, "Energy security and intergovernmental organizations" p. 4, OGEL 2 (2014), www.ogel.org. URL: www.ogel.org/article.asp?key=3459".
25. IAEA is the International Atomic Energy Agency, IRENA is the International Renewable Energy Agency, the Solar Alliance in full is called the International Solar Alliance.
26. ACER (Agency for the Cooperation of Energy Regulators), ENTSOG and ENTSO-E (the European Network for Transmission System Operators for gas and electricity, respectively). A 'regulator' is the national authority responsible for energy regulations, while a 'transmission system operator,' or TSO, is responsible for operating the transmission system on a given territory. Although there can be only one national regulator, some large countries, such as Germany, have divided their gas systems into several TSO regions. Ilaria Conti, week 9 lecture from course "Introduction to the regulation of gas markets." Florence School of Regulation, 2018, Op. cit.
27. The Paris Agreement was reached within the United Nations Framework Convention on Climate Change. For more details, please see: https://unfccc.int/process-and-meetings/the-paris-agreement/the-paris-agreement, accessed on September 15, 2019.
28. Organizations in this scenario included the European Commission's Directorate General for Energy, the IEA, and the International Energy Charter; multilateral funding mechanisms also include the World Bank, European Bank for Reconstruction and Development, Asian Development Bank, and (the Chinese-led) Asian Infrastructure Investment Bank.
29. This hypothetical Paris Energy Club is not to be confused with the private energy company membership-driven Brussels Energy Club, or the Vienna Energy Club, which coordinates multilateral organizations dealing with energy policy.
30. Prior to 2020, natural gas pipelines were often not fit for purpose for transporting biomethane (due to occasional elevated levels of chemicals related to the process of removing naturally occurring hydrogen sulfide, or H_2S). There are similar pipeline standardization issues for hydrogen (the molecules of which tend to leak from unlined metal pipelines due to their small size).

31. 'Power to X' is the conversion of electricity into gasses, liquids, or heat for storage. The electricity being used is often from intermittent sources, such as renewable energy. For more information: Pundy, Doris and Florence Schultz, translated by Daniel Eck, "How do Power-to-X technologies work," on Euractiv website, August 19, 2019, www.euractiv.com/section/climate-strategy-2050/news/how-do-power-to-x-technologies-work/, accessed on September 10, 2019.
32. "Sector coupling is the practice of powering machines and devices that would typically rely on fossil fuels with electricity instead." Schmid, Philipp, "4 areas of society that sector coupling could revolutionize," in Interesting Engineering, June 12, 2019, https://interestingengineering.com/4-areas-of-society-that-sector-coupling-could-revolutionize, accessed September 18, 2019.
33. There already exists precedent for politically oriented organizations tasking the more technically oriented organizations to assist in changing specific energy policies at the national level. In May 2014, Energy Ministers of the G7 members, plus the EU Commissioner for energy, met in Rome and approved the Rome Energy Security Initiative. "The progress report on G& Energy sector support for Ukraine," p. 1, from the G7Kitakyushu Energy Ministerial Meeting, 2016.
34. A good contemporary analogy of this hesitation is the current situation in the EU, where moves toward completing an internal energy market (or 'Energy Union') are more politically palatable than adopting EU-wide financial transfer policies within the Eurozone (often referred to as a 'Currency Union').
35. Countries involved included Norway, Iceland, New Zealand, Costa Rica, and Fijj. Details about the start of ACCTS negotiations can be found at: Ardern, Jacinda, "New Zealand leading trade agreement driving action on climate change and the environment," from the official website of the New Zealand Government beehive.govt.nz, September 26, 2019, from www.behive.govt.kz/release/new-zealand-leading-trade-agreement-driving-action-climate-change-and-environment, accessed on September 28, 2019.
36. The military action started on February 24, 2022, is in fact a continuation of the ongoing war in Ukraine begun by Russia in 2014.
37. The United States, as part of the overall negotiations related to supporting major oil exporting countries, joined the OPEC export quota system in this scenario; the broadened initiative was now called OPEC ++. National oil export quotas were partially based on cushioning certain producers from economic collapse.
38. The reader will note that this price range is higher than the one agreed by OPEC + in the first scenario.
39. Electricity generated by solar PV has certainly become more competitive and, in many cases, by 2019 has already reached grid parity or competitiveness when measured by the levelized cost of electricity. These trends over the past decade strongly suggest that, in the near future, in many parts of the world, solar PV will no longer require financial subsidies to be economically competitive. For a specific example: Roth, Sammy, "Los Angeles has lined up record-cheap solar power. But there's a problem," Los Angeles Times, August 27, 2019, on www.latimes.com/environment/story/2019-08-27/los-angeles-solar-energy-storage-cheap, accessed on August 29, 2019.
40. In 2019, it was claimed by University of Calgary researchers that hydrogen could be produced from existing oil fields. Although, in this scenario, this had not yet become a reality by 2030, scientific research in this area was ongoing. Gorey, Colm, "Breakthrough promises to turn oil fields into cleaner hydrogen factories,"

in SiliconRepublic.com, August 21, 2019, www.siliconrepublic.com/machines/hydrogen-fuel-from-oil-fields, accessed on August 22, 2019.

41. "We have a line of sight to essentially decarbonize electricity sector, and that's very important. And then we electrify as much of the rest as we can building on the low carbon electricity," Monitz, Ernest, podcast interview on the Columbia Energy Exchange, August 6, 2018, at https://energypolicy.columbia.edu/dr-ernest-monitz-shifting-dynamics-across-energy-landscape, accessed on September 8, 2019.

9 GCC economies and regional geopolitics after Russia's invasion of Ukraine

Tilak K. Doshi

Introduction

The powerlessness of the Organization of the Petroleum Exporting Countries (OPEC) in ceding market share to non-OPEC suppliers—particularly to those from US shale basins—and the sharp fall in oil prices in the second half of 2014 profoundly and adversely impacted the economic outlook for the Gulf Cooperation Council (GCC) countries.[1] The outlook was made even more precarious by the coronavirus pandemic and collapse in global energy demand in 2020. New lockdowns in Europe and the United States as the year drew to a close further impacted the poor outlook for oil and gas demand. For Gulf oil exporters, these shocks led to steep falls in foreign exchange revenues and put further stress on already stretched fiscal balances.

The Gulf Arab states are now also confronting an unstable and violent breakdown of regional order. Apart from failing or disintegrated states from North Africa to the Levant, and Yemen, there is also intensified geopolitical competition as Iran and Turkey seek to widen their spheres of influence in the region. The growing instability in the regional order is also impacting global geopolitics as the United States, Russia, and China engage with the region.

The Economic Outlook for the GCC countries

Benefitting from high oil prices in the past, GCC states were able to build extensive welfare states. Government expenditure grew exponentially to support social security, health, education, and government employment programs. The Arab Spring forced the Gulf states to further expand social support programs to head off domestic unrest. However, the steep fall in oil prices since mid-2014 posed severe economic and political challenges for them (Figure 9.1).

Source: https://www.macrotrends.net/2480/brent-crude-oil-prices-10-year-daily-chart

Figure 9.1 Daily Brent Crude Oil Prices over 10 years (April 23, 2012–April 18, 2022)

By 2016, the GCC countries, including those that had accumulated large financial surpluses, such as Saudi Arabia, Kuwait, and the United Arab Emirates (UAE), faced deepening financial stress—as measured by fiscal and current account imbalances—in coping with weak oil prices (Table 9.1). Economic growth in the GCC states significantly weakened from 2016. The general macroeconomic performance of the countries since 2016 has been one of increased government spending, low economic growth, and recurring budget deficits. However, with higher oil and gas prices, the projected GCC regional GDP growth for 2022 has rebounded to 4.7 percent compared with the global GDP growth of 4.4 percent, according to the latest IMF World Economic Outlook update.[2] Projected GDP growth in GCC slows down to 2.9 percent in 2023 compared with the IMF's outlook for global GDP growth at 3.8 percent. No doubt, the expected GDP growth for the GCC group will be a function of oil and gas prices next year, and it is likely that the World Bank's oil price forecast for 2023 is on the conservative side.

Table 9.1 GCC Selected Indicators

	2000–2015	2014	2015	2016	2017	2018	2019	2020	2021	2022	2023
GDP growth (%)	4.8	3.6	4.1	2.5	-0.2	1.9	1.1	-4.9	2.6	4.7	2.9
Current Account Balance (% GDP)	13.7	17.8	-2.4	-2.7	2.9	9.6	7	0.9	6	6.4	5.6
Fiscal Balance (% GDP)	7	1.6	-10.8	-9.9	-7.4	-3.6	-3.8	-11.7	-5.7	-2.1	-1.1

Note: GCC member countries: Bahrain, Kuwait, Oman, Qatar, Saudi Arabia, UAE
Source: World Bank, "Gulf Economic Update Fall 2021"; IMF, "MENAP Oil Exporting Countries: Transitioning to Sustainable Fiscal Position and Higher Growth", October 2019.

Oil Price Outlook at End-2020: Low-price environment amidst ample supplies

Just before COVID-19 struck, most forecasts saw oil prices a little below US$60/barrel in the short and medium term (through 2025). The IMF progressively lowered its outlook for oil prices from October 2018 to October 2019 when publishing its World Economic Outlook.[3] The US shale production boom presented world markets with an elastic supply curve for oil above the relatively low break-even price thresholds of US$45–US$60/barrel.

In mid-2020, BP lowered its benchmark Brent oil price forecasts to an average of US$55 a barrel until 2050, down from previous assumptions of US$70.[4] Speaking to investors in March, Exxon and Chevron both gave their long-term cash flow projections based on US$60 a barrel.[5] It should be noted that these are not so much price forecasts as central assumptions in scenario planning for oil companies when they invest for long-term oil and gas projects. These long-term oil price assumptions are consistent with the break-even costs of producing oil in new onshore fields in the Permian shale basin in the American Southwest, which range between US$40 and US$60 per barrel.[6]

As the virus began spreading in China in early 2020 and forced it to shut down Wuhan and other parts of the country, its demand for oil—China is the world's largest crude oil importer—fell sharply. COVID-19's spread around the world further weakened demand. By early March, the outlook for oil demand growth for 2020 was significantly downgraded. At its meeting on March 6, OPEC called for a further 1.5 million barrels per day (b/d) cut (in addition to the existing production constraints), to which nonmember countries—of which Russia is the largest producer by far—would collectively have contributed 0.5 million b/d. However, the Russians refused, arguing that further cuts would only serve to increase US market share.[7] In response, Saudi Arabia initiated a price war. This set the stage for the rout in oil prices on March 9. By the end of trading that day, the global crude oil benchmark Brent fell by about 25 percent, to US$34.36 per barrel. Toward the end of April, Brent crude had dropped to the mid-teens (Figure 9.2). The scale and speed of the price collapse was unprecedented in modern times.

On April 13, OPEC, Russia, and other oil-producing nations agreed to an unprecedented production cut of 9.7 million b/d, or nearly a tenth of global supply.[8] The agreement aimed at boosting crashing oil prices amid the coronavirus pandemic and the price war. Oil prices began their upward trajectory in the 2nd half of 2020 and gained momentum over 2021.

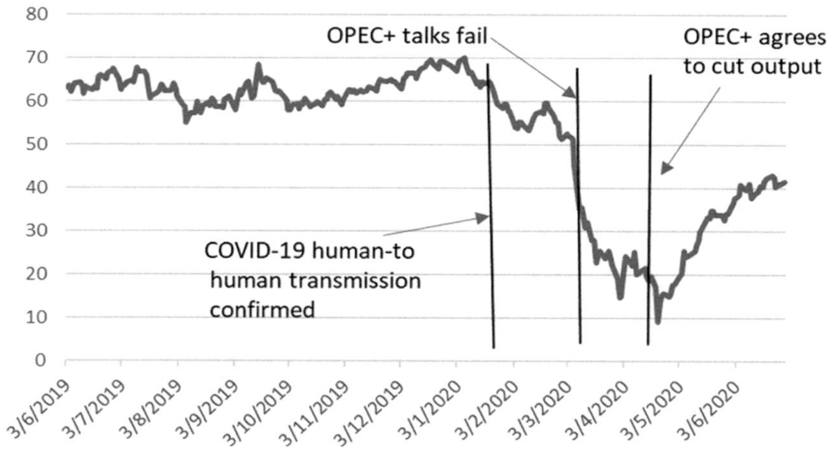

Source: https://www.macrotrends.net/2480/brent-crude-oil-prices-10-year-daily-chart

Figure 5.1 Brent Spot Crude Price (Jun 3, 2019–June 29, 2020)

The bearish oil price forecasts in the midst of the COVID-19 lockdowns (mid-2020) have now been upended by the surge in prices that gathered pace in the second half of 2021 (see Figure 9.1). The annual average Brent crude price was US$70.89 per barrel in 2021. It climbed to nearly US$130 per barrel in early March 2022 and averaged US$117 per barrel during the whole month. The OPEC+ group of producers (which includes Russia and its smaller producing allies, together with the OPEC membership led in the main by Saudi Arabia) have been gradually increasing output by a modest 400 000 b/d every month through 2021 and into 2022.

It should be noted that the oil industry has drastically cut investment in exploration and drilling since 2015 in response to tightening capital markets and investor demands for higher returns while oil prices languished. Oil and gas capital expenditures fell by almost 60% from their peak of $780 billion in 2014 to $328 billion in 2020.[9] Despite the unprecedented demand collapse caused by the COVID-19 pandemic since March 2020 and despite the endless stream of stories about robust growth of renewable energy capacity (from a very small base), the world faces a long-term supply gap for oil and gas.[10] According to energy consultancy Wood Mackenzie, only about half the supply needed to 2040 is available from producing fields; "the rest requires new capital investment."[11]

Given the collapse in upstream oil and gas investments since 2015, the International Energy Forum (IEF), in a recent report, pointed out that if upstream investments in oil and gas exploration and production do not increase by 25 percent annually over the next three years, we face a supply shock of "historic proportions."[12] According to IEF's Secretary-General, "Slashing investment in new production locks in lower total supply…it won't be long before this lower supply collides with resurgent demand. The result will be higher and more volatile oil prices and headwinds for the post-pandemic global economic recovery." The US shale sector—which saw output fall by more than 1 million b/d to less than 7 million barrels in 2020—may be hard-pressed to fill the gap on its own as the new climate change–focused Biden administration imposed punitive environmental regulations on the fossil fuels industry.[13]

Twin Shocks: the Pandemic Outbreak and Oil Price Collapse on the GCC

The onset of the pandemic and the collapse of oil prices, which had already begun trending down since early 2020, accelerated the trend in the GCC toward lower GDP growth and fiscal stress. One measure of the fiscal challenges faced by the GCC countries is the 'fiscal break-even' price—that is, the oil price at which government budgets are balanced. Kuwait, Qatar, and the UAE have fiscal break-even prices that are less than the OPEC basket oil price (used as proxy for their actual crude export realized prices) for most years. Bahrain, Oman, and Saudi Arabia have had fiscal break-even oil prices far in excess of realized OPEC prices for most years, reflecting their very high government expenditures on social welfare and government salaries. Given the surge in crude oil prices since the second half 2021, all GCC economies are forecast to realize crude oil prices in excess of their fiscal break-even prices in 2022. This will relax the governments' fiscal constraints that were increasingly onerous during the low–oil price environment of 2015–2020.

It should be noted, however, that governments typically cut planned expenditures and, thus, adjust the fiscal break-even price downward when realized oil prices trend downward. While fiscal break-even oil prices are a key indicator of fiscal pressures, an overemphasis on them, could tend to be overly pessimistic. The COVID-19 pandemic made adjusting government expenditures more difficult as the GCC governments introduced fiscal stimulus programs to maintain economic activity under the global COVID lockdowns while facing huge losses in oil revenues. With the resumption of global energy demand in the second half of 2021 and higher oil and gas prices, the fiscal constraint

Table 9.2 GCC Sovereign Wealth Funds as at First-Quarter 2022

Country	Sovereign Wealth Fund	Assets (US$ bn)
Bahrain	Mumtalakat Holding Company	18
Kuwait	Kuwait Investment Authority	738
Oman	State General Reserve Fund; Oman Investment Fund	17
Qatar	Qatar Investment Authority	450
Saudi Arabia	Public Investment Fund	620
Abu Dhabi (UAE)	Mubadala; Abu Dhabi Investment Authority	941
Dubai (UAE)	Investment Corporation of Dubai	302
Federal (UAE)	Emirates Investment Authority	78

Source: SWF Institute, Fund Rankings, Sovereign Wealth Funds, accessed at https://www.swfinstitute.org/fund-rankings/sovereign-wealth-fund

is expected to be relaxed in 2022 and most likely in 2023. Morgan Stanley, for instance, raised its third-quarter 2022 Brent crude oil price forecast to US$130 a barrel and predicted a supply deficit of about 1 million b/d persisting throughout the year.[14]

GCC countries with significant fiscal buffers in the form of large foreign exchange reserves held as sovereign wealth funds (SWFs) will be better able to accommodate budget deficits if oil and gas prices fall (Table 9.2). While the SWF buffers have significantly declined (relative to GDP) since 2014, they remain adequate for the richer GCC countries. For the GCC region on the whole, all member states are expected to be able to maintain their fixed exchange rate regimes over the medium term (next five years) even in a low–oil price environment. [15]

The smaller economies of Bahrain and Oman, which have limited foreign exchange reserves, are particularly affected by high external borrowing costs, although the former can depend on allies such as Saudi Arabia and the UAE for bailout assistance. By contrast, Oman—which has pursued an independent foreign policy and 'equidistance' with respect to relations with Iran, Qatar, and the other Gulf Arab monarchies—cannot depend on such support.[16] Thus, Moody's, along with other rating agencies, downgraded Oman's debt ratings to junk status in March 2019.[17]

While all six GCC states faced growth constraints and fiscal vulnerabilities during 2015–2020, the severity of the problems and the urgency of addressing them varied across the states. Looking forward, the richer states (Figure 9.3) with smaller indigenous populations (Table 9.3)—Kuwait, Qatar, and the UAE—will be more resilient in the medium term even if oil and gas price levels fall from their current highs. Saudi Arabia (which has a relatively large citizen population and lower per capita GDP), together with Oman and Bahrain, will face tighter fiscal constraints if energy prices trend downward.

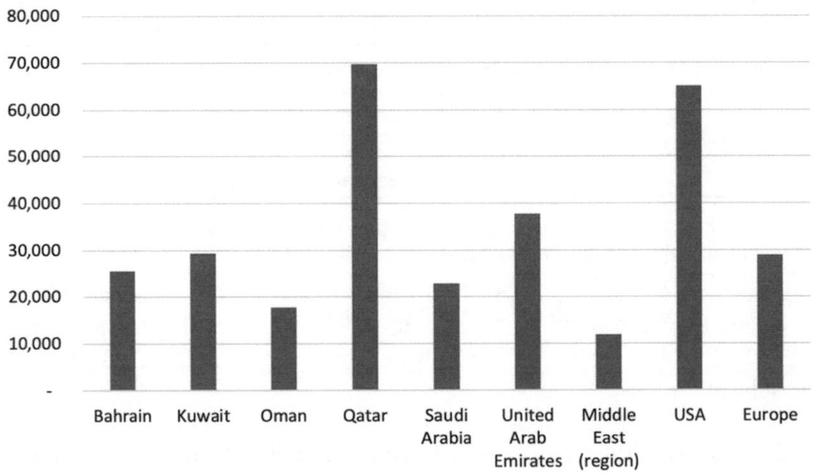

Source: IMF Database.

Figure 9.3 GDP per capita (US$ current dollars) 2019

Implications for Domestic Stability

While the Gulf Arab monarchies largely escaped domestic instability in the wake of the Arab Spring in the early 2010s—Bahrain being the exception (although the unrest there was quickly brought to heel with help from Saudi forces)—the argument that they did so because of their oil wealth is, at best, only partially correct.[18] The significant hydrocarbon resources in Syria and Libya suggest that government legitimacy and popular support in the region are not simply a function of oil wealth available to rulers. Gulf monarchies derive legitimacy from the alignment between traditional royal institutions, tribal structures, and their cultural norms. The emphasis on tradition, hierar-

Table 9.3 Populations and Expatriate Workers

GCC Populations and Expatriate Workers 2019			
	Total Population	Nationals %	Expatriates %
Saudi Arabia	34.3	63.0	37.0
UAE	9.8	15.0	85.0
Oman	4.9	50.5	49.5
Kuwait	4.2	33.0	67.0
Qatar	2.8	15.0	85.0
Bahrain	1.6	46.0	54.0

Source: World Bank Database; National Statistical Organizations; CIA Factbook.

chy, and tribal loyalties provided the Gulf monarchies with a resilient sociocultural heritage and social loyalties.

But the dual shocks of low oil and gas prices and the pandemic-induced global economic slowdown afflicted the GCC countries at a time when the urgency for promoting economic diversification, expanding employment opportunities for their youthful populations, and attaining fiscal sustainability had already become critical. This created an existential challenge domestically, and renegotiating their 'social contracts' with citizens became a critical task. There were outbreaks of public unrest in Bahrain and Oman during the protracted low–oil price period (2015–2020). Nevertheless, with the turnaround in oil and gas prices since 2021, economic growth in the GCC countries will recover significantly in 2022 as already mentioned (see Table 9.1).

Until the oil and gas price rebound since mid-2021, the leading political risk factor for the region concerned domestic social stability in Saudi Arabia, which accounts for over half of the GCC's GDP (Figure 9.4) and is its most populous member by far (Table 9.3). The Kingdom's earlier economic outlook reflected oil production curbs under the OPEC+ agreement, contractions in investment and consumption due to COVID-19-related restrictions, and continued weak oil prices.[19] In the low–oil price scenario, the fiscal deficit was expected to widen dramatically in 2021, and the medium-term outlook was for continued high deficits. However, given the upward surge in oil and gas prices since mid-2021, the fiscal deficit for the GCC in 2021 will improve to 5.7 percent of the GDP compared with 11.7 percent in 2020 (see Table 9.1).

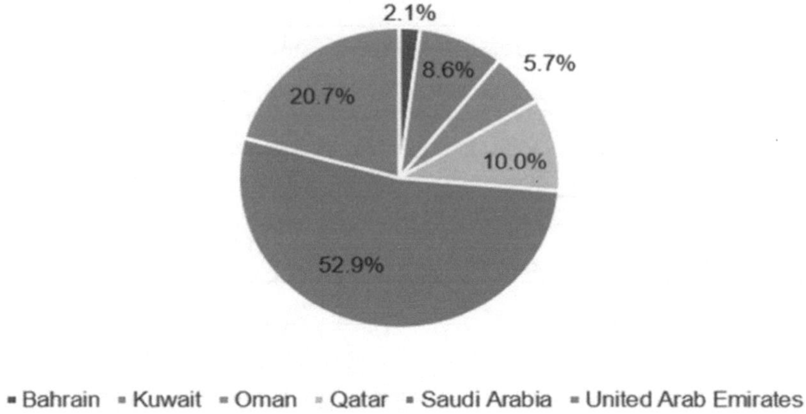

Source: International Monetary Fund, World Economic Outlook Database, April 2020

Figure 9.4 Country Share of GCC GDP 2019

Saudi Arabia announced that it could raise US$58 billion in new debt in 2021, as much as that of the previous two years combined.[20] It had already issued US$19 billion in debt in 2020.[21] The began a drawdown of foreign exchange reserves. In March 2020, the central bank's net foreign assets fell by US$27 billion.[22] Measures to manage public finances included an increase in the value-added tax from 5 percent to 15 percent from July 1, cutbacks in state spending by 5 percent (with reports of government ministries being asked to cut expenditures by 20 percent),[23] suspension of cost of living allowances for state employees, and increase of import duties on products ranging from meat, dairy, and vegetables to vehicles and building materials.[24]

A focus on austerity was expected to either delay or downsize the mega-projects associated with Crown Prince Mohammed Bin Salman's (often called 'MBS') Vision 2030 program. Saudi Aramco, the Kingdom's national oil company, delayed or cancelled many of its ambitious capital-intensive projects in downstream oil refining and the petrochemical and natural gas sectors as it focused on revenue generation and cost cutting in the medium term.[25] The company also faced the burden of fulfilling dividend payments promised to its shareholders when it launched its IPO in December 2019 while oil prices languished.[26]

The aforementioned pressures from austerity measures might help mitigate the culture of dependence on salaried tenure in the state sector among the

Kingdom's indigenous population. The Saudi monarchy is heavily reliant on a combination of large handouts of cash—in the form of public sector wages—and subsidies to shore up support for it. More than 80 percent of the Saudi budget is typically allocated to current expenditures, largely to public sector salaries and social programs. Overly drastic or rapid cuts to these carry risks of social discontent but a reduction in expectations from Saudi civil society for ready sinecures in the government sector was already very much underway by 2020. However, as mentioned, current high oil and gas prices have turned the economic outlook around dramatically for the GCC countries.

Saudi Arabia

High oil and gas prices have alleviated the immediate constraints on the trade and fiscal balance fronts facing Saudi Arabia, and the GCC generally. Nevertheless, MBS's attempts at a profound transformation of the rentier state will have major social implications, and failure by the government to deliver on economic reforms is a key domestic risk factor in the medium term. Managing heightened public expectations for the future will be crucial in maintaining public support for the Crown Prince, the Kingdom's de facto ruler. If he falters in his attempts at economic and social reforms, and if oil prices come back down after a short bullish price cycle and remain low for a protracted period, there is the real possibility that a process of 'Egyptianization' will unfold as the country becomes an increasingly impoverished welfare state.[27]

At this point, MBS's rule seems stable, and he enjoys broad support among its young population. Since assuming the role of Crown Prince in 2017, he has consolidated his position and removed or neutralized real or perceived threats to his standing, including members of the royal family, businessmen, academics, activists, and journalists. The Crown Prince has increasingly focused power on himself, at the expense of the traditional broad consensus among royal family members. Thus, stability of the Saudi regime now rests on one person, and it raises the question of a power vacuum if his rule is threatened.

The Crown Prince has overseen a process of social reforms that is popular among the country's youth (the under-30 age group, which makes up 60 percent of the population).[28] This group has been supportive of moves to root out corruption, ease social restrictions (such as allowing women to drive), and permit access to entertainment forbidden until just a few years ago. Despite the lack of reliable opinion polls in the Kingdom, it is apparent that MBS enjoys genuine support among the younger generation.[29] However, such moves are not entirely popular with older male heads of households, who still subscribe to conservative views. MBS has also neutered the religious establishment.[30]

While Saudi Arabia's long-term outlook rides on the success of his reform program, much depends on how the Crown Prince exploits the current environment of high oil and gas prices to his advantage. Similar concerns affect other Gulf states that are undertaking difficult social and economic reforms, although to different degrees.

Oman

Oman saw unemployment rise because of the cumulative impact of coronavirus-related restrictions on business activity and low oil and gas prices, and this remained the principal threat to the country's otherwise largely stable political environment. Oman's indigenous population constitutes a relatively large share of the total labor force (see Table 9.3). The burden of joblessness and low per capita incomes is, thus, felt most keenly among citizens (compared with the UAE, where an estimated 90 percent of the population consists of expatriate workers). The private sector remains unable to provide for the large young and educated workforce owing to structural barriers such as educational mismatches, private–public pay gaps, and rigid labor market regulations. This has already led to unrest. For instance, in 2018, hundreds of unemployed Omanis demonstrated in Muscat and Salalah, forcing the government to pledge that it would create thousands of jobs for citizens.[31] With higher oil and gas prices, though, Oman's economic outlook (like that of its GCC neighbors) has significantly improved.

Kuwait

Kuwait's political system, which allows an elected national assembly to determine economic policy, will prevent the government from substantially reducing social spending, despite the urgent need to do so. It has been hobbled by an impasse over its new debt law since 2017.[32] Kuwait's capital expenditure program over the past several years has been hampered by recurrent disputes between the government and legislature over large projects, and spending cuts will focus on large capital expenditure projects. But despite the large fiscal deficit expected for 2022, cuts made to recurrent spending will be restrained. Policy makers will remain concerned that a significant cut in recurrent spending could heighten popular discontent.

Previous efforts at fiscal consolidation led to public demonstrations. In 2016, government reforms to the salary and bonus schemes of energy workers triggered a three-day strike, while fuel subsidy cuts in the same year saw active protests by the Labour Union of Kuwait.[33] Labor unions are stronger and more politically active in Kuwait than elsewhere in the GCC. However, its small native population and large foreign exchange reserves mitigate the threat, and expatriates will bear the brunt of cost-cutting measures. Indeed, the country recently passed a law requiring the government to slash the foreign workforce in a year's time, a move that could see millions leave Kuwait and jobs opening up for locals. Kuwait's immediate outlook, like that of the rest of the GCC, has turned positive with the high oil and gas prices since the second half of 2021.

Bahrain

Bahrain is the smallest economy in the GCC, accounting for just over 2 percent of the grouping's total GDP in 2019 (see Figure 9.4), while its per capita income is among the lowest in the region. Alongside its GCC neighbors, its growth outlook significantly deteriorated in 2020. Non-oil activity weakened as business confidence collapsed, and the authorities cut back on public spending while its external balance of payments and fiscal position deteriorated. With the unemployment rate set to rise, the risk of social unrest was expected to grow over the medium term.

Bahrain's domestic politics is particularly fraught as tensions remain high between the Sunni-dominated government under King Hamad bin Isa Al Khalifa and the Shi'a majority population. The Kingdom's political risk profile was elevated amid intensification of the crackdown on the Shi'a opposition, with the suspension of the main opposition party, al-Wefaq, in 2016. Since the Arab Spring, when Saudi troops quelled anti-government riots, little has been resolved. Nevertheless, Bahrain's close relationship with its powerful ally Saudi Arabia provides it with a level of financial, economic, and diplomatic support that will assure regime stability. And, with a new bullish price cycle for oil and gas lifting GCC regional economic activity, Bahrain will also benefit from an improved economic outlook, at least in the short term.

The UAE

The remaining (and higher–per capita income) GCC states—the UAE and Qatar—were less severely affected by the downturn in oil prices. For the UAE, the greatest concern surrounded Dubai, which was facing its worst crisis since 2009. The tourism, hospitality, and real estate sectors were devastated, and Dubai's short- and medium-term outlooks were intimately tied to the speed of post-COVID global economic recovery. The governments of Abu Dhabi and Dubai were in talks about a support package for the beleaguered Dubai economy, reviving memories of Abu Dhabi's last bailout of Dubai in 2009 in the aftermath of the global financial crisis.[34]

With higher oil and gas prices, the UAE's medium-term outlook has become more favorable along with that of its neighbors. Among its strengths, the UAE offers the most hospitable business investment environment among the GCC countries with respect to regulations for foreign ownership, government registration and licensing, and financial market development. Its groundbreaking move to normalize ties with Israel will also generate a wealth of opportunities, not least in the tech and tourism sectors. Domestic political risk is rated very low in the UAE.[35] The government retains a strong grip on power, with the partially elected Federal National Council having little say in decision-making. High living standards among Emirati citizens suggest that public discontent will remain of marginal relevance.

Qatar

Qatar's vast assets in the SWF, combined with a huge resource base and its position as one of the world's three largest exporters of liquefied natural gas (LNG), meant that the emirate weathered the deterioration in its growth performance in 2020, after barely registering any growth in 2019. While lower oil and gas prices put pressure on the country's public finances, the government continued to prioritize maintaining jobs for locals. Qatar enjoys greater fiscal flexibility, aided by its large SWF and a relatively smaller fiscal deficit in comparison with its GCC counterparts. While the government, like its counterparts in the Gulf, will continue to promote diversification, the foundation of this growth will remain the hydrocarbon sector. The recent surge in oil and gas prices has propelled Qatar to new ambitions with respect to its LNG export capacity.[36]

Qatar's relatively small population and vast resource endowment suggests that it will maintain one of the highest per capita GDPs in the world. There are few threats to the country's stability or that of its ruling family. The country's extensive wealth and one of the world's highest per capita national incomes serve to keeps citizens indifferent to political participation. In addition, its newly minted national cohesion, forged in the wake of the blockade by Saudi Arabia, the UAE, Egypt, and Bahrain, will serve to tamp down any discontent. Upcoming events, such as World Cup 2022, will add to its economic recovery efforts.

Implications for the Regional Order

The Arab Spring, beginning in 2010, led to fundamental changes in the regional political order with the shift away from the traditional regional power centers in Cairo, Damascus, and Baghdad—which have suffered turmoil, economic devastation, and civil wars—to the Persian Gulf region. The Gulf states—particularly Saudi Arabia, the UAE, and Qatar—have used their growing economic clout based on the massive influx of revenues from high oil and gas prices from 2000 to 2014 (except for the brief plunge in prices during the 2009 global financial crisis) to develop influence in the media, diplomacy, and military spheres. The current high price cycle for oil and gas will ensure that the GCC remains active in regional affairs, which includes the challenge of facing proxy wars to contain Iranian geopolitical ambitions in the Gulf.

The Moderate GCC Sunni Camp versus Iranian and Turkish Intrusions

The MENA (Middle East and North Africa) region has been characterized by instability prior to the current turbulence brought on by the onset of the pandemic and the steep falls in oil prices. The Gulf monarchies have weathered the turbulence due to a combination of economic resources (derived from their vast hydrocarbon reserves) and political legitimacy derived from traditional tribal structures that channel social loyalties to the royal families. With the current high oil and gas prices likely to remain elevated for at least the next two years, the GCC region is now well placed to resume economic growth along with higher export earnings.[37] According to the World Bank, the strong recovery will carry into 2022 as higher oil prices improve business sentiment and attract additional investment. These favorable market conditions have successfully managed to decrease fiscal and external trade imbalances. The GCC economies are expected to have an aggregate growth rate of 2.6 percent in 2021 and to a high 4.7 percent in 2022, primarily because of stronger oil prices.[38]

Thus, for instance, Saudi Aramco doubled its 2021 net income to US$110 billion, allowing it to issue bonus shares. With profits expected to be even higher in 2022, the national oil company is planning to boost its upstream capital expenditure by US$40–US$50 billion to further expand its production capacity and cement its role as a global swing supplier.[39] The UAE and Qatar are also planning large expansions in their oil and gas production capacities in the coming few years. In the view of the Gulf oil and gas producers, the world—particularly developing countries, which account for 80 percent of the global population—will need its hydrocarbons for decades to come.

Saudi Arabia and the UAE perceive themselves as leaders of the GCC's 'moderate Sunni' camp and, in alliance with Egypt, are at the forefront of the struggle against the regional ambitions of both Iran and Turkey, which have grown at the expense of the Arab world.[40] MBS's moves in Saudi Arabia toward a more open society, as well as significant measures to curtail the role of the traditional clergy, have strengthened the Kingdom's claims toward supporting a more tolerant version of Islam.[41] The latter has been a significant component of the Kingdom's projected image in the international arena, in contrast to its rival Iran, which overtly supports a radical Islamic theology and embraces destabilizing revisionist ambitions across the region. Similarly, the UAE has made its claims to represent a vision of 'moderate, modern Islam,' a central plank in its foreign policy and soft power approaches.[42]

In the area of foreign relations, the UAE falls clearly on the side of the Saudi-led Sunni posture in regional affairs. The UAE's sizeable Iranian population mostly hails from the emigrants who left after the Islamic revolution and who do not support the current Iranian regime. The UAE has increasingly exerted influential economic and military power in the region far beyond its weight in geographical and population dimensions. A more forceful presence in the Red Sea and the Gulf of Aden supports the country's ambitions to establish a greater role in regional affairs.

The core alliance among Saudi Arabia, the UAE, and Egypt has two basic principles in its approach to foreign affairs: (1) a shared identification of security threats, primarily relating to Iran, but also increasingly Turkey, which supports the Muslim Brotherhood and (2) a non-ideological approach to the perennial Israeli–Palestinian issue that distinguishes between the plight of Palestinians and what is increasingly seen as a corrupt Palestinian leadership.[43] Continued Iranian—and increasing Turkish—intrusions into regional conflicts have led Saudi Arabia and the UAE to shore up neighboring Arab regimes with economic aid and military support. Winning favorable outcomes in regional conflicts is perceived by both countries as critical for strategically shaping the regional political order.

Their interventions in Yemen and Libya—and limited operations in Syria, Iraq, Lebanon, and Somalia against proxy forces supported by Iran and Turkey—signify this imperative. However, the financial burdens of the continued funding of a regional arms race and involvement in intractable regional conflicts (such as in Yemen) were becoming unsustainable in the context of slowing growth and low oil prices since 2016. Hence, the UAE partially withdrew its forces from Yemen in August 2019.[44] While the current high oil prices will reduce the burden on the fiscal and foreign exchange constraints binding the Gulf Sunni states, the challenges in countering Iranian proxy wars in the region, which include direct attacks by Iranian-backed Houthi rebels in Yemen on Saudi Arabia and Abu Dhabi, remain key security concerns.

Continued intrusions by Iran and Turkey into regional conflict zones pushed the Gulf Arab countries' relations with Israel closer due to shared threats and a closely aligned strategic map. Over the past several years, Israel has made remarkable progress in covert cooperation on security, intelligence gathering, and counterterrorism with the Gulf Arab countries. Progress in diplomatic relations included backchannel visits between Israeli officials and countries such as Bahrain, Oman, and the UAE. By late 2018—when Israeli Prime Minister Benjamin Netanyahu visited Oman, the first for an Israeli head of state since 1996—the increasing diplomatic exposure of this relationship between Israel and the moderate Sunni Gulf monarchies brought the relationship out into the open and signalled the momentum toward the establishment of formal relations.

The Abraham Accords

The low-oil price environment of 2014–2020, combined with the US desire to reduce its 'boots on the ground' involvement in the region, led the 'moderate Sunni' camp in the GCC to adopt a realpolitik approach to relations with Israel. In the most significant breakthrough in Middle Eastern diplomacy in over four decades, the UAE announced its agreement establishing full diplomatic, economic, and cultural relations with Israel in mid-August 2020, and Bahrain announced a similar agreement less than a month later. These were the first agreements to be signed by Arab League members since the peace accords signed by Egypt (1979) and Jordan (1994).[45] Unlike Israel's peace agreements with Egypt and Jordon, which are narrowly based on security and diplomatic relations, these agreements with the Gulf countries are expected to cover deeper economic investment and trade relations across a number of sectors, including military and cyber equipment, water and agricultural technologies, medicine and other high-technology industries. Sudan signed its normalization accord with Israel in October, and Morocco became the latest country in the region to sign a similar agreement in December.[46]

The hitherto unquestioned presumption of the regional order—that Arab states would never normalize relations with Israel without a resolution of the Israel–Palestine conflict—was jettisoned in a strategic realignment of the Gulf states against Iran. The UAE, in first announcing the normalization of relations with Israel, discarded this presumption that was the basis of the 2002 Arab Peace Initiative. By gaining Israeli commitment to suspend

US-sanctioned annexation of parts of the West Bank, the UAE obviated the charge of betraying the Palestinian cause, and by holding off on annexation in return for formal normalization of relations with the UAE and Bahrain, the then Israeli Prime Minister, Benjamin Netanyahu, was protected from criticisms on his political right flank.[47]

In a signal achievement of the dramatically changed regional political order, the normalization agreements were not accompanied by widespread street demonstrations in the cities of the Arab world—Amman, Beirut, Tunis, Algiers, or Rabat. As expected, the normalization announcements were condemned as betrayals of the Palestinian cause by leaders in Iran and Turkey.[48] The Arab League snubbed a Palestinian resolution condemning the UAE,[49] and the GCC Secretary-General called for Palestinian Authority President Mahmoud Abbas to apologize for "provocative and erroneous statements" against GCC member states.[50]

It is not apparent whether the UAE had tacit prior approval from Saudi Arabia—nor whether the UAE requested it in the first place—for the normalization agreement with Israel.[51] In the event, however, Saudi Arabia quickly approved the use of its airspace for direct flights from Tel Aviv to Abu Dhabi and Dubai.[52] It also almost certainly cleared Bahrain's normalization accord with Israel announced a few weeks later. The Kingdom itself, however, is expected to adopt a more gradual approach toward normalizing relations with Israel as it vies with Iran as the region's 'true defender' of the Palestinian cause in the eyes of its conservative constituency.[53] Oman, under its new ruler—Sultan Haitham bin Tariq—welcomed the accord between Bahrain and Israel, and the Sultanate itself is seen as a potential candidate to sign normalization agreements with Israel.[54]

The Bahrain and UAE agreements with Israel, brokered by the Trump administration, have hedged the Arab Gulf states' security dependence on the United States. By aligning with Israel, the only proximate actor willing and able to challenge Iranian and Turkish attempts at regional hegemony, the UAE strengthened its strategic posture in the region while undergoing a severe constriction in its economic growth outlook and facing a protracted low-oil price environment. The UAE–Israeli agreement enables the Emirates to access advanced weapons systems from the United States, as long as this does not undermine Israel's 'qualitative edge' in military capabilities and gains its tacit approval.[55]

Perhaps the most striking illustration of the changed perception of relations with Israel in the GCC moderate Sunni camp was signalled by Saudi Prince

Bandar bin Sultan bin Abdulaziz's (former Saudi Ambassador to the United States) interview aired by Saudi Al-Arabiya television station in October.[56] In a speech that must have been approved by King Salman, Prince Bandar launched a scathing and unprecedented attack on the Palestinian leadership, which adds Saudi Arabia and its citizens to the growing list of Arabs who regard the Palestinian leadership as 'ungrateful.' He accused the leadership of aligning with Saudi Arabia's foes—Iran and Turkey—and criticized it for accusing the UAE and Bahrain of betrayal for agreeing to establish relations with Israel. The latest Saudi media onslaught against the Palestinian leadership could be seen as a prelude to Saudi Arabia following suit with the UAE and Bahrain by establishing relations with Israel.[57] In March 2022, in a rare interview with the international media, Crown Prince Salman said, "We don't look at Israel as an enemy; we look to them as a potential ally, with many interests that we can pursue together."[58]

GCC Internal Tensions

The Gulf Arab monarchies are divided and internally conflicted. Oman has maintained a neutral stance in its relations with the two sides of the divide, with Turkey and Iran on one side and its GCC counterparts Saudi Arabia, the UAE, and Bahrain on the other. Qatar faced diplomatic isolation from the GCC heavyweights Saudi Arabia and the UAE, as well as Egypt, over differences in Qatar's choice of regional alliances with state and non-state actors, including Iran, Turkey, and the Muslim Brotherhood. Normalization of relations of the UAE and Bahrain with Israel goes far in redressing this imbalance, as growth in trade and investment relations with Israel is expected to be robust and offer significant dividends to the Gulf economies.[59] In particular, the UAE is expected to benefit from Israeli water and food security technologies, cyber and high-technology sectors, a direct shipping route between the Israeli port of Eilat in the Red Sea and Jebel Ali (in Dubai) in the Gulf, investment capital for start-ups utilizing Israeli access to US financial markets, and tourism flows both ways.[60]

Iran's intrusions through its proxy militias in the region, in particular through the many missile and drone attacks on Saudi Arabia and the UAE committed by its Houthi allies in Yemen, constitute the most dangerous flash point in the regional order now.[61] Turkey's intervention in Libya in support of the Islamist-leaning Tripoli-based government, which led Egypt to prepare deployment of its army outside its borders for the first time in almost 30 years, also constituted a dangerous flashpoint.[62] Turkey's intervention in Libya has been long and destabilizing.[63] In a televised address, Egyptian President Abdel Fattah al-Sisi said that the town of Sirte in Eastern Libya—gateway to

80 percent of the country's oil resources in the Sirte Basin—is a "red line" for Egypt and warned that advances by Turkey-backed Libyan forces on Sirte could prompt an Egyptian military intervention in support of Cairo's ally Khalifa Haftar.[64]

Saudi Arabia and the UAE have voiced their backing of President Sisi. Qatar's overt alliance and ideological kinship with Turkey, based on political support for Hamas and the Muslim Brotherhood, seems to have produced a bond that threatens not only the traditional Sunni alliance of Saudi Arabia, the UAE, and Egypt but also strikes at US interests in the region.[65] Both nations host essential US air bases while supporting Islamist political parties, increasingly cooperating with Iran and actively subverting US policy in the region.[66]

No Regional peace on the horizon

The moderate Sunni camp in the GCC, faced with the prospect of low oil prices and a constrained growth outlook over 2014–2020, is constrained in its ability to foster stability in the region. Deepening religious and ethnic tensions and profound antagonisms with Iran will produce recurrent instability. Indeed, there is no regional peace on the horizon. Saudi Arabia appears to be increasingly focused on finding a political solution to the conflict in Yemen that will allow it to withdraw from costly military operations, although the security situation on the ground continues to deteriorate and there are few signs of a durable accord being reached.[67] Tensions with Iran since the September 2019 attacks on Saudi Arabia's oil production facilities remain high, and the risk of more attacks remains elevated.

In January 2022, as if to mark President Biden's first anniversary of Middle East policies, the Iran-backed Houthi rebels in Yemen launched drone and missile attacks on oil facilities near the airport and other sensitive targets in the UAE's capital, Abu Dhabi, killing three and injuring six others.[68] The following Sunday, the US military joined with the UAE to counter another missile attack by the Houthi rebels on an air base near Abu Dhabi where some 2000 US service personnel are stationed. This involved the first firing by the US of Patriot missiles since the 1991 Gulf War. In a third attack in as many weeks, the Houthi militia launched ballistic missiles over Abu Dhabi, which were intercepted by UAE air defences, during an official visit to the country by Israeli President Isaac Herzog. The attacks on Abu Dhabi, deep in the heart of the Gulf's second richest, powerful Sunni petrostate, constitute the most serious escalation of tensions in the Arabian peninsula since the drone and missile attack carried out on critical Saudi Aramco oil facilities in September 2019 also claimed by the Houthis. That attack interrupted 5.7 million b/d of oil-processing capacity or over 5 percent of global production, although much of it was brought back online quickly.

Rounds of talks between senior Iranian and Saudi security and intelligence officials have continued and have focused on two key challenges: normalization of ties and cessation of the proxy war in Yemen. In a goodwill gesture, Saudi Arabia agreed to allow 40 000 Iranians to enter the Kingdom for the annual hajj pilgrimage. Iraq helped broker a fifth round of Iran–Saudi talks in Baghdad in April 2022. This meeting showed some progress as the two countries agreed on a general roadmap toward normalizing relations.[69] These talks were driven by the cooling of ties between Saudi Arabia and the United States after the Biden administration came to office. Nevertheless, progress on the Iran–Saudi talks remains fragile.

Relations between Qatar and its GCC neighbors, as well as Egypt, have resumed. Talks for ending the rift between Qatar and its GCC neighbors in the wake of normalization of relations with Israel by the UAE and Bahrain were seen as high priority by the US administration.[70] The three-year embargo on diplomatic and trade relations with Qatar declared in 2017 by the 'Anti-Terrorism Quartet' comprising Saudi Arabia, the UAE, Bahrain, and Egypt was ended in early 2021, partly as a move to improve prospective relations with the Biden administration.[71]

For fragile and conflict-ridden states such as Iraq, Syria, Yemen, Libya, Jordan, and Lebanon, which are already on the brink of social and economic collapse with their battered infrastructure, massive youth unemployment, and civil unrest, the impact of the pandemic and its collateral economic damage have been severe. While the oil-importing countries in the Middle East (such as Egypt, Morocco, Jordan, and Lebanon) benefitted from sharply lower oil prices through 2020, this was offset by the loss of jobs among citizens of those countries working in the oil-exporting Gulf states. This led to the loss of remittances, a major source of foreign exchange for the oil-importing countries in the region. In general, the low–oil price environment outweighed any gains to be had from lower fuel prices and have had adverse impacts on the poorer Middle Eastern countries that depend on remittances sent by their nationals working in the oil-rich states.

The significant loss in inward remittances for Egypt (which accounted for 8.4 percent of its GDP in 2018–2019) will exceed the COVID-19 impact on tourism and Suez Canal receipts (which together accounted for just over 6 percent of its GDP). Nevertheless, the economic outlook for Egypt was seen as relatively robust in late 2020 by its strong economic reform program launched in 2016 in conjunction with the IMF's loan facility of US$16 billion.[72] As MENA's most populous country with a significant number of its people below the poverty line, the risk of domestic social unrest in the wake of inflation and high food prices—particularly that of wheat, caused by the Russia–Ukraine war—cannot be discounted. With the surge in wheat and fertilizer prices after the outbreak of the war, Egypt once again faces severe trade imbalances and the mounting burden of subsidies for bread, a staple of the local diet.[73]

Enter 2022: Europe's Energy Crisis and the Russia–Ukraine War

Escalating energy prices and higher costs of living became increasingly evident during 2021 in countries such as Germany[74] and the United Kingdom,[75] which are at the forefront of the move to net-zero emissions by 2050. Germany's colossally expensive *Energiewende* (energy transition) strategy was adopted in 2010, aiming for a rapid transition away from fossil fuels toward reliance on renewables for all of the country's energy needs and net-zero emissions by 2050. In a very short period, Germany shut down most of its coal and nuclear plants and expected solar and wind energy to replace its dependence on fossil fuels. The results have not been encouraging, with the country having the highest electricity prices in the world and an increasing incidence of energy poverty with mounting household utility bills. Above all, the Green Party–driven imperatives to replace fossil fuels have led to Germany's overreliance on energy imports from Russia.

Russia accounts for 60 percent of Germany's gas supplies, as well as 50 percent of its coal and 35 percent of its oil.[76] For the European Union (EU), Russia supplies 40 percent of natural gas imports, 46 percent of coal imports, and 27 percent of oil imports. The impact of high electricity prices and unaffordable costs of heating and transport on poorer households in Europe during the 2021–2022 winter energy crisis was brought on by the EU's heavy reliance on energy imports from Russia; surging natural gas, coal, and oil prices; and an extended period of little or no wind causing renewable energy supplies to plummet.[77]

Russia recognized the east Ukrainian separatist provinces as independent on February 21 and launched its ground invasion of Ukraine three days later.[78] The invasion constituted the largest military attack of one state against another in Europe since the Second World War. Western countries and their close allies have hit Russia with a raft of sweeping and unprecedented sanctions.

Several major Russian banks were cut off from the Belgium-based SWIFT international financial transfer system. Transactions with Russia's central bank were banned by the United States, United Kingdom, and EU, effectively preventing Russia from utilizing much of its US$640 billion of foreign exchange reserves. Russia is a major global energy and commodity exporter, including that of crude oil, refined products, metals, timber, wheat, and fertilizers, and the Western financial sanctions on Russia have led to a commodity price boom and steep inflationary pressures in fuel and food prices across international markets. Russia and Ukraine together account for about 30 percent of global wheat exports and 20 percent of corn exports.[79]

Russia's reemergence in Middle East affairs

The Russian 2015 military intervention in Syria marked a pivotal moment for its Middle East policy. Largely absent from the Middle East for decades, Russia intervened to save Bashar al-Assad's regime, established a naval base in Tartus—the only such facility Russia has outside the former Soviet Union—together with an airbase in the nearby Latakia province. Russia's presence in Syria underlines its growing military foothold in the Mediterranean and its reassertion as a major player in the region's political order.[80] The geopolitical realignment and instability caused by the civil wars in Syria and US moves to withdraw from the region under President Obama opened opportunities for Russia to reestablish its relationship with the embattled Syrian regime.[81]

In addition to its growing relationships with Iran and Turkey, Russia is cooperating with Saudi Arabia over oil policy as both grappled with the emergence of the United States as the world's largest oil producer. Saudi Arabia, in turn, has upgraded its relationship with Russia beyond oil supply coordination, given its stake in the outcome of the Syrian conflict and rivalry with Iran.[82] While Russia has positioned itself as an important interlocutor to key players in the region's conflicts, the limits of its power and influence in the Middle East are apparent and its economic clout and military capabilities are far from sufficient to resolve any of the region's major conflicts. The assessment that "Russia's return to the Middle East is important, but hardly a seismic shift" is both accurate and concise.[83]

After the imposition of Western financial sanctions on Russia, Gazprom (the Russian gas monopoly) officials notified gas customers—on March 23, one day short of a month from its invasion date—that the terms of trade will henceforth be in "roubles for gas" for all "unfriendly" countries (i.e., those that imposed unilateral financial sanctions on Russia).[84] The EU claimed that paying in roubles for gas contracts denominated in euros or dollars is "against contract sanctity"; Germany and France rejected Vladimir Putin's demand that foreign purchasers of Russian gas pay in roubles as an "unacceptable breach of contract," adding that the maneuver amounted to "blackmail."

From the Russian point of view, the "roubles for gas" move was inevitable. The US Treasury Department announced on February 28 that it would "immobilize" Russian central bank assets that are held in the United States. Sanctions on Russia were widened as the G7 and EU governments moved on March 2 to block key Russian banks' access to the SWIFT international payment system and froze about half of the Russian central bank's US$630 billion worth of foreign currency and gold reserves.

Dmitry Medvedev—Russia's ex-President and now deputy head of the Security Council—said, "They are seizing assets of financial institutions and even of the [Russian] Central Bank, and are even talking about foreclosing these assets, about nationalising them in other words. Well, look, this is a war without rules."[85] As one Washington lawyer put it, the expropriation of sovereign-owned foreign exchange reserves is "the largest hammer in the toolshed" and represents an all-out economic war with no holds barred.[86]

Not only does this take away Moscow's ability to defend the rouble, this precedent will prompt a reconsideration by finance ministries across the globe—particularly in the majority of countries that have not taken sides with the United States and EU in sanctioning Russia and that may face a potential conflict with the US or EU governments in the future—about where to bank their foreign exchange reserves. OPEC producers Saudi Arabia, Kuwait, and the UAE run some of the world's largest SWFs (see Table 9.2). Doubtless, a globalist US or EU foreign policy agenda will be a new risk factor for the GCC's SWF managers. The GCC countries, some of which own the world's largest SWFs and did not support the United States and the EU in anti-Russia sanctions, must now be acutely aware of the risk of dollar-based financial sanctions that can expropriate a nation's foreign exchange reserves. Economic planners for the GCC oil and gas producers will be assessing the potential for oil and gas sales in other currencies to hedge against the dollar-holdings risk.

Despite significant pressure from the United States, the UAE abstained from a vote at the United Nations Security Council to condemn Russia's invasion.[87] Mohammed bin Zayed, de facto ruler of the UAE and Crown Prince of Abu Dhabi, chose to keep on side with fellow oil producer Russia in OPEC+. The Crown Princes and de facto rulers of Saudi Arabia and the UAE, having declined US government requests to speak to President Biden, saw no problem in talking to President Putin recently.[88]

China in the Middle East

China's emergence as an economic and military power has challenged US dominance in Asia and beyond. The country is one of the prime movers of global commodity and financial markets. Its investments in the much-hyped Belt and Road Initiative, often grossly inflated in the business press, have nevertheless grown into an extensive web of infrastructure construction and investments in over a hundred countries.[89] As a source of loans for deficit-ridden governments in Asia, the Middle East, Africa, and Europe, China has emerged as the major competitor to the World Bank and IMF, the Washington-based pillars of the post–Second World War international economic system.[90] Press reports suggest that China and Iran have concluded a 25-year strategic agreement that could see Beijing invest US$400 billion in Iran's energy and transport infrastructure, banking and telecommunications, and military cooperation and weapons development in return for oil supply at discounted prices.[91] But the 'deal' has been the subject of considerable speculation and hype.[92] The partnership document is nonbinding and more akin to a statement of intent, and it has been attacked by some quarters within Iran, including by former President Mahmoud Ahmadinejad, as "colonialist."[93]

Over the past few decades, China has expanded its economic footprint in the Gulf region and consolidated good relations with every major oil exporter, including Saudi Arabia, the UAE, and Iran. All three have a status as China's 'strategic' partner, and it has successfully negotiated a balancing act aimed at navigating regional rivalries and the security concerns of all major states in the region, including Israel, at both the bilateral and regional levels.[94] It is highly unlikely that China will jeopardize its relations with its Gulf Arab partners by pushing its strategic relationship with Iran too far. There is little reason to believe that China's posture has fundamentally changed from that expressed in its 2016 White Paper—China's Arab Policy Paper—which sought to secure economic opportunities in the MENA region while avoiding exposure to the regional rivalries among state and non-state actors.[95]

The environment of low oil and gas prices during 2015–2020 gave economic leverage to China, which, as the world's largest oil importer, benefited hugely from improving its trade balance. It also enhanced China's importance as a major direct investor and financer in significant Middle East infrastructure and energy projects. For the GCC, Chinese investment comes at a time when these states are seeking to reduce their hydrocarbon dependency and to diversify their economies. Port facilities have been important targets of investment. For instance, China is already playing a dominant role in direct foreign investments in Oman, ranging from its US$11 billion investment in the Duqm Port and Free Trade Zone on the Arabian Sea to its US$1 billion share purchase of the national power utility's transmission company.[96]

China, along with the countries in the BRICS (Brazil, Russia, India, China, and South Africa) group and most of the developing countries in Asia, Africa, and Latin America, did not adopt the financial sanctions on Russia implemented by the Western countries.[97] While China has not directly aided Russia in its war effort, it is betting that a resource-based global currency system will emerge, with rouble, yuan, and rupee convertibility tied to the value of fossil fuels, agriculture, metals, and other primary commodities exported by resource-rich countries and increasingly demanded by resource-poor developing countries.[98] China, India, and Russia are exploring alternatives to the US-dominated SWIFT interbank payments system.[99]

India struck a deal for 3 million barrels of crude oil at discounted prices from Russia for delivery in May, and is looking to secure more supplies in the weeks ahead. As one local oil analyst put it, "If Russia is offering oil at a cheaper price and the trade is between rupee and rouble, then looking at the national interest and leaving aside the geopolitical aspect, India should definitely buy the discounted oil."[100] Saudi Arabia is considering moves to conduct at least part of its oil sales to China in yuan.[101] This could signal the beginning of the end of the 'petrodollar,' one of the pillars that support the status of the US dollar as the reserve currency of the world.

President Trump, the US Shale Revolution, and the Carter Doctrine

The US security blanket became an established feature of the regional political order since Saudi King Ibn Saud met US President Roosevelt onboard a US Navy cruiser in the Great Bitter Lake of the Suez Canal in 1945. The celebrated quid pro quo trading of US military power and regime security for the unhindered flow of Saudi oil to world markets was among the pillars of the Bretton Woods global order that was constructed out of the ashes of the Second World War.

It has been argued that US strategic interests in the Middle East should wane given the country's 'shale revolution' and the remarkable surge in its oil and gas production leading to a reduction of dependence on energy imports from the region.[102] Seasoned observers such as Martin Indyk, a former US ambassador to Israel, have made the argument that given the "structural shift in American interests in the Middle East" (owing to the US shale revolution), the "Middle East isn't worth it anymore."[103]

However, it would be a mistake to make too much of this reduced import dependence. Containing terrorism, mitigating the threat of nuclear proliferation, and supporting Israel's defense needs in a volatile region remain strategic foreign policy imperatives—even as the US disengages from boots on the ground involvement in Syria, Iraq, Afghanistan, and elsewhere.[104] Under the Trump administration, the United States continued its involvement in the Middle East as an 'offshore balancer,' but with considerably more bargaining power and leverage in an age of ample oil and gas supplies.[105]

The Trump administration's 'transactional' approach to Middle East affairs was presumed to signal a progressive disengagement with the region to the detriment of the US role as security guarantor of the Arab Gulf monarchies.[106] References have been made to the Trump administration's lack of response to the Iranian attacks on oil tankers in the Straits of Hormuz in mid-2019, the September 2019 attacks by Iranian drones and missiles on Saudi oil facilities in Abqaiq and Khurais,[107] and the abandonment of Kurdish allies in Syria[108] as instances of US disengagement from the Middle East under the Trump administration. The question as to whether President Trump had abandoned the Carter Doctrine is one that concerns both US allies in the Gulf and foreign policy commentators in Washington think tanks.[109]

However, the argument that the Trump administration was 'disengaging' from the Middle East is hard to square with its actual behavior. This includes the following: President Trump's first official visit to a foreign country was to Saudi Arabia; President Trump fired Tomahawk cruise missiles into Syria after evidence emerged of the use of chemical weapons by the Bashar al-Assad regime in 2017 (in contrast to President Obama's unwillingness to enforce his self-declared "red-line" with respect to the use of chemical weapons by the Assad regime in 2015);[110] deploying Patriot missile batteries and US support troops in Saudi Arabia after the Iranian missile and drone attacks on Saudi Aramco oil facilities in 2019;[111] and the assassination of Iranian General Qassem Soleimani in Iraq in 2020.[112] In a stark reversal of President Obama's Middle East policy of distancing from the Gulf monarchies and Israel while working toward a rapprochement with Iran, President Trump's strategy sought to strongly back Israel, contain Iran's revisionist ambitions with punitive sanctions, and support the Gulf monarchies.

Indeed, if President Trump's noted unpredictability had led the Arab Gulf states to question US commitment to regional security, President Obama's distancing from its Arab Gulf allies and 'normalizing' Iran was perceived by the moderate GCC Sunni monarchies as nothing short of betrayal.[113] Most tellingly, the brokering of the Abraham Accords by the Trump administration reflects the failure of the conventional diplomatic playbook on Arab–Israeli relations adopted over the past several decades by previous administrations of both the Republican and Democratic parties.[114]

The surge in US oil production through the shale revolution made the country less vulnerable to political and social upheavals in the Middle East and increased its foreign policy leverage in achieving its strategic objectives.[115] It gave the United States the means to pursue its 'energy dominance' agenda with greater latitude to support allies and sanction rivals. The decline in US dependence on imported crude oil made it easier for the country to impose export sanctions on oil-producing adversaries such as Venezuela and Iran without the fear of a resulting spike in global oil prices. It also gave the Trump administration clout to pressure Saudi Arabia and its OPEC allies to discontinue the oil-price war with Russia in order to ensure that the US oil industry was not too adversely impacted.[116] The breakthrough in Middle East diplomacy with the Abraham Accords indicated that US leverage in the Middle East remained undiminished during the Trump administration years.

What the Biden presidency wrought in the Middle East in 15 months

As the Biden administration took office, political commentators speculated on how the new administration would wield its strategic advantages arising from its military and diplomatic assets in the region, its vast energy resource endowments, and its innovative and free market economy. There was some expectation that a Joe Biden presidency would reflect a modicum of pragmatism as the Democrats' excessive campaign promises faced the cold light of day and the real costs of radical policy decisions became apparent. Furthermore, given narrow majorities for the Democrats in Congress in the 2020 elections, it looked likely that the more extreme pledges made in the name of the Biden plan's net-zero emissions in the power sector by 2035 and in the entire economy by 2050 would be constrained.[117]

However, the first 15 months of the Biden presidency saw the exercise of wide regulatory powers and Executive Orders for reintroducing onerous regulations that the Trump administration had dumped. Biden's White House worked through politicized administrative agencies, such as the Environmental Protection Agency (EPA), the Department of Interior, and the Bureau of Land Management, to impose punitive regulations against the oil and gas industry.[118] A climate-focused Biden administration would also likely resurrect the Obama EPA's 'sue and settle' practices—deals through which environmental groups file lawsuits against federal agencies so that court-ordered 'consent decrees' are issued on the basis of a prearranged settlement agreement collaboratively crafted by like-minded climate advocates in advance behind closed doors.[119] By constraining US oil and gas production, the new administration, intent on supporting renewable energy and climate change priorities, sought to achieve radical environmental objectives to 'end' the oil and gas industry as candidate Biden had promised during the election campaign.[120]

One year after taking office, Joe Biden—with a flailing presidency struggling with sagging popularity polls,[121] soaring prices at the fuel pump,[122] and the worst inflation rates in four decades[123]—blamed the OPEC+ group of oil producers. US National Security Adviser Jake Sullivan had criticized big oil producers such as Saudi Arabia and Russia in OPEC+ for "insufficient crude (oil) production levels" back in August. The OPEC+ group promptly rejected Sullivan's request to release more oil to world markets. In February 2022, in the shortest meeting so far in its history, OPEC+ kept to its unchanged plans for modest monthly increases in the group's production schedule agreed in April 2020.[124]

While hobbling US oil and gas production, the Biden administration also worked to ease President Trump's 'maximum pressure' sanctions on Iran. Intent on salvaging ex-President Obama's Middle East legacy, Biden stated that he would return to the 2015 nuclear deal if Tehran resumes compliance. A potential resumption of Iranian exports of over 2.5 million b/d (its peak export level in 2018 before President Trump's oil sanctions were imposed) would present a key challenge for the OPEC+ group to balance global supply and demand. The Biden administration's appeasement of Iranian regional ambitions has led to a realignment of Middle East relations that threaten to upend decades of close alliance between the United States and the Sunni Arab monarchies. In particular, the Iranian threat to the regional order has led the Gulf Sunni states to hedge their traditional security relationship with the United States by closer relations with Israel, China, and Russia.

The Biden administration seems to lack an appreciation for the direct link between energy and economic power and between realism in oil policy and geopolitical outcomes. Unlike President Trump's focus on 'energy dominance' and 'America First' strategies, President Biden seems content to stymie US oil and gas production to satisfy the left wing of the Democratic party, while looking to hostile regimes like Iran and Venezuela to supply global oil markets and replace banned Russian oil exports.[125] The Saudis and Emiratis have drawn closer to Russia and China in a strategic realignment brought on by the incoherence of the Biden administration's diplomacy in the region. Under the Biden administration, the United States is in danger of losing both its own status as the world's leading oil and gas producer and its hitherto unchallenged role as security guarantor in the Middle East.

For students and scholars of Middle East geopolitics, key research questions revolve around the prospects for the eclipse of the United States as the world's leading oil and gas producer (leading to even higher global energy prices), the balkanization of global commodity trade into competing currency and regional trading blocs, and the withering of Pax Americana in the Middle East.[126] However these questions are resolved, the Biden presidency presents highly risky scenarios in global energy developments and Middle East geopolitics—scenarios that threaten to be far more disruptive than those that occurred under President Trump's watch.[127]

Notes

1. See Ramady, Mohamed, and Mahdi, Wael (eds), *OPEC in a Shale Oil World: Where to Next?* 2015 (Springer Books).
2. International Monetary Fund (IMF), 2022, "World Economic Outlook Update," January 2022. Accessed at https://www.imf.org/en/Publications/WEO/Issues/2022/01/25/world-economic-outlook-update-january-2022.
3. IMF, "Regional Economic Outlook: Middle East and Central Asia," October 2019. Accessed at https://www.imf.org/en/Publications/REO/MECA/Issues/2019/10/19/reo-menap-cca-1019#stats.
4. Ron Bousso, "BP Wipes up to $17.5 Billion From Assets With Bleaker oil Outlook," Reuters, June 15, 2020.
5. Kevin Crowley, "Investors Pressure Exxon, Chevron to Disclose Long-Term Oil Price Forecasts," *World Oil,* June 1, 2020.
6. Erin Mundahl, "Game Changer: US Shale Now Second Cheapest Source of New Oil Supply," May 14, 2019 (citing data from industry consultants Rystad Energy); Jeff Meyer, "Making Ends Meet: How the Oil Industry Is Cutting Costs to Make Up for Lower Prices," IHS Markit research, May 2017.
7. Tilak Doshi, "Never Mind Punishing the US, Russia and Saudi Arabia's Oil Price War Will Hurt All Producers," *South China Morning Post* (Opinion), March 13, 2020.
8. CBS News, "OPEC, Oil Nations Agree to Unprecedented Production Cut," April 13, 2020.
9. International Energy Agency (IEA) (2022), "Global investments in oil and gas upstream in nominal terms and percentage change from previous year, 2010–2020," October 26 2022. Accessed at https://www.iea.org/data-and-statistics/charts/global-investments-in-oil-and-gas-upstream-in-nominal-terms-and-percentage-change-from-previous-year-2010-2020.
10. Noah Browning, "World Faces Long-Term Oil Supply Gap Despite COVID Demand Destruction," Reuters, December 15, 2020.
11. https://www.woodmac.com/news/feature/explorations-future-in-a-low-cost-low-carbon-world/.

12. International Energy Forum, "New IEF Report Warns Oil and Gas Investment Cuts Will Spur Higher Prices and Volatility," December 10, 2020.
13. Tilak Doshi "Biden vs. Trump: The Battle Over American Energy Policy And Its Consequences," *Forbes*, August 8, 2020.
14. The Wealth Advisor, "Morgan Stanley Raises Oil Forecasts by $10 Citing Market Deficit," April 22, 2022. Accessed at https://www.thewealthadvisor.com/article/morgan-stanley-raises-oil-forecasts-10-citing-market-deficit.
15. IMF, "Regional Economic Outlook for Middle East and Central Asia," April 2020, pg. 2.
16. Fitch Ratings Report, "Oman Country Risk 3Q2020."
17. Reuters, "Moody's Downgrades Oman to Junk, Outlook Negative," March 6, 2019. Accessed at https://www.reuters.com/article/oman-ratings-moodys-idUSL5N20T0G4.
18. Edmund Adam, "Why the Gulf Monarchies Have Survived," The Conversation, September 2, 2020. Accessed at https://theconversation.com/why-the-gulf-monarchies-have-survived-144411.
19. For GDP, fiscal balance, and current account balance forecasts for the GCC countries, see the Data Appendix.
20. See https://english.alarabiya.net/en/coronavirus/2020/05/02/Full-transcript-of-Al-Arabiya-s-interview-with-Saudi-Arabia-s-Finance-Minister.
21. Vivian Nereim, Matthew Martin, and Reema Al Othman, "Saudi Response to Fiscal Shock Centers on Record Debt Plan," Bloomberg News, April 23, 2020.
22. Marwa Rashad and Davide Barbuscia, "Saudi Foreign Reserves Fall at Fastest for Two Decades," Reuters, April 29, 2020.
23. *Financial Times*, "Crunch Crude-Producing Nations Grapple With Price Plunge," April 23, 2020.
24. Marwa Rashad and Davide Barbuscia, "Promise of Future Prosperity Fades as Austerity Hits Saudis' Pockets," Reuters, May 13, 2020.
25. Fereidun Fesharaki, "GCC Economic Outlook and Its Implications for Asia," presentation to Middle East Institute, July 2, 2020.
26. Verity Ratcliffe and Anthony Di Paola, "Aramco Keeps $75 Billion Dividend Promise Despite Oil's Dive," Bloomberg News, March 16, 2020.
27. Steffen Hertog, "What Would the Saudi Economy Have to Look Like to be 'Post Rentier'?" London School of Economics POMEPS Studies, 2019.
28. Chiara Pellegrino, "Saudi Arabia: Between Oil and Coronavirus, the Risks for MBS," Oasis Center, July 27, 2020. Accessed at https://www.oasiscenter.eu/en/saudi-arabia-between-oil-and-coronavirus-the-risks-for-mbs.
29. *Arabian Business*, "Saudi Crown Prince Wildly Popular Among Arab Youth, Survey Shows," May 8, 2018.
30. Raihan Ismail, "How is MBS's Consolidation of Power Affecting Saudi Clerics in the Opposition?" *The Washington Post*, June 4, 2019.
31. "Unemployment Triggers Protests in Oman," *The Arab Weekly*, January 28, 2018.
32. Reuters, "Kuwaiti Parliament Unlikely to Approve Current Version of Debt Law—Speaker," April 5, 2020.
33. Devika Krishna Kumar, "Oil Rises as Kuwaiti Strike Cuts Output for Third Day," Reuters, April 19, 2020.
34. Davide Barbuscia, Saeed Azhar, Pamela Barbaglia, "Abu Dhabi in Talks With Dubai for Support Through State Fund Mubadala—Sources," Rueters, May 15, 2020.
35. "UAE Country Risk Report," Third-Quarter 2020, Fitch Ratings

36. Rania El Gamal, "Qatar Petroleum Signs Deal for Mega-LNG Expansion," Reuters, January 9, 2021.
37. Issac John, "World Bank Upbeat on GCC; Warns of Uneven Mena Growth," *Khaleej Times*, April 14, 2022.
38. World Bank, "Gulf Economic Update, Seizing the Opportunity for a Sustainable Recovery," December 2021. Accessed at https://www.worldbank.org/en/country/gcc/publication/gulf-economic-update-seizing-the-opportunity-for-a-sustainable-recovery.
39. "Saudi Aramco CEO Says Majority of Capex Will be Upstream," Reuters, March 21, 2022.
40. Michael Milshtein, "Strengthening the Stature of the United Arab Emirates in the Middle East as a Reflection of Fundamental Change in the Region," Institute of Policy Studies, IDC Herzliya, August 28, 2020.
41. Haaretz, "After Egypt Mosque Massacre, 40 Defense Ministers Pledge Support for Saudi-led Muslim Military Alliance," November 27, 2017. https://www.haaretz.com/middle-east-news/egypt/egypt-attack-births-saudi-backed-muslim-military-alliance-1.5627006.
42. Yousef Al Otaiba, "A Vision for a Moderate, Modern Muslim World," Foreign Policy, December 2, 2015.
43. Khaled Abu Toameh, "UAE: We Are Not Traitors; Palestinian Leaders Are Corrupt," Gatestone Institute, September 1, 2020.
44. James Dorsey, "The UAE Withdraws from Yemen," Research Paper, The Begin–Sadat Center for Strategic Studies, August 4, 2019.
45. Steve Holland and Matt Spetalnick, "In Break With Past, UAE and Bahrain forge ties With Israel at White House," Reuters, 16 September 2020.
46. Joe Walsh, "Trump Announces Morocco–Israel Normalization Deal," *Forbes,* December 10, 2020.
47. Michael Milshtein, "Strengthening the Stature of the United Arab Emirates in the Middle East as a Reflection of Fundamental Change in the Region," Institute of Policy and Strategy, IDC Herzliya, August 28, 2020.
48. Middle East Monitor, "Iran and Turkey Condemn UAE's Peace Agreement With Israel," August 14, 2020.
49. Khaled Abu Toameh, "Arab League Rejects Palestinian Demand to Condemn Israel–UAE deal," *The Jerusalem Post,* September 9, 2020.
50. Ismaeel Naar, "GCC Chief Seeks Apology From Palestinian Leaders After "Provocative' Statements," Al Arabiya English, September 8, 2020.
51. Stephen Kalin, Summer Said, and Felicia Schwartz, "Saudi Royal Family Divides Over Potential Embrace of Israel," *Wall Street Journal,* September 19, 2020; for an alternative view, see Tommy Stenier, "Geopolitical Competition in the Middle East: The US and Its Allies—Boots on the Ground or off Platforms," presentation to Middle East Institute, NUS, September 10, 2020.
52. Varun Godinho, "Saudi Arabia Approves Use of Airspace for UAE Flights To and From All Countries," *Gulf Business,* September 2, 2020.
53. Sune Engel Rasmussen and Aresu Eqbali, "Israel–U.A.E. Diplomatic Deal Ratchets Up Tensions With Iran," *Wall Street Journal,* August 16, 2020.
54. Rina Bassist, "Is Oman Next in Line to Normalize Relations With Israel?" Al-Monitor, August 17, 2020.
55. Al-Monitor, "UAE Official Says F-35 Request 'Legitimate,' Not Connected to Israel Deal," August 20, 2020.

56. Daoud Kuttab, "Saudi Prince Rattles Palestinian Leaders in Televised Critique," Al-Monitor, October 9, 2020.
57. Khaled Abu Toameh, "Saudi Arabia: We, Too, Are Fed Up With the Palestinians," Gatestone Institute, October 12, 2020.
58. AFP, "Saudi Crown Prince Says Israel Could be a 'Potential Ally,'" March 3, 2022.
59. Felicia Schwartz and Stephen Kalin, "Israel and the UAE Get Down to Business," *Wall Street Journal*, August 21, 2020.
60. Al-Monitor, "UAE, Israel Eye Economic Benefits of Normalisation Deal," August 20, 2020.
61. Asharq al Awsat, "GCC, EU Denounce Houthi Attacks on Saudi Arabia, UAE," February 22, 2022.
62. Mahmoud Mourad and Nadine Awadalla, "Egypt's Sisi Wins Parliamentary Approval for Possible Libya Intervention," Reuters, July 21, 2020.
63. Michael Rubin, "Egypt's Military Is Likely Headed Into Libya (and Turkey Is to Blame)," *The National Interest,* July 22, 2020.
64. "Egypt's Sisi Says Turkey/Qatar-Backed Assault on Libya's Sirte Is 'Red Line,'" *The Defence Post,* June 21, 2020.
65. Burak Bekdil, "Turkey and Qatar: Love in Bloom," Begin–Sadat Centre for Strategic Studies, July 1, 2020.
66. Richard Miniter, "Qatar and Turkey: Toxic Allies in the Gulf," Gatestone Institute, August 28, 2018.
67. Andrew England and Simeon Kerr, "Riyadh Holds Talks With Houthis in Effort to Break Yemen Deadlock," *Financial Times,* October 12, 2019.
68. Tilak Doshi, "Paralyzed by Iran and Oil: One Year Into President Biden's Middle East Policies," *Forbes,* February 7, 2022.
69. See https://www.al-monitor.com/originals/2022/04/iraq-helps-broker-iran-saudi-negotiations#ixzz7S1awQwCF.
70. Simon Henderson, "Qatar Strategic Dialogue Offers Opening to End Gulf Rift," The Washington Institute, September 11, 2020.
71. Irina Tsukerman, "Qatar's Anti-Saudi Seeds of the Islamist Quartet," Begin–Sadat Centre for Strategic Studies, July 2, 2020.
72. IMF, "Arab Republic of Egypt," Country Report 20/271, September 2020.
73. Doaa A.Moneim, "Anticipated IMF Loan to Bolster Egypt's Social Safety Net Amid Ukraine War: IMF Managing Director," Ahram Online, April 20, 2022.
74. Thomas Kohlman, "German Energy Prices Hard to Tame," DW News, December 21, 2021.
75. Thomas Colson, "Soaring Cost of Living Will be 'Deeply Damaging' for Boris Johnson, Even If He Survives Current Crisis, Warn Tories," *Business Insider,* January 20, 2022.
76. Nikolaus J. Kurmayer, "Germany to Create Strategic Coal and Gas Reserves," EURACTIV, February 25, 2022.
77. Llewellyn King, "How Europe Triggered an Energy Crisis and Now Is Paying Dearly for It," *Forbes*, November 27, 2021.
78. "Russia Has Invaded Ukraine: What We Know So Far," *The Guardian,* February 24, 2022; "Russia Recognizes Independence of Ukraine Separatist Regions," DW News, February 21, 2022.
79. "Change in Average Price of Selected Commodities From February 24 to March 14, 2022," Statista. Accessed at https://www.statista.com/statistics/1298241/commodity-price-growth-due-to-russia-ukraine-war/.

80. Yuras Karmanau, "Naval Base in Syria Cements Russia's Mediterranean foothold," AP News, September 27, 2019.
81. David Ignatius, "Obama All but Invited Putin's Bombing of Syria," *The Washington Post,* October 2, 2015.
82. Habib Toumi, "King Salman First Saudi Monarch to Visit Russia," *Gulf News,* October 2, 2017.
83. Eugene Rumer, "Russia in the Middle East: Jack of All Trades, Master of None," Carnegie Endowment for International Peace, October 31, 2019.
84. Guy Faulconbridge, "Kremlin Warns West: Rouble-for-Gas Scheme Is the 'Prototype,'" Reuters, April 3, 2022.
85. "All Russia's Big Exports Could Soon Be in Roubles, Kremlin Signals," *Asharq al Awsat,* March 30, 2022.
86. Mike Dolan, "Column: Russia Central Bank Freeze May Hasten 'Peak' World FX Reserves," Reuters, March 2, 2022.
87. Ken Klippenstein, "UAE Chooses Solidarity Between Oil Producers Over Military Allies," The Intercept, March 9, 2022.
88. Abhijit Iyer-Mitra, "Payback time! Why Saudi Arabia and UAE Refused to Talk to Joe Biden While Merrily Chatting With Vladimir Putin," Firstpost, March 10, 2022.
89. Derek Scissors, "China's Global Investment Vanishes Under COVID-19," American Enterprise Institute Report , July 16, 2020.
90. Ben Steil and Benjamin Della Rocca, "China, a Major World Bank Borrower and Competitor, Must Stop Sheltering BRI Debt From G20 Standstill," Council of Foreign Relations, May 8, 2020.
91. Farnaz Fassihi and Steven Lee Myers, "Defying U.S., China and Iran Near Trade and Military Partnership," *The New York Times,* July 11, 2020.
92. Shahram Akbarzade and Mahmoud Pargoo, "Iran–China Deal Raises More Questions Than Answers," Middle East Institute, July 27, 2020.
93. Saheb Sadeghi, "Iran Split Over 25-Year China Plan Still Shrouded in Mystery," Middle East Eye, July 17, 2020.
94. Jonathan Fulton, "Will China Become a Major Arms Supplier to Iran?" The Atlantic Council, June 9, 2020.
95. Gordon Houlden and Noureddin M. Zaamout, "A New Great Power Engages With the Middle East: China's Middle East Balancing Approach," China Institute, University of Alberta, January 2019.
96. Nawiel Jabarkhyl, "Oman Counts on Chinese Billions to Build a Desert Boomtown," Reuters, September 5, 2019.
97. Laura Aboli, "List of Countries Not Imposing Economic Sanctions Against Russia," *Australian National Review,* March 5, 2022.
98. Tilak Doshi, "The Russia–Ukraine War: A New Geopolitics Of Finance and Energy Trade Emerges," *Forbes,* April 7, 2022.
99. Dipanjan Roy Chaudhury, "India–Russia–China Explore Alternative to SWIFT Payment Mechanism," *Economic Times* (India), November 14, 2019.
100. Rajesh Roy, Vibhuti Agarwal, and and Philip Wen, "India to Buy Russian Oil at Discount Amid Ukraine War," *The Wall Street Journal,* March 16, 2022.
101. Sumer Said and Stephen Kalin, "Saudi Arabia Considers Accepting Yuan Instead of Dollars for Chinese Oil Sales," *The Wall Street Journal,* March 15, 2022.
102. Goerge Seay, "America No Longer Needs the Middle East," *The National Interest,* July 18, 2019.

103. Martin Indyck, "The Middle East Isn't Worth It Anymore," *Wall Street Journal,* January 17, 2020.
104. Middle East Monitor, "Top Army General: US to Reduce Troops in Iraq, Syria," August 14, 2020.
105. Tilak Doshi, "The Brave New World of Ample Oil," *Business Standard,* November 10, 2019.
106. Rodger Shanahan, "Trump's Hollow Strategy in the Middle East, Lowy Institute," Lowy Institute, May 27, 2017.
107. Chris Megerian and Nabih Bulos, "Trump Says 'No Rush' to Respond to Attacks on Saudi Oil Facilities," *Los Angeles Times* September 16, 2019.
108. Elias Groll and Lara Seligman, "Trump Abandons the Syrian Kurds," *Foreign Policy,* October 7, 2019.
109. Hal Brands, Stephen A Cook, and Kenneth Pollack, "RIP The Carter Doctrine 1980–2019," *Foreign Policy,* December 13, 2019.
110. Jamie McIntyre, "Inside Trump's Cruise Missile Strike on Syria," *Washington Examiner,*
April 8, 2017.
111. "Trump Orders Troops and Weapons to Saudi Arabia in Message of Deterrence to Iran," *New York Times,* October 11, 2019.
112. Namo Abdulla, "US General: Killing of Soleimani Has Deterred Iran," VOA News, June 10, 2020.
113. Yaroslav Trofimov, "Like Israel, U.S. Arab Allies Fear Obama's Iran Nuclear Deal," *The Wall Street Journal,* March 4, 2015.
114. Editorial, "The Art of a Mideast Deal: Trump Was Willing to Break With a Failed Conventional Wisdom," *Wall Street Journal,* September 15, 2020.
115. Meghan L. O'Sullivan, *Windfall: How the New Energy Abundance Upends Global Politics and Strengthens America's Power,* Simon & Schuster, 2017.
116. David Sheppard, Derek Brower and Katrina Manson, "US Puts Pressure on Saudi Arabia to End Oil Price War," *Financial Times*, March 26, 2020.
117. "The Biden Plan for a Clean Energy Revolution and Environmental Justice," https://joebiden.com/climate-plan/.
118. Steven F. Hayward, "The EPA Is Politicized—So Make It Official," *Wall Street Journal,* January 8, 2013.
119. Larry Bell, "EPA's Secret and Costly 'Sue and Settle' Collusion With Environmental Organizations," *Forbes,* February 17, 2013.
120. Bronson Stocking, "Biden Says He Will Eliminate the Oil Industry," *Townhall,* October 22, 2020.
121. Kenneth Garger, "Biden Approval Rating Tanks to New Low: Poll," *New York Post,* January 25, 2022.
122. US Energy Information Administration (EIA), "Energy Today," April 19, 2022. Accessed at https://www.eia.gov/todayinenergy/detail.php?id=52098.
123. Editorial, "Now Biden's Given America the Worst Inflation in 40 Years," *New York Post,* January 12 , 2022.
124. "25th OPEC and non-OPEC Ministerial Meeting Concludes," OPEC Secretariat, February 2, 2022. Accessed at https://www.opec.org/opec_web/en/press_room/6796.htm.
125. Sen. Macro Rubio, "Rubio Leads Colleagues in Introducing Bill to Ban Oil and Natural Gas Imports From Iran and Venezuela," March 10, 2022. Accessed at https://www.rubio.senate.gov/public/index.cfm/2022/3/rubio-leads-colleagues-in-introducing-bill-to-ban-oil-and-natural-gas-imports-from-iran-and-venezuela.

126. Tilak Doshi, “Oil and the Eclipse of Pax Americana in the Middle East,” *Forbes,* March 10, 2022.
127. Tilak Doshi, “The Coming Energy Shocks Under a Biden Administration,” *Forbes,* November 11, 2020.

PART IV

The future of energy policy: meeting the macro challenge—domestic reform or unsustainability

10 Cybersecurity and Data Protection in the power sector: challenges, perspectives, and policy approaches

Arnault Barichella

Cybersecurity risks in the power sector

Cybersecurity risks magnified by digitization of energy infrastructure

For many years, the energy industry had little exposure to cybersecurity risks due to its reliance on mechanical and analogue systems, together with so-called proprietary programs and procedures that were specially designed for each type of equipment or activity. The nature of the energy industry is such that investment cycles last for several decades, which has delayed the incorporation of digital technologies and computer software. Several factors, however, have contributed to changing this situation over time. Digital transformation in other sectors put pressure on energy firms to rationalize production through mass collection and processing of data. Moreover, the need to transfer data to entities outside of the main installations and to reinforce internal communication between industrial and management sites also became increasingly necessary.[1]

In order to address these new challenges, the energy sector chose to rely mostly on industrial control systems (ICS) and, more specifically, on supervisory control and data acquisition systems (SCADA). SCADA have made it possible to remotely manage infrastructure and equipment. They are cheaper than proprietary control systems and have helped to optimize the entire supply chain, offering consumers a broader choice of customized services. This includes real-time access to data from machinery at all levels of the energy supply chain, as well as the creation of consumer and production profiles. Such digitization has helped to boost profits and decision-making possibilities for firms and improve energy supply due to predictive maintenance. The enhanced efficiency and economic advantages have led to a 'digital revolution' in the energy sector, whereby information and communication technologies (ICTs) are increasingly installed on a large scale in energy infrastructure around the world. Nevertheless, the downside of this digital revolution has been to significantly increase the vulnerability of the energy sector to cyberattacks.[2]

This chapter will examine the impact of the digital revolution on the energy sector, in particular increased risks linked to cybersecurity. This has occurred due to a number of reasons. First, the growing reliance on ICTs and the Internet has created open networks in energy infrastructure, with an upsurge in data sharing with and transfers to external operators. The latter has amplified vulnerabilities. Although propriety and analogue systems had been fairly isolated, new devices, especially those connected to the Internet of Things,[3] are often not designed to incorporate sufficient cybersecurity protections. Second, given the long-term nature of investment cycles in the energy sector, many elements in its infrastructure were designed several decades ago, when the Internet was only just emerging, and some of the equipment will likely be maintained for a few more decades to come. Because cybersecurity was not a major preoccupation at the time, installations were not built to defend against cyberattacks through authentication procedures or encryption, for example, but focused instead on reliability and stability. Third, the fact that energy infrastructure is sometimes several decades old means that it is often problematic for operators to access the history of the composition of their equipment. This situation makes it harder to detect current vulnerabilities in installations, rendering it more difficult to take appropriate protective measures.

Furthermore, since the energy sector possesses its own unique characteristics, conventional IT protection systems borrowed from other sectors or industries may not always be transferable or effective. For example, installing an antivirus mechanism on the power grid could cause up to 20 percent of equipment to suddenly stop working, thus disrupting the continuous flow of electricity. Consequently, any software upgrade in the energy sector generally calls for prolonged testing to verify that the power supply and machinery will not be unduly affected.[4] In many cases, this has discouraged operators in the energy industry from updating their systems to protect from cyberattacks even after weaknesses are identified, resulting in protective software that is often obsolete or inadequate.

Vulnerability of electrical grids to cyberattacks

Power system operators and maintenance teams are used to dealing with disruptions caused by severe weather events or physical sabotage. Cyberattacks, however, are altogether different since they make it possible for hackers to aim at numerous vulnerabilities in the power system at the same time. In fact, only a small number of openings are necessary for a virus to propagate through an entire network.[5]

The digitization of electrical grids has accelerated over the last few years with ICTs and digital equipment constantly developing new processes; these may, however, incorporate undetected vulnerabilities that are hard to anticipate. In addition, the power supply chain is particularly susceptible to cyberattacks because electricity flows from the grid are instantaneous, increasing the risk of cascading system failure. Lloyd's insurance carried out a study in 2015 that estimated the financial impact of a large-scale cyberattack at several key points of the electrical grid in 15 US states; the resulting aggregate cost to the US economy could range anywhere between US$243 billion and US$1 trillion.[6]

The consequences would not only be financial, since the electrical grid is of fundamental importance for almost all of society's vital functions. This includes essential infrastructure for communications, health, transport, the military, government services, as well as water and food supplies. These services risk being downgraded to a bare minimum and could stop functioning altogether if emergency petrol and gas stocks run out.[7]

While the entire power system is vulnerable to cyberattacks,[8] the transmission network is a prime target for hackers due to its critical role in the effective operation of the power system as a whole. Manual procedures may help to contain the damage from a cyberattack in a local substation that is not indispensable to the rest of the network, but national or regional system operators often control electricity transmission and distribution for an entire electrical grid or large parts of the network, which makes them particularly vulnerable.[9]

In many cases, hackers are able to take advantage of human error and negligence, including the unintentional use of an infected USB key during maintenance procedures or the fact that passwords are often not updated regularly enough on equipment such as programmable logic controllers. These types of mistakes are frequently linked to a lack of training for personnel at electrical installations, while the technical expertise of potential hackers continuously progresses. Although there has been a general increase in awareness about the cybersecurity risks facing the power sector over the last few years, insufficient training remains a chronic issue.

Specificities of the civil nuclear sector in terms of cybersecurity

Due to the significant risks associated with nuclear power plants, the industry has developed a comprehensive and thorough security approach to protect against physical incidents such as sabotage, fires, or radiation. For example, communication networks and most equipment are duplicated in a number of ways—through the use of an Ethernet system, on-site installations where redundancy is applied, or additional equipment in remote locations. Several independent cables are used to transfer information about the condition of critical sites in nuclear reactors, and such information is only accepted as reliable after being verified multiple times. Likewise, nuclear plants do not send or receive any information from external entities, except for data regarding power and voltage, which needs to be regularly shared with system operators to facilitate efficient and reliable power system management. Additional security systems include 'islanding' (also relied on for other types of emergencies), whereby a nuclear installation can manage in 80 percent of cases to supply its own electricity if an attack succeeds in cutting off the power supply, thanks to a number of on-site emergency generators.[10]

Moreover, these security features have been reinforced around the world following the Fukushima nuclear incident in 2011, especially in Europe and the United States, where access to nuclear sites has been further restricted and many industrial control systems have been duplicated off-site with different configurations. Such physical security mechanisms also offer strong protection in terms of cybersecurity. They can help to significantly reduce the prospect of viruses being inserted into the critical systems of nuclear installations and contain the scale and contagion from malware during a cyberattack.

Although nuclear infrastructure in many countries was constructed before digitization, the industry has not been spared the digital revolution that has swept through the energy sector over the last few years.[11] A number of new nuclear reactor models, such as the Evolutionary Power Reactor (EPR[12]), have integrated control processes that rely on digital technologies for surveillance and remote control. The latter make it possible to transfer data in real time from more than 10 000 sensors that constantly monitor the condition of plant and machinery at critical nuclear sites, which can help to enhance security by reducing the risk of human error. Likewise, digital remote control can improve operational efficiency, leading to more cost-effective outcomes.

And yet, as with the electrical grid, this gradual digitization of the nuclear industry has also introduced new vulnerabilities in terms of cybersecurity. For instance, already in 2009, nuclear safety authorities in the United Kingdom, France, and Finland issued a joint declaration to share their concerns regarding the digitization of certain EPR systems and the associated cybersecurity risks.[13] Subsequently, all three countries chose to reduce the reliance of their EPR plants on digital systems by duplicating critical processes and reinforcing the use of analogue equipment, including at Hinkley Point in the United Kingdom, Flamanville in France, and Olkiluoto in Finland.

It should be noted, however, that other countries, including the United States, have not adopted the same level of security. Digitization of US nuclear infrastructure has been more rapid and widespread than that in Europe. For instance, the US Nuclear Regulatory Commission (NRC) launched an Integrated Action Plan in 2017, containing a series of concrete measures to accelerate the digitization of US nuclear plants, including certain critical functions.[14] Likewise, in 2018 the NRC and the Nuclear Energy Institute published an updated rule to clarify procedures for upgrading instrumentation and control systems so as to consolidate digitization of US nuclear infrastructure.[15] The first fully digitized US nuclear reactor was inaugurated in 2019 by Purdue University in Indiana; although a small research reactor, this might lead to notable changes in the US nuclear industry via application to larger reactors in the coming years.

While the economic advantages are undeniable, this digitization has nonetheless increased cybersecurity risks, despite safety mechanisms built into new digital equipment. For instance, the Wolf Creek nuclear plant in Kansas was hit by a cyberattack from May to June 2017 with malware probably stolen from the National Security Agency. Taking advantage of the digitization of industrial systems, hackers managed to exploit software vulnerabilities to infiltrate the installation's computer network. Although they did not succeed in reaching critical processes, this attack emphasized the risks associated with enhanced digitization in the nuclear industry, as well as the advantages of approaches that preserve certain analogue processes.

Cyberattack profiles in the energy sector

Over the last decade, there has been a significant increase in the number and sophistication of cyberattacks in the energy sector. These attacks have targeted not only the administrative offices of energy companies, but also physical infrastructure and installations, as well as public institutions related to the energy industry, such as ministries or departments. In fact, energy firms and institutions are now increasingly faced with cyberattacks on a daily basis, with thousands of attacks reported each year around the world.[16] The seriousness and scale can vary considerably from minor intrusions to highly destructive viruses. Despite their great variety, three main categories of cyberattacks can be distinguished:[17]

1. Cyber espionage, where the objective is to spy on activities in the energy sector in order to steal confidential data and information
2. Cyberattacks that seek to interrupt the energy supply or the provision of a service
3. Cyberattacks that seek to damage or disrupt infrastructure by compromising the integrity of systems and equipment

These categories are not mutually exclusive, since cyberattacks combine multiple characteristics in some cases. Hackers may perpetrate cyberattacks for a number of reasons, although financial motivation remains the most common factor behind the majority of documented attacks. This is typically associated with the first category of cyber espionage and data theft. These types of attacks are often conducted by criminal groups of hackers, who attempt to sell the confidential information they steal on the black market or to governments. For example, a hacker group referred to as 'Energetic Bear' spread a virus to around 250 energy firms and installations in the United States and Western Europe in 2014, stealing large amounts of confidential information since it remained operational for several years before being discovered. Likewise, another hacker group known as 'Dragonfly' launched several waves of cyber espionage operations on the energy sector in Europe and the United States from 2011 to 2014, and after 2015, with a peak of attacks in 2017 involving highly sophisticated spying malware.

Although cyber espionage can be lucrative, there are nonetheless a number of impediments that make these types of operations very challenging to carry out in practice.[18] Indeed, the configuration of industrial infrastructure in the energy sector is not easily accessible. Launching this type of cyberattack necessitates very specific expertise both in IT and in automation engineering, as well as substantial resources to prepare the attack several months in advance. Given these obstacles, it is now widely believed that powerful nations have been providing both financial and logistical support to a number of prominent cyberattacks that have impacted the energy sector over the last few years.

In this regard, geopolitical factors constitute another important motivation for cyberattacks. These are often associated with the second and third categories, which involve interruption of the energy supply, as well as damage and destruction to infrastructure, although espionage and data theft can also be an objective.[19] A prominent example remains the 'Stuxnet' virus, which infiltrated the uranium-enrichment complex of Natanz in Iran and succeeded in damaging nearly 1000 uranium-enrichment centrifuges over several years before finally being uncovered in 2010. It represented the first major cyberattack on an important energy installation, highlighting previously unrevealed vulnerabilities that astonished the energy sector at the time. Subsequent investigations suggested that the US and Israeli governments may have supported the attack, perhaps to delay Iran's nuclear program in order to win additional time for diplomatic negotiations.[20]

While this sort of assault might be interpreted as an act of war given its potentially devastating consequences, it remains highly problematic to attribute the origin of a cyber virus with certainty.[21] This is due in part to the use of false flags, which help to conceal the assailant, thus enabling state-sponsored hackers to conduct major cyberattacks without necessarily exposing themselves. Furthermore, malware is, on average, only uncovered 200 days after it infects an installation or system, delaying responses and making it even more difficult to identify perpetrators.

For example, Ukraine was targeted by several major cyberattacks in the years before the Russian invasion. This includes the 'Black Energy' virus that hit the country in December 2015, shutting down 30 power substations and, thus, depriving more than 200 000 people of electricity for several hours in eight different provinces. Electrical utilities were physically damaged and had to be run manually for several weeks after the attack. Likewise, Ukraine was targeted again in May 2017, this time by the 'XData' virus, which prepared the way for the devastating malware 'NotPetya' a month later. This extremely sophisticated virus spread to over 18 percent of Ukrainian energy firms, infecting more than 30 percent of all electronic systems in the country. It has proven difficult to assign responsibility for these cyberattacks, even if most experts believe that the Russian government was behind them, given current geopolitical tensions in the region.[22] Furthermore, these cyberattacks were not localized incidents, but spread globally, including to Western countries through firms and their subcontractors that maintain business and financial ties with Ukraine. This underlines the risk of international propagation from cyberattacks originating in the energy industry or in other sectors, which is linked to the globalization of digital technologies.

Several waves of cyberattacks also destabilized Ukraine in the lead-up to the Russian invasion in February 2022, disrupting government, military sites and the banking system, along with critical infrastructure, including the energy sector. The attacks comprised 'wiper' and 'distributed denial of service' operations, which involve saturating computer systems with high numbers of requests until breakdown, in order to close down Internet sites and destroy large amounts of data. Owing to digital interconnections, including energy infrastructure transiting through Ukraine, propagation to neighboring EU countries remains a subject of concern. What is more, the 'hybrid warfare' mobilized by the Russian army throughout the invasion of Ukraine (although not in the manner many had expected [23]) has blended cyberattacks with regular military actions, similar to the previous intrusions into Georgia (2008) and Crimea (2014).[24]

Different policy approaches to cybersecurity in the power sector

The US approach: 'security in depth'

As a response to the rising challenge of cybersecurity in the power sector, the United States has chosen a 'security in depth' approach, which involves comprehensive and rigorous standards that are applied by agencies with coercive authority.[25] Although cyber issues have been a long-term preoccupation in the United States, the 9-11 terrorist attacks acted as a catalyst that amplified and hastened the establishment of strict cybersecurity rules, including in the power sector due to its strategic significance. The 2005 Energy Policy Act[26] provided the Federal Energy Regulatory Commission (FERC) with a mandate to choose an Electric Reliability Organization (ERO) under its authority to develop security norms for the national electrical grid. FERC named a private entity: the North American Electric Reliability Corporation (NERC).[27] NERC has set up cybersecurity standards that focus on the production and transmission parts of the electrical grid (not distribution, which falls under the purview of states due to the federal nature of US legal and political arrangements).

NERC was the incumbent peak body representing the regional reliability councils prior to the 2005 Act, making it the logical and only practical choice as ERO. The 2005 Act required the ERO (i.e., NERC) to be constituted as a corporate entity. The driver behind this was to create clear, comprehensive, and legally enforceable responsibility and accountability for power system security across the United States, which represented a significant governance change due to the constitutional context. The latter was implemented in response to key recommendations from the US–Canada Power System Outage Task Force (convened to examine the Great North Eastern Blackout of 2003). The Task

Force also made several recommendations about cybersecurity, which shaped NERC's subsequent approach and work in this area.

The first version of the Critical Infrastructure Protection standards (NERC-CIPs) was launched in 2008. These standards are obligatory for more than 3300 electric utilities throughout the United States and contain some of the most rigorous and exhaustive cybersecurity rules in the world.[28] Furthermore, as a response to the continuous development of new cyber risks, these NERC-CIPs have been upgraded every few years. The eighth version was approved by FERC in 2019 and implementation began in 2020. In his second term, President Obama signed two Presidential Policy Directives[29] and one Executive Order[30] to reinforce cybersecurity for critical infrastructure and support enactment of the NERC-CIPs. Likewise, passage of the Fixing America's Surface Transportation Act in 2015[31] assigned new responsibilities to the Secretary of Energy in the event that the President triggers a grid security emergency.[32]

Despite disagreements on many issues, it should be noted that cybersecurity was one topic where President Trump chose to build on his predecessor's policies. For instance, the 2018 US National Cyber Strategy put special emphasis on securing critical infrastructure, including in the power sector. President Trump also signed an Executive Order[33] in 2017 requiring relevant federal agencies to evaluate the cybersecurity resilience of the electrical grid and provide suggestions to initiate corresponding upgrades. In 2018, the Trump administration created a new specialized Office of Cybersecurity, Energy Security, and Emergency Response to lead the Department of Energy's (DOE) coordinated responses in this area. The latter complemented the broader mandate of the Cybersecurity and Infrastructure Security Agency (CISA, within the Department of Homeland Security), established the same year. These two new structures were buttressed by another Executive Order in 2019[34] to strengthen cybersecurity competency by addressing the lack of training on this issue among federal government employees. In addition, Trump signed two further Executive Orders, in 2019[35] and 2020,[36] to ensure that the acquisition of energy sector infrastructure and bulk-power assets is carried out securely. Interestingly, both Houses of Congress also passed the Securing Energy Infrastructure Act[37] in 2019, mandating a two-year pilot program to identify vulnerabilities, as well as develop policy and technological solutions to reinforce security of the power grid. This included examining the partial return of analogue processes for some critical equipment.[38]

Since cybersecurity is a subject that enjoys bipartisan support, the Biden administration indicated its objective of continuing and reinforcing such laws and policies begun under President Trump to secure critical infrastructure, including in the power sector. Thus, in response to two of the most severe cyberattacks that recently targeted the United States, including the 'SolarWinds' cyber espionage campaign discovered in December 2020 (which seriously compromised the Energy Department), along with the hacking of the country's largest Colonial Pipeline in May 2021, Biden signed a far-reaching Executive Order. The latter set out upgraded and advanced cybersecurity requirements for all US Departments, while putting particular emphasis on private cybersecurity firms to enhance defences and transparency.[39] This was followed by a National Security Memorandum in July 2021 specifically addressing cybersecurity for critical infrastructure, with a focus on the power sector.[40] The Memorandum required CISA, in collaboration with the National Institute of Standards and Technology (NIST, within the Department of Commerce) and other federal agencies, to elaborate cybersecurity performance goals for critical infrastructure, such as electric utilities. It also launched the President's Industrial Control System (ICS) Cybersecurity Initiative, a voluntary scheme between the federal government and critical infrastructure entities with the goal of reinforcing cybersecurity standards for new systems and technologies.[41]

The US security in depth approach also involves rigorous mechanisms to ensure that cybersecurity standards are properly enacted. Hence, NERC has coercive powers that compel US electrical utilities to implement the NERC-CIPs. For example, NERC may impose penalties of up to US$1 million per day pending compliance with regulations. This has proven to be a very effective incentive over the last few years.[42] NERC also regularly conducts inspections within utilities across the United States to ensure that standards are being applied.[43] Likewise, NERC possesses an alert mechanism known as 'NERC-Alerts,' whose purpose is to notify all US electrical utilities of immediate risks to power system security and reliability, including cybersecurity risks. NERC has issued several dozen alerts over the past few years, as well as a few high-level alerts (e.g., in 2015, 2017, and 2022) in response to cyberattacks in Ukraine and the threat of global propagation. In this regard, following the Russian invasion of Ukraine, the US Congress passed a far-reaching bi-partisan bill in March 2022 which bolstered cyber defenses for various types of critical infrastructure, including in the energy sector. This involved enhancing the powers of agencies investigating cybersecurity incidents, with particularly strict new security incident reporting requirements.[44]

In addition, NERC sponsors a Grid Security and Emergency Response Exercise (GridEx) every two years. This comprehensive exercise involves federal and local government officials, together with many private industry representatives, who take part in simulated cyber and physical threats or incidents on the electrical grid. For instance, GridEx V brought together around 7000 participants from over 500 different entities across North America in November 2019, making it possible to assess in real time the resilience of cyber and physical security standards for the power grid.[45]

Public–private sector collaboration is further reinforced through the Cybersecurity Risk Information Sharing Program (CRISP), which includes most actors in the US energy industry (serving over 75 percent of electricity customers), along with the DOE. Likewise, Information Sharing and Analysis Centers (ISACs) have been in place since 1998, allowing the US government and industrial groups to work together on developing standards and detecting new risks. The ISAC focusing specifically on the electrical grid (E-ISAC) has managed CRISP since 2014 in collaboration with utilities and the DOE. Such close public–private sector collaboration in the United States has helped ensure that cybersecurity standards are tailored to the specific needs of the energy industry, improving their implementation and effectiveness.[46]

The US approach of security in depth also impacts cybersecurity in the civil nuclear sector. Following the 9-11 terrorist attacks, the powers of the NRC were reinforced, and its position as the sole national authority in this area was consolidated. In 2009, under President Obama, the NRC put in place a Cyber Security Rule, which contained comprehensive regulations for all US nuclear power plants.[47] This included the requirement to establish a cybersecurity plan adapted to the specificities of each nuclear station in order to protect all computer networks throughout the installation, covering critical systems, emergency mechanisms, as well as off-site communications. Under this Rule, competent authorities in every power plant are required to submit their cybersecurity plans and an implementation schedule to the NRC for approval. The NRC published official guidelines to facilitate enactment of the Cyber Security Rule, so that the highest standards and best practices are applied across the US nuclear industry.[48]

In June 2013, responsibilities and oversight for all NRC activities relating to cybersecurity were centralized under the aegis of the Cyber Security Branch within the Office of Nuclear Security and Incident Response. The latter conducts regular inspections to ensure effective implementation of cybersecurity plans and an appropriate level of cyber protection for each nuclear power plant through a system involving successive 'Milestones.' The latest inspection phase, referred to as 'Milestone 8,' began in 2017 and was completed in 2020.[49]

A culture of collaboration and information sharing on cybersecurity is developing between different regulatory and administrative bodies across the US energy sector. For instance, the NRC signed a memorandum of understanding with NERC in 2010 to reinforce cooperation on cybersecurity and to clarify their respective fields of responsibility. Federal agencies also participate in the Cyber Security Forum for Independent and Executive Branch Regulators, created in 2014 to help harmonize cybersecurity standards across different sectors.

The EU approach: 'comprehensive and flexible'

The EU approach to cybersecurity in the power sector is very different from the US model. It is necessarily 'flexible,' given that member states have a good deal of autonomy in interpreting and applying standards. It is also 'comprehensive' because it recognizes the interrelated nature of reliability, resilience, and information security in the power sector and, therefore, seeks to address cybersecurity issues within this wider context.[50] As a result, EU-level policies and legislation in this field are more general in nature and not as specific or detailed as those applied in the United States. This is partly because they focus on cybersecurity for critical infrastructure in general, rather than specifically for the power sector. Where they are specific to the power sector, they do not focus on cybersecurity.

EU policies in this area go back to the 2006 Programme for Critical Infrastructure Protection, as well as the 2008 Critical Infrastructure Directive;[51] both were limited to setting out broad guidelines on a general level, however. The same applies to the EU's Cybersecurity Strategy, first presented in 2013 and then updated in 2020. Moreover, the EU ratified a Directive on the Security of Network and Information Systems (NIS)[52] in 2016, which has become the main legislation for protecting critical infrastructure. It aims to define common European norms regarding operators of essential services, but is not sector specific.[53] The 2019 Cybersecurity Act[54] reinforced the 2016 Directive with new procedures to facilitate application of the NIS Directive. In particular, it created a cybersecurity certification framework across the EU for digital services, products, and processes, including those in the energy sector.

Although these recent initiatives constitute improvements, they still provide extensive flexibility to member states, each of which must develop its own national cybersecurity strategy. Likewise, the 2019 EU Regulation on Risk Preparedness in the Electricity Sector[55] seeks to develop a common approach to address a broad range of risks facing the power grid, including extreme weather events, fuel shortages, sabotage, and cybersecurity. Yet, it mandates countries to develop their own national risk preparedness plans, to be loosely managed via an Electricity Coordination Group. The only EU document focusing exclusively on cybersecurity in the energy sector is a 2019 EU Commission Recommendation;[56] this provides general policy guidelines to member states with a focus on key public and private sector stakeholders, without any binding legal force, however.

Member states are also responsible for the protection of civil nuclear infrastructure. The EURATOM Treaty, signed in 1957 by the six founding countries, allowed for the creation of the European Atomic Energy Community, whose responsibility is to ensure that nuclear energy is used in a safe and sensible manner by signatories. Since then, however, European institutions have not been able to establish common standards to protect nuclear plants from physical risks, let alone from cyber threats. As a result, responsibility for this has once again been left to member states, which enjoy extensive authority to decide on their own rules to protect domestic nuclear facilities. This is linked to the fact that the security of both the electrical grid and nuclear installations is a sensitive issue; as a result, many countries consider this to be within the purview of national sovereignty and are disinclined to share strategic information with their neighbors.

Flexibility in the interpretation and application of EU policies or legislation has led to a situation where member states across the EU have very differentiated cybersecurity frameworks. Countries such as France and Germany are leading the way, while others lag behind.[57] Greater integration of EU electricity networks and markets has the potential to expose the wider regional power system to countries with less advanced cybersecurity standards, increasing the risk of malware infiltrating the EU network and propagating to other member states. This highlights the advantages of the US security in depth approach, where the development of comprehensive and rigorous federal rules for both the electrical grid and nuclear installations reduces the danger of weak links emerging in the US power sector.

The EU's flexible approach is also reflected in the role and function of its regional regulatory body in this field, the European Network and Information Security Agency (ENISA), also referred to as the EU Agency for Cybersecurity.[58] The 2019 Cybersecurity Act provided ENISA with a permanent mandate, an enhanced budget and staff, as well as additional competences to help member states in applying the NIS Directive. It should be noted that ENISA has a mandate covering all sectors, not just the power sector like its US counterpart (NERC); at the same time, NERC's focus is wider than cybersecurity, covering different facets of power sector reliability and system security. Regardless of differences in the scope of their respective mandates, another point of contrast is that ENISA's competences are very limited compared with NERC's, as it mostly works on collecting and sharing information, offering counsel to member states, as well as promoting greater cooperation. Unlike NERC, ENISA does not possess any coercive authority to ensure compliance with EU standards, and it has far fewer budgetary and staff resources.[59]

Moreover, while ENISA coordinates pan-European cybersecurity exercises every two years, these do not concentrate specifically on the power sector and are much smaller in scale than the US GridEx. The fifth Cyber Europe exercise, which took place in June 2018,[60] focused on aviation and engaged around 900 participants, mostly from EU institutions, member states, and industry, compared with nearly 7000 participants in GridEx V. This is partly because GridEx addresses a wider range of reliability and system security preparedness issues, reflecting NERC's broader mandate within the power sector.

At the same time, the EU has established a contractual Public–Private Partnership to reinforce public–private sector collaboration on cybersecurity. This program has been managed jointly by the EU Commission and the European Cyber Security Organisation (ECSO)[61] since 2016. However, these arrangements do not focus on the energy industry and provide a looser and less binding framework when compared with CRISP and E-ISAC in the United States. While a European Energy Information Sharing & Analysis Centre (EE-ISAC) has been in place since 2015, it is mostly a private industry–driven initiative, with ENISA and a few specialized national institutions only loosely affiliated. As a result, it is less developed than its US counterparts.[62]

Furthermore, the NIS Directive requires member states to develop a competent national NIS authority, along with a Computer Security Incident Response Team (CSIRT). The Directive seeks to bring together all national CSIRTs into a common network and has also created a Cooperation Group with the EU Commission and relevant national agencies that includes a specialized work stream on energy since 2018. However, like ENISA, both the Cooperation Group and the CSIRT network lack coercive authority to enforce cybersecurity standards. Instead, member states must choose which capacities to ascribe to their CSIRTs and how to implement EU norms. Once more, this has led to a situation where the efficiency and capabilities of national CSIRTs are very different across member states, thereby creating some weak links that increase the risks of propagation.[63] This again highlights the advantages of the US security in depth approach, whereby rigorous federal mechanisms are in place to ensure that cybersecurity standards are effectively enacted.

For these reasons, implementation of the NIS Directive over the last few years has been challenging, resulting in a certain degree of fragmentation across the EU internal market. Hence, the Commission sought to upgrade the NIS Directive with a new legislative proposal in December 2021 to enhance cybersecurity requirements, reinforce reporting obligations, address the security of supply chains, and strengthen enforcement and supervisory processes. This includes measures to harmonize sanctions among member states, for example. In addition, NIS2 aims to enlarge the scope of the Directive by integrating more entities and by covering new sectors, so as to align with the sectors addressed by EU standards for physical infrastructure protection.[64] Although NIS2 clearly represents an improvement, it may not go far enough, especially in addressing the issue of weak links. For instance, despite a proposed harmonization of sanctions, responsibility still falls upon member states to set out detailed rules for their own cybersecurity paradigms at the national level. This may prolong the problem of disparate norms across Europe.[65]

While the 'flexibility' of the EU's cybersecurity approach can be problematic, it should be noted that the 'comprehensive' dimension is in fact beneficial, since it covers a range of diverse policy areas, unlike the narrower US approach. For instance, EU legislation provides cybersecurity protection for all aspects of the power system, including production, transmission, and distribution. Under the NIS Directive, this responsibility is allocated to national CSIRTs, which are mandated to adopt a holistic approach.[66] By contrast, US legislation and regulations (NERC-CIPs) do not include the distribution section of the power system, since this is a state responsibility. The problem is that only a handful of states, such as California, have enacted adequate rules covering electricity distribution. Partial regulatory coverage in this area constitutes a significant weakness, which may increase the US power system's vulnerability to cyberattack. This weakness is magnified by the growing deployment of 'smart' meters and devices among electricity consumers, each of which can provide a potential point of entry for hackers (see Section 3).[67]

Another important aspect of the EU's comprehensive approach relates to cybersecurity for renewable energies and low-carbon technologies.[68] Cybersecurity was addressed in the Clean Energy for all Europeans package proposed by the Commission in 2016. The key elements were formally adopted by the Council of Ministers in 2019 and comprised a revised Regulation on the internal market for electricity.[69] These reforms provided the Commission with a mandate to create a network code for cybersecurity in the power grid, including for the rising share of renewable energy. An expert group (Smart Grids Task Force) was formed in 2017 to prepare this network code and released its second interim report in July 2018.

By contrast, former President Obama's Clean Power Plan, announced in 2015, had not set out explicit cybersecurity rules, while the Executive Orders signed by President Biden in 2021 and 2022 to tackle climate change do not specifically address cyber threats. The same is true of individual US states, a number of which have chosen to enact their own renewable energy policies over the last few years, often without paying sufficient attention to cybersecurity. One reason for this is that many US companies in the renewable energy sector appear to be concerned that the application of too many security procedures on equipment could negatively impact productivity, innovation, and revenues. Nevertheless, the fact remains that renewable energy and low-carbon technologies have been increasingly targeted by cyberattacks over the last few years.[70] This is mostly due to the use of sophisticated digital technologies for remote control, network connection, and storage, given the intermittent nature of wind and solar power, for example.

Overall, the benefits associated with the comprehensive aspect of the EU's cybersecurity framework are apparent when compared with the narrower US approach. They cover a broader range of issues, such as the distribution sector of the power system, renewable energies, and low-carbon technologies.

The French approach: a detailed regulatory framework

Although flexibility in the EU approach has led to significant disparities across member states, it has also provided a certain margin for maneuvering, enabling some countries with sufficient resources, logistical means, and adequate infrastructure to develop their own rigorous cybersecurity paradigms at the national level. France represents a particularly salient example in this regard, since it has developed an approach to cybersecurity involving a detailed and comprehensive regulatory framework, providing a similar level of protection as, and having a number of parallels to, the US approach of 'security in depth'. The origins of France's cybersecurity policies date back to the 2008 White Paper on Defense and National Security (*Livre blanc sur la défense et la sécurité nationale*), which laid the foundations for an independent cybersecurity framework for information systems. The French policy approach to cybersecurity was further developed via the 2011 National Cybersecurity Strategy, subsequently updated in 2015,[71] and followed by a very detailed upgrade in 2018[72] with greater emphasis on the protection of critical infrastructure, including the power sector.

A key outcome stemming from the 2008 White Paper was the creation of France's National Cybersecurity Agency (*Agence nationale de la sécurité des systèmes d'information—ANSSI*) in 2009, which has become one of the most advanced cybersecurity institutions in Europe, and perhaps in the world. Indeed, the Agency possesses more staff and budget resources than NERC[73] and is charged with ensuring implementation of French cybersecurity rules. Likewise, the updated 2013 White Paper on Defense and National Security established the cybersecurity of operators of vital importance (OVIs) as a national priority.

The legal basis of France's regulatory framework was consolidated through the 2013 Military Programming Law (*Loi de programmation militaire*), which defined rigorous standards for a classified list of over 200 OVIs, comprising key infrastructure in the power sector. This list was subsequently expanded with an updated Military Programming Law adopted in 2018,[74] covering the 2019–2025 period. However, a series of sectorial decrees (*arrêtés sectoriels*) for OVIs enacted in 2016 constitute the cornerstone of the French regulatory framework. France became the first country to do this, establishing obligatory and detailed rules tailored to the specifics of each sector, such as electricity,[75] gas, and hydrocarbons, with the latest one also covering the nuclear sector.[76]

For instance, companies have three months to deliver a complete list to ANSSI of all their vital information networks. Digital technologies must be carefully classified and recorded along with each new update, and a strategy for the protection of digital and information systems must be clearly set out. ANSSI also established an alert mechanism with mandatory reporting on all cybersecurity incidents and regularly carries out thorough reviews of OVIs to verify on-site conformity. Like NERC in the United States, ANSSI is able to impose high penalties of €150 000 for individuals and up to €750 000 for legal entities.

While they share a number of similarities, the French approach is also different from its US counterpart in several important areas. For example, ANSSI is a public agency, like ENISA at the EU level, whereas NERC is a private company subject to federal regulation by FERC. Moreover, while NERC specializes in the power system, ANSSI has a much wider mandate—to protect all information systems, including in the energy sector—which also explains why ANSSI has a greater budget and more staff compared with NERC. At the same time, NERC's focus is wider than cybersecurity, covering different facets of power sector reliability and system security.[77] One advantage of the French approach is that it enables better coordination through the value chain and between the different sectors, since they are all brought together under the same common framework. However, the downside is that the energy sector possesses specific characteristics that can differ markedly from other policy areas. As a result, by specializing in the power sector, NERC may offer more timely and effective solutions for cybersecurity incidents in the electrical grid compared with the general approach favored by ANSSI.

Privacy and data protection in the power sector

Data protection in the power sector with the emergence of smart grids and smart devices

The development of smart devices[78] and smart grids represents a major aspect of the digitization of electrical networks. The objective is to enhance efficiency by 'rationalizing' energy usage, thus facilitating and empowering customer choice, which is a critical precondition for well-functioning electricity markets. Indeed, customers benefit from better access to data and information as it enables them to organize their personal energy consumption more effectively. This is becoming even more important as technological change drives the transition toward a more decentralized power system in which independent decision-making will be critical for delivering efficient, affordable, and reliable investment, operational, and end-use outcomes.

However, like most digital technologies, smart devices and smart grids also introduce new risks in terms of cybersecurity. For instance, smart grids contribute to integrating domestic and industrial electricity systems, which creates additional vulnerabilities. Moreover, the installation of billions of smart devices around the world multiplies exponentially the number of potential openings for malware within the power sector.[79] In fact, since all smart devices are connected to the grid and the Internet, where they regularly exchange data with an electricity company, every device represents a potential entry point for cyberattack. This threat is exacerbated by the fact that smart devices are in many cases designed in identical or very similar ways across countries, which means that they often share the same vulnerabilities. As a result, the downside of the mass deployment of smart devices has been to significantly increase cybersecurity risks throughout the power sector. Although this includes the propagation of viruses that could potentially disrupt the electricity supply or damage infrastructure, a seminal problem associated with these new digital technologies relates to privacy and data protection.[80]

Smart meters collect data on where, when, and how much electricity people consume. Such information is then processed and stored, along with a range of other customer information, by electricity companies in data centers. While these data collection processes are rapidly developing, their management is increasingly being outsourced through Cloud computing technologies.[81] Due to the aforementioned vulnerabilities, data collected by smart meters can be nonsecure, which may jeopardize the privacy of consumers.[82] In a number of countries, especially EU member states subject to enhanced privacy requirements, electricity companies have had to put in place safety mechanisms to ensure better data protection. In France, for example, smart meters must comply with robust privacy protection rules under national and EU legislation. This includes reduced collection and systematic encryption of any data transmitted to a data center, where systems must be strictly isolated from one another.[83]

While these measures are helpful in the case of France, smart meters installed in other countries, especially outside of the EU, often do not incorporate the same level of protection. More importantly, many experts agree that regardless of the level of safety, total protection is not possible, especially since new digital technologies may contain so-called 'zero-day' vulnerabilities. This refers to weaknesses that may not have been discovered at the time when a new technology was released or remain undetected by teams responsible for patching and updating software. Consequently, there is a risk that adequate protection has not been provided. For instance, a number of experiments conducted over the last few years highlight vulnerabilities and susceptibility to cyberattacks in smart meters, despite safety mechanisms such as encryption.[84]

The EU and France: extensive privacy and data protection

In order to manage growing data protection risks linked to new digital technologies, the EU and several of its member states have enacted, in this sphere, some of the most extensive laws and regulations in the world. It is important to distinguish between two interrelated concepts in terms of privacy rights: data protection and data security. Data protection refers to the action of limiting as much as possible the inappropriate collection of personal data; by contrast, data security involves managing the ways in which such data is processed and used after being collected.[85]

The EU has sought to create an ambitious and binding regulatory framework covering both data protection and data security, which forms part of its comprehensive approach to cybersecurity. The 1995 Data Protection Directive[86] was superseded in 2016 by the General Data Protection Regulation (GDPR), which has become the EU's key legal instrument in this area.[87] The GDPR includes provisions relating to the lawful, fair, and transparent processing of personal data; the nature and scope of data that may be processed, collected, and stored; the portability of data transfers; the right to be forgotten if citizens wish to erase or modify certain aspects of their personal data; and a requirement to provide explicit consent when data is processed for any purposes other than the reason for which it was collected.[88] The GDPR also requires companies to report data breaches within 72 hours, incorporate privacy by design in all data collection processes, conduct regular training and data protection impact assessments, as well as nominate a Data Protection Officer.

As the GDPR is a Regulation, it became binding in its entirety across all member states from May 25, 2018. Likewise, its provisions are rigorously enforced, since sanctions for breaching GDPR clauses can be as high as €20 million, or 4 percent of global annual revenues for private companies.[89] In addition to applying to all EU-based entities, GDPR provisions are also binding on any organization, public or private, that engages in the collection of EU citizens' data, regardless of its location around the world. The GDPR's substantial extraterritorial scope reflects the degree of international trade with the EU.

The EU's ambitious framework on data protection has been supplemented by rigorous legislation in this area at the national level, as well as through the establishment of specialized national institutions. In France, for example, the National Commission on Informatics and Liberty (*Commission nationale de l'informatique et des libertés*—CNIL) was founded in 1978 to establish an adequate protection of individual liberties in relation to the sensible application of new information technologies. The CNIL's mission focuses on four major axes covering both data protection and data security: inform and protect, advise and support, anticipate and innovate, control and sanction.[90] Its objectives were defined by the 1978 law on Informatics, Data Files and Liberties (*Loi relative à l'informatique, aux fichiers et aux libertés*).

The 1978 law was updated in 2004[91] to comply with new EU standards. The 2004 upgrade substantially modified the original text by expanding the range of categories that constitute 'personal data,' simplifying judicial review mechanisms, enhancing penalties for noncompliance, and reinforcing the CNIL's powers of investigation and control. This forms part of the detailed regulatory framework characteristic of the French approach to cybersecurity. Moreover, these laws help ensure the impartiality of the CNIL through strict rules concerning its management and composition.[92]

California's initiatives to offset US federal inadequacies

On the subject of privacy and data protection, the approach taken by the US federal government differs significantly from the rigorous frameworks enacted by France or the EU. In particular, current federal legislation relating to data protection is limited in scope and coverage and is not legally binding.[93] This reflects concerns that more invasive privacy and data collection regulations would unduly impede innovation and growth in the IT sector. Various stakeholders, led by influential digital technology firms, have sought to reinforce these concerns among US legislators.[94] Consequently, questions have been raised regarding the neutrality of the resulting federal legislation. For example, the 2014 Cybersecurity Information Sharing Act[95] appears to favor business interests over adequate protection of consumers' personal data.

In addition, the adequacy of federal institutional arrangements in this area is debatable. For instance, the first and one of the main federal agencies charged with privacy protection is the Privacy Office, established in 2002. However, it has been placed under the authority of the Department of Homeland Security, whose core activities may not always be compatible with ensuring privacy and data protection.[96] By contrast, the CNIL in France has a clear focus on privacy and data protection and pursues both vigorously.

Furthermore, certain laws enacted in the United States may jeopardize privacy rights in other parts of the world. For instance, the Clarifying Lawful Overseas Use of Data Act[97] (known as the 'Cloud Act'), approved by the US Congress in 2018, has considerable extraterritorial implications regarding the transfer of personal data stored in other countries that rely on US-based Cloud computing services. This may endanger data protection rights in the EU, including some of the core provisions of the GDPR. The Act has a substantial impact on the energy industry, due to its increasing reliance on Cloud computing systems to process ever larger volumes of consumer data.[98]

Such gaps in the US privacy and data protection framework at the national level have created opportunities for state-based initiatives. Although few have responded to date, there are some notable exceptions. For instance, California has successfully implemented some of the most far-reaching data protection standards in the world. It should be noted that the California Consumer Privacy Act (CCPA),[99] enacted in 2018, was inspired by and shares a number of similarities with the EU's GDPR. At the same time, California's legislation has sought to go further than the GDPR on several important issues.

For example, the state legislature passed the Privacy Customer Electrical or Natural Gas Usage Data Law in 2014.[100] The Law requires firms to ask for explicit consent from customers before exchanging or divulging data about their energy consumption to any other firm or outside entity. In addition, it sets out rigorous standards specifically designed to protect consumer data collected via smart meters. Energy companies are required to systematically utilize encryption for all types of processed data.[101] This is not remarkable in and of itself, since a number of European firms also rely on encryption to protect personal data from smart meters. What is interesting, however, is that California state law focuses on privacy protection in the energy sector and, more specifically, for data collected using smart meters and smart grids. A more recent Californian initiative on Information Privacy Connected Devices,[102] which came into effect in January 2020, requires businesses to assure information privacy for all smart devices. It reinforced data protections applying to smart meters.

By contrast, although the EU and several member states possess advanced frameworks on data protection, their legislation is more general since it covers a range of different sectors, including the energy industry. While there are benefits to both approaches, it is arguable that smart meters and smart grids generate new and complex challenges when it comes to data and privacy protection. As a result, the Californian approach has the advantage of tailored laws that focus precisely on addressing these complex issues and may, thus, offer stronger protection compared with the more general European paradigm.

In conclusion, cybersecurity and data protection are among the most significant challenges facing the power sector. Their importance is bound to continue increasing in the years to come, due to the accelerating digitization of critical infrastructure. The different policy approaches outlined in this chapter each contain their strengths and weaknesses and are often adapted to particular national or regional contexts. Enhanced international collaboration is needed to effectively address cybersecurity challenges stemming from the rapid development and globalization of digital technologies. It also offers a unique opportunity for countries to learn from each other's cybersecurity frameworks, in order to reduce the risks of global propagation.

Notes

1. Desarnaud 2017.
2. Colbert & Kott 2016.
3. The 'Internet of Things' is a concept in computer science that refers to physical objects in everyday life connected via the Internet, allowing them to identify themselves and interact with other connected objects or devices. See: Misra 2017.
4. Arghandeh & Zhou 2017.
5. D'Andrade 2017.
6. Maynard & Beecroft 2015.

7. Even if the power supply were eventually reinstated, it could take a number of weeks, perhaps even months, before a return to normal.
8. The electrical grid traditionally integrates a three-fold division between electricity production, transmission, and distribution.
9. Desarnaud 2017.
10. *Ibid.*
11. Baylon 2015.
12. Within the EU, this third-generation, pressurized water reactor is sometimes referred to as the 'European Pressurized Reactor.' However, the US and international denomination is 'Evolutionary Power Reactor,' or EPR.
13. UK Health and Safety Executive, French Authority for Nuclear Safety, and Finnish Radiation and Nuclear Safety Authority (2009), *Joint Regulatory Position Statement on the EPR Pressurised Water Reactor.*
14. NRC (2017), *Integrated Action Plan to Modernize Digital Instrumentation and Controls Regulatory Infrastructure.* An update was issued in January 2019.
15. NRC (2018), *Clarification on Endorsement of Nuclear Energy Institute Guidance in Designing Digital Upgrades in Instrumentation and Control Systems*, 83 FR 29437.
16. Many cyberattacks are, in fact, never reported by companies or institutions due to fear of reputational damage, so the total number of attacks is probably much higher.
17. Desarnaud 2017.
18. Hassanien & Elhoseny 2019.
19. While this has not been ascertained, experts suspect that a number of large-scale cyber espionage operations against the energy sector, including those conducted by the 'Energetic Bear' and 'Dragonfly' hacker groups, appear to have been supported by the Russian secret services.
20. Sanger 2012.
21. Shrobe 2018.
22. Barichella 2018.
23. The cybersecurity dimension of the war in Ukraine, while significant, has not unfolded in the way many experts had anticipated. Although Russian-backed hackers did carry out multiple waves of cyberattacks against Ukraine since the invasion began, these have primarily involved low- to medium-scale attacks including spying, psychological disruption, along with 'hybrid' warfare combining cyberattacks with targeted conventional military strikes. While there has been some spillover into neighboring EU countries, this has been relatively limited, with Moscow focusing instead on amplifying cyber espionage and disinformation against the West to foment internal divisions. This has partly been due to remarkable cyber resilience from Ukraine, combined with extensive Western IT assistance. Russia also poorly prepared its cyberattacks against Ukraine, perhaps due to the expectation of a rapid war. The impact of crippling Western economic sanctions, along with a brain drain of Russian IT professionals, have also been determining factors in this regard. However, the risk escalation must not be underestimated. See: Barichella 2022b.
24. Barichella 2022b.
25. *Ibid.*
26. Pub. L. 109–58, 109th Congress, 8 August 2005.
27. NERC's mandate is not limited to the United States and covers parts of Canada and a small section of Mexico as well.

28. Every CIP focuses on a different aspect of cybersecurity in the electrical grid, including security management controls (CIP-003-6), personnel and training (CIP-004-6), physical security of BES cyber systems (CIP-006-6), incident reporting and response planning (CIP-008-5), configuration change management and vulnerability assessments (CIP-010-2), and information protection (CIP-011-2).
29. Presidential Policy Directive 21: Critical Infrastructure Security and Resilience, February 12, 2013, and Presidential Policy Directive 41: United States Cyber Incident Coordination, July 26, 2016.
30. Executive Order 13 636: Improving Critical Infrastructure Cybersecurity, February 12, 2013.
31. Pub. L. 114-94, 114th Congress, December 4, 2015.
32. Stockton 2018.
33. Executive Order 13 800: Strengthening the Cybersecurity of Federal Networks and Critical Infrastructure, May 11, 2017.
34. Executive Order 13 870: America's Cybersecurity Workforce, May 2, 2019.
35. Executive Order 13 873: Securing the Information and Communications Technology and Services Supply Chain, May 15, 2019.
36. Executive Order 13 920: Securing the United States Bulk-Power System, May 1, 2020.
37. S.174, 116th Congress, August 16, 2019.
38. Although the US energy sector is likely to continue digitization due to strong economic incentives, this represents an interesting development that might lead to readjustments in the coming years.
39. For example, all US Departments are required to implement multifactor identification log-in systems within 180 days, hasten the transition to 'cloud' and 'zero trust' frameworks, identify which data is too sensitive to be kept in standard networks, as well as administer more thorough evaluations of critical software suppliers, with cybersecurity vendors needing to report intrusions within 72 hours of discovery. See: Executive Order 14 028: Improving the Nation's Cybersecurity, May 12, 2021.
40. National Security Memorandum: Improving Cybersecurity for Critical Infrastructure Control Systems, July 28, 2021.
41. The initiative was launched in April 2021 with a pilot targeting the power sector and has rapidly become very successful since more than 150 electric utilities covering 90 million customers have adopted or agreed to adopt enhanced control system cybersecurity technologies.
42. Barichella 2018.
43. It should be noted that these audits address the full range of reliability and system security requirements; cybersecurity is but one of them.
44 Amongst other things, the 'Strengthening American Cybersecurity Act' requires that critical infrastructure entities must report cyberattacks to CISA less than 72 hours after occurrence. See: S.3600, 117th Congress, March 1, 2022.
45. The latest exercise, GridEx VI, took place in November 2021 with fewer participants (around 3000) due to the COVID-19 pandemic.
46. NERC also holds an annual Grid Security Conference (GridSecCon), bringing together experts from both the public and private sectors to encourage collaboration through technical information and best practice exchanges.
47. US Nuclear Regulatory Commission (2009), Cyber Security Rule, 10 CFR 73.54, *Protection of Digital Computer and Communication Systems and Networks.*

48. US Nuclear Regulatory Commission (2010), Regulatory guide 5.71, *Cyber Security Programs for Nuclear Facilities.*
49. Office of the Inspector General, NRC Defense Nuclear Facilities Safety Board (2019), *Audit of NRC's Cyber Security Inspections at Nuclear Power Plants*, OIG-19-A-13.
50. Barichella 2018.
51. Directive 2008/114/EC, December 8, 2008.
52. Directive (EU) 2016/1148, July 6, 2016.
53. The deadline for transposing the requirements of the NIS Directive into national law was May 2018.
54. Regulation (EU) 2019/881, April 17, 2019.
55. Regulation (EU) 2019/941, June 5, 2019.
56. Commission Recommendation (EU) 2019/553, April 3, 2019.
57. BSA—The Software Alliance 2015.
58. Since the 2019 Cybersecurity Act, ENISA is now referred to as the EU Agency for Cybersecurity, even though the ENISA acronym is still relied on in official documents and academic texts.
59. For example, in 2019, ENISA's budget was approximately €17 million with a staff of about 60 full-time employees. By contrast, NERC had a budget of around $67 million and 200 full-time employees for the same year, in addition to many subcontractors.
60. The latest Cyber Europe Exercise, delayed because of the COVID-19 pandemic, took place in the summer 2022 and involved around 800 participants, focusing on the healthcare sector.
61. The ECSO is a nonprofit entity that brings together stakeholders working on cybersecurity from both the public and private sectors, to advance shared goals in this area at the European level.
62. Still, it should be noted that the EU has invested greater efforts to enhance information sharing between the public and private sectors over the last few years. For instance, the Commission organized a high-level event on cybersecurity in the energy sector in July 2019.
63. BSA 2015.
64. This includes sectors such as energy, banking, financial market infrastructure, transport, health, drinking water, waste water, digital infrastructure, and outer space.
65. Barichella 2022a.
66. See Annex II, subsection 1-a of the NIS Directive.
67. The NIST has published several guidelines to address cybersecurity for smart grids and smart meters; however, these represent voluntary, nonbinding standards.
68. Barichella 2018.
69. Regulation (EU) 2019/943, June 5, 2019.
70. A prominent example is the 2013 attack led by the 'Dragonfly' hacker group, which took advantage of these sophisticated digital technologies to spread malware within renewable energy companies and industrial control systems in the United States and Europe.
71. *Stratégie nationale pour la sécurité du numérique*, 2015. This was complemented in 2017 by a strategy focused on France's cyber diplomacy: *Stratégie internationale de la France pour le numérique.*
72. *Revue stratégique de cyberdéfense*, 2018. The latter was supplemented by another cyber strategy in February 2021, which concentrated more specifically on the

economic dimension with the aim of tripling France's GDP and creating 37 000 new jobs in the cyber sector by 2025, involving more than €1 billion of new investments. See: *Stratégie nationale d'accélération pour la cybersécurité*, 2021.

73. In 2019, ANSSI had a budget of approximately €100 million, with a staff of around 600 full-time employees, substantially higher than NERC's budget of $67 million and 200 full-time employees the same year.
74. Law n° 2018-607, July 13, 2018.
75. Sectorial decree on the Procurement of Electrical Energy (*Approvisionnement en énergie électrique*), August 11, 2016.
76. Sectorial decree on Nuclear Energy, March 10, 2017.
77. Although it is true that ANSSI has established an office for sectorial management of the energy and nuclear sectors, it lacks a full-fledged specialized institution similar to NERC. See: Barichella 2018.
78. 'Smart devices' comprise many different technologies that together constitute the 'Internet of Things,' including smart meters.
79. Goel 2015.
80. Boroojeni 2018.
81. Barichella 2019.
82. Skopik 2015.
83. Such data is then processed by a concentrator, which returns digital information to the smart meter through mechanisms that rely on private key encryption.
84. Desarnaud 2017.
85. Barichella 2018.
86. Directive 95/46/EC, October 24, 1995.
87. Regulation (EU) 2016/679, April 27, 2016. The EU Commission upgraded the GDPR in 2021 by reinforcing several key provisions and introducing a few notable changes. This included extending the definition of 'joint controller' and getting rid of the transatlantic Privacy Shield following multiple legal challenges; the Privacy Shield had been used to transfer EU citizens' data to the United States.
88. Kuner 2019.
89. Denley 2019.
90. CNIL 2018.
91. Law n°2004-801, August 6, 2004. The latter was subsequently completed through decrees enacted in October 2005 and March 2007.
92. A college of 18 Commissioners elect the President of the CNIL from among their members for a five-year term, subject to approval by the French Parliament. These Commissioners include high-ranking judicial officials, members of Parliament, as well as prominent experts from public administration and civil society.
93. It should be noted that the DOE-sponsored DataGuard Energy Data Privacy Program is a strictly voluntary code of conduct for the energy sector.
94. Barichella 2018.
95. S.2588, 113th Congress, July 10, 2014.
96. More recently, Privacy Offices have also been created within other federal agencies, such as the State Department or the Department of Justice. However, spreading out authority in this way has arguably diluted the influence of these Privacy Offices. Likewise, their margin for maneuver remains quite limited due to the absence of rigorous US federal legislation in this area, in contrast to the EU's GDPR.
97. H.R.4943, 115th Congress, February 6, 2018.
98. Barichella 2019.

99. AB-375, June 28, 2018. The CCPA was reinforced by another state law known as the California Privacy Rights Act, which aims to strengthen privacy rights by, for example, enabling citizens to refuse consent for sale of their personal data to third parties. The Act is scheduled to enter into force in January 2023.
100. AB-1274, October 5, 2013.
101. Barichella 2018.
102. SB-327, September 28, 2018.

References

Arghandeh, R. and Y. Zhou (eds) (2017), *Big Data Application in Power Systems*, Kidlington, UK and Cambridge, MA, USA: Elsevier Science.

Barichella, A. (2018), *Cybersecurity in the Energy Sector: A Comparative Analysis between Europe and the United States*, Études de l'Ifri, Paris, France: Ifri.

Barichella, A. (2019), *The US-EU Rivalry for Data Protection: Energy Sector Implications*, Éditoriaux de l'Ifri, Paris, France: Ifri.

Barichella, A. (2022a), *European Cybersecurity and Data Privacy: Threats and Prospects*, Policy Brief, Paris, France: Jacques Delors Institute.

Barichella, A. (2022b), *Cyberattacks in Russia's hybrid war against Ukraine and its ramifications for Europe*, Policy Paper, Paris, France: Jacques Delors Institute.

Baylon, C. et al. (2015), *Cyber Security at Civil Nuclear Facilities: Understanding the Risks*, London, UK: Chatham House.

Boroojeni, K. G. et al. (2018), *Smart Grids: Security and Privacy Issues*, Basel, Switzerland: Springer.

BSA – The Software Alliance (2015), *EU Cybersecurity Dashboard: A Path to a Secure European Cyberspace.*

CNIL (2018), *Rapport d'activité 2018: Protéger les données personnelles, accompagner l'innovation, préserver les libertés individuelles*, Paris, France: La Documentation française.

Colbert, E. J. M. and A. Kott (eds) (2016), *Cyber-security of SCADA and Other Industrial Control Systems*, Basel, Switzerland: Springer.

D'Andrade, B. W. (ed) (2017), *The Power Grid: Smart, Secure, Green and Reliable*, London, UK and Cambridge, MA, USA: Academic Press (Elsevier).

Desarnaud, G. (2017), *Cyber Attacks and Energy Infrastructures: Anticipating Risks*, Études de l'Ifri, Paris: Ifri.

Denley, A. et al. (2019), *GDPR: How To Achieve and Maintain Compliance*, Abingdon, UK and New York, NY, USA: Routledge.

Goel, S. et al. (2015), *Smart Grid Security*, Basel, Switzerland: Springer.

Hassanien, A. E. and M. Elhoseny (eds) (2019), *Cybersecurity and Secure Information Systems: Challenges and Solutions in Smart Environments*, Basel, Switzerland: Springer.

Kuner, C. et al. (eds) (2019) *The EU General Data Protection Regulation (GDPR): A Commentary*, Oxford, UK: Oxford University Press.

Maynard, T. and N. Beecroft (2015), *Business Blackout – The Insurance Implications of a Cyber-attack on the US Power Grid*, Lloyd's Insurance and University of Cambridge (Centre for Risk Studies).

Misra, S. et al. (2017), *Security Challenges and Approaches in Internet of Things*, Basel, Switzerland: Springer.
Sanger, D. E. (2012), *Confront and Conceal: Obama's Secret Wars and Surprising Use of American Power*, New York, NY, USA: Broadway Books.
Shrobe, H. et al. (eds) (2018), *New Solutions for Cybersecurity*, Cambridge, MA, USA: The MIT Press.
Skopik, F. and P. D. Smith (eds) (2015), *Smart Grid Security: Innovative Solutions for a Modernized Grid,* Waltham, MA, USA: Syngress (Elsevier).
Stockton, P. N. (2018), *Resilience for Grid Security Emergencies*, The Johns Hopkins University Applied Physics Laboratory.

11 Oil and gas development of US onshore federal lands: policy issues and research questions

Timothy J. Considine[1] and Tara K. Righetti[2]

Introduction

The management of oil and gas on US federal lands over the past several decades has been somewhat of a political football, reflecting a long-running debate between fossil fuel development, energy independence and security, and environmental conservation. With each presidential transition, agency management approaches to federal lands shift, resulting in clashes between industry and environmental interests regarding the pace of administrative approvals, legality of new administrative rules, and extensiveness of agency environmental reviews. Similarly, there are ongoing political debates in Congress about ending new oil and gas drilling on federal lands entirely or dramatically changing current leasing practices, proposals that would have extensive impacts on revenues and employment in western states. Rather than attempt to resolve these disputes or provide policy prescriptions, this chapter provides an overview of the development of federal minerals. It explains key federal leasing and permitting policies, in Section 2, and illustrates how regulatory rules may affect investment in and production of oil and gas on federal lands. Finally, the chapter previews issues related to energy and regulatory economics and politics and suggests research opportunities for applied economics.

Federal oil and gas production generates significant royalty and severance tax income and is important for economic development in several regions in the United States, particularly the Rocky Mountains, the northern plains, and Alaska. Policies that restrict leasing and permitting for oil and gas on federal lands, therefore, may significantly impact the fiscal and economic systems of these states. As a result, the phasing out of oil and gas on federal lands or new restrictive regulations that apply only to federal oil and gas development may result in distributive inequality compared with general policies that affect oil and gas operations. Estimating the net impacts on greenhouse gas emissions of such policies is difficult because investment in oil and gas can shift to nonfederal land. Shifts in investment may also make it difficult to determine the total economic impacts of such policies, depending on whether such investments are within a state or region, the nation, or international or whether investment moves to alternative fuel and generation technologies with different revenue models. The challenge of estimating the magnitude of impact on a state may be further increased by the relative cost and restrictiveness of new federal policies as compared with state and international policies. Finally, because restrictions on federal lands would disproportionately burden some states, these policies raise the question of whether the federal government should compensate states with federal oil and gas development for lost federal royalty and state severance tax revenue resulting from the policies. If so, what guidance can economists provide policy makers in crafting energy transition adjustment assistance?

In addition to evaluating the impacts of leasing and drilling bans and moratoria, there is also an opportunity for applied economics research to assess the costs and benefits of specific regulatory programs applicable to federal lands or to oil and gas generally. The institutional and historical context under which these rules and regulations are promulgated are complex and present significant challenges for cost–benefit analysis. Further complicating the analysis, new rules are frequently challenged in court and may be subsequently vacated or have their implementation delayed. There is an opportunity to evaluate the impact of these regulations both in terms of their efficiency at achieving their intended good and their economic impacts. To address these questions, economic analysis must attempt to estimate whether these policies deter investment and reduce production, and if so, to what extent. An overview of leasing and permitting regulations on federal lands appears in Section 3. Examples of specific regulatory rules and litigation that affect federal oil and gas development are included in Section 4, and an overview of recent trends in leasing, permitting, and drilling on federal lands appears in Section 5.

The fiscal and economic contribution of federal oil and gas development is another key element in policy evaluation and is the focus of Section 6. By defining the institutional context, identifying the regulatory rules in place, and understanding the fiscal and economic contributions of federal oil and gas development, Section 7 will discuss research questions that analysts may wish to consider when evaluating policies to restrict future oil and gas development on federal lands. Section 8 briefly discusses how to estimate production losses from restricting development of oil and gas on federal lands. The concluding section presents some thoughts on opportunities to conduct applied economic research that may provide policy makers with guidance on how to balance the opportunities and challenges from oil and gas development on federal lands in the future.

Institutional and Historical Context

The United States is one of the only countries in the world that permits private ownership of coal, oil, gas, and other mineral resources. Most minerals east of the Mississippi are privately owned. In the west, however, the federal government retains ownership of more than 710.2 million acres of onshore minerals that are managed by the US Bureau of Land Management (BLM) (BLM, 2020).[3] These subsurface mineral interests underlie BLM lands, but also national parks, national forests, wildlife refuges, monuments, and private surface land. The management of these lands is determined by the property clause of the US Constitution, which grants Congress authority over these lands. Congress, in turn, has enacted numerous laws related to the management of federal lands and minerals and has created agencies, including the BLM, for their management and administration.

Since the founding of the United States, there has been a trend from development to preservation of public lands. Prior to the 20th century, Congressional policy generally favored development, enacting many laws authorizing land grants, sales, and transfers of 1.275 billion acres (Alexander and Gorte, 2007). From the creation of the General Land Office in the US Treasury in 1812 to the Mineral Leasing act of 1920, Congressional legislation fostered the sale and transfer of federal lands. Minerals, including oil and gas, could be located on federal lands pursuant to the mining laws and patented—or transferred outright—to private parties. In the early 20th century, however, it became apparent that because of the patent system, the federal government was transferring away resources or tremendous economic and strategic value. Following large-scale discoveries of oil on public lands in California and Wyoming, and the US Supreme Court's upholding of President Taft's subsequent withdrawal of those lands from patent in *United States v Midwest Oil Company* (236 US 459 (1915)), Congress passed the Mineral Leasing Act of 1920. That law moved 'leasable' minerals—including oil and gas—from the patent system to the current system of leasing.

Today, a suite of laws governs the development of federal lands for oil and gas and minerals. Among these are the Federal Land Policy and Management Act (FLPMA), which requires that the BLM manage federal lands or multiple use and sustained yield; the Federal Oil and Gas Leasing Reform Act; the Federal Oil and Gas Royalty Management Act; and the Energy Policy Act of 2005. In addition, since 1964, legislation and rulemaking have expanded federal oversight of mineral extraction and transportation activities on federal lands to protect environmental quality, plants and animals, historical and cultural resources, and other amenities. Some of these may have limited impacts outside of federal lands. The National Environmental Policy Act (NEPA), for instance, applies only to major federal actions significantly affecting the human environment. Others, however, such as the National Historic Preservation Act, Clean Air Act, Clean Water Act, and species protection laws (e.g., the Endangered Species Act), are generally applicable to federal, state, and private lands.

Leasing and Permitting on Federal Lands

Leasing of federally owned mineral resources is authorized by the Mineral Leasing Act of 1920, as modified by subsequent laws, including FLPMA. To identify areas suitable for leasing, the BLM periodically undergoes a comprehensive land planning process required by 43 USC § 1712(c), resulting in a resource management plan (RMP). In addition to conducting a comprehensive analysis of potential environmental impacts, as required by NEPA, the RMP assesses the resources in the area and identifies areas that are suitable for oil and gas leasing and any conditions and limitations to that development.

After lands are identified as available for leasing in the RMP, the prospective oil and gas operator and the agency engage in an exhaustive leasing process. This process includes nomination of parcels, review by the agency, preparation of an environmental analysis, publication of a lease sale notice, and a 60-day public comment period. Upon conclusion of these stages the agency hosts a lease sale, at which the potential operator may bid on the lease (see Miller et al. 2011). Payment must be made within 60 days of the sale after lease issue, although waiting times for lease issuance can be significant. All told, this process can range from several months to many years, depending on whether an update to the RMP is needed.

Once the lease is issued, the oil and gas lessee may submit an application for a permit to drill (APD). The APD package includes information about the lessee's drilling plans, including a well plat, drilling plan, surface use plan of operations, bonding, operator certification, and onsite inspection (Ferguson et al. 2008). While obtaining an APD is generally considered the last regulatory requirement or stage before drilling commences, its issuance is not assured.

The Mineral Leasing Act also establishes deadlines for the consideration of applications for permits (30 USC § 226(p)(2)). Upon receipt of a complete APD package, the BLM must either issue the permit or defer the decision and provide the lessee with additional steps it must complete within two years. These additional steps may require additional NEPA compliance, including the preparation of an environmental impact statement, before the APD can be granted (Capone and Ruple, 2017). These additional delays may be significant. In the 2020 case of *Solenex LLC v Brenhardt*, the DC Circuit found that a 30-year delay between the issuance of a lease and its subsequent cancellation was not unreasonable considering the circumstances (see 962 F.3d 520 (2020)).

Leasing and permitting on federal lands raise several interesting issues for examination. Recently, environmental advocates have raised concerns regarding the costs to federal agencies associated with evaluating lease nominations and drilling permits, particularly nominated parcels that may not be leased, may lease at a minimum bid, or may not be developed. They argue that the current lease system encourages speculation and does not assure taxpayers a fair return from public lands. In response, in March 2021, legislators introduced the Fair Returns for Public Lands Act, which proposed amending the minimum bid, rental, and royalty rates to fully cover the cost of environmental and agency reviews. Although heralded as a move that would support energy communities and states with federal lands if passed, legislation increasing capital costs associated with development on federal lands could result in decreased leasing of federal lands or shift investment to private lands. It is unclear whether lower lease rates would be fully offset by higher minimum bids or royalties. Further, the legislation could decrease revenues to states: whereas states have a share in the federal lease bonus and royalty payments, they do not participate in lease bonuses and royalties on private lands.

Despite the significant amount of time and money required to obtain federal leases and secure an APD, the rate and pace of development are lower on federal lands than on state or private lands—even though the royalty owed on federal leases may be lower than on comparable private leases within the same region, according to the Government Accountability Office (GAO) (2017). This difference may be attributable to several factors, including longer development periods and lower holding costs. Competing contractual obligations, such as expiring lease terms on private leases, may drive decisions about whether to drill or not on federal or private lands. Operators may be more likely to defer drilling on permitted federal leases when options to extend drilling periods are longer or more certain than on comparable private leases or when the cost of delay (including payment of delay rentals) is less than the perceived benefit of waiting for more favorable economic or drilling conditions (McArthur, 2014). These varying rates of delay may further be influenced by uncertainty related to perceptions of regulatory burdens, litigation, and changes in political administrations.

Regulation and Litigation

The conditions on APDs and regulations, applicable only to federal leases, may impose additional obligations, which create a more restrictive operating environment compared with that for private and state lands. These incremental costs may relate to additional bonding beyond that required by state regulations (GAO, 1991) and environmental reviews required by NEPA, or compliance with operating regulations. For instance, on the 56 million acres on which federal minerals underlie private surface property, federal requirements for coordination with surface owners are arguably more cumbersome and restrictive than under the majority of state surface damage or split estate statutes (Dunnigan and Meyer, 2008). While most states with significant oil and gas operations require that the operator notify the landowner and reach some agreement with respect to surface damages, or else post a surface use bond, Onshore Order No. 1 obligates federal lessees to consult with surface owners at every stage of the drilling process (Dunnigan and Meyer, 2008). Onshore Order No. 1 also requires that federal lessees safeguard the environment, properly reclaim disturbed lands, assure protection of underground sources of water, and ensure that development is conducted in a manner that protects public health and safety (Onshore Oil and Gas Order No. 1, § I (5)-(9) (2007)). The BLM may require reasonable mitigation measures to ensure that the intended operations minimize adverse impacts on other uses, users, and resources, as consistent with the granted leasing rights (43 C.F.R. §§ 3101.1-2 (2016)).

Not only do federal operating regulations impose additional costs, but they may also introduce greater regulatory uncertainty because of litigation challenging federal regulations and agency decisions. In 2016, the BLM issued a new Waste Prevention Rule that replaced previous guidance related to venting and flaring for wells on federal land. This rule imposed new operating requirements, including additional inspections and replacement of pneumatic controllers and pumps, and significantly limited operators' ability to vent gas except in the case of emergencies (see 43 C.F.R. 3100; 43 C.F.R. 3160; 43 C.F.R. 3170.) Industry groups estimated that the additional costs of compliance with the rule could be as much as US$1.2 billion (see, Western Energy Alliance (2016)). Under President Trump, the BLM attempted three separate times to delay, suspend, or rescind the rule as part of his regulatory rollback agenda. Each such rescission or suspension was successfully challenged in litigation by the State of California. Concurrently, the State of Wyoming sued to vacate the 2017 rule, arguing that the agency exceeded its Congressionally delegated authority by enacting rules principally designed to limit air pollution. In 2018, the US District Court for Wyoming stayed portions of the rule, a decision that was upheld by the 10th circuit, and later, in 2020, vacated the rule. However, any reliance on the former guidance may be short lived as President Biden pursues his aggressive agenda to address climate change and reduce development on public lands.

The five-year 'roller coaster ride' of litigation and conflicting agency action is indicative of a growing trend of pursuing policy through administrative agencies, with abrupt changes from one administration to the next (*State of Wyoming v United States Department of Interior*, 493 F. Supp. 3ds 1046 (2020)). The BLM's 2015 "Hydraulic Fracturing Rule," which duplicated state law requirements and created new administrative processes (Schaumberg, 2016), similarly underwent years of rescissions and litigation. Litigations challenging agency decisions under the Trump administration have likewise been successful. Two cases in 2020 vacated more than a thousand leases issued based upon agency guidance during the Trump administration that modified agency leasing procedures related to sage grouse management areas. CEQ's NEPA modernization regulations, finalized in July 2020, have been similarly challenged in a series of cases. Uncertainty about whether newly issued rules, and decisions made thereunder, will be vacated or remanded presents challenges to estimating regulatory compliance costs and may contribute to decisions to delay drilling or shift investment from federal lands.

Leasing and Drilling

Environmental studies, litigation, and delays may increase the cost of oil and gas development on federal lands compared with that on private and state lands. The complex federal leasing and permitting processes and potential for future bans or moratoria, discussed further in Section 7, may, therefore, be potentially putting states with federal lands at a competitive disadvantage in attracting investment relative to states with oil and gas resources on private lands. These factors collectively may reduce the interest or the demand for new oil and gas leases on federal lands and have led some to argue that the relatively lower federal royalty rate of 12.5 percent compensates for the higher costs of development on federal lands. Lewis (2019) finds that shifting policies, such as the adoption of NEPA, have made federal land less desirable to develop than state and private land. Evaluating the comparative ease of development between private and federal land, however, is difficult given the heterogeneity of both state regulatory frameworks and the exercise of administrative discretion in federal agencies.

Regulatory rules may be adapted to either spur or reduce oil and gas investment on federal lands but measuring the impacts of specific regulations on leasing and drilling activity is difficult. Davis (2016) argues that the Bush administration used discretionary authority to limit environmental reviews and inspections, while the Obama administration increased environmental inspections and encouraged greater stakeholder input. Maguire (2016) applies several measures of political orientation to the US Senate, House, and Presidential leadership to test for the role of politics in oil and gas leasing activity. In an earlier study, Maguire (2012) found that economic factors were more important than political factors in the permitting of oil and gas wells. This approach, however, assumes that regulatory decisions coincide with political leadership regimes, while implementation of regulatory rules may be episodic. For example, environmentalists criticized the Obama administration during his first term for accelerating oil and gas leasing on federal lands (Goad and Goldfuss, 2013). During President Obama's second term, however, major regulatory initiatives, such as the Waste Prevention Rule, were implemented. While portions of the rule were ultimately stayed, rescinded, and vacated, litigation over the rule and the resulting uncertainty over its application continued almost throughout the duration of the Trump administration. As this example demonstrates, the impacts of specific regulations are difficult to isolate because markets, technology, politics, and legislative regimes are shifting at the same time.

Recognizing that politics, regulatory policy, and market forces all affect oil and gas investment on federal lands is important when viewing trends in leasing and drilling activity. Fewer lease sales offered by the BLM and reduced demand for new leases may have contributed to a reduction in acres of new federal oil and gas leases. For example, in 2007, there were 4.6 million acres of new federal oil and gas leases, whereas in 2015, 800 thousand acres of new federal oil and gas leases were issued by the BLM (see Figure 11.1). Of this 4-million-acre reduction in new leases, 22 percent was from Alaska, 13 percent from Wyoming, 9 percent from Utah and Colorado, and 36 percent from other onshore areas. Fewer new leases over time contribute to lower acres under active federal oil and gas leases. After reaching a peak in 2008, the acres of active federal oil and gas leases fell from 47.2 to 27.2 million in 2016, a 42 percent reduction. Politics and prices also affect the demand for new federal acres under lease. Although the number of new acres leased increased during the Trump administration, the total acreage in effect has continued to decline relative to the 2001–2016 period, according to a 2020 study by the BLM (BLM, Oil and Gas Statistics, 2020). These changes cannot be explained on the basis of commodity prices alone. As illustrated in Figure 11.1, new acres under lease peaked as oil and gas prices reached historic highs around 2008. But when oil prices recovered, following their dramatic crash in 2009, new federal leases continued to fall from 2009 to 2016, perhaps reflecting leasing management practices and regulatory rules by the Obama administration. In addition to prices, Braziel (2016) observes that initial production is another factor affecting the allocation of drilling investments across regions. Holding discount rates, prices, and costs constant, higher initial production increases the net present value of a well.

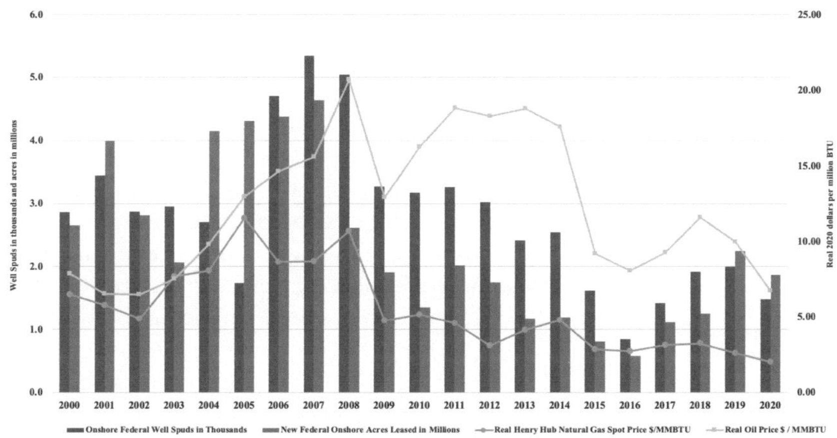

Source: US Bureau of Land Management and Energy Information Administration.

Figure 11.1 Federal leasing, well spuds, and real oil and natural gas prices

In addition to oil and gas prices (Hausman and Kellogg, 2014), regulations affecting the issuance of drilling permits may also impact drilling activity on state and federal lands. The time taken to obtain an approved APD on federal lands can be significant. For example, the average number of days to complete an APD was 307 in 2011, averaged 217 from 2012 to 2015, and 108 in 2019. These reductions in processing time could reflect the effect of administrative discretion and new efforts to streamline the approval process. At least until 2013, APD processing times were significantly longer on federal lands compared with state lands. Whereas in 2013 the average federal time to APD was 194 days, a study by Loris for the same year indicates processing times of 10 days in North Dakota, 27 days in Colorado, 14 days in Ohio, 10 days in California, and 5 days in Texas. Since then, however, in some states the gap in permitting times has narrowed because of increased environmental reviews and consultation requirements in state regulation. In 2019, Colorado passed legislation comprehensively overhauling its oil and gas regulatory laws, adding extensive new requirements for consideration of alternative locations and comprehensive impacts and providing more local government oversight of drilling (Righetti, 2020). Similarly, the state regulatory agency in California has recently denied hydraulic fracturing well stimulation permits. The number of new permits issued in both states has recently plummeted. Along with higher oil prices, shifts in both federal and state policy may, therefore, explain a portion of the recovery in federal well spuds since 2016.

Production and Income

Federal and tribal oil and gas production generates significant revenues for federal, state, and local governments. Prior to production, firms pay lease bonus payments and rents. Portions of these payments from federal leasing are shared with states. Once production commences, firms pay federal royalties, which are also shared with states, in addition to state severance and ad valorem taxes.

In the last decade, oil production on federal lands has increased by a greater factor than production nationwide. Oil production on federal lands over the past decade is summarized in Figure 11.2. Total federal oil production was 296 thousand barrels per day (MBD) in 2010 and increased to 904 MBD in 2020, a more than three-fold increase in oil production, while in the rest of the country, production doubled. The largest producer of federal oil is New Mexico, with production rising from 86 MBD in 2010 to 580 MBD in 2020. Federal oil production from other areas increased 114 MBD, with production growth in Wyoming and North Dakota partially offset by lower output in California, Utah, and Montana. Overall, oil production from federal lands at more than 900 MBD represents a significant source of world supply. Given the very price inelastic demand for oil and somewhat less but still inelastic oil supply found by Considine (2006), policies that hinder federal oil production could jeopardize US national security by enhancing the market power of the Organization of Petroleum Exporting Countries and increasing world oil prices.

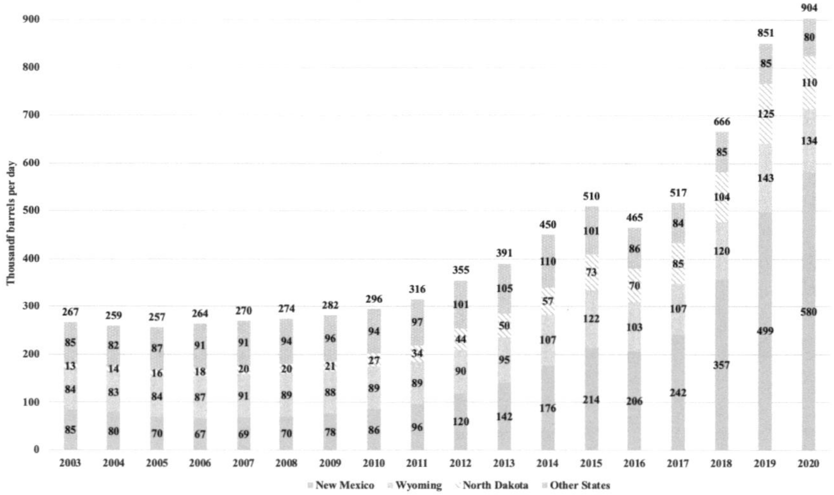

Source: Office of Natural Resource Revenue.

Figure 11.2 Federal oil production, 2003–2020

In contrast to oil, natural gas production from onshore federal lands declined from 10.8 to 8.9 billion cubic feet per day (BCFD) from 2010 through 2020. Most of the reduction occurred in Wyoming, where gas production fell from 5.3 to 3.2 BCFD (Figure 11.3). Natural gas production in the rest of the United States increased roughly by 60 percent over the same period.

Revenues from lease bonus payments, rents, and royalties are summarized in Figure 11.4. The smallest category is lease bonus payments and rents fluctuating between US$100 and US$300 million per year, except for a US$1.4 billion spike in 2018 due to a major lease sale in New Mexico's Permian Basin. Natural gas royalties peaked at US$3.4 billion in 2008 and fell to US$0.6 billion in 2020. In contrast, oil royalties increased from US$400 million to US$1.6 billion in 2020.

Approximately half of federal royalties, lease bonus payments, and rents collected are disbursed to the states. These revenues are an important source of income for the states of New Mexico and Wyoming, constituting 6.4 and 9 percent, respectively, of general revenues prior to the pandemic in 2019. Policies that restrict future development of oil and gas on federal lands, therefore, could involve some difficult fiscal decisions in western states to either cut public expenditures or increase taxation.

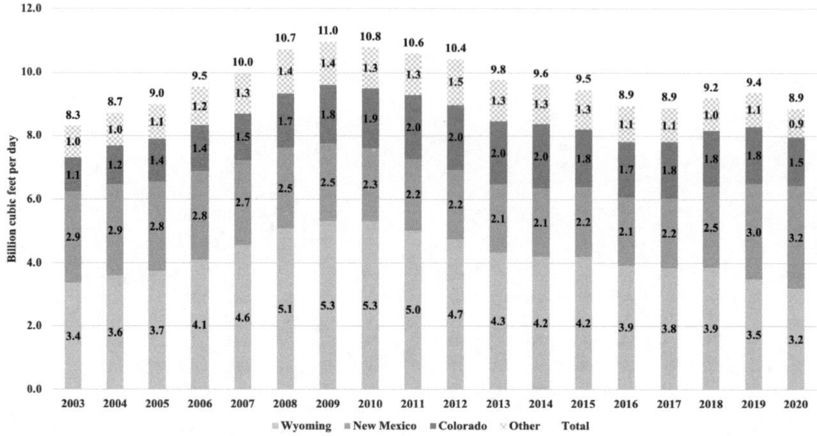

Source: Office of Natural Resource Revenue.

Figure 11.3 Federal natural gas production, 2003–2020

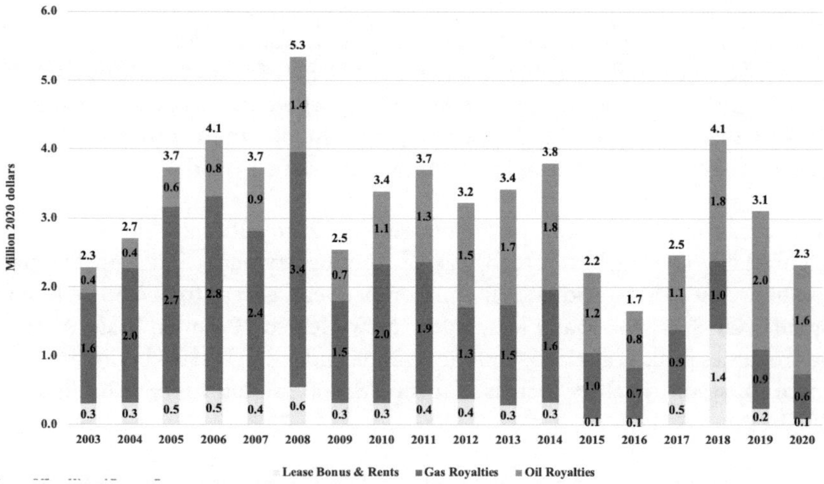

Source: Office of Natural Resource Revenue.

Figure 11.4 Resource revenues from federal lands, 2003–2020

Policy Proposals to End Leasing and Drilling on Federal Land

The potential impact of future leasing moratoria or leasing and drilling bans for new development on federal lands raise several research questions. In the past decade, both President Biden and President Obama used moratoria to temporarily suspend leasing and/or drilling. In addition, there have been numerous policy proposals to completely end new development on federal lands, including the keep-it-in-the-ground movement and the Green New Deal. Unpacking the potential impacts of proposed moratoria or bans on state and federal revenues, greenhouse gas emissions, or total oil and gas production requires a close look at how such policies are implemented and whether they are adopted in conjunction with other policies or regulations that might impact shifting of investments to private lands.

The first question is the extent to which leasing moratoria affect drilling. Most federal leases have ten-year terms. A large inventory of leases effective prior to a leasing moratorium, therefore, could allow firms to drill using an existing permit or seek permits under a prior lease, and if approved, drill new wells. Temporary leasing moratoria may, therefore, have little direct impact on drilling rates, although a moratorium could influence a firm's decision to wait and defer exercising its option to drill or apply for a permit. As discussed earlier in this chapter, decisions regarding drilling may be further complicated by uncertainty related to regulatory changes and litigation, as well as changes in state regulatory policy.

Another question is the extent to which during a lease moratoria, or in the event of a leasing ban, drilling would shift to state and private lands in other states without federal lands. A reduction in federal production would reduce market supply and slightly raise equilibrium prices. Assuming state regulations and permitting were constant, these higher prices could induce firms to increase drilling on state and private lands. However, a complete offset of the federal losses is unlikely unless the elasticity of supply from private and state lands in other states is much larger than the federal and tribal supply elasticities.

The supply from available state and private lands may be further complicated where wells are drilled in areas with a mix of federal and private mineral interests. As the size of a drilling and spacing unit increases, so does the likelihood that it will include both federal and private mineral interests. In Wyoming, for instance, the share of wells drilled on lands with mixed mineral ownership increased from 2.3 percent of wells drilled in 2012 to 36.2 percent in 2020. Where federal lands are combined—or communitized—with private lands, federal regulations apply to all the land in the unit. Policies affecting federal lands can, therefore, affect development on private and state lands (LeCates,

2018). In states with significant federal acreage, federal policies could have spillover effects on tribal, state, and private land. There is the possibility, therefore, that a federal lease moratorium or a drilling ban could reduce drilling not just on federal and tribal lands but on private and state lands as well. Identifying and estimating substitution and spillover effects could reduce some of the uncertainty surrounding the size of the net reduction in drilling resulting from a federal leasing moratorium or drilling ban.

If federal leasing moratoria or drilling bans result in a reduction in drilling activity fossil fuel production and consumption would decline. The key question: By how much? Given very price inelastic demand for oil and natural gas and price elastic supply, substantial reductions in fossil fuel consumption and related carbon emissions may be unlikely. Losses in federal production would be largely offset by higher output from nonfederal lands and from foreign producers. For example, using an estimate for the oil price elasticity of demand of -0.14 by Considine (2006) and a supply elasticity of unity at the current world oil consumption of 88 MBD, a 10 percent reduction in federal oil production would increase world prices by 0.25 percent and reduce world consumption by roughly 30 MBD and associated carbon dioxide emissions by 5.9 million metric tons. This suggests that the overall environmental benefits in terms of avoided emissions from a drilling ban would be rather small. Prest (2020) reaches a similar conclusion. These small environmental benefits should be compared with the costs in terms of lost federal investment and production. Moreover, the small changes in world prices from federal restrictions on either leasing or drilling could favor low-cost foreign producers. Federal leasing moratoria and drilling bans may, therefore, not just warrant energy transition assistance but also raise national security concerns.

Lost investment could be estimated by first determining what drilling would have been in the absence of a lease moratorium or drilling ban given expectations for prices. Developing econometric models of drilling investment would play a key role in estimating what could be lost under restrictive federal leasing or permitting policies. These models would need to control for price, cost, productivity shocks, and perhaps the aforementioned regulatory and management rules. Projections of drilling with and without a lease moratorium or drilling ban would allow estimation of lost investment.

The guiding principle of multiple use inherently involves trade-offs between resource development and environmental conservation. Greenhouse gas emission reductions are now a central element in the ongoing debate over multiple use of federal lands, so much so that there are calls to completely end future oil and gas development on federal lands. The potential impact from such proposals on greenhouse gas emissions is, however, complicated. Most of any resulting reduction in oil and gas output would likely be offset by higher non-federal and foreign production. Decreases in emissions, if any, would be paid for by significant reductions in federal royalty disbursements, severance, and ad valorem taxes in several western states with large tracts of federal land. As a result, policies that are limited to restricting oil and gas development on federal lands may be less effective and raise distributive issues compared with national environmental policies applicable to oil and gas development generally.

Estimating Production Losses

Whether due to regulation, moratoria, uncertainty, or other factors, the rig count and drilling activity were undeniably down during the first half of 2021, despite oil and gas prices that were, respectively, 8 and 18 percent higher compared with the same period in 2019. Fewer wells drilled implies lower future production. A vintage production model can be used to estimate this lost production. At any given point in time, there are thousands of wells producing oil and gas. This inventory includes many different vintages of wells, from those drilled in the current year to wells completed in previous years that are still producing. If incremental production from new wells does not change much from year to year, and if the rate of production decline from old wells is gradual, then the impact of new wells on total incremental production is likely to be small.

With unconventional oil and gas production, however, new wells are much more productive than wells drilled in the past. If the productivity of new wells is greater than production from previous vintages, then total production increases, assuming all other factors are constant. If new well completions stop completely, then total production likely will fall. The importance of new production is illustrated in Figure 11.5, which compares production from wells drilled in Wyoming after 2000 with that from those before. Production from wells completed after 2000 make up a larger share of total production each year, so that by 2020, most production is from these new vintages. Note the sharp reduction in oil production in Wyoming during 2020 when drilling activity dropped precipitously due to the pandemic and extraordinarily low prices. This illustrates the sensitivity of total production to swings in incremental output, which is a distinguishing characteristic of unconventional oil and gas production. As a result, the fiscal balance of resource-dependent states like Wyoming and New Mexico and tribal areas is very sensitive to events contributing to these swings in oil and gas production.

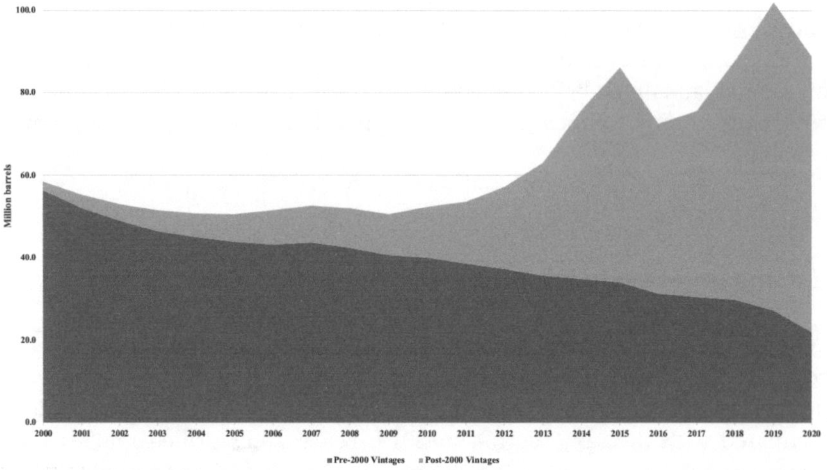

Source: Drilling Info.

Figure 11.5 Composition of Wyoming oil production, 2000–2020

The recent gains in production illustrated in Figure 11.5 can come from more wells drilled, higher output per well, or some combination of the two. Higher output per well appears to be very important. As unconventional production technology improved since 2010, first-year production per well steadily increased in many unconventional oil-producing regions. For example, first-year oil production per well in Wyoming increased from 10 933 barrels in 2011 to 79 346 barrels in 2020, a seven-fold increase. First-year production rates per well in New Mexico and North Dakota are more than 135 000 barrels in 2020.

These wide variations in first-year production across states are important to consider in modeling production decline curves in vintage models used to estimate the output losses from lease moratoria or drilling bans. Prest (2020) estimates production decline curves for federal and private lands from a panel database, but this approach may not provide adequate state-level estimates of production losses. Moreover, his classification of lands is based on surface ownership, which does not correspond with the ownership of mineral rights. A state-level analysis is important because several energy transition policy proposals contemplate compensating states for lost royalty and severance tax income resulting from policies that ban new development on federal lands. Overall, the highly productive wells in many states with federal lands suggest that restricting development of oil and gas could cause a substantial loss of production and income.

Conclusions

Despite long delays and relatively higher costs of development, oil production on federal lands has increased and is now more than 900 MBD. In contrast, federal natural gas production has declined over the last decade but remains at 8.9 BCFD. Federal lands represent a significant source of hydrocarbons for the US and world markets and revenue to state and federal treasuries. As a result, proposals to curtail production on federal lands to effect climate and environmental policy have not only implications for energy security but may also raise distributive issues that may justify energy transition assistance to states with substantial oil and gas assets on federal lands within their borders. More specifically, the impact of federal oil and gas development on greenhouse emissions is an important research question, one that involves estimating how incremental federal output affects world prices and consumption and shifts in production from private and foreign lands.

Notes

1. School of Energy Resources & Department of Economics, University of Wyoming, https://orcid.org/0000-0001-6844-9494.
2. School of Energy Resources & College of Law, University of Wyoming.
3. Federal agencies also manage some aspects of oil and gas development on tribal lands. Where this chapter refers to federal lands, it refers only to minerals owned by the federal government and managed by the BLM, as distinguished from private lands that are owned by an individual, business, or another type of non-governmental organization; state lands; offshore federal lands managed by the Bureau of Ocean Energy Management; and tribal trust lands.

References

Alexander, K. and Gorte R.W. (2007) 'Federal land ownership: Constitutional authority and the history of acquisition, disposal, and retention," *CRS Report for Congress*, RL34267, 14 pgs.

Braziel, E. R. (2016) *The Domino Effect: How the Shale Revolution is Transforming Energy Markets, Industries and Economies*, Houston, Texas, NTA Press.

Bureau of Land Management (2020),'Public land statistics 2019,' Mineral and Surface Acres Administered by the BLM, tbl.1-3, June, accessed 25 July 2021 at https://www.blm.gov/sites/blm.gov/files/PublicLandStatistics2019.pdf.

Bureau of Land Management (2020), 'oil and gas statistics,' tbl 2-8, accessed 13 October 2021 at https://www.blm.gov/programs-energy-and-minerals-oil-and-gas-oil-and-gas-statistics

Bureau of Land Management (2016) "Moab master leasing plan," accessed 26 July 2021 at https://eplanning.blm.gov/public_projects/lup/68430/88096/105439/04_Moab_MLP_Abstract_Web_508.pdf.

Capone, M.K. and Ruple J.C. (2017), 'NEPA and the energy policy act of 2005 statutory categorical exclusions: what are the environmental costs of expedited oil and gas development?', *Vermont Journal of Environmental Law*, 18, 371, 378.

Congressional Research Service (2020), 'Federal land ownership: Overview and data', accessed 25 July 2021 at https://fas.org/sgp/crs/misc/R42346.pdf.

Considine, T.J. (2006), 'Is the strategic petroleum reserve our ace in the hole?' *The Energy Journal*, 27, 3, 91-112.

Davis, C. (2016), 'BLM, the administrative presidency, and policy shifts: Policy tools affecting oil and gas operations', *Review of Policy Research*, 5 (33), 492-505.

Doughty, T. (2021), ' State of Louisiana et al v. J. Biden, Jr, et al,' accessed 26 July 2021 at https://legacy-assets.eenews.net/open_files/assets/2021/06/16/document_ew_01.pdf.

Dunnigan, K.L. and Meyer, H.C. (2008), 'Access to federal oil and gas on public lands', *Surface Use for Mineral Development in the New West*, Rocky Mountain Mineral Law Foundation, 3-11.

Ferguson, T. et al. (2008), 'How to access federal lands for oil and gas development — A best business practices primer', *Rocky Mountain Mineral Law Foundation*, 1, 9, § III.

Goad, J. and C. Goldfuss (2013), 'Chart: Obama has protected fewer public lands than Ronald Reagan, George H.W. Bush, Bill Clinton, And George W. Bush," accessed 27 July 2021 at https://thinkprogress.org/chart-obama-has-protected-fewer-public-lands-than-ronald-reagan-george-h-w-bush-bill-clinton-and-bc28c0940201/

Government Accountability Office (2017), 'Oil, gas, and coal royalties raising federal rates could decrease production on federal lands but increase federal revenue', 1-31, accessed 26 July 2021 at https://www.gao.gov/assets/gao-17-540.pdf.

Hausman, C. and R. Kellogg (2015), 'Welfare and distributional implications of shale gas', Brookings Papers on Economic Activity, accessed 25 July 2021 at, https://www.brookings.edu/wp-content/uploads/2015/03/2015a_hausman.pdf.

Herbert, G.R. (2015), 'Implementing the Utah conservation plan for the greater sage-grouse, executive order', accessed 26 July 2021 at https:// rules .utah .gov/execdocs/2015/ExecDoc156016.htm.

Lattanzio, R.K. (2017) "EPA's and BLM's methane rules," Congressional Research Service, accessed 25 July 2021 at https://fas.org/sgp/crs/misc/IN10645.pdf.

LeCates, C. (2018), 'How are federal oil and gas leases pooled and unitized', accessed 25 July 2021 at https://www.theoilandgasreport.com/2018/07/10/how-are-federal-oil-and-gas-leases-pooled-and-unitized/.

Lewis, E. (2019), 'Patchwork policies, spillovers, and the search for oil and gas', *American Economic Journal: Economic Policy*, 11, 1, 380 – 405.

Loris, N. (2013), 'Energy production on federal lands: Handing the keys over to the state', The Heritage Foundation, Policy Brief, accessed 27 July 2021 at http://www.heritage.org/research/reports/2013/06/energy-production-on-federal-lands-handing-keys-over-to-the-states#_ftn4

Maguire, K. (2016), 'Drill baby drill? Political influence on federal onshore oil and gas leasing in the Western United States', *Economics of Governance*, 2 (17), 131–164.

Maguire K (2012), 'Prices or politics? The influence of markets and political party changes on oil and gas development in the United States', *Energy Economics*, 34, 2013–2020.

McArthur, J.B. (2014), 'Stewarding public oil, gas, and hard minerals: the express and implied development rights that protect public resources', *Texas Journal of Oil Gas and Energy*, 9, 215, 227, n. 62.

Mead, M.H. (2015), 'Greater Sage-Grouse Care Area Protection', accessed 25 July 2021 at https://wgfd.wyo.gov/WGFD/media/content/PDF/Habitat/Sage%20Grouse/SG_Executive_Order.pdf.

Miller, T., M. Griffith, and R. McCrum (2011), 'Leasing federal oil and gas', *Energy and Mineral Law Foundation*, 32 §14.06[1].

Office of Natural Resource Revenue (2020), 'Revenue Data', accessed 25 July 2021 at https://revenuedata.doi.gov/query-data.

Prest, B., (2020) 'Supply-side reforms to oil and gas production on federal lands', accessed 27 July 2021 at https://www.rff.org/publications/working-papers/supply-side-reforms-oil-and-gas-production-federal-lands/.

Righetti, Tara K. (2020), 'The Incidental Environmental Agency,' 3 UTAH L. REV. 685 (2020).

Schaumberg, Peter J. (2016), 'ONRR royalty update. proposed regulations for oil and gas valuation; civil penalties', *Rocky Mountain Mineral Law Foundation*, Federal Offshore Regulatory Enforcement, Paper 13B.

United States Court of Appeals (2018), 'State of Wyoming, Western Energy Alliance, and State of North Dakota v. Department of Interior', accessed 26 July 2021 at http://blogs.edf.org/climate411/files/2018/06/50-Order-Denying-Stay-Pending-Appeal-Motions-to-Dismiss.pdf?_ga=2.50170150.1240553101.1530248915-625971117.1530248915.

Western Energy Alliance (2016) "Waste Prevention, Production Subject to Royalties, and Resource Conservation," *Federal Register*, (April 22), accessed 26 July 2021 at https://www.federalregister.gov/documents/2016/02/08/2016-01865/waste-prevention-production-subject-to-royalties-and-resource-conservation.

12 Establishing a lunar underground outpost: shifting the paradigm for future space exploration, settlement, and commerce

Greg Baiden, Louis L. Grenier,[1] Brad R. Blair, Dale Tietz and James S. Logan

Background

The approach to date, as demonstrated by the Apollo missions to the Moon, has been that of all self-contained sortie 'out and back' missions. Although unmanned robotic precursor missions were flown to better map lunar topography (Ranger) and to characterize the lunar surface environment (Surveyor), no pre-arrival infrastructure was required and lunar resources were not utilized to protect crew, extend mission capabilities, or upgrade landing sites for future visits. The dual justifications for the Apollo program were national prestige and science. The former was paramount, and the latter a distant afterthought.

The idea of establishing a permanent facility on the Moon is not new. As early as 1959, the US Army considered a permanent underground base on the Moon. But even then, neither science nor resource extraction was the priority. The real reason was Mutual Assured Destruction by weaponizing the Moon.

This chapter discusses a new approach to the establishment of planetary bases for the good of humankind using the upcoming Lunar return as an example. This approach is going to be a method for the establishment of initial settlements to provide the ability to survive each new planet's environment.

Nonterrestrial materials are paramount

History may not repeat, but it does recycle. If 17th- and 18th-century European colonists to the New World had been forced to transport every single nail, board, brick, and shingle they intended to use, plus every morsel of food they ate and every molecule of air they breathed, it is unlikely colonial societies would have ever become a reality. Instead, colonists transported themselves, their tools, and their knowledge, then utilized local resources found in the new world to build new nations.

Fast-forward to the 21st century and the same general principles apply, although this time tools will likely be sent first—to make even more tools from local resources and prepare candidate areas for survival, industrial activity, and eventual human habitation. These tools, however, will be in direct communication with each other. They will work in packs and swarms to accomplish specific tasks and generate construction feedstock material, supervised remotely by humans via telepresence.

Why cannot everything needed be transported from Earth by a fleet of giant rockets? The short answer: The cold hard physics of the Rocket Equation does not permit it. No matter how gargantuan the rocket—even if it is reusable—the fraction of rocket mass that can be dedicated to actual payload is depressingly small. The vast majority of mass in any rocket launched from Earth using current rocket technology is propellant. It should be obvious that rocketing up enough Earth materials to establish a permanent industrial presence on the Moon, much less eventual lunar human habitation facilities, is essentially a nonstarter.

Therefore, materials used to create, construct, and support industrial as well as human presence on the Moon must come from the Moon itself. Since it takes 33 times less energy to transport anything from the surface of the Moon to the low Earth orbit (LEO), rather than from Earth to LEO (the Moon has a much smaller gravity well than Earth), the ability to manufacture and transport propellant, the most critical component of the lunar industrial vision, from the Moon to LEO is the initial keystone to support an entire cislunar economy.

Water is the key

The most advanced operational rocket engines today utilize chemical propellants. Liquid hydrogen and liquid oxygen are the propellants for the most efficient rocket engines ever made. Oxygen is the most abundant substance in lunar rock. Hydrogen, unfortunately, is not present in appreciable concentrations except in lunar ice, which could, and most likely does, exist in cold traps at the bottom of permanently shadowed craters, especially at higher latitudes.

Energy is the catalyst

Harvesting water ice in shadowed craters that never exceeds minus 280 degrees Fahrenheit (95 degrees Kelvin), warming it to liquid phase, splitting it into constituent elements of hydrogen and oxygen, and then chilling the separated components into liquid propellant will take extensive amounts of continuous, robust, and reliable energy in the form of heat and/or electricity. Local solar power is not an option in permanently shadowed regions, and surface solar is inefficient given 14-day long lunar nights. Small, automated, high-energy density 'walk-away-safe' nuclear fission power plants are likely the most promising option in the shorter term for providing 24/7 power in such environments.

Humans are neophytes in deep space

The year 2022 is year 61 of human spaceflight. About 580 men and women in over 285 space missions have a cumulative experience of more than 150 person-years of spaceflight. Unfortunately, less than 0.8 percent of that experience is in deep space—beyond Earth orbit and the protective effects of the magnetosphere.

Draconian lunar environmental constraints

A coauthor (Logan) spent 22 years as a NASA space medical officer (flight surgeon). His job was to take care of the astronauts—and their families—during all phases of their careers, especially during missions and mission training. This experience has significantly informed our initial work.

Logan's First Law is this: Space is always trying to kill you. It may kill you quickly or kill you slowly, but it never ever stops trying. The Moon is one of the most unforgiving and harshest environments in the solar system—for men and machines. The only reasonable approach is to always deal with the Moon as it is, not how you want it to be. You cannot conquer, cajole, overcome, or negotiate with her. You must know her ways, respect her hazards, and adapt to her reality because she does not, cannot, and will not acknowledge yours. Your only weapon is a thorough knowledge of her many threats so that an innovative CONOPS can be evolved to evade the many ways the Moon can bite you.

Lunar operational hazards come in two major classes: physical and biological. Examples of physical hazards are thermal stress and micrometeorites.

Biological threats include ionizing radiation (from solar and galactic origins) and toxic substances. Some, like radiation and lunar regolith, are both potent physical and biological hazards simultaneously.

Physical and biological hazards

The Moon has no atmosphere or any appreciable magnetic field. As such, it is totally exposed to the ravages of the deep space environment. Its 28-day orbit is locked, meaning the same side always faces Earth. Both the lunar day and lunar night last 14 Earth days. Surface temperatures near the equator vary widely from a boiling 250 degrees Fahrenheit (120°C, 400 K) during the lunar day to a bone chilling -208 degrees Fahrenheit (-130°C, 140 K) during the lunar night. The Moon's poles, where water/ice is located, are even colder.

The Moon is a hard vacuum. The spacesuit is like a mini spacecraft. Any tear or leaky seal in the spacesuit could result in sudden incapacitation. Failure of the cooling system could result in hyperthermia. A loss of suit power or breathing consumables could also result in rapid demise. Like dangerous scuba operations, EVAs are always performed in pairs. But even then, astronauts would be unwise to stray too far from safety.

Lunar regolith

Because there is no atmosphere, the Moon is constantly pummeled by meteors and micrometeoroids traveling at an average of 17 km/s (peak of 70 km/s), which, over geologic time, creates lunar soil—known as regolith—by a process lunar geologists refer to as "gardening."

Lunar fines are a potent physical and biological hazard. Due to their very small size—as small as 1 micron—they can penetrate seals and joints of spacesuits and spacecraft. Lunar regolith has not been exposed to water in several billion years, so there is no mechanical weathering—as on Earth—to smooth out or dull surfaces.

There are a number of terrestrial dust analog disease states that are due, in large part, to a combination of very small particle sizes and intense biological reactions. Examples include Asbestosis, Silicosis, Grinder's Disease, Volcanic Ash, 9/11 Syndrome, and perhaps even Agent Orange.

Plus, if that were not enough, these small dust particles all contain nanophase iron—extremely small particles of elemental iron with a valence of zero—not +2 or +3 forms we are used to seeing on a highly oxidized Earth. In the aqueous environment of the lung, these nanoparticles will most likely be absorbed directly into the bloodstream and may, if man-made nanoparticles are any guide, be able to migrate directly into the brain via tiny passages surrounding olfactory neurons in the nose and, therefore, bypass the blood/brain barrier completely.

Space Radiation

Rather than being a benign nothingness, deep space is a seething, undulating cauldron of dangerous ionizing radiation with enough energy to destroy molecular bonds and strip electrons off atoms, creating free ions.

In space, the two major sources of ionizing radiation are galactic cosmic rays (GCR) and the solar wind. We know now that they are not rays at all but particles—ions actually—mostly protons with some heavy nuclei mixed in.

These elementary particles penetrate spacecraft, pressure vessels and space suits as well as organs and cells, ripping apart DNA of human occupants and other molecules (generating shrapnel-like secondary radiation called Spallation).

In biological systems, these ions and secondary radiation induce degenerative changes usually associated with aging, such as chronic inflammation, oxidative stress, cataract formation, damage to the extracellular matrix, and cumulative deterioration of the central nervous system. Damage to DNA results in increasing mutation rates, instability of the genome, induction of cancers, and activation of latent tumors as well as viral infections.

We know that the sun, too, can unleash horrendous bursts of protons and heavy nuclei at nearly the speed of light without much warning. These coronal mass ejections or solar particle events (SPEs) can deliver in excess of a couple of hundred rem over an hour or so—a potentially lethal dose for an astronaut. So, even on short-duration sortie missions, you can get 'fried' by a massive SPE if you are unlucky enough to be at the wrong place at the wrong time.

As an example, radiation was not an operational concern during the Apollo flights to the Moon because mission durations were short and because of one other very important factor—Luck! Figure 12.1 plots the radiation dose estimates for SPEs from May 1968 to December 1969. Arrows on the x axis denote the dates of the first five manned missions to the Moon (Apollo 7 was an Earth orbit test mission of the Command Module), including the first two landing missions on the far right.

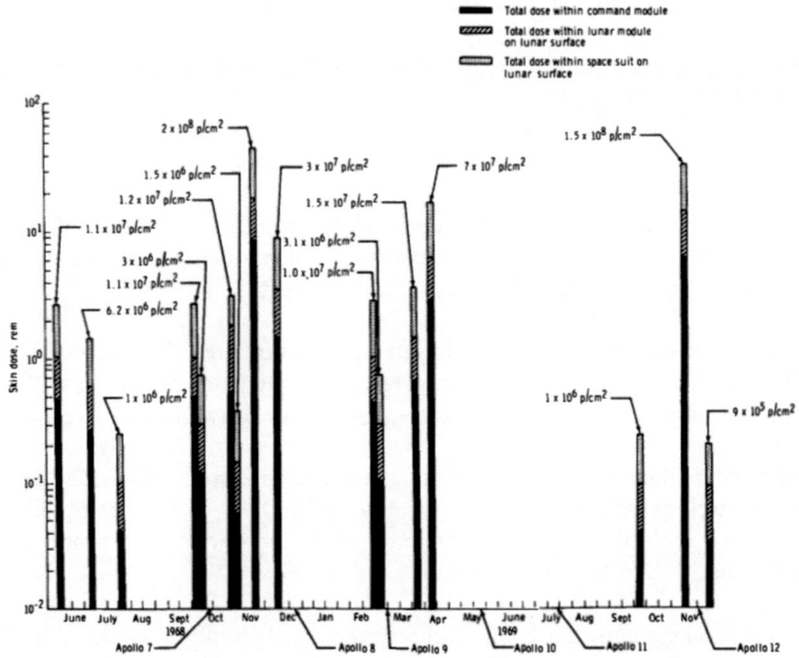

Source: Apollo Experience Report—Protection Against Radiation NASA TN D-7080 1973.

Figure 12.1 Radiation dose estimates for particle events between June 1968 and December 1969 during deep space Apollo missions to the Moon.

The particular SPEs depicted were below the threshold required to induce Acute Radiation Sickness, but several would have resulted in a dose more than twice the annual limit for radiation workers on Earth, all within a few days. But in late summer 1972 a gargantuan X-Class solar flare occurred—one of the few real "Granddaddy Flare" events in history. Had the Apollo 17 crew been on the way to the Moon in August 1972 rather than December, or worse, if astronauts had been in the lunar lander (equivalent shielding of only 5 g/cm^2), they would have received enough radiation to cause nausea, vomiting, cataracts, internal bleeding, fatigue, bacterial infection, fever, and perhaps even death due to sepsis.

Extreme solar flares are the tsunamis of space. These large 'tidal waves' are not all that rare. There is not much warning, and they can be incredibly destructive—even lethal. And they occur on top of baseline GCR exposures.

Radiation protection

On Earth, it is actually the mass shielding effect of the atmosphere that protects people, plants, and animals from GCR. To a much lesser degree, the Earth's magnetosphere provides some protection, at least at lower latitudes, but it is the atmosphere that does the heavy lifting. Over every square centimeter of Earth at sea level, there is a column of air consisting of 1032 g of mass extending from the surface to space. Therefore, our atmosphere provides a natural, passive, and constant radiation shielding equivalent to 1032 g/cm^2 (the standard unit of radiation protection equivalent).

Astronaut career radiation limits can be envisioned as a clock that spins either rapidly (in high-radiation environments) or slowly (on Earth) toward a predefined limit depending on age and gender. A goal of human operations is to take measures to slow the radiation clock as much as possible—all the way down to Earth speed if possible. Given today's technology, the only way to adequately protect crew on the Moon is through enough mass shielding on the Moon. Therefore, all human habitats and working environments will need to be buried in at least 4.12 m of regolith, preferably in solid rock. If human beings ever live or work on the Moon, they will have to live like ants, earthworms, or moles. Habitats will need to be subterranean—one way or another. Although some traditional EVA in very limited circumstances may always exist, routine surface operations by crew in spacesuits is clearly not a viable option. Although this may be heresy for space advocates steeped in science fiction depictions of lunar surface activities, the reality is that the space radiation environment effectively precludes it.

After years of being denied, deflected, or summarily ignored, the 'Elephant in the Room' has finally staggered onto center stage for good. Radiation is now the chief potential showstopper for extended-duration human missions beyond Earth orbit. We are now faced with a radiation *Perfect Storm*: The radiation environment in deep space is significantly worse than previously estimated, while, at the same time, empirical evidence mandates permissible radiation exposure limits be revised ever downward.

Implications for an optimized CONOPS

The implications of the discussed constraints force the CONOPS now described. The CONOPS will need to be forward-deployed humans in the loop using supervised remote surface and subsurface operations. These must be from radiation-protected habitats using low-latency time telerobotics combined with autonomous operations. This style of operation will be required for all future space exploration—whether the Moon, Mars, or beyond.

With the background provided regarding space hazards, this chapter will discuss why an underground permanent outpost is needed, how it might be constructed, and which terrestrial technologies can enable this outpost to be made and used to mine and generate the necessary resources to support human life on the Moon and on other planets.

Establishing a permanent underground lunar outpost and mine

Current space activity is gaining momentum with the excitement of multiple companies privately launching individuals into space. Will this exciting short-term, brief glimpse of the Earth from space grow the enthusiasm for what else space can deliver? How will the big ideas dreamed about come to fruition? Ideas like space tourism in orbiting hotels, space-orbiting solar power, and interplanetary travel, to name just a few. There is one very prominent challenge that must be dealt with to truly tame space! It has the most significant impact for all materials to be liberated to space. It comprises the issues relating to the Rocket Equation. It will necessitate the substitution of off-world materials for those formally rocketed up through the Earth's massive gravity well—at tremendous expense as well as risk. It will reverse the historical view of resource movement from Earth to space to space to Earth. If this fundamental shift in resource utilization can be achieved, it will suddenly make economically feasible projects that formerly could never achieve cost-effective closure.

The first lunar natural resource application will be energy. Water was discovered at Shackleton Crater with the L-CROSS mission. Water is a very valuable resource in space given that it can be processed to hydrogen and oxygen (rocket fuel), as discussed earlier in this chapter. Therefore, water will be the space community's first interest in using the Moon's resources as it can be provided to LEO at much less expense than bringing it from Earth. While the discovery of water was established in a gross sense, detailed exploration will be required. This should be the next focus of lunar resource utilization. Baiden and Shackleton Energy have proposed comprehensive exploration programs for the discovery and production of water, as well as the establishment of refueling stations in LEO, to support the exploration of the solar system and beyond. The idea of rocket fuel made on the Moon is a truly game-changing idea for space exploration. A water mining and processing venture such as this has many contemplating how to live and work on the Moon supporting robotic mining operations.

Future lunar inhabitants will need to concentrate on three major activities: survival, exploration, and mining, including processing. As this becomes reality the focus, while currently discovery based, will change to commercial work with mining being a key anchor. Durations of stays will change from sortie-type short-term excursions to semipermanent to permanent with long-term manning of the mining and processing operations underground. Moreover, lunar exploration below the lunar soil, in lunar bedrock, has the potential to yield a similar mineral and chemicals suite as Earth's, thus providing the resources necessary for the building of the larger projects dreamed about today in a cost-effective way.

Living and working on the lunar surface will be required in this type of operation. Safety of personnel will be a prime consideration. Hazards need to be identified and designed out where possible. The following is a preliminary list of the main necessities:

- Survival needs
- Generation of oxygen
- Generation of water
- Establishment of shelter
- Safety needs
- Radiation
- Solar Flare
- Temperature
- Micro-meteorites

The design of any lunar base will need to address these issues so that lunar inhabitants are able to survive and be protected from the environment. These environmental considerations will drive many decisions: The type of base, construction techniques, equipment, and physical layout will all need to be considered closely.

All survivalists know that the most important element of survival is shelter, once basic needs are met. In a lunar context, this is even more important. The blocking of radiation and solar flare activity and protection from the other extremes need to be adequately designed. As all these factors are considered, an underground base with sufficient depth appears to be the only feasible solution. The following are the key questions while planning this type of base:

- How would it be built?
- What technology will be needed?
- Has this type of facility been built before?
- What would be the timing of such a base?

These questions are all addressed in this chapter.

State of the art in Robotic Mining and Construction

Robotics for terrestrial mining and construction has been the topic of a large portion of public and private mining research over the last five decades, and today, it remains a hot topic for major changes in the way mining is done.

Inco Limited's Mines Research group first demonstrated that long-distance teleoperation of multiple mining vehicles for productive work was possible in 1994 at the Canadian Institute of Mining and Metallurgy Annual General Meeting. This demonstration had a teleoperator running two LHDs (digging machines) between the stage of the John Basset Theatre at the Toronto Convention Centre and Copper Cliff North Mine at Copper Cliff, Ontario, a distance of over 400 km and 4000 ft underground. The demonstration was done without any noticeable latency. What made this possible was an advanced telecommunications network that provided 600 Mb/s of wireless bandwidth developed by Dr Baiden and his research team. The success of this demonstration proved that the systems developed were able to improve safety, increase productivity, and lower costs. This demonstration led to the approval of a far-reaching program called the Mining Automation Program (MAP) to development the techniques behind robotic mining.

MAP was a joint program involving Inco Limited, Tamrock OY, Dyno Nobel Explosives, and Natural Resources Canada. The objective of this program was to build on the research originally carried out by Inco Mines Research. This program would develop both the operation center concepts for the teleoperation of mobile mining machines and the economic case for this transformational rework of mining operations. The high-bandwidth telecommunication (5G equivalent) system that could support fleet operation of mining equipment. And a second development was the ability to provide GPS denied positioning systems for underground mining. MAP, using these developments, targeted building telerobots for exploration drilling, tunnel drilling, explosives loading and ignition, material removal and transport, rock stabilization, long-hole drilling, and ore transportation systems.

MAP had many outcomes; two examples are discussed here. The first had a teleoperator running three LHDs from the safety of a centralized control center in an industrial teleoperation workstation using remote operation combined with autonomous guidance. In the second, a teleoperator ran three long-hole production drills from a centralized control room, remotely collaring the holes and automated continuous rod addition. The machines operating in these scenarios for several years regularly from distances of 25 km away with unnoticeable latency to the operator. This was all enabled by the innovative broadband telecommunication infrastructure developed by Mines Research.

The outcomes of this research are currently being applied around the world, at mines in Canada, the United States, Chile, Brazil, South Africa, Australia, and Sweden. The accomplishments of this research are of prime importance to the undertaking of future lunar operations as the hostile environment will necessitate the use of these techniques for outpost construction and the mining of water and other minerals/chemicals on the Moon.

Development of an Underground Lunar Outpost and Mine

Establishment of an international underground lunar outpost and mining facility for supplying propellant using next-generation mining robotics can lead to a permanent lunar outpost as a stepping stone to further solar system exploration and settlement. This type of early lunar outpost could easily expand to support multiple large science projects as well as commercial operations. In addition, the work has many terrestrial spin-offs, such as underwater mining and construction.

The underground habitat layout and possible construction sequence are shown in Figure 12.2. These few images are part of a large-scale study by the authors performed for the Canadian Space Agency (CSA). In this series of images, the underground outpost starts with collaring a portal into the side of a crater to establish a garage, sleeping quarters, and a research facility. The excavation of all these initial requirements will be done from the Earth-based operation center, as demonstrated by the terrestrial mining industry previously. Once these are complete, the first major component to be installed would be a collar water-lock. At this point, the outpost can begin to be habited by astronauts/

settlers. Initial lunar base predevelopment work will require an Earth-based control center for teleoperation of construction and mining robotic equipment. Several teleoperation workstations optimized for managing the latency between Earth control and lunar operation would run from a control room on Earth.

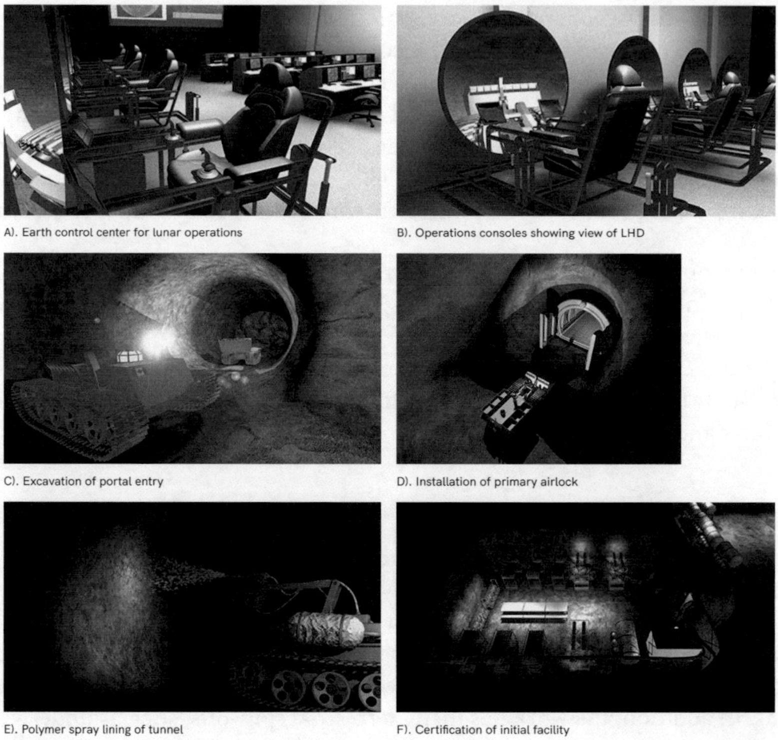

Figure 12.2 Construction sequence for early shelter habitat.

Preliminary analysis indicates that these systems offer a feasible solution to building and certifying a radiation-safe underground lunar facility. Unit energy (kW per cubic meter) for lunar excavation is expected to compare to that used in analogous terrestrial mining, tunneling, and drilling operations, enabling time, volume, and equipment productivity estimates to be derived from mining practice and modified as needed to suit the lower gravity, among other factors. It is assumed that a majority of operations will be conducted in a sealed and partially pressurized environment, reducing the wear and abrasion of equipment and enabling the use of standardized dust management practices. Ground support would be performed using a sintering process. Estimates of the amount of microwave energy required to sinter lunar regolith (see Wingo, 2007) enable calculation of the power required for structural tunnel support and sealing.

As habitation is beginning, the construction machinery can continue to advance facilities deeper underground. This can be followed by the building of science experiments such as an astro-particle observatory and/or infrared telescope. The construction scenarios shown above can be used to generate a detailed view of the CONOPS typically associated with space mission planning. These operational scenarios should be based on terrestrial mining industry experience, enabling the underground construction of development and production drifts, ramps, and 'block cave' mining operations.

Underground Lunar Mining and Processing

Achievement of a commercial mine would follow outpost establishment. Mining and processing using a preferred mining method such as block caving would be able to produce rock with entrained water. In an attached underground propellant-processing facility, the manufacture of ore (water-entrained rock) would be sent to processing elements such as heating and hydrolysis to produce hydrogen and oxygen. The products would be liquefied and stored in underground tanks for loading and transporting to LEO.

Economic Leverage of Lunar Resources

Learning to live off the land will add vitality to human space settlement and will create new jobs, industries, markets, and natural habitats as humankind expands its economic sphere. From the potential of helium 3 (He3) as a fuel for future fusion energy to the production of hydrogen, nitrogen, carbon, and oxygen to support space exploration mission logistics to future surface manufacturing of system components from aluminum, titanium, iron, silicon, ceramics, and glass, lunar resources offer a significant opportunity for the future.

> The space frontier will inevitably increase the scale of thinking and risk taking by business. When we are dealing with space, we are dealing with a technology that requires a planetary scale to stage it, decades of time to develop it, and much bigger investments to get across the threshold of economic return than is customary in business today. Business must now think in international terms and in terms of the next business generation. It must step up to the big risks with the same vision that enabled an earlier generation of builders to push railroad tracks out across the

> wilderness and lay the foundations of our modern economy Ralph Cordiner (from Webb, 1964).

Indeed, the visual of an expanding three-part sphere of influence composed of exploration, economic development, and mature economic operation can be used to describe highly successful empires—from Phoenicia to Roman to England and, finally, the United States.

The first anticipated commercial use of lunar resources is the supply of rocket propellant to government and future private users of the Moon and lunar facilities. The simple addition of an ISRU refueling station to an early lunar surface outpost would dramatically reduce the size requirements for a steady-state cis-lunar transportation system (Blair, 2002) by removing the need for the heavier, expendable first stage of a two-stage lunar lander. This approach would add robustness and sustainability to current NASA planning. Current expendable vehicle technology could be modified for reuse, collapsing the steady-state hardware requirements for any time lunar access to a reusable lunar lander and upper stage (Blair, 2002 and Diaz, 2005). Only the crew capsule would be expended upon reentry into Earth orbit. Surface mobility benefits for refuelable rover power systems are equally significant. A source of consumable fuel cell reactants on the lunar surface would enable energy-intensive applications such as mining and construction or robust and power-rich human exploration operations using a closed rover. The possible existence of platinum group metal enrichment among the diverse geologic surface environments of the Moon offers rationale for diversified commercial lunar mining (Wingo, 2004). Unique features, such as the dense nearside mascons that underlie the Lunar Mare, offer fodder to the imagination regarding the longer-term potential for underground mining.

Mining the Moon is a precursor activity to a much more robust set of long-term mature industrial operations that will take maximum advantage of the unique lunar environment. The list of valuable research activities enabled by the thermal and vacuum conditions on the lunar surface (including permanently shadowed areas) includes materials and metallurgy research, thin film technology (large scale), vacuum welding, coating, distillation, and superconductivity research, to name a few (Ruzic, 1965). Access to cold traps and the potential for large-scale (tens to hundreds of meters), passive cryogenic systems could enable a new era in low-temperature science and engineering. Active cooling to micro or milli Kelvin from one of these cryostats would require orders of magnitude less energy than used today for cryogenic research (Ruzic, 1965).

Summary

Lunar mining, or ISRU—as it has been called in the space world—is now required to become a reality. The recent finding of significant water on the Moon means that the Moon as a fuel source will change many of the plans in a positive way.

This chapter has explored how a lunar outpost might be established, how mining might occur, how terrestrial techniques will likely become the basis for future mining equipment and systems on the Moon, and why these facilities are important for astronaut/settler long-term health and safety.

The creation of outposts on the Moon and mining and processing appear to be feasible given techniques that have already been explored. Moreover, the concepts will be required to continue the human journey of exploring the solar system and beyond.

Next Steps: Future Research Initiatives

Making the CONOPS a reality is going to require several steps. The first, most pressing, will be the creation of a Lunar De-risking Facility to conceive, experiment, and build the terrestrial precursor to the subterranean lunar outpost. This work must coincide with progress in establishing the needs of a lunar settlement, such as energy.

Lunar De-risking Facility

Prior to building such an outpost on the Moon, it makes sense to create a terrestrial Lunar De-risking Facility. This has been proposed as the International Institute for Space Mining (Baiden and Tietz, 2010). The concept is to create a terrestrial testbed to simulate the conditions of space and the Moon in a large 250 m cubed underground tank facility. This facility would be flooded to provide large-scale conditions of weightlessness, space vacuum, and thermal characteristics on Earth to simulate robotic construction under these conditions on the Moon from Earth.

A concept of the facility has been developed by Baiden. Within the facility would be an underwater/underground construction simulator for teleconstruction of a lunar underground base. This physical simulator would support real conditions for robotic construction of the base in weightless conditions.

Additional chambers would allow the largest thermal vacuum chamber in the world due to being constructed in a large rock cavern.

Establishment of a Lunar Outpost

The establishment of radiation-protected subterranean lunar habitats for extensive lunar resource extraction and processing will turbocharge space exploration and settlement. It will also seed an exponential expansion of cislunar commerce, paving the way for breakthroughs in human survival and growth in the solar system and beyond. While initial uses of the Moon will likely emphasize on energy and spacecraft propellant production (and storage), critical materials derived from lunar feedstock will play an ever increasing role in celestial as well as terrestrial civilization.

Energy is the key to human survival on and off Earth. Technologies emanating from the challenges of lunar settlement will radically enhance energy management and multiply potential energy strategies on earth. Technical breakthroughs required for successful off-earth settlement will undoubtedly spin off innovative applications for other energy modalities as well—fusion, fission, geothermal, wind, tidal, biofuels, and magnetics, to name a few.

Potentially, the most significant impact of non-terrestrial material-manufacturing capabilities will be the liberation of humankind from the cold, hard physics of the Rocket Equation. Substitution of off-world materials for those formally rocketed up through the Earth's massive gravity well—at tremendous expense as well as risk—will reverse the historical arrow of resource movement from earth to space to space to earth. This fundamental shift in resource utilization will suddenly make economically feasible projects that formerly could never achieve cost-effective closure.

Non-terrestrial materials manufacturing could usher in the long-anticipated Age of Space Solar Power, in which carbon-free energy could be generated by solar power satellites, built in space with space-based materials, and beamed almost anywhere on earth 24/7. This technology would be nothing less than transformative for an increasingly troubled planet.

There is no energy shortage in the solar system; only an innovation and creativity shortage in the realm of human endeavors.

Acknowledgement

At the time of republishing and updating this article, first written 20 years ago, our distinguished colleague and co-author, Mr. Brad Blair, passed away in June 2022. It is fitting that this vision of the future of settlement and mining of the moon and beyond is a part of his legacy.

Brad committed his life to space exploration encouraging all young and old to take on the challenge for humankind. Brad was a true visionary space explorer who dreamed, like us two, of a permanent human presence in space.

The NSS National Space Society paid a well thought of tribute to him:

https://space.nss.org/national-space-society-mourns-the-passing-of-brad-blair/

May your vision of space exploration and the means to get there continue unabated, Brad. We dedicate Chapter 12 to the memory of Brad Blair.

Greg and Louis

Note

1. The views expressed by the author are based on 36 years of professional engineering experience covering the aerospace and space sectors and do not necessarily constitute an official endorsement from the Canadian Space Agency or the Government of Canada on current established space policy and future directions of the space program. The content of this chapter are reflections from a group of multidisciplinary experts providing guidance material for potential strategic directions.

References

Baiden, G.R., 1996. "Future robotic mining at INCO Limited: The next 25 years", Bulletin Can. Inst. Min. Metall., Montreal, 89, pp. 36–40.

Baiden, G.R., 2005, "Telerobotic Experiments for Mining", Bulletin Canadian Institute of Mining and Metallurgy paper.

Baiden, G.R., 2017, "Geospatial mapping and surveying robotics for both GPS and GPS denied environments", UG Mining Technology Conference, Sudbury, Canada.

Baiden, G.R., 2017, "Tele-robotics for hang-up assessment and removal – an idea whose time has come", Society of Mining Engineering Annual Meeting, Denver, CO.
Baiden, G.R., 2021, "Mining on Earth the Analogy-From Prospecting to Product", LSIC Excavation and Construction Workshop, Johns Hopkins.
Baiden, G.R. and Bissiri, Y., 2007, "An Innovative Approach using Telerobotics for Intelligent Block Caving Operations", IFAC MMM Symposium Proceedings, Quebec City, Quebec, Canada, August.
Baiden, G.R. and Bissiri, Y., 2005, "An Intelligent Algorithm for a teleoperation operation: Multiple machines and multiple operators", IEEE, ICOM05 Conference Proceedings, category: Intelligent computation, May.
Baiden, G.R. and Henderson, E., 1996, "LHD Tele-operation and Guidance - Proven Productivity Improvement Tools", Bull. Can. Inst. Min. Metall., 87, pp. 47–51.
Baiden, G.R. and M. Scoble, 1992, "Mine-Wide Information System Development", Bull. Can. Inst. Min. Metall., 85, 960, pp. 65–70.
Baiden, G. and Tietz, D., 2010, "International statute for Space Mining", confidential presentation.
Baiden, G.R. and Tietz, D., 2016, "International Institute for Space Mining – A space mining de-risking facility", FEDNOR workshop, Sudbury, Canada.
Baiden, G., Scoble, M. and S. Flewelling, 1993, "Robotic Systems Development for Mining Automation", Bull. Can. Inst. Min. Metall., 86, 972, pp. 75–77.
Baiden, G.R., Strom, R. and Preston, C., 1997, "Mining automation program", Bulletin Can. Inst. Min. Metall., Montreal, 90, pp. 71–77.
Baiden, G.R., Bissiri, Y., Seguin, G. and Persingher, M., 2007, "Effects of Adding Vibrotactile Feedback on Operators' Cognitive Load in Mobile Vehicle Teleoperation", The Journal of Field Robotics, Wiley, September.
Blair, B., Diaz, J., Duke, M., Lamassoure, E., Easter, R., Oderman, M. and Vaucher, M., 2002, "Space Resource Economic Analysis Toolkit: The Case for Commercial Lunar Ice Mining", Final Report to the NASA Exploration Team, Center for the Commercial Applications of Combustion in Space, Colorado School of Mines, Golden, Colorado, December 20.
Cohen, M.M., 2002, "Selected Precepts in Lunar Architecture", IAC-02-Q.4.3.08, 53rd International Astronautical Congress, The World Space Congress - 2002, 10–19 Oct 2002/Houston, Texas.
Cordiner, R., 1961, "Competitive Private Enterprise in Space", Chapter 10 in *Peacetime Uses of Outer Space*, Simon Ramo (editor), McGraw Hill Book Company, pp. 213–240.
Dartnell, L., Desorgher, L., Ward, J.M. and Coates, A.J., 2007, "Martian sub-surface ionising radiation: biosignatures and geology", Biogeosciences, 4, 545–558.
Diaz, J., Ruiz, B., Blair, B., Harsch, M., Duke, M., Parrish, C., Lueck, D., Mueller, R., Whitlow, J., Boucher, D., Nock, K., Penzo, P., Sanders, J., Baird, S. and Romig, K., 2005, "STARLITE - Space Transportation Architectures and Refueling for Lunar and Interplanetary Travel and Exploration", NASA Grant NAG9–1535, Center for the Commercial Applications of Combustion in Space, Colorado School of Mines, Golden, Colorado, June 5.
English, R.A., Benson, R.E., Bailey, J.V. and Barnes, C.M., 1973, "Apollo Experience Report – Protection from Radiation", Technical Note TN D – 7080, March.
Hofmann, M. and Bergamasco, F., 2020, "Space Resources Activities from the Perspective of Sustainability: Legal Aspects", Global Sustainability 3. https://doi.org/10.1017/sus.2019.27.
Jablonski, A.M. Ogden, K.A., 2005, "A Review of Technical Requirements for Lunar Structures - Present Status", International Lunar Conference 2005.

Poole, R.A., Golde, P. and Baiden, G.R., 1999, Remote operation from surface of Tamrock Datasolo drills at Inco's Stobie mine, Bulletin Can. Inst. Min. Metall., 89, pp. 47–50.

Poole, R., Golde, P., Baiden, G. and M. Scoble, 1997, "Multiple Machines-Single Operator on Surface at Inco's Stobie Mine", Bulletin Can. Inst. Min. Metall., Montreal, 90, pp. 63–67.

Poole, R., Golde, P., Baiden, G. and M. Scoble, 1998, "A Review of Inco's Mining Automation Research in the Sudbury Basin", Bulletin Can. Inst. Min. Metall., Montreal, 91, pp. 68–74.

Ruzic, N., 1965, *The Case for Going to the Moon*, G.P. Putnam's Sons, New York, 240 pp.

Santomartino, R., Zea, L. and Cockell, C.S., "The Smallest Space Miners: Principles of Space Biomining", Extremophiles, 26, no. 1 (January 6, 2022): 7. https://doi.org/10.1007/s00792-021-01253-w.

Steffen, O., 2022, "Explore to Exploit: A Data-Centred Approach to Space Mining Regulation", Space Policy 59 (February 1): 101459. https://doi.org/10.1016/j.spacepol.2021.101459

Vagenas, N., Scoble, M. and G. Baiden, 1996, "Mobile Machine Automation in Underground Metal Mining", Int. Jnl. Mineral Resources Engineering, Imperial College Press, London, 5, 1, pp. 43–55.

Vagenas, N., Scoble, M. and G. Baiden, 1997, "Mobile Machine Automation in Underground Metal Mining", Bulletin Can. Inst. Min. Metall., Montreal, 90, pp. 57–62.

Webb, J., 1964, Administrator, National Aeronautics and Space Administration, Keynote Speech at Armed Forces Communications and Electronics Association, May 20, Washington, DC.

Wingo, D., 2004, *Moonrush: Improving Life on Earth with the Moon's Resources*, Apogee Books Space Series 43, Softcover, 260 pp.

Wingo, D., Woodcock, G. and Maxwell, M., 2007, "Lunar Outpost Development and the Role of Mechanical Systems for Payload Handling, Deliverable Under NASA Contract NNL06AE27P", Skycorp Incorporated, Huntsville, AL 35801, February 10.

Xu, F., 2020, "The Approach to Sustainable Space Mining: Issues, Challenges, and Solutions", IOP Conference Series: Materials Science and Engineering 738, no. 1 (January 1): 012014. https://doi.org/10.1088/1757-899X/738/1/012014.

13 Questions to ask before we commence mining in space: what, where, when, why, who, and how?

Carol A. Dahl

Introduction

Minerals are thought to have developed an unimaginably long time ago, starting with the Big Bang. Human mining of these old materials is much more recent. The oldest-known mine to recover materials is thought to be a silica mine in Egypt that operated 100 000 years ago, when humans still lived on a flat Earth (Guinness Book of World Records, 2022). The notion of mining from space started even more recently in the imaginations of science fiction writers, as in *Edison's Conquest of Mars*—first published in serial form in 1898 and later as a book (Serviss, 1947). Such fanciful books, TV series, and movies over the next century or so introduced many themes needed to be considered to turn space mining from science fiction to science fact.

Dahl (2022) reviews many such themes in science fiction. They include the dangers of collisions with asteroids, propulsion systems, planet gravity aiding propulsion, finding and returning space materials, dealing with low or no gravity and atmosphere, robotic mining, orbiting and surface space stations, enforcement of property rights, international regulation of space mining, corporate social and environmental responsibility, and interplanetary mining and trading networks. These issues, and more, will need to be resolved to make space mining a reality. Meanwhile, science fact has been mounting as well. For example, Lewis (1996, 2015) and numerous others provide us with a more factual account of why space mining might be just around the corner with a wealth of clever suggestions on how it might be done.

A space station on the Moon seems to be getting closer as well. The Deep Space Gateway Project to put a crewed space station in lunar orbit has a targeted launch of 2024 and is part of the multicountry Artemis Project. China has also announced targets for a research station on the Moon in conjunction with international partners and a later mission to Mars (China National Space Administration, 2021). From the private sector, both Elon Musk and Jeff Bezos have expressed interest in developing future space colonies (Hamilton, 2021). If or when these and numerous other efforts succeed and lead to sustainable space mining are interesting and challenging questions. The theme of this chapter is to speculate on the information required to answer such questions. Thus, I will indicate what we have already done and speculate on questions of what, where, when, why, who, and how—still required to be determined to make these space mining imaginations a reality.If or when these and numerous other efforts succeed and lead to sustainable space mining are interesting and challenging questions. The theme of this chapter is to speculate on the information required to answer such questions. Thus, I will indicate what we have already done and speculate on questions of what, where, when, why, who, and how—still required to be determined to make these space mining imaginations a reality.

As with mining on Earth, the space mining supply chain will start with finding prospective resources. I will start there, too, and in Section 2, consider exploration and some of what we know about resources in space and where they are. Once we have identified prospective targets, we will need to know how to get to the minerals. In Section 3, I will explore propulsion in space. If we can get there, to start mining operations, we will need to move materials in space. In Section 4, I consider the rocket equation and its implications on moving things in space.

Moving things in space will be essential, but knowing how to generate something we want to move is even more essential. Thus, in Section 5, I consider issues in developing mines to produce and process materials. Low or no gravity and atmosphere will present challenges for mining operations and human inhabitants as our closest potential space mining sites are the Moon and near-Earth asteroids (NEAs). Although robots and artificial intelligence are likely to play an important role in our mining operations, they may not be able to do it all. In Section 6, I consider the need for humans in space and their habitat requirements.

Once we know how to produce, but before we launch into production, we will also need to consider why we want to produce. Many reasons are cited for why we should mine space, including reducing environmental damage from mining on Earth, tapping into the vast resources of space as earthly resources become depleted, allowing space habitation as population pressures increase on Earth, and improving material benefits and technology for future generations (Gilbert, 2021). For the private sector to commence operations, markets will need to provide profits commensurate with the risks taken. This will depend not only on the costs of producing the material but also on the market structure and demand for the product. Section 7 will consider such demand issues along with a generic spatial market simulation model to focus on needed information. In addition to economic issues in any large commercial mining operation, there remain questions on the role of the government, which will be outlined in Section 8. A brief sum up is contained in Section 9, with congratulations on accomplishments to date and encouragement to keep exploring the final frontier. Supplementary material and additional documentation are available in Dahl (2022).

How will we know what is out there and where it is?

The search for minerals on Earth is called prospecting. Dahl (2022) summarizes many prospecting methods on Earth, most of which have potential space applications. Early on, earth prospectors looked for surface signs that signaled mineral ore. For visual confirmation in space, we more often use telescopes from Earth and its artificial satellites, employing photometry, which measures the brightness of objects, or spectrometry, which considers the different wavelengths to identify elements in space (ProfRob, 2015).

Such visual measures may also be used from spacecraft orbiting space bodies, and we can use geophysical and geochemical methods if we are orbiting or on the surface of space bodies as well. Dahl (2022) describes some of these methods. Magnetometers are used to measure differences in magnetic intensity, which may signal mineral deposits. Gravity meters detect differences in gravity and help determine the density of the material beneath them but do require a celestial body with gravity. In electromagnetic surveys, an AC current on or above the surface creates a magnetic field. Measuring the intensity of the field gives information on the conductivity and composition of underground materials. Seismic surveys, typically using thumpers or blasts, create mechanical waves through a solid object and measure the characteristics of the waves reflected back. Radiometric techniques (e.g. Geiger counters and gamma ray scintillators) use radioactive emissions to determine rock age, radioactive mineral deposits, or other associated materials.

However, visual and other observations from on high do not necessarily tell us what is underground. That requires samples. From space, our early physical samples came from meteorites, while, more recently, we have brought home small amounts from the Moon, Mars, some asteroids, and a comet (Dahl, 2022). Geochemical methods require such samples. Colorimetric analytical techniques treat samples with the resulting color indicating the composition. Treatments include chemicals and fluorescent lights. Materials may also be dissolved in acids or other agents that precipitate out materials. See Dahl (2022) for such prospecting methods, references, and other advanced techniques that not only require samples but also skilled technicians to implement them.

The discussion so far suggests we know how to prospect for materials in space. Many of the prospecting methods we use on Earth have been or could be modified to work in space. However, the methods applied so far in space have been close to the surface, with the deepest drilled cores only about 3 meters deep. If the objects are not homogeneous, much deeper core samples will need to be taken. Crawford (2019) argues that deeper core samples, say to 100 meters and more, will be much more complicated, requiring in-person human oversite.

So, we do have methods to look for the materials, so where should we look? The most likely near-term targets are the Moon and NEAs, followed by Mars and its planets, Deimos and Phobos. Some knowledge of asteroid composition comes from the study of meteorites. Asteroids that have not been sampled, which means practically all of them, are typically categorized by their spectral type. Metzger (2013) indicates three types of asteroids of relevance to space mining—C, S, and M. Type C is likely to contain water, metal, and organic or carbonaceous compounds. Their components might be converted into hydrogen, oxygen, and methane for rocket fuel and carbon dioxide to grow plants and create plastics and rubber that might be crafted along with metal into parts, perhaps with the use of 3D printers. Type S may contain the platinate group of metals (PGMs). Some of these precious metals sell for millions of dollars a metric tonne on Earth, making them candidates to mine for return to Earth. Type M asteroids may include PGMs, but with more iron and nickel. These two less valuable but plentiful minerals on Earth will more likely be used in space for colonization or as hardware for larger missions as they are very expensive to get to space but comparatively cheaper to mine on Earth. However, if Earth shortages and costs provided the right incentives, they might eventually be sold on Earth as well. For more on detecting, estimating population, identifying, and characterizing asteroids, see Anthony and Emami (2018).

So, we have places where to look and likely techniques to look with, but we still have a lot to learn about what is out there and need to be able to get to these places. One of the biggest challenges in getting to these places is the propellant needed to escape Earth's gravity. Dahl (2022) provides some information on the historical uses of propellants. The Saturn V burned a special kerosene

(RP-1) with liquid oxygen (LOX) for takeoff and burned liquid hydrogen (LH2) with LOX for higher stages. The U S Space Shuttle (1981–2011) burned a solid aluminum-based rocket fuel with LOX for takeoff followed by burning LH2 with LOX. The Falcon Heavy (first launched in 2019) uses RP-1 and LOX as fuel, while SpaceX's Starship (expected first launch in 2022) will be the first to use liquid methane (CH4) and LOX as fuel.

Although hydrogen is the most efficient fuel for use by chemical oxidation, it has to be kept very cold to keep its mass manageable (Boring, 2017). When storage is needed on long flights, hydrazine-related compounds based on ammonia have been used (Fletcher-Wood, 2016). However, given its toxicity, greener alternatives to hydrazine products have been sought after (European Space Agency, 2001). Another big disadvantage of using these chemical reactions for thrust is the excessive weight of the fuel needed to escape Earth's gravity. The weight to reach low Earth orbit might be 85% propellant, leaving 15% for the rocket and payload (Petit, 2012). The small percentage of payload severely limits the weight of equipment, accompanying humans, and return samples.

Besides propellant, applications that need electricity in space include electric control and maneuverability of launch vehicles, spacecraft, shuttles, landers, and rovers as well as research and astronaut equipment (Halpert, Frank, and Surampudi, 1999). Five common methods of generating electricity in space for such uses are solar photovoltaics (PVs), often coupled with batteries; fuel cells; ion thrusters; radioisotope thermoelectric generators (RTGs); and fission power systems (FPS). These methods have their advantages and disadvantages.

The hydrogen and oxygen needed for fuel cells are heavy, as are solar panels. Thus, for shorter missions, fuel cells have the advantage, while for longer ones, solar is the lighter option (Borogove, 2019). Ion thrusters are another option for propulsion in space but are too weak for takeoff and only work in a vacuum. In them, electricity is used to ionize a fuel, often xenon. The ions are accelerated and ejected to provide thrust (NASA Glenn Resarch Center, 2017).

Nuclear energy has also been employed almost from the beginnings of space programs. RTGs, sometimes called nuclear batteries, are used to provide heat and electricity for use in space (US Office of Nuclear of Energy, 2021). In them, the heat of radioactive decay, usually of plutonium 238, is converted into electricity using thermocouples (NASA's Jet Propulsion Lab, n.d.). If the heat is used directly, the units are called radioisotope heat units. These units do not have enough power for takeoff. Fission has been used occasionally in space, but again not as a propellant. With all of these nuclear techniques, a very small amount of fuel goes a long way, but there are always safety concerns from potential radiation leaks. Fusion—popular as a propellant in the science fiction world—has been the subject of much research for decades, but has only created a positive energy balance for a few seconds. Given the high amount of potential energy it could produce, mastering fusion could be a game changer in space travel (Starr, 2021).

Dahl (2022) gives more detail and documentation on the aforementioned and other technologies and their evolution. Lewis (2016) provides a good summary on how we might produce propellants in space. The historical record shows that we can get to space, especially within our solar system, where we would most likely begin our mining ventures. But can we move enough equipment and materials into space to develop mining operations and get the processed products to market? I will speculate on this capability in the next section.

Moving materials in space

Now, although we can get to space, defying Earth's gravity is not easy or cheap. Dahl (2022) notes that the US Space Shuttle had a payload of 25 000 kg into low Earth orbit at an estimated cost of US$54 000/kg, which has dropped in some recent private sector flights to as low as US$3000/kg. US Apollo 17 landed around 16 500 kg on the Moon. The total fuel needed was more than 2.9 million kg. What we have brought back is rather sparse. Six trips to the Moon using powerful Saturn rockets from 1969 to 1972 only netted the United States 382 kg (842 pounds) of moonrock (NASA, 2022a). Other non-crewed missions have netted even less. Not much by earthly mining standards.

To better understand such logistics, let's see what rocket scientists tell us about moving mass around the solar system. In leaving Earth, you need to accelerate enough to escape Earth's gravity. This acceleration, or change in velocity, is designated as delta v or Δv and is measured in kilometers per second (km/s). We have numerous estimates of optimal Δv for various celestial objects of interest: Δv to low Earth orbit starts at about 9.4 km/s; with another 6.4 Δv, we can land on the Moon; and with 8 or so more Δv from LEO, we could get to the potential mining targets in the main asteroid belt between Mars and Jupiter (Taylor, McDowell, and Elvis, 2018).

If landing on a celestial object with gravity, you will also need some Δvs to slow down and not crash land. If the body in question has an atmosphere, the friction of the atmosphere will slow a craft passing through it. The atmosphere will increase the Δvs needed to leave such a body but decrease the Δvs needed to land. Relying on the atmosphere to slow the craft for landing is called aerobraking, which requires heat shields to avoid incineration.

With space exploration and study, we have been accumulating more information about the difficulty or Δvs to get to different objects. Asterank has a database of more than 600 000 asteroids, which gives Δvs and other collected information, including orbital information and spin (Asterank, 2022). NASA (2022b) gives the Δv from LEO for more than 17 000 NEAs. About 2000 have a Δv of 5.5 or less, which is less than that for going to the Moon.

When traveling in space, inertia is important; every time you want to change directions, speed up, or slow down, you will need to change velocity, where velocity is both a speed and a direction. If you want to orbit or land on an asteroid or other celestial body, you also need to synchronize your movement and direction with the object, requiring more changes in velocity. These Δvs can be added up across all the maneuvers required to reach a required space destination.

The big challenge with propellants is demonstrated by Tsiolkovsky's ideal rocket equation, which shows how Δv is related to the rocket mass, including payload (M_{s0}) and fuel mass (F_0), and the exhaust velocity of the rocket (v_e)—assuming no drag and constant fuel burn over time—is

$$\Delta v = v_e \ln\left[\frac{Ms_0 + F_0}{Ms_0}\right] \tag{13.1}$$

(Infogalactic: The Planetary Knowledge Core, 2015; Spakovszky, 2007).

The velocity (v_e) we get from a ship of given weight and fuel burn depends on physical principals relating to its design. Dahl (2022) rearranges this equation to glean some further insights on Δv and fuel use. If the interest is on fuel burn, solve the aforementioned equation for fuel to get

$$Ms_0 \exp\left(\frac{\Delta v}{v_e}\right) - M_{S0} = F_0 \tag{13.2}$$

Thus, fuel use increases linearly with the mass of the ship, including payload, but exponentially with Δv.

The most likely mining prospects near term are the Moon, near-Earth objects (NEOs), and Mars. NEOs are asteroids and comets with orbits that bring them within about 1.2 AU of the Sun. Since Earth and Mars are 1 AU and 1.5 AU, respectively, from the Sun, NEOs will sometimes be in Earth's neighborhood and closer than MARS. We have demonstrated a capability to get to these places.

The large amount of fuel needed to leave Earth's gravity is one of the challenges that will need to be overcome if we want to move crew and equipment from Earth to outer space. Much of the current research is addressing this problem by focusing on generating as much of the needed material in space as possible.

Developing, producing, and processing material

Once we have done our homework and found mineable deposits of ore, defined as material containing commercially viable amounts of the desired material, we can proceed. We will have already confirmed we have the technology on how to get to the material, collect, process, and get our final output to market; confirmed our market is commercially viable (more on that later); and made a final investment decision. It is, then, time to get shovels or boots, or perhaps both, on the ground.

For small operations of loose material on or very near the surface, materials may be scrapped or raked up being careful to contain the results from floating off if there is no gravity. Excavators that chew and collect material are a likely option and could handle more solid materials as well. Augers may be another option and have already been used in space for sampling. See Longchen et al. (2014) for the use of augers in space sampling and optimal drill structure. On Earth, augers may have bits up to a meter across and go to depths of around 100 m (Bhattacharyya, 2020). As always, our methods will have to adapted to low gravity, harsh conditions, and the available energy supply. Explosion-driven impactors have been used in space to loosen material near the surface for collection.

Humans have brought materials back from the Moon, Mars, and asteroids, albeit in very small amounts. All these efforts were aimed at material very near the surface, no more than a few meters deep. For the United States, the Apollo astronauts were the miners, and tools included scoops and rakes to gather material, hammers to break off rock chips and drive in core tubes, and drills to get core tube samples from greater depth. Individual samples were put into sample bags, accumulated into larger sample bags, and boxed to be transferred back to Earth (Lunar and Planetary Institute, n.d.).

For larger operations, we can again consider our earthly options. I mention some here. For more detail on these operations, see Dahl (2022). For depths of up to 300 meters, open pit mining is typically used on Earth. First remove any non-ore overburden; break up the ore to get it out of the mine, often by drilling holes and blasting; and use equipment with huge scoops, called draglines, to drop the ore onto local transport—conveyor belts or trucks—to get it to a local processing location. The ore is typically crushed or ground into a fine powder for further separation to get out the valuable material (Matters, n.d.). This separation process uses gravity, magnetic, or electrostatic properties for the initial separation and is called beneficiation (Lewis, 1996). If there are no environmental issues, the dross separated out from the valuable material may be left in piles, where gravity exists, or be left to float off into space if no gravity will hold it down; otherwise, it will need to be safely disposed of.

Water or other liquid solvents are often essential for mineral recovery. The aqueous methods suggested by Elbelawi et al. (2021) include placer, dredging, hydraulic, and in situ leaching. With in-situ leaching, chemicals may be pumped underground to dissolve materials to be pumped to the surface. If the method is used in space, such chemicals would need to be brought from Earth or generated locally. An alternative in situ technique is to use heat to liquefy the mined material, so it can be pumped to the surface. Many believe that water will be one of our first mining targets. Given the cold temperatures and low gravity in space, if it exists in free form, it will be underground ice. If this water is in the form of ice, in situ thermal will be a natural alternative and can be accomplished using energy generated locally.

Material samples already retrieved from space give us some ideas about mining in space. Except for the US moon samples, all used robots. Given the difficult conditions on our near-mining targets, it seems that robotic mining will be the likeliest near-term option. Previous missions suggest we can get to our targets and collect samples, while advances in artificial intelligence continually advance that probability. Yet, these samples were tiny and no processing was done on them. Can we do this collection at scale, add in processing, and do it at commercial levels is the question.

As surface mineable ore gets deeper and deeper, eventually surface mining is no longer viable and we need to move underground, which adds considerable expense and complication to the process. Underground space mining does not seem as likely near term, unless it is done to also create habitat in mined out areas. It has even been suggested that hollowed out asteroids could be converted into ships for habitat, transportation, and ore transfer.

On Earth, underground mining operations vary considerably depending on the minerals being sought; whether the sought material is in soft or hard rock; and the geology, configuration, and orientation of the deposit, along with related geology and economics. But a few generic ingredients are the basis for all modern underground mining operations: Tunnels are needed to get miners and material from the surface to the ore; the tunnels need to be structurally sound, with reinforcement added if needed; ventilation, heat control, and power sources need to be provided for; and underground passages need to allow access to the ore bodies and to tunnels to the surface. Ore bodies are typically drilled and blasted to loosen the ore so that it can be moved to the surface by truck or conveyor for further processing.

Dahl (2022) describes, references, and gives applications for a variety of underground mining techniques commonly used on Earth. The two most popular techniques in underground soft rock mining are (1) room and pillar (a more selective technique) and (2) long wall (a bulk method). Hard rock underground mines more typically contain metals and gems, with method depending on the layout and properties of the ore, mineral sought after, and host rock. The methods are often categorized in two ways: (1) bulk mining versus selective mining and (2) whether underground artificial support is needed in open areas.

Bulk or unselective methods are typical with large deposits of low-grade ore, where all the ore is mined, and include block caving (supported), sublevel caving (supported), and vertical crater retreat (unsupported). Whereas in the more expensive selective mining, high-grade ores spread throughout the deposit are mined, leaving the low-grade ores in the ground. Selective mining methods include a number of unsupported stoping techniques with supported methods, including cut and fill as well as bench and fill. Techniques may vary in the same mine across different areas and at different times as the characteristics of the deposits being mined change. Such tailoring of the method to the mine in space, if needed, will prove to be yet another challenge.

The goal of processing at the mine is to concentrate the ore, separating the valuable compounds from the gangue. This processing is tailored to the material being mined. The three stages of processing at the mine are typically comminution, which breaks the ore into finer pieces by crushing and grinding and may even start underground; beneficiation, which separates the ore from the gangue waste; and further concentration of the ore.

Usually, the ore is not the end product needed but will need to be further processed by smelting or refining (e.g. iron will be extracted from iron ore). Such extractive facilities are often not available at the mine. They may even be in another company or country. The four typical categories for extracting metals are based on the method used: heat, dissolving in aqueous or water solutions, electrolysis in salt solutions, and use of halides.

Even this very brief introduction of mining, with more details in Dahl (2022), suggests that humans have developed an amazing number of complicated processes to recover elements from Earth at very low concentrations. Many such processes require large amounts of water and gravity. A few processes have been applied on a very small scale on the ISS, the Moon, Mars, some asteroids, and a comet. Study after study I have encountered suggests this will be one of the big questions: Can we do this collection and processing at scale in a harsh space environment and do it at commercial levels?

Needs for humans and habitats in space

On Earth, we may have started with picks and shovels, but most mined material operations are now highly capital intensive with large economies of scale and a trend toward increasing automation and robotics. Advantages of this automation include better and safer human working conditions, the ability to mine increasingly harsher environments, and lower labor costs. Teleoperations can allow one operator to control multiple operations, reducing time loss from transporting humans and shift changes. Real-time data collection and monitoring lead to higher productivity through better control of logistics, processes, and equipment maintenance along the supply chain (Mueller and Susante, 2012). Robotics used in space could have similar benefits, as the environment is even harsher with much higher labor, transport, and fuel costs.

While robotics in mining has increased substantially in recent decades and we have returned small samples from space using only robots, the question is this: Can we dispense with humans present at space mining operations altogether? If not, are humans willing and able to live in harsh space environments? Thus, we need to know whether robotics can operate independently of close human supervision in large complicated operations. Mueller and Susante (2012) provide a number of actual terrestrial examples of automation improvements, including remote control of excavation and loading (some from a distance of many kilometers), driverless trucks, and improved software and sensors for information gathering. Their reference to Moore's Law also reminds us that these methods continue to improve. They argue that such applications will be leveraged and adapted for space at relatively low costs.

In early applications, the extraterrestrial mining done will likely be to replace expensive earth-based resources with local space resources for local use, called in situ resource use (ISRU). Mueller and Susante (2012) provide a summary of the main functions of ISRU related to lunar and Mars exploration, which will also be applicable once we are past the initial exploration stage. These functions are (1) continued prospecting to determine the size and location of various resources; (2) production and storage of water, air, and energy for propulsion and equipment operation; and (3) construction, repair, and adaptation of hardware and infrastructure.

It seems likely that for sustainable commercial space mining at least some nearby human support will be required. Dahl (2022) considers some of the needs and possibilities of space habitation. Two basic venues usually considered for human habitation in space are bases on or under the surface of a space body and stations that orbit around a space body. The government-sponsored US Skylab (1973–1974) and USSR/Russian Mir station (1986–2001) are earlier orbiting examples. Subsequently, the ongoing multicountry ISS (1998 with planned retirement for 2030 or beyond) has been the result of the collaboration between 15 countries (Taylor, Flatow, and Koerth, 2022). More recently, the private sector has been involved in the ISS, with private companies delivering astronauts and supplies. As of now, we have no inhabited stations orbiting other space bodies, although a number of uninhabited crafts have done so.

Ganapathi et al. (1993) surveyed the habitats envisioned before and after the U S Apollo Program (1961–1972). They found that the early studies characterized the need for temperature control and protection from meteorites and radiation. As information mounted from the missions, regolith was investigated for its protective abilities. Studies considered how soil properties and seismic activity would affect habitat design. Such habitats could be prefabricated on Earth, likely based on design of the ISS habitation modules, or they could be built in space from in situ materials (e.g. concrete, basalt, glass, aluminum, iron, and titanium). All of them would require space-processing capabilities. For longer stays, water would be recovered locally. It could provide water and oxygen for human consumption and oxygen and hydrogen for propellant. In reviewing more recent suggestions, this earlier comprehensive review seems to provide the basics of most of the more recent design suggestions. See also Baiden et al. (2022) for their vision of a lunar base.

Both the public and private sectors and coalitions between them have plans for putting humans back in space. With the high cost of such space activities, there have been increasing tendencies toward such coalitions. For example, the Artemis missions led by US NASA—with coalition partners including Canada, the European Space Agency, and Japan—have also chosen five private companies to help with the mission: Blue Origin, Dynetics, Lockheed Martin, Northrup Grumman, and SpaceX (Witt and Rowe, 2021). Artemis III plans to return humans to the Moon to build a permanent-crewed base camp. The camp would provide a staging area to support ongoing research on science, local resource use, and other knowledge needed for a future permanent base on Mars and other future space activities, including travel, habitation, and mining ventures. A related agreement is the 2020 Artemis Accord with 16 governments including the five Artemis partners agreeing to cooperate for the peaceful exploration of space (Government of Canada, n.d.).

For longer-term mining operations requiring sustainable human settlements, the same two aforementioned basic choices have been imagined—large orbiting stations, such as those suggested by O'Neill (1976), or surface habitats, such as those envisioned by Lewis (1996)—starting with the Moon or Mars. Both would start with basic materials and equipment from Earth and would continue to grow into sustainability by processing and using materials in space.

One more recent suggestion is the use of 3D printing (also called additive manufacturing) to build habitat as well as manufacturing in space. NASA has been successfully experimenting with 3D printing on the international space station since 2014 using polymers and resins (Government of Canada, n.d.). ESA recently announced that it was teaming up with the private sector to test 3D printing technologies using lithographic techniques from scrap metals in microgravity (Listek, 2021).

Humans have demonstrated that they can live in space for short time periods. The big questions related to human habitation for mining will be developments in robotics, the needed local human presence, the long-term physical and psychological effects from living in space, and the economic rewards and habitat environment needed to entice the needed human presence at the mining site (Hollingham, 2014)

Economic feasibility and the private sector: markets for mined space materials

Knowing what is out there, where it is, and how to exploit it is not enough. For an entity to undertake space mining, the expected benefits must exceed the expected costs. In this section, I focus on economic feasibility for the private sector and in the next section consider what might be a role for the government.

With a mature space mining industry, a heavy component from the private sector is likely, so understanding economic rewards will be an essential component. Such rewards will depend on space markets and how they will evolve. Let us start with a very simple basic model for Earth. The mining sector produces one output and there is no space market, yet. Earth is Market 1 and later space will be Market 2. Represent demand and supply in Earth's market and equilibrium by the following equations:

$$Qs_1=S_1(P_1) \tag{13.3}$$

$$Qd_1=D_1(P_1) \tag{13.4}$$

$$\text{Equilibrium } Qs_1(P_1)=Qd_1(P_1) \tag{13.5}$$

In a competitive market, price on the supply curves should represent the extra cost of that last unit, so shifting costs will shift the market. With no space market, we can graphically represent this model in a traditional supply and demand framework and show equilibrium price in the market as follows:

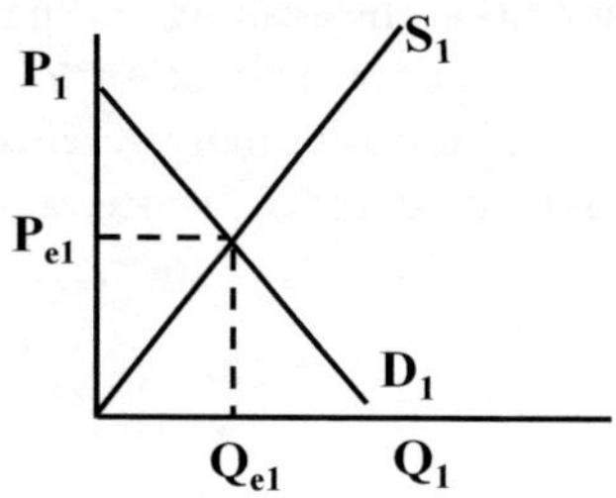

Figure 13.1 Model with no Space Market

This model represents a competitive market with neither side of the market having control over price. Dahl et al. (2020) start from such a model to simulate how mining a metallic asteroid and bringing back asteroid material would affect the price of the asteroid material on Earth ($P_{a1,t}$). $Q_{a,t}$ is the amount of asteroid material brought back in year t. They develop earth demand and supply equations over time by extrapolating from existing data and inject the asteroid material into Earth's market to determine the price of asteroid material in each year. They use the simulated data to compute the net present value of the project for each metal as follows:

$$NPV = \sum_{t=b}^{b+20} \frac{P_{a1,t} \times Q_{a,t}}{(1+r)^t} - \sum_{t=0}^{b+20} \left(\frac{C_t}{(1+r)^t} + \frac{c_t \times Q_{a,t}}{(1+r)^t} \right) \tag{13.6}$$

To solve for the net present value (NPV) of our project, we need to know all the values in the aforementioned equation. Where b is first year, the project delivers the final product to Earth's markets, C_t is the fixed capital cost spent in year t, c_t is the annual unit operating cost in year t, and r is the required rate of return. Given the riskiness of space ventures, many believe that r is likely to be higher than 20%. Since their asteroid has eight metals, they make this computation for all eight metals and conclude it is difficult to make profits using demonstrated technologies and costs to bringing their whole asteroid back and processing it on Earth.

Current thoughts call for bringing the basic starting materials from Earth with the means to start generating additional materials in space as soon as possible. Metzger, Muscatello, Mueller, and Mantovani (2013) call this procedure of bringing the basics and mining and processing other materials "in situ bootstrapping." Water, regolith, and other basic materials seem to be the mostly likely first products to be produced in space. They provide a nice survey of the literature on bootstrapping (also called self-replicating), beginning in the 1980s. They note that improvements in robotics, 3D printing, and the likelihood of water on the Moon suggest that those costs would be considerably lower now than in earlier estimates. They consider mass and energy balances but do little with cost estimation.

So, now let us add a space market that introduces demand (Qd_2) and supply (Qs_2) of space materials into the aforementioned model. The unit cost of transporting materials from Earth to space and back is τ with no transport costs within each markets. With arbitrage between the two markets, $P_2=P_1+\tau$ and we can write Qs_2 and Qd_2 as functions of P_1. Miners in both markets can deal in both markets, as can demanders. Our new model will be as follows:

$$Qs_1=S_1(P_1) \tag{13.7}$$

$$Qs_2=S_2(P_1) \tag{13.8}$$

$$Qd_1=D_1(P_1) \tag{13.9}$$

$$Qd_2=D_2(P_1) \tag{13.10}$$

$$\text{Equilibrium } S_1(P_1)+S_2(P_1)=D_1(P_1)+D_2(P_1) \rightarrow S_2(P_1)= D_1(P_1)+D_2(P_1)-S_1(P_1) \tag{13.11}$$

See the situation in the market below. We have Earth supply S_1 and total demand in both markets is D_1+D_2. In the middle, we have space supply (S_2). Put these two graphs together on the right to show equilibrium condition on the right of the arrow above. Note that at prices of c and above, Earth has the whole market and quantity demanded for space materials falls to 0. The graph on the right shows the equilibrium price on Earth as P_{e1} and space production as Q_{se2}. At this price, the graph on the left shows Earth consumption (Q_{de1}) and Earth production (Q_{se1}). Note that Earth quantity demanded is less than Earth quantity supplied, so the Earth supplies some material to the space market (Q_{se1}-Q_{de1}). Space only supplies the space market. We can also compute space price as $P_2=P_1+\tau$.

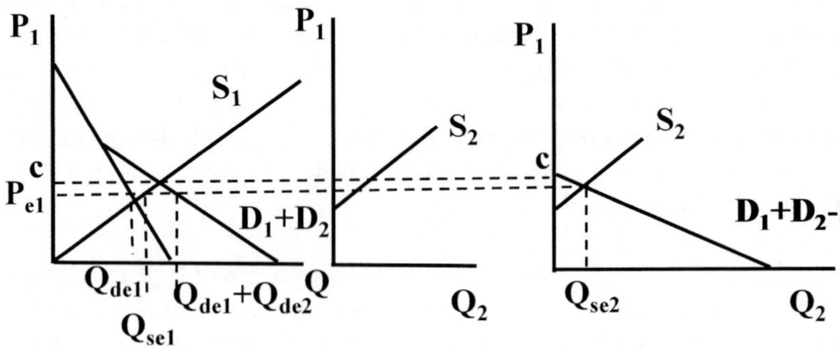

Figure 13.2 Model with Space Demands and Supplies

Kargel (1994) and others have suggested that precious metals such as gold and PGMs might be profitably mined on asteroids for earth return, but only if processed in situ or on the asteroid. He acknowledges, however, that we do not know the technology to separate PGMs on asteroids, nor do we know what the mission would cost. Andrews et al. (2015) find a project profitable that allows platinum return to Earth with other materials sold in space. In the aforementioned model, if we increased earth costs or lowered supply costs, we could easily represent a case where space was a net exporter to Earth. You could play around with the diagrams and also come up with cases where space supplied the whole market. To compute NPV for space in Equation (13.1) over the life of the project, we need to forecast the space price, quantity, and operating costs, including transport and processing for each year, and pick the appropriate discount rate.

If we can always write the demands and supplies in terms of P_1, it is fairly easy to get some intuition by visually determining who is selling how much to whom. However, as we generalize the aforementioned markets, all sorts of complications will arise. If markets are no longer connected, arbitrage conditions need not hold. Transport costs on Earth (τ_{11}) and in space (τ_{22}) will not be zero. Transport cost from Earth to space (τ_{12}) and from space to Earth (τ_{21}) may not be the same, as aerodrag and shielding may give a lower cost from space to Earth. When we leave Earth's gravity, our ship must use fuel to overcome the pull of gravity, but when we enter Earth's gravity, our ship must use fuel to resist the pull of gravity to slow down and not crash on landing. With no atmosphere, the energy needed to speed up or slow down would theoretically be the same. With aerodrag, the transport costs from Earth to space are likely to be higher than the return. Further, in some cases, demand and supply nodes may be priced out of the market. Equality equilibrium conditions in the model in these markets may yield negative quantities. To prevent this, we will need to require all quantities to be greater than or equal to zero.

In the modeling, we have only one space market supplying material. For some time there has been debate about whether the Moon or the NEAs would be that first market. For example, Lewis (2015) has long been a proponent of mining NEAs. Prado (1999) summarizes some arguments in favor of NEAs: without gravity many NEAs have lower Δvs to get and return materials with less risk of ship and equipment crashing into them; without a molten core and gravity, materials on NEAs might be less mixed than on the Moon and easier to process; lighter-weight equipment can be employed with little or no gravity on most NEAs, reducing launch weight; on small NEAs, it will be easier to provide solar power 24X7, instead of roughly half a month of dark followed by half a month of light on most places on the Moon; faster-rotating NEAs are likely to have somewhat less extreme temperatures; and sentimental attachment to the Moon may cause more social opposition to potentially defacing it.

Others favor the Moon as our first target. The Moon is closer (around 3 seconds round trip radio contact, around 6 days round trip for space travel), making it easier to launch rescue missions, make crew rotations, and remotely control mining operations. The Moon is always nearby, and we do not have to wait weeks for orbital launch opportunities. With more gravity, its environment would be a bit more similar to Earth and mining methodologies using gravity might need less modification. A counterargument to asteroids' lack of gravity is that, at a cost, we could create artificial gravity on asteroids if needed. It was once thought that the Moon had little water. More recent evidence suggests it has free water, whereas water on asteroids is bound up in chemical compounds requiring much more complicated processing. We know more about the Moon, and information gathered in the last decade suggests that it is more favorably endowed with needed minerals and water than once thought. As we have been involved with the Moon for many decades, programs, institutions, and interest groups will be supportive of mining the Moon and press to move forward (Prado, 1999; Spudis, 2014).

From an economic point of view, we could create a general model of the various mining targets and see what the model suggests is most profitable. Suppose we could have n_j demand nodes and n_i supply nodes. Let the supply equation at node i be as follows:

$$Qs_i=S_i(Ps_i) \text{ for } i = 1, \ldots n_i \tag{13.12}$$

Let the demand equation at node j be as follows:

$$Qd_j=D_j(Pd_j) \text{ for } j = 1, \ldots n_j \tag{13.13}$$

Let the transport cost from supply node i to demand node j be τ_{ij} and the flow of materials from i to j be x_{ij}. If markets i and j are connected or a product is being shipped from i to j, then arbitrage requires that $P_j=P_i+\tau_{ij}$ or $P_j-P_i-\tau_{ij}=0$. If they are not profitably connected ($x_{ij}=0$), then there is no required relationship between the prices in i and j. A slick way to conveniently generalize this requirement is

$$(P_j-P_i-\tau_{ij})x_{ij}=0 \tag{13.14}$$

Next, we need the equilibrium conditions. Supply from each node has to equal its demand. Thus, supply from node i is

$$S_i(P_i)=\sum_{j=1}^{n_j} x_{ij} \text{ for all i} \tag{13.15}$$

And demand from node j is

$$D_j(P_j)=\sum_{i=1}^{n_i} x_{ij} \text{ for all j} \tag{13.16}$$

Also, we cannot have negative prices or negative product flows, yielding three more sets of constraints:

$$x_{ij}\geq 0 \text{ for all i and j} \tag{13.17}$$

$$P_i\geq 0 \text{ for all i} \tag{13.18}$$

$$P_j\geq 0 \text{ for all j} \tag{13.19}$$

This more general model would be solved for all the trade flows, $x_{ij,}$ along with quantities and prices at all supply and demand nodes. If all the inputs can be determined—Equations (13.12), (13.13), and τ_{ij} for all i and j—the aforementioned model can be set up as a mixed complementarity problem (MCP) and solved in a variety of mathematical programming languages, including AMPL, AIMMS, GAMS, JUMP, and Pyomo (Jusevičius et al. 2021). See Murphy et al. (2016) for some history and modeling examples applying MCP.

See Dahl (2022) for other recent space project cost studies as well as additional intuitive cases and descriptions for the aforementioned model and ways to complicate the general model further. For example, we could add time to trace out the estimated variables both spatially and temporally; we could add economies of scale in transport with unit cost a function of amount transported; we could add more products, allowing for complements and substitutes in demand and supply.

Coming up with these inputs is quite challenging, but as with technologies, we can start with what inputs would be for Earth and try to imagine how they would change for space and over time. For example, Dahl (2020) has surveyed estimates of demand and supply for various minerals, and Dahl et al. (2020)

use the estimates to create demand and supply equations that change from year to year. They use estimated costs of returning an asteroid to cislunar space and adjust them as best they can to return them to Earth. They do sensitivity tests given the high uncertainties. As the costs were based on estimates for governments, they include hypothetical cost reductions over time, as space mining will likely be conducted by the private sector.

The aforementioned model is a spatial simulation model of a competitive market. For a survey of such models for mineral industries, see Labys and Yang (1991). But market power could prevail in some markets. If the market is not competitive, the model could be modified to represent other market structures. For example, Sommariva (2015) assumes a market with the space miner having 5% of the PGM market, with all firms identical Nash Cournot players. Such suppliers choose their profit maximizing quantity given the quantity of other players. Dahl (2022) suggests other spatial market structures that could be modeled, including a spatial Stackleburg model in which one player dominates and knows how other Nash Cournot firms will react and a model where a dominant firm behaves as a monopolist facing the other market players that are competitive. The information embedded in the aforementioned models would be needed in all these market structures as well.

Although we do not know how the space markets will evolve, mining the Moon or asteroids is often cited as supplying demanders in space markets not on Earth. So, who might demand space resources for use in space? Of course, the mining industry itself will need resources. Space tourism is a possibility. However, the market so far is very thin, with only a handful of flights at exorbitant costs (Dahl, 2022). Servicing existing and adding to Earth's artificial satellites seems like a highly likely potential market. Cleaning up all the existing space debris orbiting the Earth seems worth some consideration as well, although it would likely require some policy intervention.

In addition to the technical risks, Dahl (2022) summarizes some further economic risks. Future space markets are highly speculative. If they are mostly government-funded missions, as in much of the past, they will likely be quite small. If they are to supply materials for burgeoning space colonies, they could be quite spectacular. If space colonies do evolve, as many expect, the next big question would be: When? We can ask similar questions about costs. They are high but falling. The questions to ask: How far and how fast will they fall? Additionally, we all know that "On time, on budget" is a dream not often fulfilled. For example, Sovacool et al. (2014) surveyed more than 400 large electricity infrastructure projects from 1936 to 2013 and found that cost overruns averaged more than 60%, with 75% of the projects suffering cost overruns.

Given the questions on both sides of the market, the question of funding also becomes an important point. On Earth, consortiums of banks and development agencies often fund large-scale mining projects in harsh conditions. Lenders hire technical consultants who often make site visits to monitor the status of projects. Will they be willing to fund projects that are only built and operated robotically? If not, will venture capitalists be able to come up with the cash?

Market volatility is another risk. Most recent studies consider water for space and, perhaps, PGMs for Earth. While I suspect water prices on Earth are fairly stable, it is not clear what they will be in space. If the water is used to service existing space activities, water use should be more predictable; if it is for building space colonies, we might expect the boom and bust of building cycles. We know more about price volatility in the PGM market on Earth. For example, between 1986 and today, platinum price started at around US$30 million per tonne, dropped to around US$20, shot up to over US$65, and fell back to around US$30 (Dahl, 2022).

Role of Governments

As the private sector moves closer to mining space, it will consider not only commercial but also other risks. As space is a commons, property rights are ambiguous and markets may fail. Companies may not want to take the risk and enter. Alternatively, entering companies may not take the effect of their operations on other companies, and too many companies may enter into what economists call the tragedy of the commons. Nor may such companies worry about liability for negative externalities or sustainability issues in a commons such as space debris or nuclear waste. With such commons, there is a needed role for governments to develop mechanisms for allocating property rights.

Companies will need to comply with both national and international laws but may be hesitant if those laws do not exist, are ambiguous, or are contradictory. Lee (2012) suggests that legal risks include unclear property rights relating to mining operations, extracted material, and intellectual property; regulatory risk includes any ambiguities, potential delays, or other surprises in obtaining needed government approval and permits as well as ambiguities in liability and contractual enforcement. Legal frameworks providing clarity on these issues are not yet very mature. At the international level, Lee (2012) also indicates that there are six relevant international treaties that may pertain to space. The first is the Nuclear Test Ban Treaty, which entered into force in 1963 and prohibits nuclear explosions in Earth's atmosphere, outer space, and under the sea. The second treaty, more directly focused on space, is popularly called the UN Outer Space Treaty and entered into force in 1967. The treaty neither allows nor disallows space mining, so does not provide clarity on property right issues (Greenspon, 2016).

Shortly thereafter, the third UN treaty (the Rescue Agreement) called on signatories to help each other rescue and return endangered astronauts and space objects to the launching country. It came into force in 1968, but does not indicate who will bear the costs of any rescue missions.

The fourth multilateral treaty, the 1972 UN Convention on the International Liability for Damage Caused by Space Objects, ascribes liability to launching states for space objects causing damage on Earth, in space, and to aircraft on Earth. The fifth multilateral space treaty relates to the registration of objects launched into space and came into force in 1968. The UN 1979 Agreement Governing the Activities of States on the Moon and Other Celestial Bodies, effective 1984, more specifically targets the Moon and is often called the Moon Agreement. It stipulates that the Moon and its resources are to be used for peaceful purposes as the common heritage of all humankind. There is to be no private or state ownership, nor weapons or military bases allowed. Interestingly, the only countries that have soft landed a craft on the Moon—Russia, the United States, and China—have not ratified the agreement. See Dahl (2022) and Lee (2012) for additional nonbinding UN principles, resolutions, and guidelines. See Froehlich (2018) for an overview of national space laws by major country, region, and objective.

Although national space laws typically do not address mining, there are two fairly recent laws that do: the United States in 2015 (US Congress, 2015–2016) followed by Luxembourg in 2017 (Boring, 2017). In both laws, the space mining company seems to get what it captures from the space commons, which poses potential property rights issues that may discourage potential entrants or entice too many entrants (K. W., 2018). These laws have been criticized as being in conflict with international law (Xu, 2020). Froehlich (2018) further notes that the US law has been criticized as being a wish list from industry with inadequate safety regulation. The United Arab Emirates also has a recent mining law that encourages space activities but does not explicitly address mining and requires permits for all space activities (UAE Federal Law No. (12), 2019).

Lee (2012) indicates that the two biggest issues in current international space law that could prevent a space industry from developing are this property rights issue and the related common heritage provisions, or how much of the mining rewards will have to be shared. He noted that the 1982 Convention on Law of the Sea was not put into effect until the stance on sharing was softened. He notes that this conflict, arising largely between the industrial and developing states, is one of a number of other competing interests that will need to be resolved: environment versus development, international regulation versus free market, and hard law with strict regulation and enforcement versus soft law relying more on guidelines and voluntary compliance. See Lee (2012) for more on the relationship between international and space law, lessons learned from the 1961 Law on Antarctica and the 1994 Law of the Sea, and recommendations for a more comprehensive regulatory approach, including information disclosure on any nuclear devices in space, safety regulations, end-of-life cleanup of operations, and enforcement and dispute settlement mechanisms.

With strong economic incentives and the appropriate legal and regulatory framework in place, it is likely that the private sector will then lead the charge on space mining. However, when there are positive externalities in a market, we believe the market will produce less than the optimal amount, and we will still likely want the government to be involved in space-supporting scientific research as well as space mining endeavors. For example, government space programs, careers, and support inspire students to choose careers in STEM disciplines (science, technology, engineering, and math). Scientific research is helping us better understand Earth's evolution and its relation to the solar system, as well as climate on Earth and other celestial bodies. Advances in biology, geology, geophysics, and radio astronomy are all potential public benefits of space activities (Crawford, 2019). Further, NASA indicates more than 2000 spin-off benefits related to space research, including pollution-digesting bacteria and high-powered lasers (NASA, n.d.). More specific to the mining sector, positive externalities are likely to include advances in batteries, propulsion systems, mining methods, and materials. We will also have more information on detecting and deflecting potentially dangerous space objects.

Conclusions

It is once again an exciting time for space travel with the potential for space mining. We have lots of questions, lots of ideas, and some answers to fuel this enthusiasm. Those involved in the space industry should be congratulated for some remarkable accomplishments bringing us closer to a space mining age. In this chapter, I have explored some of their accomplishments. They have demonstrated we can leave Earth, we can survive short periods of time in space, we can get to potential mining sites, and we can bring back materials. What do we need to know to build these first steps into a sustainable mining industry?

Resources in space seem to be astronomical, but we need to do a lot more prospecting to know more about what exactly is out there and where it is. And, if we find it, can we mine it? The mining industry should also be congratulated. Over centuries, it has developed ever more complex techniques to process ever poorer quality ore. We need to know how we can adapt, scale up, and supplement this Earth technology to mine and process space material, manufacture it into useful objects, and move it to where it will be used. Such operations are likely to require additional know-how and a great deal of energy.

Another big question is the role of robots and humans. If humans are required on-site long term, there is much we still need to know about providing protective and acceptable habitats. If robots are to do it all with remote control, we will need to develop smarter robots that can deal with complex operations and communication and operating systems that can deal with the communication time delays to far off operations.

We will also need to know why we should want to mine space and who will do it. If the private sector is allowed to, and expects to make a profit commensurate with the perceived risks, it will do it. To understand revenues, mining operators will need to understand evolving mineral markets on Earth and in space. With space colonization, the markets are likely to be large; without colonization, we will be more restricted toward the Earth and its orbiting infrastructure, along with scientific missions to space. Even if the technologies and markets exist, the cost of generating enough energy and equipment to process and move materials to and from space is still a big question mark. For example, so far the best we have done to LEO is on a Falcon 9 rocket at US$3205 per kilogram (Jgalt, 2020).

Governments have their own reasons for being in the space race—from national prestige and scientific discovery to national security. Although we expect the private sector and markets will do the mining, governments should still play a role on the commercial side of activities where markets will fail. As space is a commons, governments will need to provide a legal and regulatory framework to fairly allocate property rights. They will need to provide safety, liability, and environmental regulation and develop regulatory enforcement and dispute settlement mechanisms relating to commercial operations in space. As space is a global commons, property rights and equitable sharing of our common heritage will require cooperation at an international level.

An additional reason we likely want governments to support space mining is that it has the potential for significant positive externalities. Moving dirty mining operations to space could improve the environment on Earth; it could provide material for space colonization, relieving population pressure at home; and ultimately improve the material well-being of future generations.

So, will it happen? If so, when? I believe it will, but when is anyone's guess. If the planned space activities in the next two decades are accomplished, I believe we will have a much clearer idea of what to expect. Humans have passed through various ages. Although the stone age is past, we still use stones; although the bronze age is past, we still use bronze; although the iron age is past, we still use iron. The information age is still upon us. Let us hope that it yields the information we need: what, where, when, why, who, and how to produce the materials we need for the space age to flourish.

References

Andrews, Dana G., Bonner, K. D., Butterworth, A. W., Calvert, H. R., Dagang, B. R. H., Dimond, K. J., et al. (2015). Defining a successful commercial asteroid mining program. Acta Astronautica, 108, 106-118. https://doi.org/10.1016/j.actaastro.2014.10.034.

Anthony, Niklas and Emami, M. Reza. (2018). Asteroid engineering: The state-of-the-art of near-earth asteroids science and technology. Progress in Aerospace Sciences, 100, 1-17. https://doi.org/10.1016/j.paerosci.2018.05.001.

Asterank. (2022). Asterank. Asterank. Retrieved May 22, 2022, from http:// www.asterank.com/.

Baiden, Greg, Grenier, Louis, Blair, Brad, and Tietz, Dale. (2022). Lunar underground mining and construction: A terrestrial vision enabling space exploration and commerce. In J. Considine (Ed.), A Research Agenda for Energy Politics. Edward Elgar.

Bhattacharyya, Sekhar. (2020). Introduction to mining engineering: Auger mining. PennState College of Earth and Mineral Sciences. Retrieved May 22, 2022, from https://www.e-education.psu.edu/geog000/node/880.

Boring, Nicolas. (2017). Luxembourg: Law on use of resources in Space adopted. Library of Congress. Retrieved May 22, 2022, from https://loc.gov/item/global-legal-monitor/2017-08-22/luxembourg-law-on-use-of-resources-in-space-adopted.

Borogove, Russel. (2019). Why did the Soyuz 7K-LOK use fuel cells rather than solar panels? StackExchange. Retrieved May 22, 2022, from https://space.stackexchange.com/questions/37237/why-did-the-soyuz-7k-lok-use-fuel-cells-rather-than-solar-panels.

China National Space Administration. (2021). International lunar research station (ILRS) guide for partnership. Retrieved May 22, 2022, from http://www.cnsa.gov.cn/english/n6465645/n6465648/c6812150/content.html.

Crawford, Ian. (2019). The future exploration of the Moon. Royal Astronautical Society, London, U.K. Retrieved May 22, 2022, from https:// ras.ac.uk/ events-and -meetings/future-exploration-moon.

Dahl, Carol A. (2020). Dahl mineral elasticity of demand and supply database (MEDS). Division of Economics and Business Working Papers. Colorado School of Mines. Golden, Colorado. Retrieved from http:// econbus -papers .mines .edu/ working -papers/wp202002v2.pdf

Dahl, Carol A. (2022). Needed info to mine space. Draft, Mineral and Energy Economics Program, Colorado School of Mines. Golden, Colorado. Retrieved from http:\dahl.mines.edu\Dah22.pdf

Dahl, Carol, Gilbert, Ben, and Lange, Ian. (2020). Mineral scarcity on earth: Are asteroids the answer? Mineral Economics, 33(1-2), 29-43. https://doi.org/10.1007/s13563 -020-00231-6.

ESA Earth Observation Portal (Eoportal). (2022). Minimize Lunar Gateway of NASA's Artemis Program. European Space Agency. Retrieved May 22, 2022, from https:// directory.eoportal.org/web/eoportal/satellite-missions/l/lunar-gateway.

European Space Agency. (2001). Green propellant for space propulsion. European Space Agency. Retrieved May 22, 2022, from https:// www .esa .int/ Applications/ Observing_the_Earth/Green_Propellant_for_Space_Propulsion.

Fletcher-Wood, Rowena. (2016). Hydrazine: Rowena Fletcher-Wood discovers the many uses for a toxic compound. Royal Society of Chemistry. Retrieved May 22, 2022, from https://edu.rsc.org/magnificent-molecules/hydrazine/2000023.article.

Froehlich, Annette (Ed.) (2018). Space resource utilization: A view from an emerging space faring nation: Springer Cham.

Ganapathi, Gani B., Ferrall, Joseph, and Seshan, P. K. (1993). Lunar base habitat designs: Characterizing the environment, and selecting habitat designs for future trade-offs. Pasadena, CA: NASA Jet Propulsion Lab. Retrieved from https://spacearchitect.org/ pubs/NASA-CR-195687.pdf

Gilbert, Alex (2021). Mining in space is coming. Retrieved May 22, 2022 from https:// www.milkenreview.org/articles/mining-in-space-is-coming.

Government of Canada. (n.d.). The Artemis program: humanity's return to the Moon. Government of Canada. Retrieved May 22, 2022, from https:// www.asc-csa.gc.ca/ eng/astronomy/moon-exploration/artemis-missions.asp.

Greenspon, Andy. (2016). Precious metals in peril: Can asteroid mining save us? Harvard University. Retrieved May 22, 2022, from https:// sitn .hms .harvard .edu/ flash/2016/precious-metals-peril-can-asteroid-mining-save-us/.

Guinness Book of World Records. (2022). The world's oldest mine. Guinness World Records Limited. Retrieved May 22, 2022, from https://www.guinnessworldrecords .com/world-records/oldest-mine.

Halpert, Gerald, Frank, Harvey, and Surampudi, Subbarao. (1999). Batteries and fuel cells in space. Interface, 25-30. https://doi.org/10.1149/2.F06993IF.

Hamilton, Isobel Asher. (2021). Jeff Bezos and Elon Musk both want to colonize space. Here are the 6 biggest problems with their plans, from thinning bones to toxic plants on Mars: Business Insider.

Hollingham, Richard. (2014). The effects of space travel on the human body. BBC Future. Retrieved May 22, 2022, from https://www.bbc.com/future/article/20140506 -space-trips-bad-for-your-health.

Infogalactic: The Planetary Knowledge Core. (2015). Tsiolkovsky rocket equation. Infogalactic. Retrieved May 22, 2022, from https://infogalactic.com/info/Tsiolkovsky _rocket_equation.

Jgalt. (2020, May 11). Lowest cost per kg for LEO launch by 2025. Retrieved from https:// www .metaculus .com/ questions/ 4390/ what -will -be -the -lowest -cost -per -kilogram -in -us -dollars -to -deliver -a -payload -to -leo -or -beyond -before -2025/ #: ~: text = For %20example %2C %20a %20flight %20to ,to %20LEO %20is %20about %20 %243%2C205.

Jusevičius, Vaidas, Oberdieck, Richard, and Paulavičius, Remigijus. (2021). Experimental analysis of algebraic modelling languages for mathematical optimization. Informatica, 32, 283-304. https://doi.org/10.15388/21-INFOR447.

K. W. (2018, June 12). Who owns what in outer space. Economist. Retrieved from: https://www.economist.com/the-economist-explains/2018/06/12/who-owns-what -in-outer-space.

Kargel, Jeffrey S. (1994). Metalliferous asteroids as potential sources of precious metals. Journal of Geophysical Research: Planets, 99(E10), 21129-21141. https://doi.org/10 .1029/94JE02141.

Labys, Walter C. and Yang, Chin-wei. (1991). Advances in the spatial equilibrium modeling of mineral and energy issues. International Regional Science Review. https:// doi.org/10.1177/016001769101400104.

Lee, Ricky. (2012). Law and regulation of commercial mining of minerals in outer space. Dordrecht Springer Netherlands.

Lewis, John (1996). Mining the sky: Untold riches from the asteroids, comets, and planets. Reading, MA, USA: Addison Wesley.

Lewis, John. (2015). Asteroid mining 101: Wealth for the new space economy. Deep Space Industries Incorporated.

Lewis, John S. (2016). In-space production of storable propellants. Deep Space Industries. Retrieved from https:// ntrs .nasa .gov/ api/ citations/ 20190001542/ downloads/20190001542.pdf

Listek, Vanesa. (2021). In-space metal 3d printing from incus to be tested by ESA. 3DPrint. Retrieved May 22, 2022, from https://3dprint.com/285706/in-space-metal -3d-printing-from-incus-to-be-tested-by-esa/.

Longchen, Duan, Songcheng, Tan, and Hui, Gao. (2014). Study on auger drilling technology for sampling drilling in the lunar stimulants. Procedia Engineering, 73, 212-217. https://doi.org/10.1016/j.proeng.2014.06.190.

Lunar and Planetary Institute. (n.d.). Lunar science and exploration. Lunar and Planetary Institute. Retrieved May 22, 2022, from https://www.lpi.usra.edu/lunar/ samples/apollo/tools/index.shtml.

Matters, Mining. (n.d.). Introduction to mining. https://miningmatters.ca/docs/default -source/ mining -matters - - -resources/ activities -and -lesson -plans/ introduction -to -mining.pdf?sfvrsn=2d1fbd98_2

Metzger, Philip. (2013). The type of asteroid to mine, Part 1, 2, and 3. Retrieved May 22, 2022, from https://www.philipmetzger.com/type-of-asteroid-to-mine-part -1/, https://www.philipmetzger.com/type-of-asteroid-to-mine-part-2/, https://www .philipmetzger.com/type-of-asteroid-to-mine-part-3/.

Metzger, Philip T., Muscatello, Anthony, Mueller, Robert P., and Mantovani, James. (2013). Affordable, rapid bootstrapping of the space industry and solar system civilization. Journal of Aerospace Engineering, 26.2, 18-29. https://doi.org/10.1061/ %28ASCE%29AS.1943-5525.0000236.

Mueller, R. P. and Susante, P. J. van. (2012). A review of extra-terrestrial mining robot concepts. Paper presented at the Earth and Space 2012 Conference: Engineering, Science, Construction, and Operations in Challenging Environments, Pasadena, CA, USA.

Murphy, Frederic, Pierru, Axel, and Smeers, Yves. (2016). A tutorial on building policy models as mixed-complementarity problems. INFORMS Journal on Applied Analytics, 46(6), 465-481. https://doi.org/10.1287/inte.2016.0842.

NASA's Jet Propulsion Lab. (n.d.). Power and thermal systems. Retrieved May 22, 2022, from https://rps.nasa.gov/power-and-thermal-systems/power-systems/.

NASA. (2022a). Lunar rocks and soils from apollo missions. NASA. Retrieved May 22, 2022, from https://curator.jsc.nasa.gov/lunar/.

NASA. (2022b). Near-earth asteroid delta-v for spacecraft rendezvous. NASA. Retrieved May 22, 2022, from https://echo.jpl.nasa.gov/lance/delta_v.rendezvous.html.

NASA. (n.d.). NASA spinoff. NASA. Retrieved May 22, 2022, from https://spinoff.nasa.gov/.

NASA Glenn Resarch Center. (2017). NASA - ion propulsion. NASA Glenn Research Center. Retrieved May 22. 2022, from https://www.nasa.gov/centers/glenn/about/fs21grc.html.

Petit, Don. (2012). The tyranny of the rocket equation. U.S. National Aeronatics and Space Administration. Retrieved May 22, 2022, from https://www.nasa.gov/mission_pages/station/expeditions/expedition30/tryanny.html.

Prado, Mark. (1999). 7.2.2 asteroidal vs. lunar materials utilization. Retrieved May 22, 2022, from https://www.permanent.com/asteroids-vs-moon-private.html.

ProfRob. (2015). Photometric surveys vs. spectroscopic surveys. StackExchange. Retrieved May 22, 2022, from https://physics.stackexchange.com/questions/169734/photometric-surveys-vs-spectroscopic-surveys).

Serviss, Garrett P. (1947). Edison's conquest of Mars. Los Angeles, CA, USA: Carcosa House (currently available for download at https://www.gutenberg.org/files/19141/19141-h/19141-h.htm).

Sommariva, Andrea. (2015). Rationale, strategies, and economics for exploration and mining of asteroids. Astropolitics, 13(1), 25-42. https://doi.org/10.1080/14777622.2015.1014244.

Sovacool, Benjamin K., Gilbert, Alex, and Nugent, Daniel. (2014). An international comparative assessment of construction cost overruns for electricity infrastructure. Energy Research & Social Science, 3, 152-160. https://doi.org/10.1016/j.erss.2014.07.016.

Spakovszky, Z. S. (2007). Thermodynamics and propulsion: The rocket equation. Massachusetts Institute of Technology. Retrieved May 22, 2022, from https://web.mit.edu/16.unified/www/SPRING/propulsion/notes/node103.html.

Spudis, Paul D. (2014). Moon first - mine the asteroids later. Smithsonian Air & Space Magazine (May 22, 2022).

Starr, Michelle. (2021). Finally, a Fusion Reaction Has Generated More Energy Than Absorbed by The Fuel. ScienceAlert. Retrieved May 22, 2022, from https://www.sciencealert.com/for-the-first-time-a-fusion-reaction-has-generated-more-energy-than-absorbed-by-the-fuel.

Taylor, Anthony, McDowell, Jonathan C., and Elvis, Martin. (2018). A Delta-V map of the known Main Belt Asteroids. Acta Astronautica, 146, 73-82. https://doi.org/10.1016/j.actaastro.2018.02.014.

Taylor, Christie, Flatow, Ira, and Koerth, Maggie. (2022). Date set for international space station's burial at sea. Science Friday. Retrieved May 22, 2022, from https://www.sciencefriday.com/segments/international-space-station-end/.

U. S. Congress. (2015-2016). U.S. Commercial Space Launch Competitiveness Act. (H.R.2262) https://www.congress.gov/114/plaws/publ90/PLAW-114publ90.pdf.

U. S. Office of Nuclear of Energy. (2021). What is a radioisotope power system? U.S. Department of Energy. Retrieved May 22, 2022, from https://www.energy.gov/ne/articles/what-radioisotope-power-system.

UAE Federal Law No. (12). (2019). On the regulation of the space sector. https://www.moj.gov.ae/assets/2020/Federal%20Law%20No%2012%20of%202019%20on%20THE%20REGULATION%20OF%20THE%20SPACE%20SECTOR.pdf.aspx.

Witt, Monica and Rowe, Jena. (2021). NASA selects five U.S. companies to mature Artemis Lander concepts. NASA. Retrieved May 22, 2022, from https:// www.nasa.gov/press-release/nasa-selects-five-us-companies-to-mature-artemis-lander-concepts.

Xu, Fengna. (2020). The approach to sustainable space mining: issues, challenges, and solutions. Paper presented at the IOP Conference Series: Materials Science and Engineering.

Index